Sustainable Strategic Management

Sustainable Strategic Management

Second Edition

Jean Garner Stead
and W. Edward Stead

M.E.Sharpe
Armonk, New York
London, England

The EuroSlavic fonts used to create this work are © 1986–2013 Payne Loving Trust.
EuroSlavic is available from Linguist's Software, Inc.,
www.linguistsoftware.com, P.O. Box 580, Edmonds, WA 98020-0580 USA
tel (425) 775-1130

Library of Congress Cataloging-in-Publication Data

Stead, W. Edward.
Sustainable strategic management / by Jean Garner Stead and W. Edward Stead.—Second edition.
   pages cm
Includes bibliographical references and index.
  ISBN 978-0-7656-3544-0 (hardcover : alk. paper)—ISBN 978-0-7656-3545-7 (pbk. : alk. paper)
1. Sustainable development. 2. Strategic planning. 3. Management. I. Stead, Jean Garner.
II. Title.

HC79.E5S717 2013
658.4'012—dc23   2013005479

Printed in the United States of America

The paper used in this publication meets the minimum requirements of
American National Standard for Information Sciences
Permanence of Paper for Printed Library Materials,
ANSI Z 39.48-1984.

IBT (c) 10 9 8 7 6 5 4 3 2 1
IBT (p) 10 9 8 7 6 5 4 3 2 1

SUSTAINABLE FORESTRY INITIATIVE

Certified Sourcing
www.sfiprogram.org
SFI-01234

In Memory of our dear friends,
Nancy Robinson and Bill Gathings.
You were too young when you left us.
We miss you terribly.

In Honor of our precious grandchildren,
Grant Thomas Green and Allison Grace Green.
You are our posterity, our future generation.
We love you so much.

May we be guided by wisdom from the past
and motivated by hope for the future.

Contents

List of Table, Figures, and Case Exhibits   xi
Preface   xiii

1. **The Emergence of Sustainable Strategic Management**   **3**
   Case Vignette 1: Creating Value Through Sustainability
        at Eastman Chemical Company   3
   The Changing Economic Worldview   7
   Pursuing the Triple Bottom Line   10
   Coevolution and Organizational Survival   11
   Transformational Change: A Critical Pathway
        to Organizational Sustainability   14
   From Strategic Planning to Sustainable Strategic Management   15
   Chapter Summary   26

2. **In Search of Sustainability**   **28**
   The Science of Sustainability   28
   The Issue Wheel: Carrying Capacity Meets the Human Footprint   33
   Ecological Sustainability: Management Happens on Earth   38
   Social Sustainability: Searching for Equity   46
   Sustainability: A New Way of Thinking   54
   Chapter Summary   56
   Case Vignette 2: The Meaning of Sustainability
        at Eastman Chemical Company   57

3. **Environmental Analysis for Sustainable Strategic Management**   **60**
   The Coevolving Factors Determining Environmental Turbulence   61
   The Coevolving Sectors of the Macro Environment   63
   Traditional Industry Analysis   70
   Business Ecosystems: Ideal Structures for Sustainable
        Strategic Management   77

The Coevolving Markets of the World   88
Environmental Forecasting   91
Chapter Summary   95
Case Vignette 3: A Brief Environmental History
    of the Chemical Industry   96

4. SSM Resource Assessment   **99**
The Resources of the Firm   99
SSM Resource Assessment Data-Gathering Tools   109
Analyzing and Evaluating Resources and Capabilities
    to Build Core Competencies   117
Creating Stakeholder Value via Eco- and Socio-Efficiency   121
Beyond Eco- and Socio-Efficiency: Eco- and Socio-Effectiveness 125
Chapter Summary   128
Case Vignette 4: Eco-Efficiency at Eastman Chemical Company 129

5. SSM Competitive Level Strategies   **131**
The Nature of Competitive Level Strategies   131
SSM Competitive Level Strategies   139
Strategies Dependent on Relative Competitive Position
    and Market Type   149
Chapter Summary   166
Case Vignette 5: Product Stewardship at Eastman
    Chemical Company   167

6. SSM Corporate Level Strategy   **170**
Corporate Expansion Strategies   172
The Build or Buy Decision   183
Retrenchment and Restructuring Strategies   187
SSM Corporate Portfolio   190
Chapter Summary   201
Case Vignette 6: Corporate Strategy at Eastman
    Chemical Company   202

7. Choosing and Implementing SSM Strategies   **206**
Choosing Portfolios of SSM Strategies   206
Instilling SSM Value Systems   214
Creating Meaning Beyond Profit   217
Designing Self-Renewing Learning Structures   221
Establishing Transformational Change Processes   224

Chapter Summary   226
Case Vignette 7: Strategies, Structures, and Processes
     for Implementing SSM at Eastman Chemical Company   227

8. Organizational Governance and Strategic Leadership in SSM   **231**
Establishing Effective Corporate Governance Mechanisms
     for SSM   231
Emerging Perspectives on Organizational Leadership   239
Effective Business Ecosystem Leadership   245
Building Trusting Relationships   246
Chapter Summary   247
Case Vignette 8: Strategic Leadership at Eastman
     Chemical Company   248

Bibliography   251
Index   270
About the Authors   286

List of Table, Figures, and Case Exhibits

Table

3.1	Sectors and Elements of the Global Macro Environment	65

Figures

1.1	The Closed Circular Flow Economy	8
1.2	The Open Living System Economy	9
1.3	The Triple Bottom Line	11
1.4	Organization–Environment Coevolutionary Spiral	13
1.5	Coevolution of SSM	17
1.6	SSM Coevolutionary Process	19
1.7	Hierarchy of Strategies	23
2.1	The Issue Wheel	34
3.1	Sectors of the External Environment	64
3.2	Interactions Among Global Risks	66
3.3	Traditional Industry Analysis	72
3.4	Stages of Industry Coevolution	76
3.5	Coevolutionary Industry Analysis	79
3.6	Business Ecosystem Structure	82
3.7	Multiple Scenario Analysis	93
4.1	Resource Assessment	100
4.2	Coevolution of Capital	102
4.3	Closed-System Value Chain	110
4.4	Open-System Value Chain	113
4.5	Coevolution of Eco- and Socio-Effectiveness	115
4.6	Eco- and Socio-Effectiveness	126

5.1   Foundations of Competitive Strategy   132
5.2   Hierarchy of SSM Strategies   140
5.3   Coevolution of SSM Strategies   141
5.4   Corporate Portfolio of SSM Competitive Strategies   150
5.5   Whole-Pyramid Strategic Thinking   164
6.1   Corporate Strategy Capital Allocation   171
6.2   Whole-Pyramid Portfolio   198
6.3   BCG Growth Share Matrix   199
7.1   Competitive Level Strategic Choice   212
7.2   Corporate Portfolio of Core Competencies   213
7.3   Standing for Sustainability   217
8.1   Performance Gap Analysis   238
8.2   SSM Evaluation and Control   239

Case Exhibits

1.1   Eastman Chemical Company's Sustainability Evolution   4
6.1   Eastman Product Portfolio 2009   204
6.2   Eastman Product Portfolio 2012   205

Preface

Strategic management is like all business disciplines in that it has deep roots in the traditional economic model that portrays organizational success as exclusively synonymous with economic success. Firms succeed when they cover their costs, improve their sales, and earn a profit, and they fail when they do not. This has not changed, and it is not likely to change in the foreseeable future. The financial health and performance of a firm has been and will always be critical for its success.

What has changed is that in today's sustainability-dominated world where pervasive concerns for mother nature and society are rapidly escalating, firms are expected to earn their financial returns in ways that benefit society and/or protect the natural environment. As would be expected of a major trend in any field, the growing concern for more sustainable business practices has recently permeated the walls of business schools when the Association to Advance Collegiate Schools of Business (AACSB) established a sustainability standard for its members. Because of this, strategic management scholars are now responsible for teaching their students how to develop and implement strategies that not only earn financial rewards for their firms but also serve the social and ecological needs of the planet that we call home.

And that is where this book comes in. It is the first book to integrate sustainability into strategic management. It covers the full gamut of strategic management concepts and processes that would be expected in any quality strategic management book, and it does so in a way that thoroughly weaves sustainability into each and every one of them. Students using this book understand things such as: why reducing materials and energy intensity is an effective functional-level strategy, why socially differentiated products command premium prices, and why a business ecosystem pursuing a vision of social and ecological responsibility can dominate its market. Further, because the book is relatively short, reasonably priced, and very thorough in its coverage of strategic management concepts and ideas, it can be used either as a stand-alone text for graduate and undergraduate strategic management courses, as a supplement to another book, or as one of a group of short texts.

Two scholars whose deep influence on us has added untold value to our work over the years are Ed Gray and Herman Daly. Ed Gray is one of the pioneers in the field of business and society, Herman Daly is one of the pioneers in the field of ecological economics, and both were primary advisors to Jean during her PhD program at LSU. The seeds of sustainability that these gentlemen planted in us over 30 years ago have grown and matured throughout our careers, and their ideas and their spirit are deeply embedded in this and our other books. Thank you, Ed, and thank you, Herman. You will always be in our hearts and minds.

Many people at East Tennessee State University (ETSU) have contributed valuable time, energy, and ideas to this book. We would like to thank our graduate assistants, Harold Riddle, who helped with our research in Chapter 2, and Brett Sloan, who helped with the author questionnaire. We would also like to thank Michelle Sullivan, our departmental administrative assistant, for the hard work she put in on our manuscript, and Andrew Childress, a senior accounting student, who helped us conceptualize some key points in Chapter 3. And as always, we would like to thank our dean, Linda Garceau, for her support, and our department chairperson, Phil Miller, for his willingness to take on more than his share of the load so that the rest of us can prosper.

One person at ETSU who deserves our special thanks is Al Spritzer, former dean and current endowed chair holder in our college. Al has supported and encouraged our writing endeavors for over thirty years. He encouraged us to write what was in our hearts when we were young professors and he was a young dean, and his support has never wavered, even after he chose to step down as dean twelve years ago. Recently, Al has done all that he could to support our efforts to integrate sustainability into the college's curricula, research, and service activities, and we are truly grateful for all that he has done for us.

At the top of Al's contributions to our sustainability efforts was his introduction three years ago of our book, *Management for a Small Planet*, to Jim Rogers, chairman and chief executive officer (CEO) of Eastman Chemical Company. This was the beginning of a very fruitful sustainability partnership between Eastman and ETSU. Both Jim Rogers and chief sustainability officer (CSO) Godefroy Motte (twice) have visited the campus to speak to and interact with our students and faculty, and the Corporate Sustainability Group, including group leader Anne Kilgore and group members Bill Heise, Kristin Ketron, and Mark Schurger, have worked directly with students in ETSU's capstone strategic management classes on projects related to Eastman's sustainability advantaged products, such as Tritan BPA-free plastic. We want to thank all these Eastman folks from the bottom of our hearts for your willingness to work with our students. You have given them an experience that they could have never gotten without your involvement. And we especially want to thank Bill, Kristin, and Mark, who put in huge amounts of time designing and evaluating the student projects and visiting classes to answer questions and provide guidance to the students.

The case vignettes that appear in each of the eight chapters in this book are also a big part of our sustainability partnership with Eastman. These case vignettes clearly demonstrate many of the key concepts we cover in this book. We especially want to thank two Eastman people who went the extra mile to ensure the quality of the vignettes: CSO Godefroy Motte, who took very valuable time out of his busy day to interview with us for the case; and Bill Heise, who read all of the vignettes and made very valuable suggestions regarding their accuracy and efficacy.

As with our last book, we want to thank our Auburn support group, Gregg and Martha Shepherd and Mike and Linda Davis (whose worry about our ever getting past Chapter 5 was a big motivator). We said last time that you turned what could have been the drudgery of many long, lonely workdays into meaningful fun and friendship. Well, you did it again. War Eagle! guys, and thanks for everything.

We have written five book prefaces beginning with the first edition of *Management for a Small Planet* in 1992, and each one has included a paragraph about our hopes and dreams for our only child, Garner Lee. She was 12, 16, 24, and 29 when the first four prefaces were written, and she will be 33 when this one is published. During that time she has lived in Tennessee, South Carolina, Indianapolis, New York City, and she now lives in the Silicon Valley. She completed high school, graduated from college, earned a master's degree, established a career, found her soul mate, and got married while we were writing those first four prefaces, and a common thread through all of them was her desire to have her own family. That dream is now a reality. Garner Lee and Mike now have two beautiful children—our grandchildren—Grant Thomas Green, three years, and Allison Grace Green, seven months. And this is where our hope in the future lies. This is our posterity, our own future generation.

Peaceful solutions,
Jean and Ed

Sustainable
Strategic
Management

1

The Emergence of Sustainable Strategic Management

Case Vignette 1

Creating Value Through Sustainability at Eastman Chemical Company

Jim Rogers, chairman and chief executive officer (CEO) of Eastman Chemical Company, contemplated the question and then responded, "Sustainability is an area where we can show our hearts but use our brains. We show our hearts by doing things that protect the next generation of the world that we live in—things like reducing greenhouse gases, volatile organic compounds, and energy use. Sure, this saves us money, but we know it is the right thing to do. However, the fun part is when we get to use our brains, which involves looking for ways to drive growth with sustainability. Doing this means giving our customers what they want so that they can ride the sustainability wave with us. We want to be right there alongside our customers helping them drive sustainability as a competitive advantage."

Rogers went on to say, "Sustainability is a mega trend sweeping over our industry and many others. It makes sense for our business, it makes sense for our world, and it is very consistent with Eastman's culture of continuous improvement, innovation, and responsibility." He pointed out that Eastman has made significant progress in its sustainability efforts over the past year, including naming Godefroy Motte chief sustainability officer (CSO). According to Rogers, Motte, who is located in the Netherlands, "brings with him Europe's pioneering sustainability thinking and a personal passion for sustainability."

In commenting on his firm's commitment to sustainability, Motte said, "Eastman is an advanced materials and specialty chemical company developing innovative, sustainable solutions to improve the world. As such, sustainability has become an integral part of what we do—it is part

Case Exhibit 1.1   **Eastman Chemical Company's Sustainability Evolution**

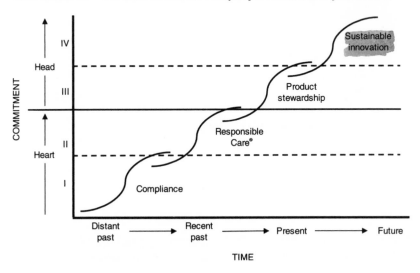

of our DNA. Thus sustainability has become an important driver of our new product developments. We are working hard to create value through environmental stewardship, social responsibility, and economic growth both now and for future generations." Motte further points to the fact that Eastman's sustainability efforts are not new. He said, "We've been an active participant in the chemical industry's voluntary Responsible Care® initiative for nearly a quarter of a century. After all, sustainability is an attitude and not just an activity to participate in from time to time."

Motte expanded on Roger's point that Eastman's commitment to sustainability has coevolved to include both doing what is right for current and future generations—working from the heart—and creating innovative new products that protect nature, improve society, and create economic value for Eastman and its customers—working from the head. He said that he sees Eastman's sustainability journey as progressing through four stages: Compliance, Responsible Care®, product stewardship, and sustainable innovation (see Case Exhibit 1.1).

Both Rogers and Motte described the first two stages as coming from the heart—doing what is right regardless. Compliance, obeying the law, is certainly the right thing to do, but it is also quite expensive. Nonetheless, they both pointed out that compliance was the primary sustainability focus of the chemical industry until the 1984 explosion at Union Carbide's pesticide plant in Bhopal, India, which killed thousands of people and exposed hundreds of thousands to methyl isocyanate and other deadly chemicals.

This incident and others like it, along with an increasingly complex and expensive regulatory environment, became imminent threats to the chemical industry in the 1970s and 1980s. Thus, in the late 1980s, chemical firms, including Eastman, joined together under the auspices of the American Chemistry Council (known then as the Chemical Manufacturers Association) and established the Responsible Care® program, which helped shift the industry's sustainability focus from regulatory compliance to voluntary ecological and social responsibility. Not only did Responsible Care® significantly improve the image of the chemical industry during some of its darkest days, it also encouraged firms to find ways to create value via improved ecological and social performance (i.e., energy reduction, resource reduction, pollution prevention, materials substitution, employee safety, community safety, improved community relations, etc.).

Such efforts are now central to the design and function of Eastman's products and processes. For example, the firm was named an EPA Energy Star® Partner of the year in both 2012 and 2013, was actively involved in the European Chemical Industry Council's (CEFIC) Build Trust program, and reported its sustainability activities to the Global Reporting Initiative for the first time.

Motte believes that Eastman has fully embraced the two heart stages and is currently operating in the first head stage—stage three—product stewardship. This stage involves the firm's taking full stewardship of the value chain by working with customers to provide sustainable solutions and by providing life cycle analysis (LCA) data to help customers reduce their footprints. Tritan™, a BPA-free plastic for containers, and Perennial Wood™, an ecologically safe alternative to pressure-treated lumber, are two examples of what Eastman refers to as "sustainably advantaged" products that have recently emerged in this stage.

Eastman now wants to move into stage four, sustainable innovation, which involves establishing ecological and social sustainability all along its value chain and serving customer needs in all global markets, including the base of the economic pyramid. For example, the HydroPack™ (discussed further in Case Vignette 5) resulted from a partnership between Eastman and its customer Hydration Technology Innovations to provide clean drinking water for disaster victims. Also, Eastman is currently working with a diaper manufacturer to develop a more affordable, eco-friendly diaper, which is a desperate need for BoP customers. In commenting on Eastman's desire to fully embrace stage-four sustainability, Motte said, "It is an opportunity to use our creativity and innovation to be part of the solution, for our world today and for future generations."

Eastman's sustainability journey is typical of firms in its industry. All organizations survive by successfully adapting to changes in the business environment, and the environment of the chemical industry has become progressively more sustainability demanding over the past half century (Hoffman 1999). The dangers of its products and by-products were exposed by Rachel Carson in *Silent Spring* in 1962, and they were again brought to the headlines in the 1970s and 1980s with issues like Agent Orange, Love Canal, and Bhopal. Chemical tragedies like these eventually led to a regulatory environment in the industry that was oppressively expensive. Firms in the industry responded to these dire events and costly regulations by implementing strategies and processes designed to reduce both their regulatory burdens and their costs of environmental management. Strategies implemented included reducing or eliminating wastes and toxins, reducing energy, and making other improvements in their environmental performance. Thus, firms in the industry began seeking competitive advantages via total product stewardship. Today chemical firms in the industry are beginning to seek competitive advantages by innovating new products and processes that will allow them to expand into previously ignored markets, including those heavily populated markets at the base of the pyramid (BoP).

Unfortunately, sustainability is not just a chemical industry issue. If it were, achieving it would be simple. But **sustainability**—typically defined as providing a high quality of life for current and future generations—is a global issue that involves all people and all business organizations. Sustainability is more a global vision of the future than a specific state of being, and it is usually portrayed as having three interdependent dimensions: the economy, the society, and the natural environment. The interactions among these dimensions are complex, and many of these interactions lie outside the realm of traditional business models.

Sustainability has grown from a fringe issue in the 1970s to a central issue in the global consciousness today (Aburdene 2005; Edwards 2005; Hawken 2007; Senge et al. 2008; Speth 2008). Paul Hawken (2007, 12) says, "Social and cultural forces are currently converging into a worldwide movement that expresses the needs of the majority of people on Earth to sustain the environment, wage peace . . . and improve their lives." Of course when an issue becomes central in society, it becomes an important part of the business strategy landscape (Kiron et al. 2013). Peter Senge (2011) says that the rising sustainability consciousness is a "profound shift in the strategic context" of business organizations, and two recent surveys of global business executives bear him out. In the first survey (Kiron et al. 2012), 90 percent of the 2,874 responding executives said that implementing sustainability strategies is now or soon will be a competitive necessity for their organizations, and 70 percent said that they have put sustainability on their strategic agendas within the past six years. In the second survey (Kiron et al. 2013), 50 percent of the 2,600 responding executives said that they had changed their basic business models to incorporate sustainability because of the strategic opportunities that it provides them, a full 20 percent increase over the previous year's survey. Data such as these leave little doubt that the 2012 survey researchers were correct when they concluded, "The sustainability movement [is nearing] a tipping point" (Kiron et al. 2012, 69).

The Changing Economic Worldview

Reaching that tipping point has taken humankind about 350 years. Since the beginning of the Industrial Revolution, humans have built their hopes and dreams on a worldview that unlimited economic growth is possible and desirable forever. This belief in the possibility and desirability of unlimited economic growth has led to the global belief that more production and consumption are good regardless of the environmental and social consequences. Gross domestic product (GDP) is viewed as a measure of pure good, regardless of what actually constitutes it. Indeed, in today's world, personal and societal welfare are measured almost solely on economic growth factors.

So this longstanding worldview encourages humans to produce and consume, produce and consume, produce and consume, at breakneck speeds. Whereas doing so in early economic history when few nations and few people were participating in economic activity is understandable, humans today clearly realize that their economic activities are threatening the very resources and systems that support quality human life on the planet. If humans continue to foul the air and water, degrade the land, ignore the poor and disenfranchised, and exploit the natural beauty, they are in danger of leaving a world to their future generations that is not as hospitable to humans as the one they inherited from their ancestors.

At the heart of the worldview that has guided strategic decision makers over the past 350 years is the image of the economy as a closed circular flow (see Figure 1.1). This framework depicts the production–consumption cycle in which resources are transformed by business organizations into products and services that are purchased by consumers. Note in the model that resources flow in one direction and money flows in the other. The problem with the closed circular flow model is not what it depicts, but what it ignores. Depicting the economy as closed implicitly assumes that the economy is isolated and independent from the social system and ecosystem. Under such an assumption, the economy is not subject to the physical laws of the universe, the natural processes and cycles of the ecosystem, or the values and expectations

Figure 1.1   **The Closed Circular Flow Economy**

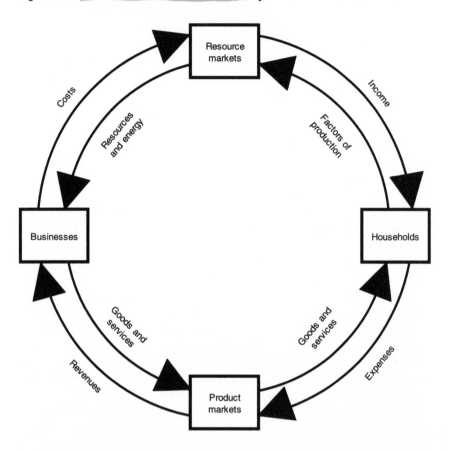

of society. Assuming these away leaves humankind with a mental model of an economy that can grow forever as self-serving insatiable consumers buy more and more stuff from further and further away to satisfy a never-ending list of economic desires without any serious social and ecological consequences.

Unfortunately the economy is not isolated from the earth's other subsystems as depicted in the closed circular flow model. Now is the time to break free from the mythic drive for economic growth in favor of a new economic worldview, one based on the image of an interconnected global community of people functioning in harmony with one another and with nature. Long-term economic health is possible under this worldview only if the social system and ecosystem can support it. Thus global economic activity has to function within the natural and social boundaries of the planet. The earth is the ultimate source of natural and human capital for the economic system. Thus, a healthy

Figure 1.2 **The Open Living System Economy**

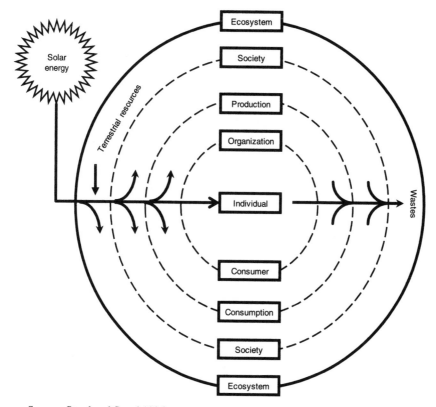

Source: Stead and Stead 1996.

flow of economic activity can be sustained for posterity only if strategic decision makers operate under the paradigm that the economy serves the needs
of the greater society within the limits of nature.

Figure 1.2 depicts such a worldview. In this model, the earth is a living
system. As such, its survival is dependent on achieving a sustainable balance
within its various subsystems. The most basic living subsystems on the planet
are the individual organisms that inhabit it, and the most dominant of the
planet's individual organisms is humankind. Because of this dominance, the
decisions made by human beings are major forces influencing the ultimate state
of society and nature. The ability of human beings to make effective decisions
about how they interact with one another and with the planet depends on the
accuracy of the mental processes they use to make those choices. At the heart
of these mental processes are the underlying assumptions and values human

beings hold. Thus, human values and assumptions have a huge influence on the state of society and nature.

Of course, humans make their decisions in a variety of collective contexts. Decisions are made in the context of families, business organizations, educational institutions, governmental agencies, and interest groups, to name but a few. In the economic realm, individuals make decisions as members of organizations that produce goods and services, and they make decisions as part of the collective of consumers who purchase and use these goods and services. These collectives of organizations and consumers make up the economy, the subsystem that encompasses the production–consumption cycle depicted in the closed circular flow model. However, unlike the closed circular flow model, this model is open to the greater social system in which the economy is embedded and the greater ecosystem to which all humankind is bound. Thus, the model depicts the solar flow of energy that provides fuel for the earth's subsystems to operate, it depicts the terrestrial resources in nature that provide the materials and energy necessary for economic activity, and it depicts the wastes that are generated during economic activity that must somehow be absorbed back into the ecosystem. Nature provides the framework for this model. As with nature, waste is considered lost profit and value is created by design. Feedback becomes the most valuable source of capital, and the more it is used, the more abundant it becomes. Limits are positive forces that encourage innovation and continuous improvement, and diversity brings choice, resilience, and sustainability. In other words, within this model, organizations can create more value by emulating what they once sought to conquer: nature (Kiuchi and Shireman 2002).

Pursuing the Triple Bottom Line

Thus, managing organizations in the open environment depicted in Figure 1.2 requires a very different management framework from the one grounded in neoclassical economics that says organizations function in a closed economic environment that is separate from society and nature. This new framework is founded on the premise that sustainability is achievable only if organizations can earn their economic profits in ways that are socially and ecologically responsible. Thus, whereas in the neoclassical framework managerial success is defined solely by managers' contributions to the financial profits of the firm, in the open system framework, these profits are earned in ways that also contribute to the good of society and the natural environment.

A popular framework designed to capture managerial commitment to all three dimensions of sustainability is the **triple bottom line** (Elkington 1997) (see Figure 1.3). Firms pursuing the triple bottom line are committed

Figure 1.3  The Triple Bottom Line

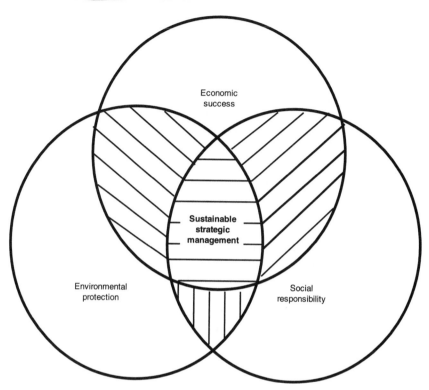

to economic success that both enhances and is enhanced by their concerns for the greater social and ecological contexts in which they exist. Because organizations are generally familiar with the bottom line concept, the triple-bottom-line image can be more easily integrated into current organizational cultures. Further, the framework allows managers to more clearly focus their organizational initiatives at those points where economic success, social responsibility, and/or ecological health intersect. Thus, using the triple bottom line as a managerial framework allows organizations to map out a future that is consistent with the three tenets of sustainability, and it allows organizations to more clearly define the roles and responsibilities of managers in achieving that future.

Coevolution and Organizational Survival

Coevolution is a biologically rooted theory demonstrating that interdependent entities evolve and change in concert with one another over time (Ehrlich and Raven 1964; Lovelock 1979, 1988). Coevolution has emerged as a valid framework in organizational science because it unites seemingly dichotomous explanations of why some organizations survive and others do not. Frameworks such as strategic choice and the resource-based view explain that organizational survival is primarily a function of strategic management efforts. Others, such as population ecology and institutional theory, explain that organizational survival is primarily a function of environmental forces. Coevolution ties these perspectives together because it holds that organizations and their environments are locked into perpetual cycles of mutual change and adaptation. In today's world the business environment is becoming increasingly more dynamic and complex, and organizations are adapting to this by developing more flexible, innovation-driven structures and processes (Flier, Van Den Bosch, and Volberda 2003; Lampel and Shamsie 2003; Lewin, Long, and Carroll 1999; Lewin and Volberda 1999, 2003a, 2003b; Pfeffer 1993; Porter 2006; Volberda and Lewin 2003).

Coevolutionary relationships demonstrate six characteristics: specificity, reciprocity, simultaneity, adaptability, boundary spanning, and permanence (Porter 2006). Of the six, the dynamics between reciprocity and permanence are particularly important for understanding the true nature of environment–organization coevolutionary cycles. By itself, reciprocity portrays the cycle as a two-dimensional circular process in which environmental changes lead to organizational adaptations, which lead to environmental changes, which leads to organizational adaptations, and so on. However, the two-dimensional circle of reciprocity does not fully portray the fact that the coevolutionary dance between organizations and their environments is a perpetual process that leaves each entity permanently changed.

By shifting the image of the coevolutionary relationship between environmental selection and organizational adaptation from a two-dimensional circle to a three-dimensional spiral, we can more thoroughly understand the perpetual ever-changing processes going on between organizations and their environments (see Figure 1.4). Whereas circular dynamics imply that organizational selection-adaptation cycles may eventually lead back to the same place, spiral dynamics demonstrates that the reciprocal environment–organization change process results in both the organization and its environment continuously morphing into something different over time.

Spiral dynamics says that changes in human consciousness result from spiraling coevolutionary processes such as the ones that occur between organizations and their environments. These higher levels of consciousness naturally emerge in order to help humans adapt and survive life's changes, and each of these coevolving shifts in human consciousness is accompanied by a shift in core values. Thus, human consciousness evolution is a process

Figure 1.4   **Organization–Environment Coevolutionary Spiral**

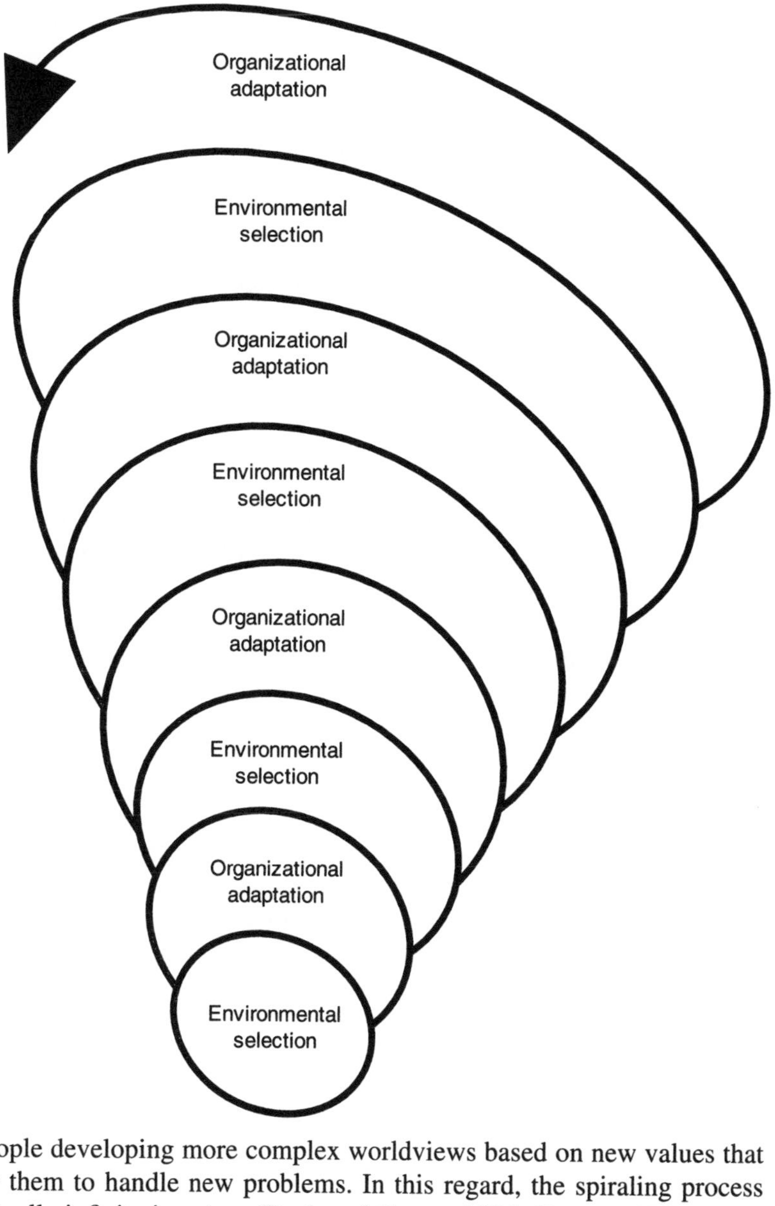

of people developing more complex worldviews based on new values that allow them to handle new problems. In this regard, the spiraling process is virtually infinite in nature (Beck and Cowan 1996; Graves 1970; Wilber 1996, 2000).

As discussed earlier in the chapter, sustainability is at the heart of a current transcendence in human thoughts and values worldwide. People are openly, pervasively, and in some cases desperately seeking a higher quality of life for themselves and their children. Because the drive for sustainability is now a central global theme, it has emerged as a central theme in the business environment. Coevolution teaches that organizations wishing to survive during this environmental transcendence will need to create transformational change processes that allow them to develop and deeply ingrain into their cultures sustainability-centered values, ways of thinking, and ways of doing things.

Transformational Change: A Critical Pathway to Organizational Sustainability

Organizational change efforts targeted at the shallower levels of an organization's culture are generally adaptive, incremental, and focused on changing artifacts and norms so that the firm can do what it currently does better than it did before. However, as change touches the deeper values and beliefs levels of an organization's culture, transformational change processes are required. These employ deep dialogue processes that allow the organization to closely examine and change its underlying values, beliefs, and assumptions, redefining the essence of who it is and what it does.

Transformational change is discontinuous rather than incremental, and it leads organizations to entirely different qualitative states. Organizations attempting transformational change cannot expect to be successful by taking the slow linear steps associated with incremental organizational change efforts. Rather, transformational change requires fundamental efforts designed to completely shift the consciousness of the firm to a different level based on new values, beliefs, and ways of doing things. This shift to a **new consciousness** can be accomplished only by changing the values that underlie the current organizational consciousness (Beckhard and Pritchard 1992; Senge 1990).

Successfully infusing sustainability into an organization's culture requires the organization to establish transformational change processes that allow it to examine and redefine its core values, the nature of its work, and its relationships with its stakeholders at all levels—economic, social, and environmental (Dunphy, Griffiths, and Benn 2007; Freeman, Pierce, and Dodd 2000; Gladwin, Kennelly, and Krause 1995; Post and Altman 1992, 1994; Stead and Stead 1994). Post and Altman (1992, 13) said years ago, "Internal paradigm shifts and transformational change are necessary as companies attempt to adjust to the rapidly changing world of green politics and markets." More recently, Dunphy, Griffiths, and Benn (2007) pointed out that business organizations have been largely responsible for transforming the planet into the hyper-growth, environmentally and socially challenged planet we know today. Now it is time for these organizations to transform themselves in ways that will allow them to better contribute to planetary health, social responsibility, and human quality of life. Thus, as sustainability concerns continue to move into the forefront of the issues facing humankind, organizations across the globe wishing to join the sustainability revolution will need to become adept at designing and implementing socially and ecologically responsible transformational change processes.

From Strategic Planning to Sustainable Strategic Management

The prosperous years following World War II led to the tremendous growth of corporations and the emergence of **strategic** (or **long-range) planning**. Prior to this, most firms engaged in business-level policy formulation, an internal process of integrating business-level functions and efficiently allocating resources among them. However, the Arab Oil Embargo of 1973, described by E. F. Schumacher (1979) as the watershed economic event of the twentieth century, stimulated top managers to begin to integrate the external environment into their planning processes. Strategic planning is typically a top management process characterized by annual planning retreats and planning reviews spanning five-year planning horizons. This top-down annual activity is a purely rational process involving scanning the environment, planning where the firm wants to go, and deciding on the steps to take to get there. Strategic planners provide extensive data analyses of both the internal and external environment to executives who allocate resources to implement the strategic plan. In this process, strategy formulation is viewed as a separate process from strategy implementation, and thinking about strategy is viewed as separate from doing it (Rothaermel 2013).

As was demonstrated with the chemical industry example at the opening of this chapter, increased environmental turbulence during the 1980s meant that top managers had to begin to scan and adapt to environmental changes more often than once a year at the planning retreat. The strategic management process emerged in response to this increasing need for environmental vigilance. **Strategic management** is a continuous process that involves the efforts of top managers to fit their organization to its environment by developing **competitive advantages** built on **capabilities** that are not easily duplicated (Barney 1991) in order to achieve organizational goals. Traditionally the primary intent of strategic management has been to facilitate a firm's ability to use adaptive learning (Senge 1990) to increase market share and competitive position within well-defined industry boundaries. Thus, traditional strategic management focuses primarily on improving "what is."

The shift from strategic management to **sustainable strategic management (SSM)** necessarily begins with a shift in thinking regarding the basic relationship between the economy, society, and the natural environment. As previously discussed, strategic managers now and into the future will have to guide their organizations away from the assumption that unlimited economic growth is both possible and desirable on a finite planet and toward the assumption that economic activity can exist over the long term only if it protects and improves the lives of the planet and its people. Thus, underlying SSM is the basic assumption that the economy is an open subsystem that exists within the larger social system and ecosystem (Figure 1.2). In this economy the industry boundaries have shifted from defined and predetermined to blurred and open as the once separate and distinct markets of the world have joined together in a coevolutionary dance that is changing each and all forever.

SSM is both by definition and practical necessity a cumulative, coevolutionary relationship between business, the society in which it operates, and the planet on which it exists. Because concern for the long-term health and welfare of humankind has increased along with stakeholder demands for more sustainable business practices, organizations have begun to incorporate sustainability into their strategic management processes. It is from this practical environmental reality that the necessity for SSM has emerged in the twenty-first century.

SSM is a **spiraling, integrative process** that expands and lifts the scope of traditional strategic management. Spiraling because SSM is a higher level, more socially and ecologically responsible strategic framework that has emerged from the upwardly spiraling coevolutionary interactions between the sustainability-rich business environment and the strategic interests of business organizations. Integrative because SSM incorporates both the industrial organizations (I/O) model (McGahan and Porter 1997) and the resource-based model (Barney 2001) that explain alternative views of how firms gather and use information necessary to choose and implement successful strategies.

In the I/O model the external environment, especially the industry environment, is seen as the primary determinant of firm performance, thus the strategic positioning of the firm within an attractive industry is critical in determining above-average returns. The firm's unique resources and internal capabilities, on the other hand, are seen as the primary determinants of superior firm performance in the resource-based view of the firm. Thus, the effective deployment of resources to build core competencies, resulting in competitive advantages, is the essential ingredient for success in this view of firm performance (Hitt, Ireland, and Hoskisson 2009). In SSM the reciprocal, coevolutionary interactions between the business environment and the firm's capabilities result in improved triple-bottom-line performance. The positioning of the firm in an attractive market coevolves with building unique resources

Figure 1.5   **Coevolution of SSM**

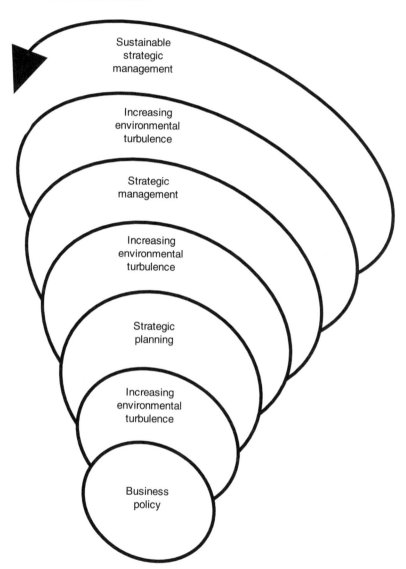

and capabilities that cannot be imitated by competitors, which, in turn, results in superior performance. The SSM process expands the scope of traditional strategic management to include the greater society and ecosystem, representing the next coevolutionary stage in the business, policy, and strategy field, as depicted in Figure 1.5.

SSM requires that strategic managers engage not only in **adaptive learning**; they must also employ **generative learning** (Argyris and Schön 1978; Senge 1990). In adaptive learning processes, organizations search their environments for relevant data, interpret these data by filtering them through familiar, well-established organizational mental models, and then take actions to adapt to their environment based on these interpretations. Adaptive learning is generally effective when firms make familiar or routine changes resulting in incremental innovations. However, when the familiar, well-established organizational mental models employed in adaptive learning do not provide adequate guidance for strategic decision makers, generative learning processes that allow them to think in new and different ways become necessary. These challenges and changes in currently held organizational mental models require a deep examination of the underlying values and beliefs upon which they are based, and this examination provides the impetus for radical innovation.

Thus, SSM requires the development of a new way of looking at the world based on an understanding of the coevolutionary social, ecological, and economic systems that link issues and events in the organization's environment. This forces strategic managers to focus on interrelationships and dynamic processes of change rather than linear cause and effect, enabling them to look beyond traditional industry borders and strategy models and ask, "What can be?"

SSM Concepts

Thus, sustainable strategic management has emerged from a spiraling coevolutionary dance between business organizations and their sustainability-rich environments. **Sustainable strategic management** involves a set of processes and strategies that include strategic analysis, strategy formulation, and strategy implementation that are economically competitive, socially responsible, and in balance with the cycles of nature. These three stages of SSM represent the reciprocal processes of strategic analysis (defining the firm's vision, mission, and goals and scanning the firm's external and internal environments), formulating strategies at the business unit level, corporate and enterprise level, and implementing SSM strategies through effective organizational design and transformational strategic leadership (see Figure 1.6).

Strategic Visions

The SSM process begins with a **strategic vision** based on sustainability. A strategic vision is a shared image painted in words that portrays the ideal

Figure 1.6 **Sustainable Strategic Management (SSM) Coevolutionary Process**

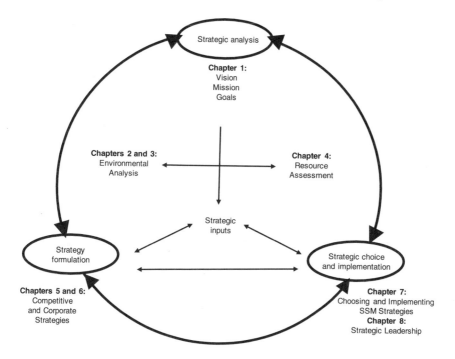

future of the firm. A shared strategic vision of the future is meant to stretch a firm by articulating some ambitious but attainable future state that will help to motivate employees at all levels and to drive strategies. The vision captures the firm's aspirations, pervading the whole organization with a sense of being a part of something larger. A shared vision can be described as big-picture thinking with passion. An inspiring vision, such as one based on the core value of sustainability, helps employees find meaning in their work because they see their personal aspirations captured within the firm's strategic vision (Collins 2001; Collins and Porras 1994). For example, in 1994 Ray Anderson, the founder and late CEO of Interface Global, the world's leading producer of soft-surfaced modular floor coverings, challenged his employees with a bold vision: "To be the first company that, by its deeds, shows the entire industrial world what sustainability is in all its dimensions—people, process, product, place and profits—by 2020 . . ." (Interface Global 2008). Two decades later, this passionate vision still leads the firm. Ray Anderson's commitment to and passion for sustainability continues to inspire and motivate Interface's employees because it provides them with a sense of being a part of something larger. This is big-picture thinking with passion. It empowers all of Interface's organizational members to think that together they can change the business world through their collective actions.

In sum, authentic strategic visions: (1) reflect the core values, beliefs, and aspirations of the firm; are simple, positive, and intrinsic; (2) account for the personal visions of organizational employees; (4) come from the heart; (5) are perceived as achievable via hard work and dedication; (6) are exhilarating, inspiring, and challenging; (7) are motivational during hard times for the firm; (8) serve as foundations for developing organizational missions, goals, and strategies; and (9) serve as a basis for determining what information organizations consider important and how they measure success (Collins 2001; Collins and Porras 1994; Parker 1990; Senge 1990). Thus, powerful, well-crafted strategic visions are shared images of the future that guide the firm's decision-making processes and act as mirrors that reflect the appropriateness of organizational actions.

Missions

The organization's **mission** is formulated within the context of the strategic vision and defines the organization's unique purpose. It addresses the question of why the firm exists, and it legitimizes the firm in the eyes of society. The mission statement sets the organization apart from others of its type and identifies its scope of operations in product/market terms and the customers it intends to serve (Hitt, Ireland, and Hoskisson 2009). In other words, the mission statement defines the organization's business, and as the firm's business changes so will its mission. For example, Henry Ford's original mission was to make the automobile accessible to every American, while today Ford's mission is to provide personal mobility for people around the world (Rothaermel 2013). It is interesting to note that Bill Ford (Ford's chairman) and Alan Mulally (Ford's CEO) have engaged in generative learning by questioning the fundamental assumption of their founder's mission of being in the automobile business. The current mission statement is not product focused (it does not even mention the automobile), but instead is now focused on the customers' needs for personal mobility. It leaves open how it plans to fill these needs in the future. Even if it ventures into personal flying devices, Ford's mission would still be relevant. Thus, the questioning of the fundamental assumption of what business it is in has led to a redefinition of Ford's business that does not have to include the automobile.

For a dominant, single-product-line firm, the mission focuses on customer groups (who is being satisfied), customer needs (what is being satisfied), and how customer needs are being satisfied (via the firm's core competencies) (Abell 1980). However, defining the business in a diversified, multiple-product-line firm requires that the mission focus on the entire portfolio (collection) of businesses in terms of the purpose of the portfolio, the scope of the portfolio, and balance of cash flow within the firm's portfolio of businesses. For example, General Electric (GE) is a diversified conglomerate with businesses that span numerous industries and markets such as energy, technology, infrastructure, and finance. Given such a diverse portfolio of businesses, GE defines its reason for existence (purpose of its portfolio) as a means to solve problems for customers, communities, and for GE itself. Reinforcing this capability to solve problems is a culture built on imagination, building, and leading (Rothaermel 2013).

Goals

Visions and missions form the foundation for the formulation of **goals** (or **strategic objectives**) that specify the long-run results that the organization seeks to achieve. Goals provide a broad, general direction for the firm within a well-defined time frame. Goals may be related to financial objectives such as sales growth, revenue growth, or cost reduction as well as to nonfinancial objectives such as reduction of greenhouse gases or employee development (Dess, Lumpkin, and Eisner 2008). Due to sustainability's broad, abstract nature, the formulation of specific sustainability goals is critical for the success of SSM. Only by translating sustainability into specific performance targets can strategic managers begin to actively manage in a sustainable manner. These goals should provide an index for measuring the firm's progress in all three dimensions of its triple-bottom-line performance.

For example, Eastman Chemical Company has formulated short-term (1–3 years), mid-term (3–5 years) and long-term goals (5–10 years) to measure its triple-bottom-line performance. One of its long-term environmental goals is to reduce energy intensity by 25 percent from 2008 to 2018. Eastman has formulated a mid-term social goal of expanding its value chain engagements in ways that focus on strategic sustainability issues with designers, academia, government, nongovernmental organizations, and others with potential influence. It has also formulated a mid-term economic goal to ensure that two-thirds of its revenues from new product launches are advantaged on assessed sustainability criteria. Thus, by formulating specific goals in terms of its triple-bottom-line performance, the strategic managers at Eastman Chemical are providing direction and an index to measure progress for all employees in terms of moving toward their sustainability vision of "accelerating value creation across all three dimensions of sustainability . . . by leveraging technical capabilities now and for future generations" (Eastman Chemical Company 2011).

Strategies

Strategies are means to achieve goals. A strategy is a comprehensive plan that matches the opportunities and threats in the external environment with the firm's strengths and weaknesses, in order to develop competitive advantages that achieve organizational goals. **SSM strategies** expand the strategic focus to include the coevolutionary opportunities and threats that emerge from the greater society and ecosystem as well as the economic environment. SSM strategies are integrative strategies designed to provide long-term competitive advantages to organizations by simultaneously leveraging the three dimensions of sustainability. SSM strategies are multilevel and multidimensional, designed to create opportunities for firms by attending to the economic, ecological, and social dimensions of their products, services, and processes from cradle to cradle (McDonough and Braungart 2002).

SSM strategies vary in content depending on their scope and strategic level, and they can be conceptualized as a hierarchy of strategies (Figure 1.7), where **enterprise level strategy** (Freeman and Gilbert 1988) represents the overarching moral and ethical foundation of corporate strategy, answering the question, "What do we stand for?" In SSM, the firm stands for sustainability (Stead and Stead 2000). Enterprise level strategy is not specifically formulated like other strategy levels, but results from the strategic decision-making behavior of the top management team. These strategic managers establish the firm's shared values, which in turn form the basis for its **corporate culture**. At the **corporate strategy level** in a diversified firm the strategic focus is on managing the scope and emphasis of the firm's portfolio of businesses, while the focus at the **strategic business unit (SBU)** or **competitive strategy level** is on how to compete in a particular product/market segment. A SBU is a large division (often with multiple product lines) of a diversified firm that has varying degrees of profit and loss responsibility.

Each SBU has an array of **functional level strategies**, such as financial, human resource, marketing, or operations strategies, where resources are deployed in order to build **core competencies**, unique capabilities that competitors cannot easily imitate. These core competencies then become the cornerstone upon which the firm's competitive level strategy is built. When core competencies are exploited in the marketplace via the firm's competitive strategy, they afford the firm a unique **competitive advantage** that provides superior performance relative to competitors. Given that SSM strategies are formulated within the foundational context of the triple bottom line, many of a firm's competitive advantages will be sustainability-based advantages.

Figure 1.7 **Hierarchy of Strategies**

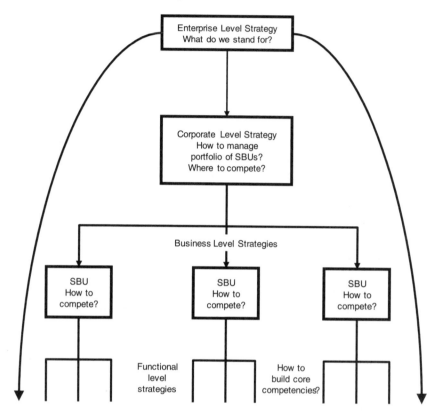

SSM Planning Processes

Formulating SSM strategies is a transformational planning process that requires managers to use generative systems thinking. In the traditional models managers from the top of the firm take an active role in the strategy formulation process. The planning goal is usually the incremental improvement in market share within existing industry boundaries, a focus on "what is," which reflects an adaptive organizational learning process. Crafting SSM strategies requires a shift in the mental model of strategic managers from the closed view of the economy (Figure 1.1) to the open systems view of the economy (Figure 1.2) as a coevolving subsystem of the greater society and ecosystem, reflecting a shift to generative learning. This outside-the-box thinking enables strategic managers to structure their firm's strategy formulation processes around the emerging core value of sustainability. This open systems planning model requires the involvement of many managers, suppliers, customers, and other important stakeholders representing the collective wisdom of the firm. Such an open process facilitates the transition from adaptive to generative organizational learning, allowing for the continuous questioning of fundamental assumptions and values related to why and how the firm is doing business. Such a planning process requires developing myriad internal and external economic, social, and environmental alliances, networks, and relationships with other firms, governments, interest groups, communities, activists, and so forth.

The SSM planning process provides a context in which intended strategies are formulated and emergent strategies are embraced. **Emergent strategies** (Mintzberg and Waters 1985) are unplanned, bottom-up strategic initiatives that emerge from either the internal or external environment. Whereas intended strategies are formulated via a rational, top-down planning process, emergent strategies are unexpected initiatives that may lead to goal accomplishment. Such strategies are successful only if the organizational culture is formed around an attitude of "expect the unexpected" implanted with the ability to react strategically. For example, a Starbucks store manager developed an iced drink in response to customer requests. Although originally told by corporate management that Starbucks was only in the coffee business and they were not interested in iced drinks, the employee, with the help of an internal champion, persevered. The top management team reluctantly agreed to the introduction of Starbucks Frappuccino. This iced drink has turned into a billion-dollar business for Starbucks. This bottom-up strategic initiative at Starbucks demonstrates the importance of **planned emergence**, where the top management team develops systems and structures that facilitate the emergence of bottom-up strategic initiatives that achieve organizational goals (Rothaermel 2013).

Planned emergence is the essence of the SSM planning process where the collective wisdom of the firm provides inputs for the planning processes, allowing firms pursuing SSM to rewrite industry rules and to think beyond existing industry boundaries, enabling them to ask "what can be." Thus, the SSM strategy formulation processes expand organizations' ability to create their own future by encouraging organizational members to question the underlying assumptions and values on which the strategy is formulated.

SSM Stakeholders

It is essential that the firm's **stakeholders**, those individuals, groups, and entities that affect or can be affected by the organization's purpose and actions (Freeman 1984), participate and provide inputs into the SSM strategy formulation process discussed above. Stakeholders include both internal stakeholder groups of employees, stockholders, top managers, and board of directors, and external stakeholders that include customers, regulators, suppliers, competitors, advocacy groups, alliance partners, creditors, insurers, communities, governments, and so forth. Input from these stakeholder groups provides the information necessary to formulate strategies that can create shared value with its multiple stakeholders across the firm's value chain (Porter and Kramer 2011). There is often a symbiotic relationship among stakeholder groups where mutual benefit accrues to multiple stakeholders. This interdependence among stakeholders such as the one between employees, customers, suppliers, shareholders, and communities must be acknowledged and strategically managed by the top management team.

Strategic Leaders

Strong strategic leader commitment is the primary driver of sustainability agendas in business organizations (Kiron, et al. 2013). Strategic leaders, such as chief executive officers, have broad responsibility for determining the long-term direction of the organization, and they are the managers who are ultimately held responsible for the economic success of the firm. Strategic leaders must be able to anticipate, envision, adapt, and empower others to implement the strategic changes necessary to create the organization's future. CEOs guide the development of the internal capabilities of the firm in order to make goal achievement possible, and they also manage the strategic processes required to advance their firms toward their visions. This requires that they meaningfully influence the behaviors, thoughts, and feelings of the people around them. The ability to attract, develop, and manage the human and intellectual capital of their firms is a critical leadership skill required to manage knowledge and to create and commercialize innovation. Introducing SSM processes into firms adds social and ecological dimensions to the traditional bottom-line economic roles and responsibilities of CEOs. Given this increase in complexity, many firms have developed heterogeneous **top management teams** composed of people with various functional level backgrounds, education, and experience to help manage triple-bottom-line performance.

Succeeding in establishing and maintaining SSM processes requires a type of strategic leadership that differs significantly from the patriarchal, autocratic leadership models of the past (Doppelt 2003; Nahavandi 2009; Schumacher 1973; Senge 1990). Rather, managing the transformational changes necessary for sustainable strategic management will require transformational leadership, which Nahavandi (2009, 206) defines as "leadership that inspires followers and enables them to enact revolutionary change." Jim Post (2007, 16–17) says, "Leadership is . . . the essential determinant of whether the future of the corporation will be one of transition, transformation, or revolution."

The most powerful economic decision makers in the world are strategic managers in business organizations. These are the people who guide the world's economic machine, deciding what to produce, how to produce it, how to distribute it, and where to distribute it for all of the world's economic products and services. Thus, collectively, strategic managers contribute significantly to the structure and welfare of society as well as the amounts and types of energy used, resources consumed, wastes generated, and pollution created. Given this high level of influence that strategic managers have on the planet's economic, social, and environmental systems, it is critical that they take a leadership role in helping to institute the transformational changes that will allow humankind to transcend into a community of economic, social, and ecological balance that can be sustained for generations to come. If the assessments of Hawken (2007), Edwards (2005), Speth (2008), Kiron et al. (2012), and others are correct, then the changing competitive landscape dictates that this is the ideal time for organizations to become social change agents that can contribute significantly to a planet that is fiscally, socially, and ecologically welcoming for all human beings now and in the future.

Chapter Summary

We introduced the book with a brief look at the history of sustainability efforts at Eastman Chemical Company, a medium-sized global chemical firm that manufactures specialty chemicals, plastics, fibers, and so forth. We will return to Eastman's sustainability story throughout the remainder of the book in ways that demonstrate the sustainable strategic management frameworks and concepts we introduce.

Sustainability has grown from a fringe issue into a pervasive global movement. This is largely because for far too long human economic behavior has been rooted in the unrealistic belief that unlimited economic growth is possible and desirable forever. Only recently have humans come to believe that earthly resources and processes are in danger if human economic activity is not brought back into balance with the planet's stressed natural resources, biophysical systems, and social systems. This shifting economic perspective means that business organizations will need to shift their thinking from the traditional single-bottom-line perspective to a triple-bottom-line perspective. Such a shift normally requires organizations to completely transform their cultures. Coevolution teaches that successful transformation to triple-bottom-line organizations is a continuous upwardly spiraling process that matches the perpetual environmental transcendence going on around it.

Sustainable strategic management has emerged from the coevolutionary interactions between organizations, the society they are a part of, and the planet they exist on. It involves developing a set of processes and strategies in organizations that are economically competitive, socially responsible, and in balance with the cycles of nature. In building an SSM portfolio, organizations must incorporate sustainability into their visions of the future, they must build sustainability into their missions and goals, and they must develop the capabilities and create the strategies that allow them to accomplish those goals, fulfill their missions, and make progress toward their visions. They must also build sustainability-infused planning processes, and they must establish sustainability as a critical aspect of their relationships that they build with stakeholders. This requires strategic leaders who are committed to the principles and practices of sustainability and who have the capabilities to guide their firms in their transformations to triple-bottom-line motivated and designed organizations.

2

In Search of Sustainability

As we begin our journey into sustainable strategic management, we want to explore a basic question: Where will sustainable strategic management (SSM) lead humankind? That is, if economic institutions were to universally adopt SSM processes, what would the potential outcome be? The short answer to this question is that sustainable strategic management will contribute to humankind's pursuit of **sustainability**, the point at which humankind "meets the needs of the present without compromising the ability of the future generations to meet their own needs" (WCED 1987, 8). But what does this mean? What are the underlying principles and dimensions of sustainability, and what will be required for sustainability to happen?

In an effort to address these questions we will examine the concept of sustainability in some depth in this chapter. In doing so, we are establishing sustainability as both an ideal end state for a world dominated by business organizations pursuing the values, principles, and practices of SSM, and a viable transformational process that can help humankind to achieve this end state. Thus, sustainability is a journey toward this vision. However, as we proceed, we want to advise the readers that sustainability is a complex, transdisciplinary, multidimensional concept. It is not something that humankind is close to achieving or even fully understanding. As such, achieving sustainability will require that humans think differently—not just act differently—about the relationships between the economy, the society, and the natural environment.

The Science of Sustainability

We begin our discussion by briefly presenting some of the basic scientific concepts that help ground sustainability in well-established scientific frameworks with regard to the relationships between economic activity, society, and nature. We contend in this section that the Earth is a living system, that the relationships among the Earth's components are coevolutionary, that economic activity on Earth is subject to the laws of thermodynamics, and that economic activity on Earth is metabolic in nature.

The Earth Is a Living System

The Earth—humankind's home—is a living biosociophysical system subject to constant coevolutionary change processes as it renews, reproduces, and regenerates itself and its component subsystems. As an open system, the Earth has processes in place that help it maintain a dynamic balance among its component subsystems, each of which is also open and in search of balance among its own component subsystems. Living systems exchange information, matter, and energy with their environments in order to counteract uncertainty and decay. They receive feedback from their environments that helps them balance inputs and outputs to maintain a dynamic equilibrium. Living systems are morphogenetic, meaning that they can renew, reproduce, and/or regenerate themselves. Living systems have some purpose, goal, or final state that they seek. Living systems are complex; they are composed of a finite number of component subsystems, each of which processes information, matter, and/or energy. These component subsystems are highly interdependent and cannot be treated as isolated entities. Living systems are irreducible wholes; their survival is threatened when their component subsystems break down. Further, living systems are synergistic, displaying certain properties that could never be anticipated by analyzing their component subsystems; they are different from the sum of their parts (Boulding 1966; Schumacher 1977).

The component subsystems of living systems exist in nested hierarchies, with each subsystem contained in a larger system. These hierarchies of subsystems exist at different levels of physical, social, and/or spiritual complexity. Each level both includes and transcends the previous level. Thus, the Earth is an irreducible whole whose survival is threatened if any of its component subsystems break down. Figure 1.2 (see page 9) represents a nested hierarchy of component subsystems associated with economic activity on Earth. As such, all of these subsystems—individuals, organizations, the economy, society, and the ecosystem—are qualitatively different from those below and above it, and the demise of any of these subsystems would gravely threaten the survival of the others. Thus, achieving sustainability in any of these subsystems means achieving a sustainable balance among all of them. As a living system, the Earth both encompasses and transcends the matter, plants, animals, people, societies, and organizations that compose it. From its environment it imports sunlight, which provides the energy for resource development and life itself. Humankind's survival depends on the delicate interaction between the atmosphere, oceans, land, species, and other subsystems that compose it (Boulding 1966; Schumacher 1977).

The Earth's Subsystems Coevolve

A useful framework for understanding the dynamics of sustainability is Gaia theory, which provides a strong scientific basis for understanding the coevolutionary nature of the Earth's component subsystems (Ehrlich 1991; Lovelock 1979, 1988). In Greek mythology Gaia was Mother Earth, the wife of Uranus (the universe) and birth mother of life on the planet. Gaia theory founder James Lovelock chose the label because it best represented his idea that the Earth is a living super organism. Gaia theorists point out that the living system Earth was actually born with the big bang of creation some 15 billion years ago, when the energy necessary for the formation of the universe was released. Some 4.5 billion years ago the Earth became a discernible hot, gaseous ball, and since then it has changed dramatically in terms of chemical content, geological activity, and the evolution of life. Research in Gaia theory has demonstrated that these three have not changed separately, but rather have coevolved on the planet. For example, the oxygen content of the atmosphere has increased over the eons to 21 percent—enough to support large mammals such as humans—as a result of interactions among the Earth's living and nonliving components. In this and many other ways, the Earth's living organisms have continuously interacted with their natural environments to change and regulate chemical, atmospheric, and climate processes in much the same way that a plant or animal self-regulates its internal state. These symbiotic coevolutionary relationships generally involve a complex choreography of both cooperation and competition. Thus, Gaia theory has clearly established that the relationship between the Earth's biological and physical forces is one of mutual influence.

Gaia theory also points to the fact that humankind's environmental sensitivity need not be altruistic. Although environmental debates are often couched in terms of "saving the planet," research results from Gaia theorists make it clear that the planet does not need saving. It can take care of itself. What is threatened via ecological, social, and economic degradation is not the planet but humankind and its way of life. Thus, achieving sustainability will require balanced, complex interactions involving both cooperation and competition among all of the planet's component subsystems, or the human condition will suffer as a result. Gaia theory provides an elegant metaphor that emphasizes a key principle of ecology: that all living things operate together. It is a metaphor that can help human beings to better understand their place in the overall ecological scheme. It brings the phrase, "system of systems" (Boulding 1956, 202) to life. If people were to perceive the Earth as a living, breathing, coevolving being that exists through a beautiful and intricate dance of forests, rivers, oceans, atmosphere, microbes, plants, and animals, their perspectives of human activities would likely change. James Lovelock (1988, 14) says, "In Gaia we are just another species. . . . Our future depends much more upon a right relationship with Gaia than with the never-ending drama of human interest." Eckhart Tolle (2005, 21) agrees, saying that the only way to avoid the environmental crisis generated from humans' egoistic pursuit of material wealth is to "evolve or die" as a species.

The Economic Subsystem Is Entropic

As mentioned, survival for living systems is based on their ability to exchange energy, wastes, and information with their environment. It is a process of constantly swimming upstream against time, seeking order in a sea of chaos. This process is subject to the laws of thermodynamics, a set of principles governing the movement and transformation of energy in the universe (Daly 1977; Georgescu-Roegen 1971). The first law of thermodynamics, the conservation law, says that the amount of energy released by the big bang is a constant in the universe. Energy cannot be created or destroyed; it can only be transformed from one state to another. The amount of energy generated during this transformation depends on the temperature difference between the states (hence the term "thermodynamics"). The second law of thermodynamics says that every time energy is transformed from one state to another, some of its available energy to do work is lost. This process is called **entropy**. Entropy occurs when stored energy becomes cooler, less concentrated, and/or less ordered when it is applied to do work. When energy is no longer available to do work, when it has degraded to the point of being useless, it becomes waste.

Whereas entropy is a certainty for the Earth, there is little certainty about the path or time it will take. These will depend on how efficiently humankind uses its available energy and how well it responds to the changes in its environment. The Earth and its living subsystems can survive and increase in orderliness while there is sufficient power from the sun as long as people respond correctly to signals from the environment. Climate change, smog, cancer, water shortages, genocide, and energy crises are just a few signals that indicate the need for changes in how humans interact with the planet. The more serious these problems get, the more difficult they will be to deal with. However, if people respond appropriately to these signals, the species can survive and develop for eons to come. In a true biophysical sense, strategic managers, who control the majority of global economic activity, make decisions that directly influence the rate of the entropic flow of resources and energy.

The path that entropy will take is directly related to economic activity on the planet. To this point humankind's economic system has survived by using processes that rapidly transform energy and natural resources from their low-entropy natural state to create high-entropy products, services, and wastes. In the economic system, money and energy flow in opposite directions. For example, the farmers' money goes to town in exchange for the fertilizer they need to power their crops; the manufacturers' money goes to the utility company in exchange for the power they need to produce their products. However, while money stays within the economic system, energy often exists outside the system. Sunlight, nonrenewable resources, and other sources of energy that power the economy do not enter the economic cycle until they are purchased and/or converted to fuel. Further, the wastes that occur as a result of converting energy into economic wealth are also considered external to the system. Thus, it seems reasonable to assume that the entropy law should be at the heart of future economic theory and practice. If it is not, it is virtually impossible to effectively account for the true value of natural resources, the intrinsic value of life, and the actual cost of pollution and overpopulation in economic activity. Essentially, assuming that economic activity is not subject to the entropy law leads directly to the fallacious assumption that unlimited economic expansion is forever possible (Daly 1977; Georgescu-Roegen 1971).

The Economic Subsystem Is Metabolic

One of the most enlightening frameworks for understanding the impacts of a high-entropy economy is **industrial metabolism** (Ayres 1989, 1994). Just as living organisms have metabolic processes for transforming the energy they import from their environment into life-maintaining processes, economies can also be viewed as metabolic because they extract large quantities of energy-rich matter from the environment and transform it into products for consumption. Industrial metabolism involves all the processes used to convert resources, energy, and labor into products, services, and wastes.

Whereas the metabolic processes necessary to maintain life in the ecosystem are balanced and self-sustaining, metabolism in the economic system is grossly out of balance with its environment. Resources that literally take eons to renew (such as oil) are being used at nonrenewable rates because only a small percentage of the resources used in economic activity remains in the system for any length of time (basically as durable goods). Most materials are used to produce food, fuel, and throwaway products that pass through the economic system from extraction to production to consumption to waste very rapidly. These wastes are often toxic and harmful to the natural environment. The damage is done not within the economic system per se, but in the atmosphere, water, and gene pool that have no current economic value.

Entropy occurs at all points in the metabolic process, including extraction, production, and consumption. However, most of the loss comes at the point of consumption. Most foods, fuels, paper, plastics, lubricants, solvents, fertilizers, pesticides, cosmetics, pharmaceuticals, and toxic heavy metals are discarded as wastes after a single use, as are thousands of other products and their packaging. Many of these are very difficult and expensive to recycle, so not only do people use too many of them, but they are also not likely to use them again.

The basic message from the industrial metabolism framework is that the metabolic processes in the economy need to achieve the same type of balance that is possible in the ecosystem when it is absent of economic activity. Just as the ecosystem can sustain itself indefinitely by importing sunlight and using it to power a system that operates almost totally by recycling materials, economic systems also need to incorporate sustainable energy transformation processes. Achieving this balance will require total materials recycling. That is, the four segments of the materials flow cycle—the natural environment, raw materials and commodities, productive capital, and final products—must achieve a balance via processes such as recycling, remanufacturing, reconditioning, and so forth.

The Issue Wheel: Carrying Capacity Meets the Human Footprint

From a biophysical perspective, sustainability is defined by the planet's **carrying capacity**—the amount of production, consumption, resource depletion, environmental degradation, and wastes the planet can realistically absorb without threatening the coevolving systems that support human life—the atmosphere, geosphere, hydrosphere, and biosphere. The Earth's carrying capacity dictates the maximum size of the **human footprint**—the resources and energy used and wastes and degradation created by humans in the conduct of their daily lives on the planet. When the size of the human footprint exceeds the planet's carrying capacity, the human-friendly balance of the Earth's natural systems is threatened. In this section, we will attempt to elucidate why and how the current human footprint is out of balance with the Earth's carrying capacity and thus putting significant stress on the planetary subsystems.

The current human footprint results from the interactions among three highly interrelated, coevolving variables: population growth, human affluence (as measured by the growth in per capita gross domestic product [GDP]), and

Figure 2.1   **The Issue Wheel**

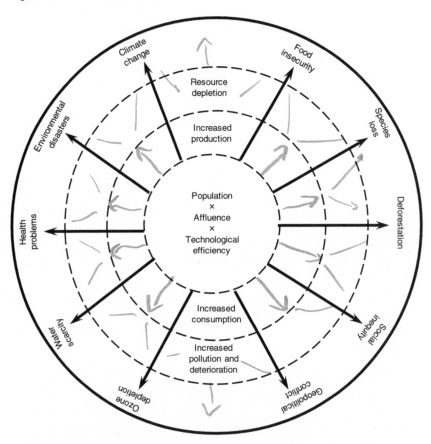

Source: Adapted from Stead and Stead 1996.

the impact of technology on the natural environment (as measured by the materials, energy, and wastes generated to create each unit of GDP) (Ehrlich and Ehrlich 1990). Like a wheel, the environmental and social issues faced today begin with the interactions among these three central variables and radiate out into the larger society and ecosystem. As Figure 2.1 depicts, population growth, affluence, and technology efficiency interact to create rapidly increasing production and consumption. As humankind produces and consumes in order to meet the demands of an exponentially growing number of people, it continues to deplete its resources and foul its nest with its own wastes and pollutants. The resulting problems include environmental catastrophe, water scarcity, loss of species, failed political states, environmental injustice, climate change, food insecurity, land degradation, geopolitical conflict, deforestation, social inequity, disease, and a lower quality of life for many in the present and for posterity.

Population

The global population in 2012 reached over 7 billion. The United Nations projects that the world population will increase to 8.9 billion people by 2050 with nearly all of this growth in developing and undeveloped markets. Each year 79.3 million human beings are added to our small planet, which is still only 25,000 miles in circumference. The human population has tripled in the past 72 years, and there were 10 times as many people on the Earth in 2000 as there were in 1700. Approximately 95 percent of population growth is occurring in undeveloped and developing markets (especially in Africa and Asia). It is projected that by mid-century Africa will add 21 million people to the planet annually, and Asia will add 5 million. Some countries have had annual population growth rates above 3 percent, a rate that would double their populations in less than 25 years. These countries include Niger, Afghanistan, Uganda, Timor-Leste, the Palestinian territories (West Bank and Gaza), Liberia, and Burkina Faso (Engelman 2011).

Although overpopulation is primarily portrayed as a problem for undeveloped and developing markets, the human footprint concept demonstrates that overpopulation is an issue in the world's developed markets as well. Overpopulation occurs when a region, nation, or community exceeds its human footprint and cannot sustain itself without rapidly depleting its resources, degrading its environment, and/or importing energy and resources from elsewhere. Today 7 billion people are stomping all over the planet's carrying capacity. Given that by 2050, 2 billion more humans will be "walking" on the planet, it seems crucial that they quickly find ways to reduce the size of their collective footprint on small planet Earth.

Affluence

In addition to exponential population growth, world GDP increased on average 46 percent per decade from 1980 to 2005 (Speth 2008). There are increasingly more humans on this planet who want to consume like those in the developed markets of the world. Worldwide, private consumption expenditures—the amount spent on goods and services at the household level—topped US$20 trillion in 2000, a fourfold increase over 1960. In 2009, global output for consumptive purposes rose by 6.6 percent, led by China's 9.1 percent and India's 7.4 percent (Gardner 2011). China, India, and the rest of the developing markets of the world will eclipse the developed markets in a dramatic shift in the balance of economic power over the next fifty years. Forecasts are that China will overtake the eurozone in 2012 and the United States by 2016 to become the largest economy in the world. India is in the process of overtaking Japan and is forecast to pass the eurozone in about 20 years. Over the next half century, the average GDP per capita is predicted to grow by roughly 3 percent annually in developing markets, as compared to 1.7 percent in the developed markets (Mead 2012).

In the developing and developed markets of the world the increasing size of the footprint is largely due to the ecological excesses of affluence. By one calculation, there are now more than 1.7 billion members of "the consumer class"—nearly half of them in the developing world. China and India alone claim more than 20 percent of the global total—with a combined consumer class of 362 million people. Developing markets also have the greatest potential to expand the ranks of consumers. China and India's large consumer sets constitute only 16 percent of their populations, whereas in Europe the figure is 89 percent. Indeed, in most developing markets the consumer class accounts for less than half of the population, suggesting considerable room to expand. This new, emerging consumer class represents a global trend where consumers are seeking to imitate a lifestyle and culture that became common in the developed markets of Europe, North America, and Japan in the twentieth century, a lifestyle where well-being is directly correlated with the amount consumed (Worldwatch Institute 2011). In affluent markets people buy too much, eat too much, use too much, and owe too much. This lifestyle based on the excessive consumption of goods has been described as a sociological phenomenon labeled hyper-consumption (Barber 1995).

Take China, for example. Auto sales increased by 60 percent in 2002 and by more than 80 percent in the first half of 2003. Each day 11,000 more cars merge onto Chinese roads. By 2015, 150 million cars are expected in China, 18 million more than were driven in the United States in 1999. If China's car ownership and oil consumption rates were equal to the U.S. rates, 80 million more barrels of oil a day above current production levels would be needed. These numbers are especially troubling because China's car population is expected to reach 1.1 billion by 2030 (Brown 2008).

The fact is that economic growth statistics like these are generally reported with glee because the global economy is currently functioning under the illusion that everyone on the planet can consume all they want forever. This has been a dominant assumption of economic theory since Adam Smith published *The Wealth of Nations* in 1776. Of course, when Smith published his theories in the early days of the Industrial Revolution, unlimited growth was a relatively harmless assumption. There were less than a billion people inhabiting the Earth in 1776, and very few of them in very few places were actually involved in significant economic activity. There certainly seemed plenty for everyone forever at that time. However, the current rapidly growing population and rapidly growing economic marketplace has changed the situation drastically. Today we live in a "full" planet. If there are 8.9 billion people in 2050 (a mere 37 years) living in a world full of growth-oriented economic systems, the human habitat will not be able to manage the stress without making significant changes in the way humans live and the way business is practiced.

Sustainability cannot be achieved unless the understanding of economics goes beyond the current thinking that economic growth is the only important measure of individual well-being. Sustainability involves the need to create for posterity an ecologically balanced and socially just economic system that provides humans with the goods, services, economic justice, and meaningful employment necessary for a high quality of life. Thus: **At the heart of sustainable strategic management is the understanding that the impacts of economic activity should be measured on their ecological and social as well as economic outcomes.**

Technological Efficiency

One of the keys to stemming the size of the human footprint is to create production, transportation, and consumption technologies designed to have little or no impact on the Earth's biophysical systems as humans pursue economic growth. For many, improved technological efficiency represents the saving grace from planetary ecological catastrophe. They believe that the road to ecological salvation is paved with environmentally improved technologies that use less energy and fewer resources and generate fewer wastes while churning out a never-ending stream of products and services. In fact, there have been and continue to be important advances in green technology.

For example, enhanced energy efficiency from numerous sources ranging from improvements in lighting and air-conditioning technologies to improvements in automobile engine efficiency provides double dividends by lowering energy costs and carbon dioxide emissions. Research and development of alternative energy sources, such as solar collectors and hydrogen fuel cells, and improvements in current technologies, such as carbon capture and storage technologies for coal-generated energy systems, hold serious promise for a more energy efficient future.

However, the surge in human population threatens to offset any savings in resource use from improved efficiency, as well as any gains in reducing per capita consumption (Worldwatch Institute 2011). As we will demonstrate in the next section, despite current improvements in energy efficient technology, there are still large global increases in carbon emissions. Further, statistics show that the Earth's temperature continues to rise, toxins and pollutants continue to plague the planet, species continue to disappear, and many critical natural resources that sustain human life, such as clean air and water, are declining. Thus, skepticism abounds with regard to the potential for technology alone to provide the way out of humankind's ecological and social ills. The following sections will specifically address the ecological and social dimensions of sustainability.

Ecological Sustainability: Management Happens on Earth

In his classic article, Kenneth Boulding (1966) compared the Earth to a spaceship because it is a relatively closed system with little ability to import inputs or export outputs. As Figure 1.2 depicts, the Earth's only significant input is solar energy, and the Earth presently has no way to dispose of wastes beyond its own boundaries. For billions of years this limited openness was sufficient to support a robust biophysical balance. However, as discussed above, the increased production and consumption associated with a growing population in a growth oriented global economy flies directly in the face of ecological balance. Thus, the planet's wild places are disappearing, its resources are being depleted at increasingly rapid rates, it is being degraded by an overflow of dangerous pollution and wastes, and its climate is changing in alarming ways.

Depleting Resources

The 4.5 billion year coevolution of the Earth's biophysical systems has resulted in an abundance of natural resources, such as fossil fuels, high-grade mineral ores, trees, rich agricultural soils, groundwater stored during the ice ages, and millions of species. Natural resources are critical to humankind's survival because, ultimately, they are the only capital humans have. They are the basic sources of material wealth, financial wealth, and psychological wealth. However, the news on how well humans are protecting the planet's natural capital—its collection of life-supporting natural resources and processes—is not all that encouraging. There is the potential for severe water and cropland shortages leading to food insecurity in the coming years. Forests, wetlands, species, upper atmospheric ozone, and fossil fuels and essential minerals are also disappearing at alarming rates.

Water security is a fundamental requirement for human survival and development. Today, around 1.4 billion people live in closed river basins where water use is greater than discharge levels, thus exceeding the area's carrying capacity for water, and creating severe ecological damage. By 2025, 1.8 billion people could be living in countries and regions with absolute water scarcity, and two-thirds of the world population could be living under conditions of water stress (UNEP 2007). Groundwater levels are estimated to drop 1 to 3 meters in India and China, which possess the most irrigated lands in the world. Water withdrawals are expected to increase by 50 percent by 2025 in developing markets and 18 percent in developed markets. The Middle East and North Africa are considered the most water-stressed regions in the world. Water stress is a serious human development problem with an alarming potential for geopolitical conflicts over access to water (Roudi-Fahimi, Creel, and De Souza 2002; UNDP 2007).

Wetlands are also vital to the planet's ecological balance because they help to stem floods and erosion, replenish groundwater aquifers, and facilitate the settling or removal of inorganic matter and organic microbes. Further, wetlands are rich in biodiversity. Half of the world's coastal and inland wetlands have been lost over the past century, and 60 percent of the world's rivers have fallen victim to construction, channeling, draining, and/or pollution. The devastation caused by Hurricane Katrina was significantly enhanced because the vast wetlands that once protected New Orleans and Baton Rouge from the brunt of tropical storms have largely disappeared due to stream channeling and development. The economic losses suffered from Katrina amounted to more than US$125 billion.

Species extinction rates today are estimated to be roughly 100 times higher than past ages based on analysis of fossil records. Estimates are that these extinction rates will increase to the order of 1,000 to 10,000 times over the coming decades (United Nations Environment Programme 2007). According to Brown (2008) we are experiencing the sixth great extinction in civilization, with the last one occurring 65 million years ago when an asteroid hit the planet. Now, for the first time in history, a mass extinction is being caused by one of the planet's own species—human beings. The Millennium Ecosystem Assessment, a four-year study of the Earth's ecosystem services by 1,360 eminent scientists, found that 15 of the 24 primary ecosystem services were currently being degraded or pushed beyond their limits. For example, world fisheries have been depleted, with 75 percent of the world's fish stocks either fully or overexploited. This is of critical concern in terms of food security since fish are the major global source of human protein (Brown 2008).

Other species face extinction as well. According to Brown (2008), 20 percent of the world's mammals, 12.5 percent of all birds, 33 percent of all amphibians, and 70 percent of all assessed plants are considered at risk. Since 1990, 25 percent of the honeybee population has vanished in the United States, and up to 90 percent of the world's feral honeybee population has disappeared. Data also indicate the decline in genetic diversity in both plants and animals. For example, at least one breed of livestock has become extinct every month for the past seven years. The state of farm animal diversity is critical for the people in undeveloped and developing markets where farm animals are not only sources of food but are also capital that can be sold in times of need (Nierenberg 2007).

Stratospheric (upper atmosphere) ozone depletion continues to occur everywhere except over the tropics. Huge holes in the planet's upper ozone layer, which shields the Earth's inhabitants from the debilitating effects of the sun's ultraviolet rays, have been discovered over the past several decades. The ozone hole has steadily grown in both size (up to 27 million square kilometers) and length of existence (currently from August through early December) over the past two decades (NWS 2012).

The world's forests shrank by 1.3 percent (520,000 square kilometers) from 2000 to 2010 (Normander 2012). About 4.2 percent of the world's natural forests—161 million hectares (398 million acres)—disappeared during the 1990s. Even more disturbing is that 152 million of these hectares were lost in the world's tropical rain forests, which were once referred to by Brazilian environmental martyr Chico Mendes as "the lungs of the planet" because they absorb so much carbon dioxide and produce so much oxygen (UNEP 2007). As these forests disappear, so do the habitats of most of the Earth's species, the water and watersheds for billions of people, and the first line of defense against climate change.

These problems stem largely from the current destructive nature of the interactions among the economic, social, and ecological systems. The forests are being harvested and shipped to developed and developing markets where they are converted into paper and wood for furniture, homes, and so on. By 2030, China will have 1.46 billion people who will consume twice as much paper as is produced worldwide today (Brown 2008). The pulp and paper industry is the single largest consumer of water used in industrial activities and is the third greatest industrial greenhouse gas emitter. Between 2000 and 2005, around 10 million acres of forests were lost per year in South America, which incorporates the mighty Amazon forest where the majority of the species on the planet live. However, the good news is that the rate of deforestation has declined during the first decade of this century (Normander 2012).

Nonrenewable fossil fuels are also being exhausted at incredible rates, and this trend is forecasted to continue. World energy consumption is projected to increase by 57 percent from 2004 to 2030, with energy demand increasing 95 percent in developing markets and 24 percent in developed markets. In terms of oil, the current consensus among oil market experts is that the world will meet the 93 million barrel a day peak extraction rate—the rate beyond which demand cannot be met—sometime around 2020 (U.S. Department of Energy 2007). Global oil production has struggled to keep up with increased demand recently, particularly from Asia. In China alone consumption has risen by over 4 million barrels per day in the past decade, accounting for two-fifths of the global rise. In 2010 world oil supplies were down because consumption exceeded production by over 5 million barrels per day for the first time ever.

Coal is the most abundant fossil fuel, and it has surpassed oil to become the largest contributor to global carbon dioxide emissions of all fossil fuels. In 2009 coal accounted for 29.4 percent of energy consumption, its highest level since 1970 (Kitasei 2011). Increased use of coal in developing markets will account for approximately 85 percent of the total growth in world coal consumption by 2030. China continues to be the largest coal market in the world with a total world coal consumption of 46.9 percent. China burns about 3.7 billion tons of coal each year, or roughly 3 times what it consumed in 2000 and 3.5 times what the United States consumes. China will soon account for half the coal burned on the planet. China, already the world's number one emitter of carbon dioxide, has now become the world's largest energy consumer. Although many of the world's most polluted cities are in China, it continues to build new coal plants at a blistering rate (Thompson 2011). Further, not only is humankind depleting its supplies of fossil fuels, it is also quickly depleting its supplies of minerals such as copper and iron ore that are used in industrial activities.

Increasing Pollution

The Earth has no significant potential for exporting its pollution and wastes beyond its atmospheric boundaries, as we discussed above. Thus, humans are left to release the wastes that result from their consumption and production processes into the air they breathe, the water they drink, and the ground they live on and produce food on. In the true biophysical sense, humans are transforming low-entropy natural resources into high-entropy wastes at a rate that exceeds the Earth's carrying capacity, causing the pollution of our air, land, and water, the essential resources that sustain human life.

Access to clean water is a fundamental requirement for human life and development. Besides using water at irreplaceable rates as mentioned above, humans have poured toxic chemicals and other waste products into the Earth's waterways over the years. Human and animal wastes, agricultural wastes, and industrial wastes are too often dumped into the Earth's aboveground and underground waterways with little regard for those who are downstream. Many substances, such as nitrates, pesticides, petrochemicals, arsenic, chlorinated solvents, radioactive wastes, and human wastes, find their way into rivers and waterways and eventually flow into the oceans. For example, every day 2 million tons of sewage, industrial wastes, and agricultural wastes are discharged into the world's waterways, the equivalent of the weight of the entire human population. The UN estimates that the wastewater produced annually is 6 times greater than all the water in all the rivers of the world. Worldwide, 2.5 billion people live without improved sanitation, and 1.2 billion people (1 out of 3 in rural areas) defecate in the open, posing an extreme human health risk (Ross 2010).

Not only are humans fouling their nests by dumping their human wastes into the water, they are also dumping wastes into the oceans at a rate that has increased threefold since the 1960s. An estimated 46,000 pieces of plastic litter are floating on every square mile of the Earth's oceans. Conservation groups estimate that more than a million seabirds and 100,000 mammals and sea turtles die globally each year by getting tangled in or ingesting plastics. There are more than 200 dead zones—areas so contaminated that they cannot support marine life—in our oceans, a one-third increase in two years. The most severe cases exceed 20,000 square kilometers (about the size of the state of Maryland) and are located in waters such as the Gulf of Mexico, the Baltic Sea, the Arabian Sea, the Bay of Bengal, and the East China Sea (Halweil 2007).

One of the most troubling water issues is the pollution of groundwater in agricultural regions due to the huge amounts of fertilizers, pesticides, and animal wastes that mix with rain and seep into the underground aquifers from which farmers and communities get their drinking water. Unfortunately, this problem shows no signs of abatement. For example, pesticide use has increased fivefold in Latin America since 1980 due to the increased demand for fresh produce all year long in high-income markets. Americans pour approximately 2.2 billion pounds of pesticides on their farmlands each year, and fertilizer use is up 10 percent worldwide (Speth 2008). Contamination of groundwater is particularly troubling because once polluted it is expensive and sometimes impossible to clean.

Many of humankind's wastes are buried. The images of overflowing landfills and garbage barges looking for communities willing to take their trash are fresh in the human psyche. In fact, the **throwaway society** we know today was deliberately conceived in the United States not long after World War II to generate more employment and economic growth by making disposable products. The rationale was that if more products are produced and thrown away, then more jobs will be created to replace them, and more economic growth will result. Little did the decision makers over 50 years ago understand that the throwaway society would set the economy on a collision course with the planet's ecological limits. Most of the world's major cities have reached a crisis in waste disposal. For example, the last landfill in Toronto, Canada, closed in 2002, and it now ships 750,000 tons of garbage each year to Wayne County, Michigan (Brown 2008).

Not only are landfills overflowing, the economic and environmental costs of getting the garbage to the landfills is rapidly becoming prohibitive. The simple reality is that the world has run out of cheap oil to move things like garbage around from place to place. The city of New York, for example, is currently using 600 energy-intensive tractor-trailer rigs to move (primarily to New Jersey) the 12,000 tons of garbage generated by its citizens daily. If these rigs were to be strung together each day, they would constitute a nine-mile long tractor-trailer truck convoy, contributing significantly to fuel consumption, air pollution, carbon emissions, and traffic congestion. In addition to oil, humankind's current fascination with throwaway products will assure that future generations of humans suffer from shortages of numerous other natural resources discarded by their ancestors (Brown 2008).

Although they do not come close to matching the amount of chemical and solid wastes generated, nuclear wastes represent a very serious hazardous waste disposal problem. Developing markets are expected to see a robust expansion of nuclear power generation between 2004 and 2030, with China's annual growth rate forecast to be 7.7 percent and India's 9.1 percent (U.S. Department of Energy 2007). Yet, many of the wastes and by-products from nuclear processing facilities and power plants are dangerously toxic and will be so for hundreds of thousands of years. Further, none of the countries that produce nuclear wastes have come up with an acceptable solution for their disposal. For example, in the United States a battle over the appropriateness of burying nuclear wastes under Yucca Mountain, Nevada, has raged for decades, and there really seems to be no end in sight. In the meantime, millions of containers of nuclear wastes are stored on the grounds of U.S. nuclear power plants and processing facilities awaiting final disposal.

Changing Climate

During the Industrial Age, there has been an unprecedented increase in the presence of potentially dangerous greenhouse gases (GHG) in the atmosphere. Atmospheric concentrations of carbon dioxide (the most prominent GHG) are increasing by 1.9 parts per million annually. The growth rate in GHG emissions from 2000 to 2010 was faster than in previous decades. The annual increase in GHG emissions reached 1 billion metric tons for the first time in 2002, and this happened three more times between 2003 and 2010 (Mulrow 2010). Fossil fuel burning, biomass burning (i.e., burning the rain forests to clear them for grazing land), agricultural activities, and declining forest cover are infusing large quantities of carbon emissions and toxins into the atmosphere every day.

Of the many insidious environmental issues contributing to the oversized human footprint of today, climate change is clearly the most notorious and immediate. Climate change is occurring because of the increases in greenhouse gases in the atmosphere, especially carbon dioxide. These gases trap solar heat in the Earth's atmosphere just as the transparent roof on a greenhouse traps solar heat, hence the term, **greenhouse gas**. Essentially, climate change is occurring because of changes in the planetary carbon cycle—the cycle by which carbon molecules are created and exchanged among the Earth's biophysical systems. The carbon cycle remains in balance so long as the amount of carbon in the cycle does not exceed the carbon budget, which is the amount of carbon that can be naturally absorbed by the cycle's carbon sinks (the atmosphere, waterways, plants, and soil). Because of the huge rise in carbon emissions from the burning of fossil fuels during the Industrial Revolution, more carbon is being trapped in the atmosphere. This creates an abundance of carbon dioxide that remains in the atmosphere, keeping more of the Earth's heat from escaping and resulting in rising temperatures now and into the future. Further, such excesses of carbon in the cycle have the potential to weaken the natural carbon sinks, reducing the carbon budget and stimulating even more rapid changes in climate.

When the current excessive greenhouse gas emissions of the developed world markets are combined with the emissions from the accelerating economic engines of China, India, and other developing markets, aggregate carbon emissions are forecast to continue to increase worldwide during the twenty-first century. China's carbon dioxide emissions have increased approximately 6 percent a year since 1971, a trend that is projected to continue (Mulrow 2010). Predictions indicate a potential stabilization point for atmospheric carbon dioxide in excess of 750 parts per million, with possible resulting temperature increases in excess of 5 degrees centigrade. Such rates would exhaust the entire twenty-first century carbon budget by 2032. Beyond a warming threshold of two degrees centigrade above the pre–Industrial Revolution era, there could be a large-scale reversal in human development resulting in irreversible declines in social and human capital. If the 2 degrees centigrade threshold is crossed, poverty, malnutrition, and serious health consequences will be encountered, as Figure 2.1 depicts. Climate change poses five specific risks for human development from increased oceanic temperatures leading to more weather-related disasters, reduced agricultural productivity, increased water insecurity, reduced ecosystems and biodiversity, and increased adverse human health consequences (UNDP 2007).

Several of these consequences are already being felt. The oceans have warmed significantly over the past 40 years, and much of that warming has taken place in the oceans' deepest regions. According to scientists, deepwater warming is a clear sign of impending temperature increases. Further, as the ocean waters warm, there is a greater likelihood of an increase in both the quantity and intensity of tropical storms because there is more warm water over which they can form and gain strength. Studies have found that hurricane winds have increased about 50 percent in the past 50 years. The increased tropical storm activity could have devastating consequences for many countries, including Pacific and Caribbean island states that could literally disappear because of the storms and the rising sea levels. Scientists believe that up to 330 million people could be displaced by storms and rising tides resulting from temperature increases in this century (Löw 2010).

The cover story of the November 11, 2012, *Bloomberg Business Week*, "It's Global Warming, Stupid," was a loud call connecting global warming and the increase in natural disasters. The article contends that Hurricane Sandy beckons an examination of climate change and its impact on both the economy and people. In the northeastern United States, Sandy's path left at least 40 dead and economic losses expected to climb as high as US$50 billion. Eight million homes were left without power and hundreds of thousands of people were evacuated. More than 15,000 flights were grounded, and factories, stores, and hospitals were shut. Lower Manhattan was left dark, silent, and underwater.

In fact, nowhere in the world is the rising number of weather catastrophes more evident than in the United States. From 1980 through 2011, there were five times as many severe weather incidents in the United States as in the previous 30 years, causing losses totaling US$1.06 trillion. During that same period, weather catastrophes rose by a factor of 4 in Asia, a factor of 2.5 in Africa, a factor of 2 in Europe, and a factor of 1.5 in South America. July 2012 was the hottest month in the United States since record keeping began in 1895, and two-thirds of the continental United States suffered drought conditions during the summer of 2012 (Barrett 2012).

Climate change transforms ecosystems and reduces biodiversity. Although some species will be able to adapt to the warmer temperatures, a 3 degree centigrade increase in warming could put 20–30 percent of land species at risk of extinction (UNDP 2007). Ironically, one of Lovelock's (1979, 1988) most significant findings in his research on Gaia theory was that biodiversity is an important ingredient in climate regulation. Thus, as species extinction rates increase due to climate change, the resulting loss in biodiversity may be reflected in more climate disasters and rising temperatures. It is a coevolving vicious reinforcing cycle that could spiral out of control if it has not already. If humankind does not find some way to effectively deal with climate change now, then future generations will suffer greatly from our lack of action. Clearly, this is a problem that humankind has already willed to its children.

Social Sustainability: Searching for Equity

Socially, achieving sustainability will require effectively dealing with a plethora of social issues facing communities and nations worldwide. Included among these issues are population growth, the economic gulf between developed, undeveloped, and developing markets, human rights, human health, gender equity, education, food security, urbanization, and community viability. As discussed in Chapter 1, unlimited economic growth is a cornerstone assumption of conventional economics. From a social perspective, the logic of this assumption goes something like this: If the economic pie gets bigger, then more people can get wealthier until eventually everyone has enough, therefore solving the issue of distributive equity both within and between nations. Thus, conventional economics believes that the fair distribution of wealth will happen when the whole world gets aboard the economic growth train.

However, ecological economics provides a very different view of this issue. In addition to addressing the appropriate scale of the economy and the efficient allocation of natural resources, ecological economics directly addresses the distribution of wealth within and between countries because inequitable wealth distribution results in so many social (and environmental) injustices. As Daly and Farley (2004, 267) explain, the distribution of wealth and income is "a fundamental dimension of justice in society." Distributive inequity and injustice are primary contributors to overpopulation. Increases in income eventually lead to decreases in both mortality rates and fertility rates. In today's world, many regions have increased incomes enough to reduce mortality, but they have not yet increased incomes enough to reduce fertility. Thus, a situation develops "where rapid population growth begets poverty and poverty begets rapid population growth. In this situation countries eventually tip one way or the other. They either break out of the cycle or they break down" (Brown 2008, 5). For example, in Sudan women have five children each on average, and the population of 45 million is growing by 2,400 per day. "Under this pressure, Sudan—like scores of other countries—is breaking down" (Brown 2008, 124). In fact, a billion people live in countries where the population will double by 2050.

The less developed regions account for the vast majority of the world population (81.3 percent), where the more developed regions have 18.7 percent of the world population. More and more of the world's inhabitants are coming to reside in the less developed regions, increasing from 67.7 percent in 1950 to a projected 86.4 percent in 2050 (UN 2004). This unequal population distribution provides business organizations with opportunities for new labor and consumer markets not available to them in the slow-growth developed markets of the world with their aging populations.

Unfortunately, these new sources of labor and consumers come with myriad social issues exacerbated by their rapid population growth and rapid depletion of resources. Issues such as poverty, economic injustice, food insecurity, violence against women, environmental injustice, infant mortality, inadequate access to reproductive health care, and urbanization coevolve with natural resource issues such as water and cropland scarcity/pollution, deforestation, and species diversity resulting in an environmental context drastically different from the developed markets of the world. These coevolving issues make improving the quality of life of citizens in markets experiencing rapid population growth a tough uphill battle. Thus, in order for organizations to take advantage of these new, emerging consumer and labor markets, they will have to add health care, education, water scarcity, social and economic injustice, food insecurity, and so on to their management agendas in the twenty-first century. In the following section, we explore these social issues in more detail.

The Injustice of Distributive Inequity

Wealth is defined as the total value of the assets held by an entity, such as a person, household, organization, or nation, at a given point in time. The wealth created from global economic activity has come at high human and environmental costs that are borne disproportionately by the poor and marginalized people of the world. According to Lester Brown (2008, 107), "The social and economic gap between the world's richest one billion people and its poorest billion people has no historic precedent. Not only is this gap wide, it is widening." The world is socially divided into polar opposites, twin peaks (Quah 1997). The poorest 40 percent of the world's population accounts for only 5 percent of global income. The richest 20 percent of the population accounts for three-quarters of world income. Not surprisingly, 90 percent of the world's wealth is concentrated in North America, Europe, and the rich Asian Pacific countries (Shah 2010).

There are even distributive inequity issues in the developed markets that generate 75 percent of global income. For example, in the United States the income gap has continued to widen. Data indicate that the top 1 percent of American wage earners currently capture more of the real national income than do the lower 50 percent. The incomes of this top group grew 275 percent from 1979 to 2007 while the incomes of other American households only grew 62 percent (Francis 2012). Research indicates that average Americans are struggling harder to get by while rich Americans are getting richer and the rate of poverty is increasing. The working poor, primarily dual-income families that still cannot make ends meet without public assistance, are being "nickel and dimed " while trying to provide food for their families as global food prices continue to rise (Ehrenreich 2001). Thus, even affluent countries of the world have population segments that can be characterized by high rates of poverty, disease, and ecosystem destruction.

Daly and Farley (2004, 262) say that wealth is a "historical result of whose ancestors got there first, of marriage, of inheritance, plus individual ability and effort and just plain luck." They do not take issue with these per se, but they strongly believe that without also accounting for the huge distributive inequities of wealth that exist in the world today, achieving sustainability will be impossible. It is no surprise that statistics on the distribution of wealth mirror those for income distribution where the top 10 percent of adults own 85 percent of global household wealth (Davies et al. 2008). Wealth is an important measure of economic well-being for several reasons: It provides the citizens who hold it with a cushion against adverse events such as illness and unemployment, it provides them with capital for entrepreneurial efforts and other investments, and it increases the income they have available for food, shelter, and other needs and wants. There is a very high disparity of wealth among the citizens of the world, even though incomes have been rising in the developing markets, such as in urban China. In fact, global wealth is more concentrated than income both within and between countries, with the lowest level of wealth found in the poorer countries that lack any sort of social safety nets. India and China, if current growth continues, will move up in the global distribution of wealth, while Africa, Latin America, and the poor parts of the Asian Pacific region will continue in poverty. "Thus wealth may continue to be lowest in areas where it is needed the most" (Davies et al. 2008, xii).

Along with the distributive inequity of income and wealth come issues with social and environmental justice. Unfortunately, even though environmental and social justice have been endorsed over the past 60 years by numerous international conventions, including the United Nations, millions of people are still denied these human rights daily. Life expectancy is now declining in many parts of the poverty-stricken world, indicating that even the most basic human right—survival—is threatened in places. More and more impoverished environmental refugees are fleeing their homes because of land degradation, water scarcity, and climate disasters. Some societies are so stressed over basic resources and their inability to meet the basic needs of their people that their political systems are failing. Brown (2008) believes that these are the early signs of decline in our civilization.

Food Insecurity

The stresses on the ecosystem are having a serious effect on global food security. Brown (2008) notes that food insecurity is a tipping point that has brought many civilizations down over the ages. He explains that several converging trends are impacting farmers' abilities to meet the world demand for food. Falling water tables, loss of cropland to nonfarm uses, and extreme climate events such as droughts, heat waves, fires, and floods have resulted in a world grain production that has fallen short of consumption for the past eight years. Approximately 70 percent of human calories are supplied by grain, but forecasts indicate continuing and significant price increases for grains, much of which can be attributed to climate change. One billion people worldwide are hungry and are being pushed over the edge by skyrocketing food prices. The droughts of 2012 have exacerbated the increasing cost of food and its distribution, both of which have the greatest impact on the poor (Weil 2012).

Cropland is decreasing because farming has become so efficient. Today, due to the intense consolidation and specialization of the industry, sociologists have designated many areas in rural America "food deserts" because the population is totally dependent on convenience stores and lacks access to fresh produce (McKibben 2007). Consider the irony of Midwesterners going to local food banks for cornflakes to feed their children, all the while surrounded by fields of corn grown to feed livestock for meat consumption. The results for rural communities in undeveloped and developing markets could be even more devastating than the food deserts in the United States as, globally, farming communities decline and the rural poor migrate to urban slums.

Three major problems are associated with growing crops on a centralized, global scale that add to the world's food insecurity: water resources are limited, the entire system is fossil fuel based, and there are increased risks of spoilage and disease. Regarding the first, as discussed earlier, water scarcity and pollution are happening at frightening speeds across the globe, and 70 percent of the water used by humanity goes for crop irrigation. Regarding the second, agriculture has become global and totally fossil fuel dependent at every stage of the production and delivery chain. Bill McKibben (2007, 63) says, "Our food arrives at the table marinated in oil—crude oil. Cheap and abundant fossil fuel has shaped the farming system we've come to think of as normal." Food travels anywhere between 1,500 and 3,000 miles from the farm to the table. Airfreight not only contributes 10 to 30 times more carbon per mile than trucking, it also increases the price of food, putting even more pressure on global food security. From 1980 to 2001, the distance our food traveled increased 25 percent (Halweil 2004; McKibben 2007).

Regarding the third issue, increased contamination of the food supply, the recent cases of E. coli and salmonella bacteria in fruits, vegetables, and meats sold in the United States demonstrate that the centralized food system poses inherent risks of disease. The consolidation of the poultry industry, for example, is the underlying culprit for the spread of avian flu, and more than half the poultry sold in Britain is contaminated with salmonella because of the industrialized process of stacking the birdcages on top of one another, thus forcing the birds to consume the wastes from the cages above (McKibben 2007).

The United Nations reports that close to 1 billion people, mostly in poorer nations, get fewer calories than they need for proper nutrition, while approximately 1.6 billion, mostly in wealthier nations, get more calories than they need. Humans, on average, obtain about 48 percent of their calories from three grains—wheat, corn, and rice. In the United States the average grain consumption per person is 800 kilograms. Most of this grain is actually consumed by livestock that is in turn consumed by people. On the other hand, in India each person consumes only 200 kilograms of grain, but most of that is consumed directly with little available for feeding livestock (Brown 2008).

Statistics like these make it clear that there is a strong coevolutionary relationship between wealth and food security. As Lester Brown (2008, 107) says, "Hunger is the most visible face of poverty," and the faces that it can be seen on the most are those of children. Six million Ethiopian children under the age of five are at risk from malnutrition. As previously noted, there is also a strong coevolutionary relationship between the natural environment and food security. For example, the severity of the Ethiopian situation was exacerbated when rains that allow Ethiopian farmers to plant a second crop did not come. Also, desertification is spreading in Ethiopia, providing little hope that the land can sustain the expanding population (Dinnick 2008).

Fareed Zakaria (2008, 3) says, "The 50 countries where the Earth's poorest people live are basket cases that need urgent attention." This raises an important question: Should the rest of the world try to save these sinking nations, or should it engage in what Garrett Hardin (1974) called "lifeboat ethics," where each of the more affluent nations, like lifeboats with limited capacities, must decide whether or not it has the capacity to pull any of these 50 struggling nations to safety without sinking itself. Hardin argues that the carrying capacity of the lifeboats is just like the carrying capacity of the Earth, and if all 50 of these countries swimming in the water are allowed in, it may overload the lifeboats, resulting in complete justice coupled with complete catastrophe. According to Hardin, the harsh ethics of the lifeboat become harsher when considering the reproductive differences between countries along with the land's carrying capacity to feed expanding populations. Most of these 50 struggling countries also have failing social and political systems. How should the world respond? These are difficult ethical questions that must be asked by a global business community moving toward a vision of a sustainable world. Politically, global poverty and income inequity exacerbate tensions between the rich and the poor, leading to increased geopolitical conflicts and stresses that create a politically unstable world.

Health, Gender, and Educational Inequity

The gap between the rich and poor of the world is also reflected in disease patterns. The poorest billion suffer the most from infectious diseases such as malaria, dysentery, tuberculosis, respiratory infections, and HIV/AIDS. Infant mortality in the 50 poorest countries is 85 deaths per 1,000 newborns, while in affluent countries it averages 8 per 1,000 (Brown 2008). The HIV/AIDS epidemic has taken its toll on the poor who lack basic health care, especially the 16.6 million children who have been orphaned by the AIDS epidemic. In 2010 approximately 34 million people worldwide were living with HIV/AIDS, with 68 percent living in sub-Saharan Africa (Avert 2012). Of those, only 1 million were being treated with antiretroviral drugs. The virus affects all facets of these people's lives. Families break down when an adult becomes infected, and currently more than 20 percent of adults are infected in the region. And the most heartbreaking effect may be the orphans created by the epidemic. As Lester Brown (2008, 111) says, "There is no precedent for the number of street children in Africa." Another serious impact of the HIV/AIDS epidemic in sub-Saharan Africa is that it is breaking down the ability of many of the region's communities to resist famine, so the spread of the virus and the spread of hunger are caught in a deadly reinforcing downward spiral.

More women are infected with HIV/AIDS than ever before in every region of the world. In the regions where women do not have a position of power in making decisions about sexual relations, the infection rates are rampant. This gender inequity is a widespread global problem because in many cultures women are seen as inferior individuals whose primary purpose is to serve as vessels for male sexual pleasure and childbearing. Women brave enough to acquire birth control pills in undeveloped and developing regions often have to hide them from their husbands or lovers for fear that they will be accused of interfering with the men's right to control their fertility. In many parts of the world women have no choice but to continue to have unprotected sex (Jordan 2007). Undervaluing, abusing, and otherwise discriminating against women is also a worldwide problem. One of the most egregious outcomes of gender inequity is violence against women, whether it is verbal, physical, sexual, or economic. In many parts of the world women are seen as mere property with no rights.

Levels of income, education, legal rights, and political involvement are lower for women than men throughout most of the world (Jordan 2007).

Another income–gender gap issue involves literacy rates. Whereas the developed markets of the world can boast that almost all of their adult citizens are literate, the illiteracy rates in many undeveloped and developing regions are alarmingly high. Of all 793 million illiterate adults in the world, two-thirds are women who are concentrated in three regions of the world—south and west Asia, sub-Saharan Africa, and the Arab states (CIA 2012).

The digital divide exacerbates the gap in literacy rates, regardless of gender. The Internet has the potential to diffuse education into the farthest corners of the globe. Unfortunately, this promise is not currently being fulfilled. For example, whereas nearly 78.6 percent of the population in North America has Internet access, only 6.2 percent have access in Africa (Internet World Stats 2012). The irony revealed in statistics like these is that those who could benefit the most from Internet access, the poor with little or no access to schools, libraries, and the like, are the ones with the least Internet access. The digital divide will likely continue until some of the underlying social, political, and economic issues are addressed in poor countries (Guillén and Suárez 2005).

It is also important to note that literacy rates within the wealthiest nations often vary significantly with levels of income, thus creating undeveloped markets within their borders. For example, low incomes, poor health, inadequate housing, and substandard education characterize the Southern Appalachian region in the United States. Consequently, the region is an undeveloped market and subculture that exists within the broader context of mainstream America. Nearly 17 percent of the people of Southern Appalachia live in poverty, only 27 percent have graduated from high school, and functional illiteracy rates of 30–50 percent are not uncommon in the region. Child hunger rates are also alarming in Southern Appalachia, with upwards of 20 percent of the children in the poorest counties of the region not always having enough to eat (Legg 2013; Stead, Stead, and Shemwell 2003).

Research indicates that income levels are clearly related to literacy rates. Research on students entering kindergarten in the United States, for example, revealed that the average math and reading scores for African American children, 36 percent of whom live in poverty, and Hispanic children, 29 percent of whom live in poverty, were 20 percent lower than the scores for white children, 11 percent of whom live in poverty. The researchers note that by age four the average child in an affluent family hears 35 million more words than a child in a poor family. Thus, by the time children from lower income families enter school, they are already behind and generally remain so throughout school, reinforcing the cycle of poverty and illiteracy within one of the wealthiest countries in the world (Winerip 2007).

Urbanization

A large proportion of the economic activity is centered in urban areas due to the lack of infrastructure in rural areas (Porter 1998). Further, the majority of the world's population resides in urban areas. Approximately 3.5 billion people (50 percent of the world's population) live in cities today. This number has increased tremendously since 1950 when only 30 percent of the world's population lived in cities. Approximately 180,000 individuals move to cities each day, and by 2050 it is forecast that approximately two-thirds of the world's population will live in cities. Asia and Africa will account for 86 percent of that growth (Xinhua 2012). China, especially, has seen rapid urbanization where 47 percent of Chinese now live in cities, up from 17 percent in 1980 (University of Minnesota 2012).

Currently, approximately 1 billion people live in urban slums worldwide. In these areas, people live without basic necessities—sanitation, shelter, clean water, and sufficient living space (Jorgenson and Rice 2012). People are migrating into the cities looking for ways to meet their basic needs, but these urban areas lack infrastructure and public health facilities for the increasing number of poor. More than 200 cities in undeveloped and developing markets have grown beyond 1 million inhabitants, stressing the local, political, economic, and social infrastructures. The result is expanding urban slums where disease, hunger, violence, and a high risk for environmental disasters like flooding are prevalent. In addition, the psychological stress of living in overcrowded slums that lack meaningful contact with nature leads to a measurable decline in human well-being. Such declines have the potential to threaten political and social stability, tipping societies into chaos (Delgado 2007).

Shifting Geopolitical Power, Conflicts, and Failing Political Systems

The expanding global economy has resulted in a diffusion of political power in the world. The great transformational growth in economic and political power in countries such as China, India, and Brazil signals that some of the political and economic power long held by the developed nations of the world, particularly the United States, is now shifting to emerging markets. As previously discussed, by 2040 the emerging markets in China, India, Brazil, Russia, and Mexico will generate more economic output than the historically dominant G-7 countries of the United States, the UK, Italy, France, Germany, Japan, and Canada. Currently, emerging-market countries own 80 percent of the world's foreign exchange reserves. Zakaria (2008) calls this future the post-American world, where rising powers reject being integrated into the global system the "western way" and are instead choosing to enter on their own terms, thereby reshaping the system itself.

Jeffery Sachs (2008) says that the real paradox of rising globalization is that the global economy is integrated while global society is politically divided. Sachs believes this provides the greatest threat to the survival of civilization because it makes it virtually impossible to get the global political coopera- tion necessary for dealing with the issues created by the rapid growth of the global economy. Sachs says that we are now crowded into an interconnected society of global trade, migration, geopolitical conflicts, pandemics, and global terrorism.

Research indicates that the state failure rate is increasing. "Failing states are now an integral part of the international political landscape" (Brown 2008, 123). States fail when governments can no longer provide basic needs and security (education, health care, food, etc.) for their people. Revenues can- not be generated to finance government, and societies become fragmented, frequently erupting into civil war. Society is ruled by groups such as the warlords in Afghanistan, the tribal chiefs in Somalia, or the street gangs in Haiti. Currently the Central Intelligence Agency estimates that more than 20 states are failing, while the British government classifies 46 states as fragile (CIA 2012). It is not surprising that 17 out of the top 20 failing states are experiencing rapid population growth, and that 14 of them have 40 percent or more of their populations under the age of 15 (Brown 2008).

There is a tight coevolutionary link between insurgency movements, unemployment, environmental degradation, and failing states. The top three failing states are Sudan, Republic of the Congo, and Somalia. However, state failure is not always confined to national boundaries. For example, genocide in Rwanda spilled over into the Republic of the Congo, drawing several other countries into the conflict. The war eventually claimed the lives of 3.9 million people. Clearly, at some point, political instability such as this has the potential to spread and to disrupt the global economy (Brown 2008). Natural disasters, disease, drought, financial collapse, and populism do not stop at the border. These issues, and others, flow in an interconnected world. The risk posed by state failures is not just about terrorism. State failures matter because at the end of the day, if states cannot manage and control these pressures, who will? After all, the number of lifeboats is limited (Hardin 1974).

Sustainability: A New Way of Thinking

As can be gleaned from the discussion above, there are many barriers to achieving sustainability, and they are complex, incredibly intertwined, seri- ous, and, some say, overwhelming. At the biophysical level, the entropy law provides the absolute physical wall beyond which human activity on Earth will not be possible. In order to bring the economic system into sync with the Earth's natural entropic processes, humankind must find ways to slow down the high-entropy energy, resource, and waste processes that result from current economic activities. This means overcoming several biophysical barriers, including: finding safe and/or plentiful substitutes for the nonrenewable resources and toxic chemicals now in use, developing the efficient use of clean, renewable energy sources, developing better processes for recovering, recycling, and disposing of wastes, developing more efficient production processes, and developing closed-loop networks of industrial ecosystems throughout the globe.

Further, sustainability is not just a biophysical problem. If it were, then maybe it would be easier to confront. However, as we discussed, sustainability is a human development problem, with all of the ethical, cultural, social, religious, political, civil, and legal implications that entails. Slowing population growth to sustainable levels will require addressing an array of issues including gender equity, economic equity, health care, education, birth control, social mores, and religious principles. Curtailing slash-and-burn destruction of the rain forests will not stop without addressing issues like democracy, human rights, property rights, and international trade. Solving the problems of the unsustainable megalopolises around the globe means addressing all these same issues and many others, such as how to finance sustainable public transportation systems and how to find employment for the millions of poor who migrate to these cities every year. Adding to the complexity is the fact that these are not just the problems of the current generation; they are the problems of those not yet living. They are the problems of our children and our children's children. They are also the problems of the other species on the planet, both current and future.

When viewed from the lens of rational thought and scientific inquiry that has dominated the way humans have viewed the universe for the past 350 years or so, the odds of coming up with solutions to the problems related to the interface between business, society, and the natural environment seem tenuous at best. The idea that Adam Smith's "economic man" will ever willingly surrender his quest for castles and gold so that people he will never know can have a comfortable place to live in a safe society with clean air to breathe, adequate soil for food, clean water to drink, and the opportunity for creative self-expression is essentially ludicrous within the present framework of the materialistic, ego-centered, growth-oriented, mechanical, mental models that are currently driving human thought processes.

E.F. Schumacher's famous saying, "small is beautiful," was meant as a challenge to the way humans think about their relationship with each other and with nature. The slogan challenges humankind to give up the bigger-is-better, grow-forever mindset that dominates the current materialistic world in favor of a belief that the long-run survival of the human species on the planet depends on finding a sustainable balance among the planetary economic, social, and ecological subsystems for posterity.

A sustainability-based mental model of the world would define truth using assumptions very different from the current ones underlying the mental model that unlimited economic growth on a finite sphere is both possible and desirable. Assumptions required for a mental model based on sustainability are: The planet is home to humankind, and as such it should be kept clean, healthy, safe, and well managed. A healthy economy and a healthy ecosystem are intricately and irreversibly interconnected. Humans are both a part of nature and, because of their superior intelligence, the chosen stewards of nature. Humans have ethical responsibilities that are intragenerational, intergenerational, and interspecies. The ecosystem is finite with limited resources and limited regenerative and assimilative powers. Irreplaceable parts of the natural capital, like other species and the ozone layer, are nonsubstitutable. Unlimited economic growth forever is impossible because the laws of thermodynamics govern interactions between the ecosystem and the economic system. Humans are multidimensional beings who can learn to appreciate aesthetic as well as economic value and can learn that wisdom, intellectual development, and spiritual fulfillment are as important as material well-being. And last, the economic system should internalize all ecological and social externalities.

In short, we believe that achieving sustainability is not just about changing how humans do things; it is about changing how humans view things. If humans are ever to see the light of sustainability, it will not be because they were simply rational, logical, and scientific; it will be because, in addition to these things, they were able to change the underlying mental frameworks that guide the way they see the planet and their place on it. And, through enlightened business executives questioning the underlying assumptions of why they are in business, we envision the global business community stepping up to be the change agents needed to move humankind toward creating a more sustainable world for future generations.

Chapter Summary

At the heart of sustainable strategic management is the understanding that business organizations should be measured on their ecological and social as well as economic outcomes. The human-friendly Earth we know today is an irreducible whole whose survival is threatened if any of its coevolving nested component subsystems break down. From an economic perspective, organizations are nested in the economy, which is nested in the society, which is nested in nature. Breakdowns in any of these subsystems can lead to a collapse of the whole system, rendering the planet much less human friendly.

This is important because the current human footprint is greater than the planet's carrying capacity. That is, the negative coevolutionary impacts of rapid population growth and unchecked economic growth are exceeding humankind's efforts to improve technological efficiency. The results of this imbalance include environmental degradation, depleting resources, increasing pollution, energy issues, and climate change (which has revealed its hand with a special vengeance lately). Socially, population is growing exponentially, economic inequities and gender inequities are rampant across the globe, a high percentage of the world's population lacks access to basic health care and education, and nations around the globe are failing due to poverty, disease, drought, and endless war. It is clearly time for a change, not only in the way we do things but also in the way we view things. At the center of this new lens is sustainability, the promise of a high quality of life on a healthy, equitable planet for current and future generations, with the global business community taking a leadership role in this sustainability journey.

Case Vignette 2

The Meaning of Sustainability
at Eastman Chemical Company

As discussed above, sustainability is about the vision of providing a meaningful quality of life for the billions of people who inhabit this planet now and in the future. It is both an ideal future state and a set of processes for pursuing that state. It has strong scientific roots, and it has economic, social, and ecological dimensions. It is simple enough to understand that sustainability will require providing economic opportunities and social justice in ecologically sensitive ways for the current and future residents of the planet, but finding ways to translate this ideal of enduring planetary affluence, freedom, and natural balance into profitable organizational strategies is not so simple. And yet, given the central role of global business in the world's economic, social, and ecological health, bringing the principles and practices of global sustainability down to the organizational level is critical. This was John Elkington's (1997) intention when he conceived the idea of the triple bottom line (discussed in Chapter 1), which ties the economic performance of firms to their ecological and social performance. Since it appeared, the triple-bottom-line framework has become a standard in the business world.

Eastman Chemical Company has adopted a triple-bottom-line perspective for its definition of sustainability based on CEO Jim Rogers's vision of being "recognized as a company with a genuine and deep-rooted commitment to sustainability." In a talk to a group of university students, Eastman's chief sustainability officer, Godefroy Motte, said, "At Eastman, we strive to do business by creating value through environmental stewardship, social responsibility, and economic growth, now and for future generations. That's how we define sustainability. Sustainability is an attitude and not an activity to participate in from time to time. It is an opportunity to use our creativity and innovation to be part of the solution, for our world today and for future generations."

With regard to the environmental stewardship arm of its triple bottom line, Eastman has made a strong long-term commitment to continuously improve its environmental performance. For example, it has established for itself tough short- and long-term targets for continuously reducing energy consumption, greenhouse gas emissions, volatile organic compound emissions, hazardous wastes, and toxic releases, and it is investing significant time, energy, and money into developing innovative new products that are more eco-friendly (such as Tritan™ and Perennial Wood™ mentioned in Case Vignette 1). According to its 2011 sustainability report, "Eastman's continued commitment to sustainability serves to minimize our environmental footprint and conserve natural resources. Sustainability is integrated into every area of our business—for the benefit of our customers, our stockholders, our employees, and the world at large."

The social responsibility arm of Eastman's triple-bottom-line performance begins with its employees. The firm is committed to the personal safety and security of all its employees and to the safety of its products and processes at every stage of its value chain. In 2010, the company achieved its best ever Occupational Safety and Health Administration (OSHA) recordable safety rating (0.53) for injuries requiring treatment beyond first aid. In commenting on this, Jim Rogers said, "There are many factors that contribute to such performance, but the most important factor is the commitment that each employee makes to work safely and to watch out for the safety of the other person. The benefits of this safety emphasis extend to our homes and communities, as well." Eastman supports employee self-development, and it provides employees with significant training, development, and educational opportunities. In addition, it has a strong commitment to employee health and well-being, and it deeply values diversity in the workplace. For example, Eastman provides its employees with an integrated health program that includes access to on-site fitness centers and information and research from Eastman's personal health-care team. Along with personal health-care representatives, Eastman's collaborative focus on health care has helped numerous employees to live healthy lives and prepare for and respond to major life events. Eastman is also very committed to the communities in which it operates. It believes that it has a responsibility to protect the health and vibrancy of these communities. For example, it has established Community Advisory Panels that allow it to have continuous open dialogue with its communities, and it encourages all employees to volunteer to serve the greater needs of these communities.

Recall from Case Vignette 1 that while Eastman believes in its heart that sustainability is the right thing to do, it also believes that the real fun of sustainability lies in using corporate brainpower to find innovative ways to drive economic growth with sustainability. This is the centerpiece of sustainability at Eastman today. Again quoting the 2011 sustainability report: "Sustainability is, and will continue to be, an important lens for identifying business development opportunities for our company. The impact of environmental constraints on ever-stressed natural resources is supporting our commitment to embed sustainability in our product development and innovation processes. That is why we strive to provide our customers with solutions that provide performance, value and an improved environmental footprint. We will continue to build our portfolio of sustainably advantaged products to accelerate our efforts to deliver innovative, sustainable solutions to our customers throughout the world."

3

Environmental Analysis for Sustainable Strategic Management

The sustainable strategic management (SSM) process begins with identifying opportunities and threats in the external environment and then formulating effective strategies for dealing with them. **Opportunities** arise when a firm can take advantage of conditions in the environment to formulate strategies that enable it to achieve its goals and outperform its competitors, while **threats** are conditions in the environment that impede goal achievement. Scanning and analyzing the firm's external environment is increasingly complex due to the turbulent coevolutionary environmental forces affecting business organizations.

Environmental turbulence has been a constant for business organizations for the past four decades. E.F. Schumacher described the Arab oil embargo of 1973 as the watershed economic event of the twentieth century. "Things will never be the same again," Schumacher (1979, 5) said, and they have not. The embargo provided the small crack that many organizations (e.g., Japanese auto manufacturers) needed to gain a stronger foothold in the international market, and the global economic race was on. With the world's two most populous countries, China and India, now in the race, the demand for oil and other natural resources is rising and will continue to rise for the foreseeable future. A key point exposed by the 1973 embargo is that the causes and effects of environmental turbulence go beyond the boundaries of economic activity, spilling into the arenas of politics, social welfare, and ecological concerns. Incredible advances in technology have paralleled the explosion of global economic activity since the embargo. The growth and change in information technology has transformed the way humans work, communicate, and live, and no industry has been immune from its effects. Further, there have been increasing social and environmental demands from citizens worldwide, leading to unprecedented levels of consumer advocacy, social activism, and legislation aimed at changing the way organizations do business. These complex, interrelated economic, geopolitical, technological, social, and ecological demands define the twenty-first-century business environment that organizations must be capable of adapting to if they want to survive and thrive.

The Coevolving Factors Determining Environmental Turbulence

Over thirty years ago, Igor Ansoff (1979) noted that four factors make the modern business environment different from the past. First of all, the **scope of the marketplace** for business is growing on a global scale, and it is becoming increasingly more fragmented due to inequities in economic, social, and ecological justice. Stuart Hart (2005) says that today's global business environment has expanded because three formerly very differentiated economies are now merging: the money economy of developed and developing markets; the traditional, village-based economy of undeveloped markets; and the economy of the natural world in which the other two are embedded. Whereas these economies were at one time separate and distinct from one another, they are now in a common global arena where they are coevolving with one another. For example, purses handmade by indigenous South American villagers from recycled aluminum pull tabs are now available for very high prices in chic boutiques across the United States. Examples such as this demonstrate that products and wealth are being transferred between the money economy and the traditional economy, and more aluminum from the natural economy is being reused in the process. Over time, coevolutionary processes like this will lead to more consumer satisfaction in the money economy, more wealth and more meaningful work in the village economy, and less waste and damage for the natural environment. Clearly, the coevolutionary nature of these markets will create both business opportunities and threats for twenty-first-century organizations.

Ansoff's second factor was that the number and complexity of **critical success factors** necessary for organizational survival are increasing significantly. Today managers must not only focus on putting the right products and/ or services in the right markets, they must also focus on myriad nonmarket stakeholder concerns such as human rights, global poverty, climate change, complex regulatory frameworks, technological change, and resource constraints. More than ever, business organizations are being called upon to close the gap between the needs and increasing demands of civil society and the solutions offered by the public sector (Laszlo 2008). Esty and Winston (2008) have said that increasing stakeholder pressures for more social and environmental responsibility have manifested into what they call the "green wave" of stakeholder concerns. This green wave is supported by Ernst and Young

(2011), which found that half of the shareholder proposals in 2011 focused on social and environmental issues, indicating a growing concern about these issues among equity stakeholders. Also, 95 percent of the respondents to a *Business Week* poll agreed that businesses should serve multiple stakeholders and multiple purposes; those polled believed that sometimes organizations should sacrifice profit in order to make things better for their workers and communities (Huff et al. 2009).

Ansoff's third factor was that today's business environment is characterized by **high-speed change**; and the fourth was that change in the current business environment is **novel and discontinuous** rather than linear. Taken together, the speed and discontinuity of change mean that predicting the future based on the past is very difficult, even impossible at times. For example, the Internet almost instantaneously transformed the business world by creating an unprecedented level of transparency. Now stakeholders have the ability to self-organize via the Internet around particular issues that target corporations (Laszlo 2008). Stories criticizing companies such as Walmart and Coca-Cola over issues such as unfair labor practices and the overconsumption of water now easily move from the Internet blogosphere to Wall Street. Because of this rising transparency, Esty and Winston (2008, 16) said that "full accountability is the emerging norm." Not only does the virtual world increase the demand for firm transparency, it also poses threats in terms of cyber security, a complex, emerging risk consisting of online data and information security and critical information infrastructure breakdown (World Economic Forum 2011). This type of discontinuous change makes it clear that it is more important than ever for organizations to develop generative (creative) learning processes that encourage questioning and changing the mental frameworks they use in their current decision-making processes.

Thus, the competitive landscape for global businesses today is complex, discontinuous, rapidly changing, and composed of coevolving developed, developing, and undeveloped markets, all of which are embedded in the natural environment. There are now multiple, increasingly powerful stakeholders representing social, environmental, as well as economic interests in global corporations. Organizations that can realign their value chains to account for the needs of these increasingly influential sustainability-oriented stakeholders will have business opportunities now and into the future. Taking advantage of these opportunities will require that organizations develop capabilities to formulate strategies that create stakeholder value as a source of competitive advantage in the turbulent business environment.

Given the complexity of today's business environment, it is imperative for strategic managers to develop environmental scanning cultures within their organizations. Determining environmental opportunities and threats should result from the collective wisdom of the firm's stakeholders. Successful sustainable strategic management requires that opportunities and threats be identified, and it requires that they be analyzed in terms of the underlying assumptions on which they are based. Although the external environment is typically segmented into two sectors (macro and industry) for analysis purposes, this does not mean that these environmental forces are mutually exclusive. The fact is that the coevolutionary forces in the environment are so dynamic and interrelated that environmental analysis must be based on systems thinking, focusing on developing information flow, feedback loops, analytical processes, dialogue processes, and so forth, that will allow organizations to recognize, understand, and capitalize on the environmental turbulence that surrounds them.

The Coevolving Sectors of the Macro Environment

The **macro environment** is sometimes referred to as the remote or general environment because it affects virtually all organizations, and strategic managers have little or no influence over it. In other words, the macro environment is the context in which business takes place—the broader, global economic, technological, demographic, social, and political forces that are embedded within the finite ecosystem. As we discussed in Chapter 2, the entropy law places the ultimate physical constraint on humankind's activities here on Earth. It is within this broader understanding of these biophysical laws that SSM analysis of the macro environment takes place. The following section describes the coevolving sectors that are scanned for data analysis in the macro environment, as Figure 3.1 depicts.

A scan of the **economic** sector includes factors such as economic growth, inflation, unemployment, interest rates, and exchange rates. The economy and financial system are now global and highly interdependent, and they are embedded within the finite ecosystem, which affords the firm both opportunities and threats. A scan of the **ecological** sector would entail understanding the ecological impacts of the firm on the natural environment, including gathering pertinent data on resource depletion, pollution, energy use, and climate change. **Sociocultural** factors would include factors such as social values, norms, and beliefs that guide a society's behavior, while a scan of the **demographic** environment would include factors such as population growth, the distribution of individuals in a society in terms of age, sex, ethnicity, income, location and other personal attributes that determine buying patterns. For example, understanding population characteristics can help strategic managers understand the needs of current customers and determine how many potential customers they may have.

Figure 3.1   **Sectors of the External Environment**

Technological change creates both opportunities and threats to the firm. As we discussed above, the Internet has had a major impact on the transparency and accountability of the firm. Technological innovations, such as the growth of digital and mobile devices, require strategic managers to rethink current strategies. The globalization of the economy requires new ways of thinking about global governance and its relationship with the **political/legal** environment in which firms compete. Although understanding the impacts that laws and the legal system have on firm performance is essential, it is becoming increasingly difficult to analyze due to the fact that the relationship between government and business varies so much in the various coevolving global markets. Table 3.1 summarizes the elements of these six global sectors.

Clearly, these macro environmental forces cannot be analyzed in isola-

Table 3.1

Sectors and Elements of the Global Macro Environment

Sectors	Elements
Economic	• GDP • Inflation and interest rates • Saving rates • Sovereign debt/exchange rates • Deficits/surpluses
Ecological	• Resource depletion and pollution • Destruction of ecosystems • Climate change • Species extinction • Energy • Natural disasters
Social	• Gender/educational equity • Sustainability movement • Attitudes re: life-work balance • Workforce diversity • Consumer confidence in business
Demographic	• Population size • Population distribution • Income distribution • Age distribution
Technological	• Increased transparency from the Internet • Digitalization • Mobile communication • Cloud computing • Information explosion
Political/Legal	• Regulation/Legislation • Failed states • Geopolitical unrest • Global governance

tion from one another because they are highly coevolutionary. According to Laszlo and Zhexembayeva (2011), the coevolving trends of declining resources, the radical transparency required of business organizations, and increasing stakeholder expectations are redefining how firms create value. Thus, a system-level perspective of the interrelationships among the forces of a macro environment is required for an effective SSM environmental scan. Let us examine some examples of how these six macro environmental forces coevolve with one another over time to generate both opportunities and threats for business organizations.

The World Economic Forum (2012) data on the biggest global risks for 2012 clearly demonstrate that the economic, social, and political sectors of the macro environment are converging and coevolving (see Figure 3.2).

Figure 3.2   **Interactions Among Global Risks**

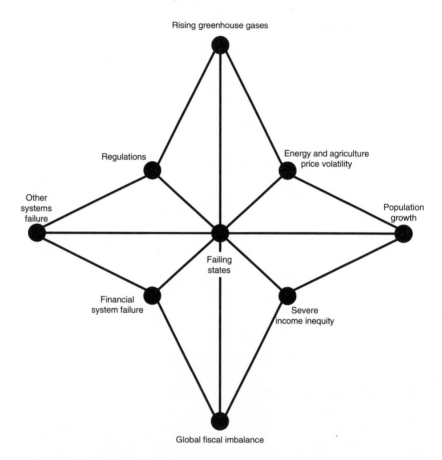

Source: Adapted from World Economic Forum 2012.

Specifically, the data show highly interrelated global risks arising from economic disparity, global governance failures, critical systems failures, chronic fiscal imbalances, unsustainable population growth, and rising greenhouse gases. Noting that the benefits from globalization are not yet being equitably shared, researchers believe that the economic disparity both at the national and international levels is leading to social fragmentation, failed nation states, and the resurgence of nationalism. To meet these challenges, improved global governance is crucial, yet it has been difficult to achieve, resulting in failures such as the lack of international agreement at the Copenhagen Conference on climate change. According to the report, this demonstrates the paradox of the twenty-first-century business environment: The divergent interests and differing cultural values that make global governance so necessary are the factors that make achieving it so difficult (World Economic Forum 2011, 2012).

Further, clusters of coevolving global risks are embedded within those discussed above. One such cluster is concerned with the macroeconomic forces of currency volatility, fiscal crises, and asset price collapses. These are arising from the increasing wealth and influence of emerging economies such as China and India as well as the high levels of debt in the more developed economies such as the United States and the European Union. Combined with these macroeconomic imbalances is another cluster of risks that includes failed states, organized crime, and corruption arising from economic disparities, terrorism, and war that are all taking place in a hyper-connected virtual world. In 2009, the value of global illicit trade was estimated to be US$1.3 trillion, and this leads to huge costs for legitimate business and traps countries into cycles of poverty, violence, and instability (World Economic Forum 2011, 2012).

The ecological limits of the planet's resources to support the world's growing population characterize another cluster of risks. Global demand for food, water, and energy is expected to rise by 30–50 percent in the next two decades, while economic inequity within and between nations is expected to grow, leading to geopolitical conflicts, social instability, and irreversible damage to the ecosystem that supports human life (World Economic Forum 2011, 2012). In fact, the number of natural disasters in the world may double during the next 10 to 15 years due to rising temperatures, which has made climate change and its resulting human and economic impacts the number one threat of the insurance industry (Boykoff 2011).

Another cluster of risks arises from shifts in the demographic sector where there is a convergence of global economic markets, the desire of firms to expand globally, and the social and economic dislocations. Eighty-five percent of the world's population lives in developing countries today (Galindo and Massena 2011). The average age of the population in these countries is very young, so the working-age population is expected to grow rapidly. This represents major opportunities for business with respect to new labor and consumer markets. However, when high population growth is combined with water and other resource stresses, "population cluster bombs" are created that could send social and political shock waves to neighboring countries or regions, thus increasing threats arising from organizations' increased scope of operations. The World Economic Forum (2012) has identified population cluster bombs in 14 countries encompassing 450 million people worldwide. On the other hand, due to the low birthrates and high longevity in the industrialized countries, there will be a bulge of people aged 50 to 90 years old. This global graying of the population is having a tremendous impact on health care, social services, pensions, and so forth in the industrialized world where a smaller population of young people must support these services. In order for strategic managers to take advantage of the new labor and consumer markets in the developing countries, they will have to add health care, education (especially of women), family planning, water, infrastructure, and so forth, to their strategic agendas. For only if the population is healthy and educated can business take advantage of the opportunities that these new markets offer.

The very nature of these clusters of risks demonstrates, as seen in Figure 3.2, the coevolutionary nature of the macro environmental forces of economy, society, politics, technology, and ecology in the firm's external environment.

There are other opportunities and threats that arise out of the coevolutionary interactions among society, economy, and ecology. Numerous scholars have noted that a fundamental shift in human consciousness is taking place today. Regardless of whether it is called the "great emergence" (Tickle 2008), the "blessed unrest" (Hawken 2007), "SEE Change" (Waddock and McIntosh 2011), or the "sustainability revolution" (Edwards 2005), a rise in consciousness is definitely happening in regard to the relationship between the health of the planet and the people who inhabit it. The new consciousness involves a complex network of social, ecological, economic, cultural, political, and intellectual dimensions with sustainability at its heart. Hawken (2007, 12) expressed it this way: "The movement expresses the needs of the majority of people on Earth to sustain the environment, wage peace, democratize decision making and policy, rejuvenate public governance . . . and improve their lives." Senge (2011) said that society's rising sustainability consciousness is a "profound shift in the strategic context" in which organizations must do business. Edwards (2005) describes the movement as a transformation from the industrial revolution to the sustainability revolution. Speth (2008) describes a revolutionary new sustainability-based consciousness arising that focuses on concerns for the Earth and its people. Aburdene (2005) says that this rising consciousness is a new "megatrend" that is bottom-up, participative, and spiritually charged.

The rise of social entrepreneurship is indicative of this transformative change in consciousness, reflecting the coevolving environmental forces from the economic, social, and ecological sectors of the macro environment. Generally, **social entrepreneurship** is considered to be proactive initiatives that address social or environmental issues through the delivery of a product or service that catalyzes social change. Social entrepreneurs are **change agents**, creative problem solvers who turn problems such as unclean water into market opportunities (Waddock and McIntosh 2011). They can be found within divisions of large corporations, heading up their own enterprises, or working within a group from the citizen sector. The **citizen sector**, the millions of groups across the globe that are mission-driven to address critical social and ecological needs, is changing the way society's problems are being solved. Globally there has been a dramatic increase in these social entrepreneurs, and there has been a 300 percent increase in these groups in the United States since 1982 (Drayton and Budinich 2010).

Consider the social entrepreneur, John Danner, cofounder and CEO of Rocketship Education, a network of charter elementary schools that are bridging the achievement gap—the staggering difference in academic performance between poor and privileged children. Danner, a Silicon Valley entrepreneur and onetime public school teacher in Nashville, Tennessee, believes he has the answer to closing the literacy gaps that were discussed in the previous chapter. He has a revolutionary school model that combines unique educational and financial features into a hybrid approach where Rocketship students, "Rocketeers," who are overwhelmingly poor, Latino, and Spanish-speaking, have outscored the California state averages on standardized exams. The "Rocketeers," in some cases, have performed as well as students in nearby Palo Alto public schools, where Stanford University professors send their children. Danner's vision is to take his revolutionary school model and expand it into the nation's largest chain of charter schools, reaching 50 cities by 2020. He believes he has the solution to one of the major social sustainability issues—the literacy gaps resulting from the inequitable distribution of income and wealth (Layton 2012).

Today, social entrepreneurs, such as John Danner, and the citizen sector organizations (CSOs) that they found, are partnering with business organizations to creatively and profitably address some of the most pressing ecological and social problems. The organizational learning that takes place within firms who partner with these CSOs allows them to innovate new products and services for new markets, promoting powerful and widespread social change along with increasing organizational revenues. For example, Starwood Hotels and Resorts, which operates five historical haciendas in the Yucatan, has collaborated with local citizen groups to establish 27 enterprise development workshops associated with the haciendas, to enable communities to earn income by reviving traditional Mayan jewelry. They also source 90 percent of the produce and 100 percent of the poultry and pork from local farmers (Jenkins 2007). This type of multisector collaboration between CSOs and business firms provides a vehicle for firms to discover market opportunities, to increase profits, to gain knowledge, and to be an agent of social change (explored further in later chapters).

The central key to their success is that these partnerships are able to create jobs and improve the living conditions in the local communities where implemented. **Glocalization** is a term popularized by Thomas Friedman (1999, 2004) to recognize the need for local communities to maintain strong local cultural and economic identity as the global economy grows. The central idea of glocalization is that the integrated global economy is here to stay, and in order to be competitive, communities must keep their local economies, cultures, and ecosystems healthy and viable. Doing so starts with building the community around healthy, locally owned enterprises. Such enterprises meet local demand, provide local jobs, are less stressful on the natural environment, and circulate more of their wealth in the local community. Thus, healthy communities want to build entrepreneurial capability and to rely on the global economic system only for goods and services that cannot be produced locally. This is a process of building communities from the inside out—from the local to the global. Thus, as Michael Porter (1998, 77) says, "Paradoxically, the competitive advantages in a global economy lie increasingly in local things— knowledge, relationships, and motivation that distant rivals cannot match." And, the increasing interest in the going-local and slow-food movements is indicative of people's desire to build stronger communities in which to live by purchasing locally. Thus, the rising global consciousness is reflected in the emergence of social entrepreneurs, the going-local movement and the rise of the citizen sector–business partnerships that call on the business community to be active agents for social change.

In sum, scanning the sectors of the macro environment entails analysis of the coevolutionary relationships between the economic, sociocultural, political/legal, technological, demographic, and ecological trends that may afford both opportunities and threats for business organizations. The ability to discern whether these coevolutionary forces will provide opportunities or pose threats requires strategic managers to engage in double-loop learning, questioning the fundamental assumptions of how they view their firm's strategic position in the world.

Traditional Industry Analysis

Given the coevolutionary nature of the environmental analysis process, gathering data on the competitive or industry environment is done simultaneously with the scan of the macro environment. Data from these environments are aggregated for analysis to determine the major opportunities and threats facing the firm. There is an emerging view of industry analysis that shifts from a static view of an industry analyzed within well-defined industry borders to a dynamic, symbiotic view of a business ecosystem composed of a group of firms involved in a coevolving system of competition and cooperation (Moore

1996, 2006). As we will see later in the chapter, the business ecosystem is the fundamental industry structure for SSM. But first we will discuss traditional industry analysis and demonstrate how it differs from the emerging view of industries as ecosystems.

Defining the Industry: Where Are the Boundaries?

In traditional industry analysis, an industry is generally considered a group of firms producing the same or related products or services that are close substitutes for each other, thus serving the same customer needs (Hill and Jones 2009). Others view industry as a simultaneous consideration of the firm's products, customers, geography, and stages of the value chain (de Kluyver and Pearce 2012). An industry is typically characterized as a broad economic sector, such as the automobile industry, made up of various market segments, such as the green automobile segment (Grant 2008). In defining the industry boundaries, the choice of **horizontal scope** along product lines, **vertical scope** along the value chain, and **geographic scope** determine where the boundaries will be drawn (Ghemawat 2010). Thus, strategic managers must make critical competitive choices in defining the industry boundaries within which the firm will compete.

Industry analysis is traditionally portrayed as a static perspective of "what is" within the industry. This suggests that strategic managers scan the product market segments in which they compete for opportunities and threats without much regard for context. In traditional industry analysis, the structure of the industry determines the rules for competing, which in turn directly influence the conduct and economic performance of the firms in the industry. Strategic managers' primary focus in this case is on increasing market share within the defined industry boundaries, and the competition is defined as those firms that directly compete in individual product and/or service categories. Cooperative relationships are typically limited to those with direct suppliers and customers. The capabilities to create value are viewed as residing in a single firm, and organizational performance is measured primarily in terms of how well the individual firm is managed with respect to its economic sustainability (Moore 1996). Thus, within this traditional paradigm of industry analysis, strategic managers will often rest their decisions on familiar mental models that allow them to adapt to change within well-defined industry boundaries. This process often leaves managers with narrow, static pictures of current and future reality. These static pictures restrict managers' ability to readily recognize the need for fundamental change, which may threaten the future survivability of their firms. The following section discusses the specific characteristics of traditional industry analysis.

Figure 3.3 **Traditional Industry Analysis**

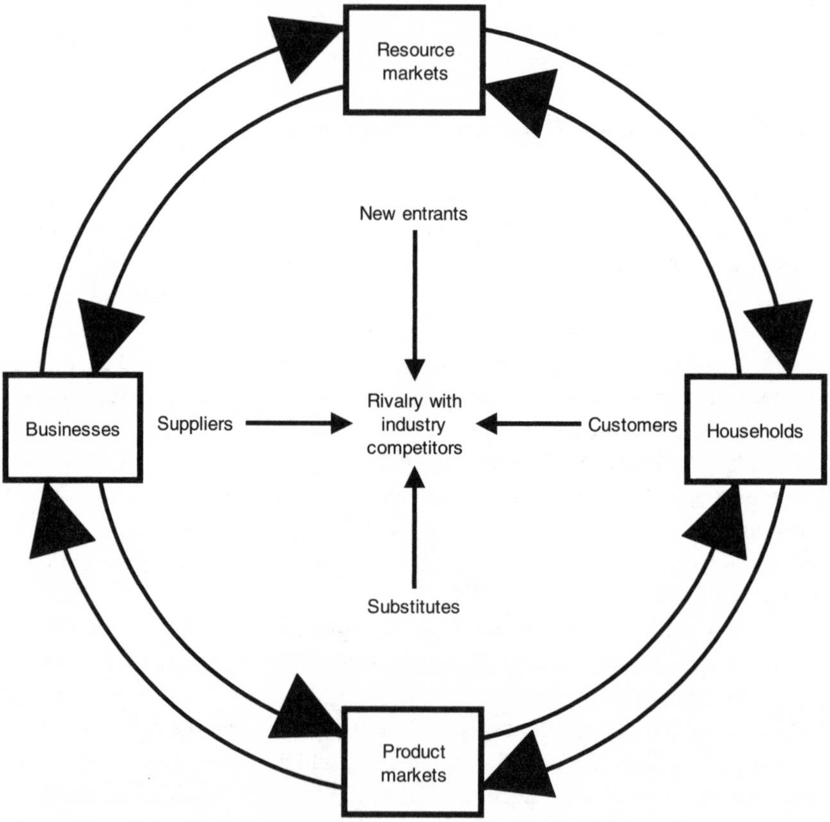

Source: Adapted from Michael E. Porter's (1980) Five Forces Model.

Competitive Forces Influencing Industries

Forces from the industry environment directly impact the firm, and the amount of influence the firm has over its industry is dependent on the dominance of its competitive position. Michael Porter's (2008) **Five Forces Model** is traditionally used as a framework for analyzing the competitive forces within the industry. Like so many other models used to make strategic decisions today, the implicit assumption of this classic model is that the industry is operating within an economy closed to the greater society and ecosystem, as Figure 3.3 depicts.

According to Porter (2008), five forces shape industry competition, and these in turn influence the conduct and performance of the firm. Once industry borders have been identified, then the five competitive forces within the industry can be analyzed, as Figure 3.3 demonstrates. These forces are: (1) the risk of entry from potential competitors, (2) the intensity of rivalries among established firms within the industry, (3) the bargaining power of suppliers, (4) the bargaining power of customers, and (5) the threat of substitute products. Porter argues that the stronger each of these forces is, the more limited the ability of established companies to earn greater profits. Whereas weaker competitive forces can be viewed as opportunities, stronger competitive forces are threats. After the analysis, firms can choose strategies that allow them to capitalize on their competitive opportunities and/or minimize their threats in order to create competitive advantages.

Potential competitors are firms that are not currently competing in the industry but have the potential to enter if they choose. The risk of entry of potential competitors is a function of the height of the barriers to entry, those factors that make it costly for firms to enter an industry. Barriers to entry include economies of scale, brand loyalty, absolute cost advantages, customer switching costs, access to distribution channels, capital requirements, and government policy. Accordingly, high barriers to entry into the industry increase the costs for potential competitors to enter, thus minimizing the threat from potential competitors, while low barriers to entry increase the threat from potential competitors (Porter 2008).

The **bargaining power of suppliers**—those firms that provide the necessary inputs of resources, labor, and services—is the ability of suppliers to raise prices or reduce quality that directly impacts economic profits and product quality downstream. Thus, powerful suppliers are a threat. Suppliers are the most powerful when the inputs supplied are unique with few substitutes, when there are only a few suppliers, when switching costs are significant, and when suppliers threaten to enter their customers' industry by forward integration (Porter 2008).

The **bargaining power of customers** is determined by the ability of buyers to bargain down the prices charged in the industry or to raise costs by demanding better quality products or services. Customers are powerful when they purchase in large volumes and when the products in the industry are standardized, thus decreasing switching costs. Customers can also be a powerful force when they threaten to enter the industry and produce the product themselves, supplying their own needs rather than those of their customers (Porter 2008).

The **threat of substitute products**, the products or services of different businesses that can satisfy similar customer needs, is another competitive force. If the industry has few close substitutes, such as with the microprocessor, then the threat is weak. However, if the substitute is lower in price and has a higher quality/performance than that of the industry's products or services, it becomes a greater threat. For example, as the quality of video conferencing has improved, it is becoming an increasing threat to air travel due to its lower costs (economic and carbon) and improved performance.

Porter's final force is the **intensity of the rivalries** among existing firms that reduce economic profits through strategies such as price cuts, new product introductions, and intensive advertising. Rivalries are high when many firms are approximately the same size, when industry growth rate slows, when overcapacity exists, and when firms are unable to differentiate their product offerings (Porter 2008). Thus, the number and size distribution of firms in the industry determine its competitive structure. A **fragmented industry** (monopolistic competition) consists of a large number of firms producing differentiated products with low barriers to entry and few economies of scale, while a **consolidated industry** (oligopoly) has a high concentration of a few firms, many economies of scale, and other barriers to entry.

Other Industry Factors

After analyzing the competitive forces within the industry and identifying the market segments in which the firm has chosen to compete, other factors that need to be analyzed include the firm's strategic group, profiles of competitors, and stages of industry evolution. The firm's **strategic group** includes the firms that have similar strategic approaches to the market. These are the organization's closest competitors whose products customers view as direct substitutes and who are the greatest threat to the profitability of the firm (Hill and Jones 2009). Strategic group analysis includes the identification of the characteristics of the strategic group and the firm's position within it. Take the automobile industry, for example, where four general strategic groups can be identified according to their price and breadth of their product line: Ferrari, Lamborghini, and Porsche are in the most expensive segment with the narrowest product lines; BMW and Mercedes have slightly lower prices and broader product offerings; Kia and Hyundai are in the lowest price segment with a narrow product line; and a broadly segmented group consists of Toyota, Ford, General Motors, Honda, Chrysler, and so on. Firms may choose to enter new groups, such as Mercedes and BMW entering the sports utility group and Hyundai offering upscale models to compete directly with Toyota's Camry and Honda's Accord, but mobility among groups depends on barriers such as brand or technology (Dess, Lumpkin, and Eisner 2008).

A **profile of competitors** within the strategic group is essential competitive intelligence for strategy formulation because these are the firm's direct competitors. Close to 80 percent of American corporations have some type of competitive intelligence activities, and spending on these activities was forecast to reach US$10 billion by 2012 (Hunger and Wheelen 2011). Effective competitor profiles enabling strategic managers to think like their competitors entail understanding: (1) what drives the competitor, as shown by its vision and future goals; (2) what the competitor is doing and can do, as demonstrated by its competitive and corporate strategies; (3) what the competitor believes about the industry, as revealed by its assumptions; and (4) what the competitor's capabilities are, as demonstrated by its strengths and weaknesses (Porter 1980). Gathering competitive intelligence about competitors enables strategic managers to anticipate competitive moves and build competitive strategies that are not only retaliatory to competitors' moves, but also increase the firm's market share and competitive position.

The **stage of industry coevolution** influences strategy formulation since each stage provides both opportunities and threats to the firm. The task for strategic managers is to anticipate how the changes in competitive forces from the coevolutionary nature of the industry will affect the firm and then to formulate competitive strategies that will capitalize on the opportunities and counter the threats emerging from each stage of the industry life cycle. The content of the firm's competitive strategy must change as the industry coevolves through its life cycle.

As Figure 3.4 demonstrates, the firms in the industry can be thought of as coevolving through stages beginning with the **embryonic and pioneering stage** where products/services have vague, poorly specified features and are unfamiliar to consumers. When consumers become more aware of the industry and its products/services, the industry firms coevolve into the **establishment and growth stage**, where demand is expanding, new customers are entering the market, and barriers and rivalries are relatively low thereby attracting new competitors. With revenues increasing at a growing rate, the industry firms seek to establish competitive positions by building brand recognition through differentiated products. But eventually demand slows, competition stiffens, and weak firms disappear from the industry. This characterizes the coevolution into the **shakeout and maturity stages**. During these stages, those firms that have not been able to build a core competence and establish themselves during the growth stage are shaken out of the industry. The market becomes saturated, barriers to entry begin to increase, competition intensifies due to overcapacity, and there are few opportunities to attract new customers. It is now that demand, sales, and revenues become negative as the industry moves into the **decline stage** (Hill and Jones 2009). The identification of the stage of industry coevolution is important since the appropriate competitive strategy will vary as the industry firms coevolve, creating different opportunities and threats at each stage that must be addressed in strategy formulation.

Figure 3.4   **Stages of Industry Coevolution**

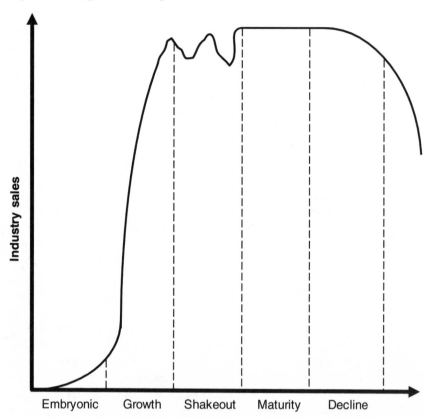

Stages of industry coevolution

In sum, traditional industry analysis views the industry as the fundamental unit of analysis, with well-defined industry borders consisting of product/ market segments within a closed economic system. Thus, the competitive arena is determined by defined industry borders and selected market segments. An analysis of the competitive forces influencing the industry, coupled with strategic group analysis and competitor profile data, provide important competitive data for strategy formulation. Understanding the cycle of industry coevolution also provides critical input for strategy formulation. After the industry data are gathered, they are then aggregated with the data gathered in the analysis of the macro environment to generate the data set from which strategic managers can analyze the major opportunities and threats facing their firms.

Business Ecosystems: Ideal Structures for Sustainable Strategic Management

Sustainable strategic management, however, requires a framework for industry analysis that reflects the symbiotic relationship that the firm has with the greater society and ecosystem. With a primary focus on competitive dynamics, traditional industry analysis virtually ignores the nonmarket context in which competition takes place. However, today's sustainability-rich business environment provides organizations with a strategic context that is complex, discontinuous, rapidly changing, and composed of coevolving developed, developing, and undeveloped markets, all of which are embedded in the natural environment (Hart 1995). There are multiple, increasingly powerful stakeholders representing social and environmental as well as economic interests in global corporations. It is therefore imperative for SSM that traditional industry analysis be expanded to account for this discontinuous, complex environment in which firms compete.

In SSM coevolution provides the framework into which the larger context of the business landscape can be incorporated in the environmental analysis process (Mahon and McGowan 1998; Moore 1993, 1996). Whereas in traditional industry analysis, the structure of the industry influences the conduct of the firm, which, in turn, influences the performance of the firm, in coevolutionary industry analysis these three factors are seen as circular, interactive, and spiraling (see Figure 1.4), meaning that the structure of the industry both influences and is influenced by the conduct and performance of firms. In coevolutionary industry analysis, industry boundaries are blurred and the industries in which the firm competes are to a certain extent a matter of choice.

In order to effectively respond to this shift in strategic context, organizations must develop self-renewing change-oriented structures that encourage organizational members to continuously explore ways to improve the sustainability performance of current products/services, and to innovate new, more sustainable products/services (Volberda and Lewin 2003). Such structures provide frameworks for enhancing the social, human, and natural capital of organizations while simultaneously meeting customer needs and creating economic value for the firm. The **business ecosystem structure** (Moore 1993, 1996) provides such a framework. Within the business ecosystem structure, the industry is viewed as a community of coevolving firms that have coalesced around some form of innovation and/or shared vision. As with traditional predator/prey interactions, these organizations formulate and implement strategies to compete (to eat) and to cooperate (to avoid being eaten). Competition is not between individual firms so much as it is between communities of firms sharing complementary products and/or services, similar processes and capabilities, and—most important—a shared vision. Cooperation among the organizations in the ecosystem extends beyond direct suppliers and buyers to include all the participants in the value-creating community, including the relevant stakeholders. They are interdependent in that they coevolve with one another, leading to a shared fate (Moore 1993) or a "strategic community of destiny" (Gueguen, Pellegrin-Boucher, and Torres 2006).

The business ecosystem structure can be viewed as a public good because it facilitates collective actions in networks where multiple contributors with differing interests can join together in a common cause (Iansiti and Levien 2004a; Moore 1996, 2006). These structures can also be viewed as enterprises tied together and extended by shared strategic visions and codes of conduct (Post, Preston, and Sachs 2002a, 2002b). Thus, business ecosystems guided by strategic visions of sustainability can provide the organizing structures for firms to be agents of social change for a more sustainable world (Bies et al. 2007).

Business Ecosystems Defined

Business ecosystems are networks of niches occupied by ecosystem members connected by shared platforms. At the heart of successful business ecosystems are clearly defined, forward-looking visions shared by all ecosystem members rather than by well-defined boundaries resulting in specific industry practices. These members are generally composed of an **ecosystem leader (keystone firm)** and its niche players, and their roles are to collectively focus their entrepreneurial efforts on complementary, value-creating functions within the ecosystem (Moore 1993, 1996, 2006; Iansiti and Levien 2004a, 2004b).

The shared platforms are sets of solutions made accessible to ecosystem members by ecosystem leaders through established standards and interfaces within the ecosystem. Ecosystem leaders draw the boundaries and define the relationships among ecosystem members, and they provide these platforms so that they and their niche players can effectively cocreate value. These platforms allow ecosystem members to develop shared **ecosystemic competencies** that enable the business ecosystem to preserve lasting competitive advantages (Gueguen, Pellegrin-Boucher, and Torres 2006; Iansiti and Levien 2004a, 2004b; Moore 1993, 1996, 2006). Other scholars have described the sustainable competitive advantages from strategic networks such as business ecosystems as collaborative advantage (Kanter 1994), organizational advantage (Nahapiet and Ghoshal 1998), and interorganizational competitive advantage (Dyer and Singh 1998).

Each member's contribution to the business ecosystem is developed some-

Figure 3.5 **Coevolutionary Industry Analysis**

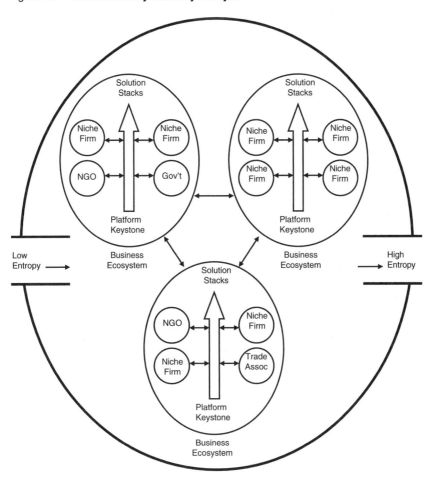

what independently in a modular design as Figure 3.5 depicts. Essentially, the various entrepreneurial niches of the ecosystem members are viewed as self-contained modules that have been aligned around the ecosystem's shared vision. These modules define the contributions of each member to the business ecosystem. This modularity of contributions is often envisioned as **solution stacks** that build upon one another and interact at designated system interfaces. For example, a solution stack could consist of a micro-processor, operating software for the system, and trained employees who are searching for a technical solution to a problem. **Modularity** is a major determinant of ecosystem structure and definition. Once the interaction between the module and its interface with the system is established, then the task structure develops to accomplish the work. Thus, as modularity increases with disruptive technological change, the number and diversity of firms within the business ecosystem tends to increase. Visions, values, and ideas provide the organizational blocks for building the definition of the business ecosystem where sharing, trading, competing, and volunteering establish a new coevolving economic community (Iansiti and Levien 2004a, 2004b; Moore 2006).

Consider for example the Walmart ecosystem. Walmart is the keystone firm, the ecosystem leader, and it has shaped the vision of its business ecosystem around low cost and ecological sustainability. Walmart's Retail Link platform provides its ecosystem members with a platform that can be used to solve fundamental shared problems and create value for thousands of its business ecosystem members (Iansiti and Levien 2004b). It has invested close to US$4 billion in building up its Retail Link system, which has been in operation since 1991. More than 10,000 Walmart suppliers use Retail Link to monitor sales of their goods at the store level and replenish inventories as needed. The Retail Link inventory system also integrates into one of the largest data warehouses around. Walmart uses this integrated system to make more than 10 million transactions daily available to every Walmart store by 4 a.m. the next day (Goleman 2009; Kanter 2009).

Walmart has traditionally focused on improving its supply chain efficiencies. Implementing Retail Link has resulted in Walmart growing its business from US$45 billion in 1993 to over US$400 billion today while increasing the robustness of its ecosystem by adding thousands of niche suppliers. Walmart's commitment to ecological sustainability and low cost has resulted in the development of a new sustainability index that requires its 100,000 global suppliers to calculate and disclose the total ecological costs of their products. Walmart aggregates these into a single ecological rating that customers will see right next to the product's price. Additionally, in an effort to move toward greater social sustainability and to improve its social image (which has historically been quite tarnished), Walmart's suppliers will also have to furnish data on workers' wages, human rights, and the contributions they are making to communities. Thus, it is Walmart's intent to embody in its sustainability index all the environmental, health, and social impacts of the products it sells throughout their life cycles, therefore highly encouraging its ecosystem members to move toward more sustainable business practices if they wish to remain in the Walmart business ecosystem (Goleman 2009; Kanter 2009). In this way, Walmart uses its leverage as the business ecosystem leader to shape the vision and values of increased sustainability within the system.

Business Ecosystem Fundamentals

Fundamental to business ecosystems are the concepts of collaboration and space (Iansiti and Levien 2004a, 2004b). **Collaboration** is necessary to create a system of complementary capabilities and members in order to create value for multiple stakeholders. **Space** (also known as market space, white space, opportunity space, or blue oceans) is the concept of new market domains that exist in the minds of the ecosystem entrepreneurs. Blue oceans, as character-ized by Kim and Mauborgne (2005), denote unknown market spaces where demand is created, not fought over as within traditional industry borders. This provides for value innovation that results from thinking outside of traditional industry borders to the business ecosystem as a whole, thus creating oppor-tunities to create new market space leading to systemwide change (Laszlo and Zhexembayeva 2011).

Thus, the business ecosystem is a cooperative structure that facilitates the development of complementary businesses and other organizations within a given space (Moore 2006). In essence, this multisector, multistakeholder structure guided by a shared vision creates space where ecosystem members can explore what is possible. Thus, the business ecosystem structure is ideal for open innovation and change. An innovation trajectory can be expected of all ecosystem members because their value added comes from their ability to innovate on their own. Many executives today are looking for ways to delegate more of the management of innovation to networks of suppliers and other stakeholders that interact with each other to cocreate products and services. By combining specialization by the niche players along with collaboration with other stakeholders within the ecosystem, in what is technically called **distributed cocreation**, the business ecosystem structure provides innovative opportunities for all participants (Bughin, Chui, and Johnson 2012).

The rise of the Internet as a participatory platform has facilitated the growth of **open innovation** based on collaboration with business ecosystem members. For example, in 1998 LEGO launched an educational product, Mindstorms (programmable bricks), in a partnership with MIT Media Lab. An enthusiastic community of adults and children embraced the product and began to share product designs online, creating the online LEGO Gallery. The organizational learning from this successful product launch led the company to investigate more ways to harness the creative efforts of its customers in product design and development by having the customers suggest new product designs and rewarding them financially if their ideas proved marketable (Bughin, Chui, and Johnson 2012). This type of open innovation ranges from incremental improvements in current products and processes to disruptive changes that create new market space for the business ecosystem members to explore.

Figure 3.6   **Business Ecosystem Structure**

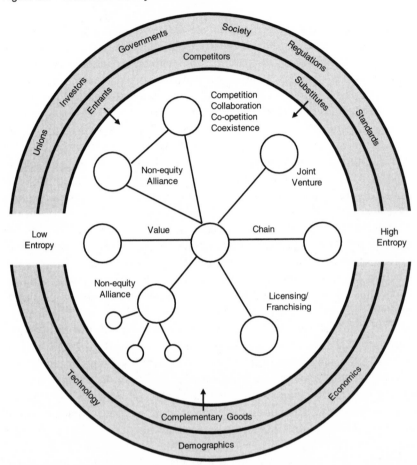

Figure 3.6 demonstrates these collaborative relationships within a business ecosystem.

The business ecosystem structure allows members to focus on managing their own niches due to the stable, well-defined relationships with other members. This frees up human energy, time, financial resources, and so forth that would be used to manage the relationship complexities in more uncoordinated systems to be invested directly in vision-driven innovation and market creation. Of course, this assumes that widespread trust underlies the relationships within the business ecosystem (Putnam 2000; Tymon and Stumpf 2003), and it assumes that members of the ecosystem will share in its stewardship. If trust and shared stewardship are not present, then negative relationship complexities can develop within the ecosystem, which threaten its long-term survival since all parts of the system must remain healthy in order for the ecosystem to thrive (Iansiti and Levien 2004a; Moore 2006).

Building trust becomes increasingly difficult as the heterogeneity of the organizations within the business ecosystem grows. Business ecosystems involve a set of relationships that may include competitors, other business organizations, citizen sector organizations (CSOs), nongovernmental organizations (NGOs), trade associations, sustainable enterprise economies (SEEs), and so forth (Drayton and Budinich 2010; Waddock and McIntosh 2011). Many of these partners from the citizen sector help to creatively and profitably address pressing ecological and social concerns. These ecosystem partners essentially serve as social entrepreneurs that act as change agents and creative problem solvers that can turn social and ecological problems into market opportunities. Partnerships with these citizen sector stakeholders open up avenues for the business ecosystem members to explore new market space, to lower costs, and to develop innovative opportunities along with addressing critical social and ecological needs (Drayton and Budinich 2010).

Other stakeholder partnerships, such as industrial ecology networks where all the firms are committed to collaboratively slowing the entropic process, are increasing as well. Industrial ecologies involve a set of interorganizational arrangements where two or more organizations attempt to recycle material and energy by-products to one another. Whereas these industrial ecologies typically begin as waste exchange arrangements for the purposes of pollution prevention and cost reduction, coevolution would suggest that such networks will likely expand to address resource depletion, overconsumption, biodiversity, community health, and human rights issues (Starik and Rands 1995).

Led by founder and CEO, Howard Schultz, Starbucks has established a strong business ecosystem around a vision of sustainability. Starbucks leads a business ecosystem with niche players that include ecologically responsible growers paid fairly for their crops, indigenous workers paid fairly for their labor, paper products manufacturers helping to improve the recycled content and recyclability of Starbucks wastes, and a network of NGOs and CSOs, including Conservation International, Earthwatch, the African Wildlife Foundation, and the U.S. Green Building Council. In an effort to expand the company's grower-support program, Starbucks recently bought a 593-acre coffee farm in Costa Rica. The farm will help support growers and their families while allowing Starbucks to create new blends of coffee to sell. CEO Howard Schultz has committed to buying only ethically sourced coffee by 2015. Starbucks also attends to its human capital by providing affordable health care, even for its part-time employees. Starbucks has captured 52 percent of the coffeehouse sales market, demonstrating that sustainability-focused business ecosystems can certainly create value by developing synergy around the core value of sustainability (Ottman 2011).

The ecosystem leadership provided by Starbucks, the keystone firm, is key to the success of its diverse multicontributor system. Successful business ecosystems like this have leaders who have the ability to translate a shared vision, based on platforms and standards, into collective action, using both organizational and community-based learning structures. Together as a stakeholder community, the ecosystem members are able to cocreate their future (Moore 2006). In addition to Starbucks, Apple, Google, Amazon, Walmart, Facebook, and Microsoft are also keystone firms and play the leadership roles in their business ecosystems. They provide platforms that connect millions of customers to thousands of content creators and other partners within their ecosystems, thus creating value-sharing opportunities for all of the niche players in the ecosystem (Iansiti and Levien 2004b).

Traditional business models are being challenged with the pervasive digitization of business and the social networks that create total connectivity and transparency. The business ecosystem is one such new model that has emerged to better explain the current reality of competition with its multiple stakeholder demands. The business ecosystem view of industry is a more realistic view of the twenty-first century business environment in which collaboration between networks of multisector organizations creates value for all the niche members within the ecosystem. The embedded business ecosystem culture of disruptive innovation coupled with its focus on planned emergence gives the business ecosystem the power to cocreate new solutions to society's problems, creating shared value for multiple stakeholders.

Business Ecosystem Health and Performance

The health and performance of business ecosystems can be determined by their productivity, robustness, niche creation, and ability to innovate (Iansiti and Levien 2004a, 2004b; Moore 2006). **Productivity** is a measure of the ecosystem's ability to continuously innovate new products and services using fewer resources ("doing more with less"). The ecosystem must be **robust** enough to withstand unexpected shocks from environmental turbulence. A robust ecosystem affords its members a greater degree of predictability and survival. The ability to create more niches attracting new business ecosystem members supports the ecosystem's ability to absorb shocks and to stimulate innovation. The nature of the relationships between niche players and the keystone firm determines the degree of stability of the ecosystem. **Coupling strength** determines the switching costs of moving between ecosystems for the niche players (Iansiti and Levien 2004b). In loosely coupled ecosystems, such as Google, niche players move between ecosystems with relatively low switching costs, while switching costs are high for the niche players in the tightly coupled Apple ecosystem.

In a healthy ecosystem the entropic flow is slowed because as the diversity of the business ecosystem grows, the ability for ecosystem members to **co-create** valuable new sustainable solutions to meet customer needs increases. Also, through the stakeholder engagement processes necessary in the business ecosystem structure, relationships are built through collaboration, which is the glue that holds the ecosystem together. Increasing levels of trust are likely to develop between ecosystem members over time, which slows the entropic flow of human time and energy necessary to maintain social capital, a source of competitive advantage (Tymon and Stumpf 2003). Continuous customer feedback, as LEGO discovered, is also critical if the business ecosystem is to remain relevant and maintain its ability to innovate where customers have more direct control over the design of the goods and services they consume and the processes that are used to make them. Customers provide a source for organizational learning and innovation, thus providing the potential to slow the entropic flow. By linking multitudes of suppliers with the world's largest retailer, the Walmart Retail Link platform has provided cost-saving ecological efficiency throughout its business ecosystem.

Co-opetition and Business Ecosystem Competitive Dynamics

The business ecosystem structure represents an emerging competitive model that can be categorized as **co-opetition**, a network of key players who cooperate and compete with one another in order to create maximum profitability for the network (Nalebuff and Brandenburger 1996). The collaborative, competitive nature of business ecosystems creates a highly competitive environment in which potential competitors may arise from traditionally noncompetitive sectors. The coevolutionary dynamics of the structure enhance the importance of the collaborative value within the network. Therefore, within this competitive model it is necessary for firms to go beyond purely competitive strategies and integrate the value of collective, collaborative strategies with all their complexities and reciprocal interdependencies (Gueguen, Pellegrin-Boucher, and Torres 2006).

Co-opetition provides the structure for ecosystem members to explore new market space and to identify more opportunities through collective strategies. Co-opetition is based on three concepts: (1) complementary firms, even if competitors, are seen as a means of promoting the ecosystem's resources, (2) arbitration between competitive and collective strategies occurs where firms protect their own interests while identifying opportunities within the ecosystem network, and (3) ecosystem members play multiple, diversified roles over time (Gueguen, Pellegrin-Boucher, and Torres 2006).

Consider the Apple ecosystem and the emerging competitive dynamics in the smartphone and tablet space. Apple's Steve Jobs initially introduced the iOS platform with its iPod family of products in a preemptive move that discovered new market space. After the new space was discovered, Apple moved in to establish the foundations that let the ecosystem expand. Apple, however, established and operated the core contribution and established the platform of its iOS ecosystem alone. After the vision took off, Jobs then encouraged its expansion by bringing in independent artist recordings, podcasts, and e-books, by pulling in third-party manufacturers of add-on hardware, and by comarketing with computer companies like Hewlett Packard. Jobs, however, protected the iOS ecosystem by maintaining his digital rights management system, a barrier to entry that prevents non-Apple music players from being used with the iOS platform (Isaacson 2011). Apple has expanded its iOS based product line into phones and tablets where relatively clear modularity and defined relationships exist among its ecosystem niche players.

Therefore, Apple cooperates with its ecosystem partners, but it also protects its interests from competing ecosystems. The niche players within the Apple ecosystem are tightly coupled with Apple, often being described as a walled garden. This tightly coupled ecosystem demonstrates the necessity for business ecosystems to develop and to protect their resources and capabilities that determine the business ecosystem's competitiveness, while building collaborative relationships with ecosystem members and with other ecosystems. This is the essence of co-opetition within and between business ecosystems.

On the other hand, Larry Page, cofounder and CEO of Google, has developed a loosely coupled ecosystem that is often described as an open garden. The Android platform, now rebranded as Google Play, is an open-source mobile operating system that competes directly with Apple's closed iOS platform. The rebranding of the Android platform is a strategy to consolidate and integrate its content ecosystem, which currently offers books, music, and movies, so it can more effectively compete with Apple. Currently, the Android platform powers approximately 69 percent of the smartphone market, thanks to Google's ecosystem member, Samsung, which accounts for 40 percent of Android device sales (Seeking Alpha 2013).

In fact, Samsung's unprecedented success with Android smartphones and tablets has Google executives worried that Samsung will attempt to renegotiate its mobile-ad arrangement. A majority of Android devices come preloaded with various Google applications that generate the company a considerable amount of ad revenue. Samsung is said to receive more than 10 percent of revenue from its advertising partnership with Google (Efrati 2013). The fear is that Samsung could become a threat if it gains too much ground on other manufacturers, so Google executives are now considering bringing other manufacturers into the ecosystem to ensure that they can keep Samsung's leverage in check by providing legitimate competition. In addition, Larry Page has recently acquired Motorola Mobility as sort of an insurance policy against Samsung's leveraged position. Google is working with Motorola to develop a new high-end smartphone to legitimately compete with Apple's iPhone and Samsung's Galaxy line of devices. This positions Google to introduce a new line of Google-branded smartphones and tablets. For now however, Google and Samsung continue to view each other as ecosystem partners in the never-ending battle against Apple, but their collaborative relationship may not last forever, demonstrating co-opetition within the Google ecosystem (Graziano 2013).

The competition between the Apple ecosystem and the Google ecosystem is intense. Before he died, Steve Jobs declared thermonuclear war against Larry Page and Google for copying his patents on his iPhone and iPad, suing Samsung, the manufacturer and Google ecosystem member, for US$2.5 billion, thus beginning the patent wars between ecosystems (Bosker and Grandoni 2012). In discussing the conflicts over patents, Eric Schmidt, cofounder and executive chairman of Google, says the patent wars prevent innovation, since there are an estimated 200,000 patents that overlap, allowing one ecosystem the ability to stop the sale of a competing ecosystem's product. According to Schmidt, even though the competition between ecosystems is intense, Apple and Google still remain very good partners, ". . . literally talking all the time about everything" (Etherington 2013, 1), thus demonstrating the collaborative dynamics of co-opetition between ecosystems.

The Microsoft partner network, another competing ecosystem with Apple and Google, provides a platform to make resources available to a wide variety of technology companies so they can build a business around Microsoft technologies. Microsoft has recently entered the tablet space with its Intel-based surface tablet that will run Windows 8 Pro. The Microsoft Partner Ecosystem consists of the 640,000 partners, vendors, and service providers that build or sell solutions based on Microsoft's platform. These partners include systems integrators, original equipment manufacturers, independent software vendors, value-added resellers, telecommunications companies, Internet hosting services, marketing agencies, and resellers (Ligman 2010). As of 2009, this ecosystem was generating $8.70 in revenue for the ecosystem niche players for every dollar that Microsoft made (Del Nibletto 2010). Thus, the Microsoft business ecosystem provides opportunities for all of its members to prosper.

The strategic approaches that these three competing business ecosystems take are varied in terms of their platforms and core competencies. In turn these keystone players define their ecosystem boundaries quite differently, as Figure 3.6 depicts. Although Microsoft wants computing to continue to be tied to the desktop, they have recognized that the future is in mobility and are introducing tablets and phones. For Apple, it is all about closed information appliances, products differentiated by design with lots of third-party apps and computers anybody can use. When consumers buy Apple products, they buy its ecosystem. The challenge is for Apple to introduce new products that create new market space. As for Google, all roads lead to the Internet, a place synonymous with Google and its core competence in search (Krebs 2011). Thus, the essence of competitive dynamics is in the interplay between the competitive and cooperative strategies employed by the three ecosystem leaders as they create their business ecosystem's future.

In sum, the collective actions within the business ecosystem provide organizations with platforms and relationships that allow them to be more effective agents of social and ecological change (Bies et al. 2007). The members of business ecosystems can come together to do something for the planet and its people that none could do alone. A shared vision based on sustainability shepherded by an effective ecosystem leader can build and maintain the relationships in the ecosystem that hold the modular, entrepreneurial niche players together. This gives them the capability to cocreate solutions to the world's problems by targeting opportunities in the world's coevolving markets and by rewriting traditional industry rules. In such healthy business ecosystems, dialogue, collaboration, information sharing, trust, complementary capabilities, niche creation, and trajectory innovations are clearly present. They provide the necessary platforms for formulating and implementing new strategies for managing in sustainable ways in this coevolving, multistakeholder, multisector world—strategies that accurately reflect "what is" and creatively explore "what can be."

The Coevolving Markets of the World

A coevolutionary view of market analysis within the business ecosystem structure is required in SSM environmental analysis. As discussed earlier in the chapter, the global business environment has coevolved from three highly differentiated economies: the money economy of the developed and developing markets of the world; the traditional, village-based economy of the undeveloped world; and the economy of the natural world in which the other two are embedded (Hart 2005). As Chapter 2 discusses, significant wealth and income inequities exist both within and between the markets of the world. Thus, a country such as China will have coevolving undeveloped, developing, and developed market segments all functioning within its borders.

Although markets are often characterized by their geographical location (i.e., the undeveloped markets of Africa or the developing market of India), they are more accurately portrayed in terms of their specific demographics and varying socioeconomic factors. The coevolving undeveloped, developing, and developed markets of the world offer major opportunities and challenges for businesses that have an SSM portfolio of businesses. However, building strategies for competing within these markets will require firms to engage in dialogue-based generative (creative) learning processes that allow them to think and act differently regarding these unique markets.

Developed Markets

The developed markets of the world currently house the richest 25 percent of the world's population and control 75 percent of the world's income and purchasing power (Milanovic 2002). These markets, which include the United States, Canada, the European Union, Japan, and others, are the world's largest producers and consumers of goods and services, and they have controlled the global marketplace for most of its history. As discussed in Chapter 2, the human footprint in the developed markets is very large. For example, the developed market in the United States, with less than 5 percent of the global population, uses about a quarter of the world's fossil fuel resources—burning up nearly 25 percent of the coal, 26 percent of the oil, and 27 percent of the world's natural gas. Although consumption continues its rapid pace in the developed markets of the world, nearly half of the 1.7 billion people in the consumer class are in the developing markets. A lifestyle and culture that became common in Europe, North America, Japan, and a few other pockets of the world in the twentieth century is going global in the twenty-first century (Worldwatch Institute 2011).

The footprints of corporations in many of the resource-intensive industries such as chemicals and energy are extremely large, and these industries are typically based on older technologies that have limited environmental performance improvement potential (Hart 2005). Thus, the primary need in the developed markets of the world is to reduce corporate and consumer footprints while providing consumer value through sustainable, innovative products and services that enable consumers to reduce their footprints.

Within the developed markets of the world, growth segments have emerged in response to the rising public concern about social and ecological issues and their resulting impacts. "Green has gone mainstream because more people are worried about sustainability-related issues than ever before" (Ottman 2011, 3). For example, 84 percent of American adults can be considered some shade of green, mirroring their counterparts around the world. Both the organic food market and the organic nonfood market (organic fibers, pet foods, personal-care products, etc.) have grown rapidly over the past few years, and the number of sustainable product introductions is also growing very rapidly (Ottman 2011). This reflects the fact that "today's marketers increasingly realize that consumers really fear the planet is losing its ability to sustain human life; they fret about their own immediate health, and that of their children" (Ottman 2011, 3). Innovative, sustainable products designed to meet the needs of the socially and environmentally conscious segments of the market afford firms many opportunities to create triple-bottom-line value.

Undeveloped and Developing Markets

Undeveloped and developing markets provide unique opportunities and challenges for businesses to make positive contributions in moving toward a sustainable world. As previously discussed, approximately 85 percent of the world's population lives in undeveloped and developing markets of the world, mainly in the rural areas of China, India, Africa, and Latin America. These markets are typically village-based, traditional economies where people live at a subsistence level, primarily off the land, with little involvement in the cash or money economy (Hart 2005). The traditional, undeveloped markets are characterized by rural poverty, isolation, disease, exponential population growth, and environmental degradation.

This untapped market of the world's poorest poor has been labeled the **base of the pyramid (BoP)** (Hart 2005; Prahalad 2006; Prahalad and Hart 2002). Approximately 4.6 billion people in these markets live on less than US$4 per day and about 1.4 billion of them live below the international poverty line of US$1.25 per day (Hart 2005; World Bank 2008). The BoP markets are not homogeneous, but rather are segmented by different characteristics across regions, countries, and industry sectors, making them fragmented and making it difficult for them to obtain economies of scale when entering. All the BoP markets do, however, share a common defining characteristic: They are the part of the world population that has historically been excluded from the market economy. The lack of formal integration of the BoP markets into the formal economy has resulted in a low socioeconomic market of the world's poor that primarily operates in the informal economy. According to Ted London and Stuart Hart (2011), the BoP market that contains the majority of humanity can be characterized by (1) those living in the informal market, (2) heterogeneity across multiple dimensions, (3) the poorest of the world's poor with the least amount of income, and (4) local enterprises that are not connected to the formal economy. These characteristics require formulating strategies quite different from developed market strategies.

The BoP market is estimated as a potential US$1.3 trillion market that potentially offers numerous win–win opportunities for businesses to earn a profit while helping to alleviate poverty (Hart 2005; London and Hart 2011; Prahalad 2006; Prahalad and Hart 2002). For example, the global low-income health-care market provides major opportunities for strategic managers to address critical social needs and create economic value for the firm. The market is currently worth US$202 billion, and it is expected to grow exponentially because of emerging business and social innovations. Also, the market for low-income housing in urban slums is estimated to be worth US$1 trillion and growing (Drayton and Budinich 2010).

Interestingly, even with all of the wealth and purchasing power in highly developed countries, they often have income and wealth inequities that lead to pockets of undeveloped markets within their borders. As Chapter 2 discusses, the urban inner cities and the rural Appalachian region of the United States have historically demonstrated many of the characteristics of undeveloped markets. This is largely due to insufficient retail penetration in these areas; they have significantly fewer supermarkets, department stores, and pharmacies per capita than their higher income counterparts. This lack of economic activity results in cycles of poverty and social problems such as domestic violence, drug abuse, and crime. Restoring economic and social health to these undeveloped market segments offers numerous opportunities for businesses to become profitable through triple-bottom-line performance that serves the local community (Dean and McMullen 2005; Porter 1995).

As previously discussed, a large consumer class has emerged in the developing markets where industrialization has brought increasing consumer demand for goods and services. As Hart (2005) notes, developing markets represent the collision of the money economy with nature's economy, where meeting future consumer demands without exceeding the carrying capacity of the planet is the major challenge. Thus, the developing markets of India, China, Indonesia, and so forth consist of the rural, isolated poor, the urban slum dwellers, an increasing number of refugees, and the increasingly affluent, all involved in a coevolutionary dance that creates opportunities and challenges for the firm. The coevolution of these once distinct markets results in myriad social and environmental issues (as discussed in Chapter 2). Finding sustainable solutions to these issues provides numerous business opportunities for organizations, allowing them to contribute to the preservation of human, social, and natural capital while earning a reasonable profit for their efforts.

Environmental Forecasting

After scanning and monitoring the macro and industry environments for signals of environmental trends and changes, strategists then develop projections of anticipated outcomes and assess the importance of the forecasted environmental changes on their strategies. Forecasts are critical because they shape strategic managers' views of their future. As previously discussed, the novel, discontinuous, nonlinear, change-oriented business environment makes predicting the future based on the past very difficult. This renders traditional forecasting techniques much less effective for predicting future trends unless they are combined with forecasting techniques that are not based on using the past as the sole predictor of the future. Thus, managers should be very cautious about limiting their forecasts to single quantitative point estimates as the only possible future outcome in today's unpredictable, turbulent environment.

Multiple scenario analysis is a forecasting technique that creates a climate that fosters more creative, out-of-the-box thinking within the organization (see Figure 3.7). The use of multiple scenario analysis was originally developed at Royal Dutch Shell during the late 1960s to prepare managers to think more clearly about the future (Swartz 1991; Wack 1985a, 1985b). Multiple scenario analysis has coevolved over the past decades into a forecasting tool that allows managers the flexibility to develop several paths to the future. The use of scenario analysis reflects the recognition by managers that the future is unpredictable. A **scenario** is a flowing narrative (rather than a quantitative point estimate) that depicts a possible path to the future. Each scenario in multiple scenario analysis is a story based on a particular mental model of the future. Scenarios may be anticipatory, helping strategists predict and understand risk, or exploratory, helping strategists discover new market space. Thus, taken together, multiple scenarios provide a picture of the general direction of change an organization will face in the future. Building scenarios for sustainable strategic management requires an analysis of stakeholder impacts and anticipated stakeholder expectations that will help organizations to be prepared for dynamic, coevolving sustainability-based issues such as climate change (Laszlo 2008). General Electric's (GE) ecomagination strategy is based on the scenario of an increasingly carbon-constrained world that GE views as a major business opportunity.

For example, Allen Hammond (1998) constructed three scenarios for 2050 by analyzing persistent long-term demographic, economic, social, environmental, and security trends that were likely to shape and constrain the future. These three scenarios, which reflect very different mindsets and worldviews, were developed to explore alternative possibilities for how the future may unfold. The scenarios are: (1) Market World—a future based on the belief that market forces and new technology, once unleashed, are sufficient to bring rising prosperity and a brighter future to humankind; (2) Fortress World—a grimmer future in which uneven economic growth creates islands of prosperity surrounded by oceans of poverty and despair, a future of growing environ-

Figure 3.7 **Multiple Scenario Analysis**

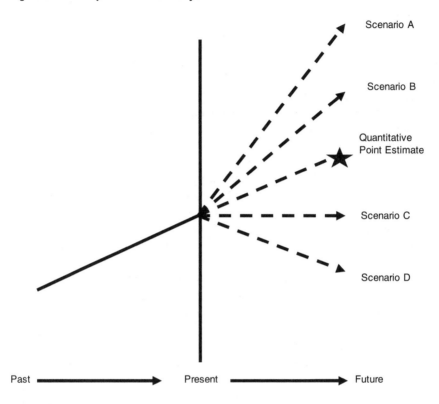

mental degradation, conflict, violence, and social chaos; and (3) Transformed World—a future in which fundamental social and political changes offer hope of fulfilling human aspirations. Hammond argues that all three scenarios are plausible, and that the choices we make as human societies now will determine which world—which trajectory into the future—ultimately comes to pass. SSM is based on the vision of a transformed world, a sustainable world for present and future generations, where the business sector becomes engaged in cocreating solutions for pressing societal and ecological issues.

Another example of scenario analysis is the Millennium Ecosystem Assessment (MA) called for by former United Nations Secretary-General Kofi Annan. Initiated in 2001, the objective of the MA was to assess the causes and consequences of ecosystem changes for human well-being and to determine the scientific basis for actions needed to conserve and sustain these ecosystems for humankind. The MA has involved the work of more than 1,360 experts worldwide. The MA scenarios were designed to incorporate more realistic and detailed ecological dynamics than previous global scenarios by considering social and ecological feedbacks (Carpenter, Bennett, and Peterson 2006).

The MA provides estimates for some key indicators of human health, including global population and the per capita regional availability of water and food production. The scenarios explored two global development paths (globalized versus regionalized societies and economies) and two different approaches for ecosystem management (reactive and proactive). In reactive management, problems are addressed only after they become obvious, whereas proactive management attempts to maintain ecosystem services for the long term.

The following scenarios were selected to explore contrasting transitions of global society up to the year 2050 (Carpenter, Bennett, and Peterson 2006): (1) Global Orchestration—a globalized world with reactive ecosystem management with an emphasis on equity, economic growth, and public goods such as infrastructure and education; (2) Order from Strength—a regionalized world with reactive ecosystem management with an emphasis on security and economic growth; (3) Adapting Mosaic—a regionalized world with proactive ecosystem management with an emphasis on local adaptations and learning; and (4) TechnoGarden—a globalized world with proactive ecosystem management and an emphasis on green technologies.

The MA scenarios were developed with a focus on conditions in 2050. Under all four MA scenarios, the projected changes in the underlying driving forces result in significant growth in consumption of ecosystem services, continued loss of biodiversity, and further degradation of ecosystem services. Demand for food is projected to grow by 70–80 percent, demand for water by 30–85 percent, and poverty and child malnutrition will continue to be prevalent due to economic disparity. There will be an absolute decline in the natural capital that supports human life, including freshwater resources and biodiversity. The bottom line of the MA findings is that human actions are depleting Earth's natural capital, putting such strain on the environment that the ability of the planet's ecosystems to sustain future generations can no longer be taken for granted. Although the projected future is bleak for coming generations, the assessment shows that with appropriate actions it is possible to reverse the degradation of many ecosystem services over the next 50 years, but the changes in policy and practice required are substantial and not currently under way (Corvalan, Hales, and McMichael 2005). Changing the course of this forecasted future requires collective global action by multiple stakeholders with business leadership to improve ecosystem management and to build the capacity to address global challenges, including long-term climate change, poverty, and disease.

Scenarios such as these may also be used to assist in business ecosystem definition and redefinition. Looking into possible futures described by the above scenarios provides the context to: (1) rethink organizational missions in light of a shared vision of sustainability; (2) expand the business ecosystem's scope and redefine its businesses to address critical social and environmental issues; and (3) help cocreate solutions for the well-being of future generations. Various strategies may be tested against a number of different futures. They may be descriptive, describing the future without commenting on its desirability, or they may be normative, incorporating the scenario users' interests and motivations. Today, computer modeling is regularly incorporated into scenario building. This takes advantage of the best features of both approaches—the rigor of modeling and the creativity of scenario building.

The most important outcome, however, of the process of scenario building is strategic managers' learning and development (Chermack and Swanson 2008). The art of scenario building is an organic process where learning advances in a coevolutionary fashion. Scenarios provide a process that stimulates thinking about the future and creates dialogue about strategic issues. Moreover, it builds a consensus based on the strategists' mental models of the future. The process surfaces inconsistencies in the mental models of strategic managers, and it provides an environment that enhances the ability to cocreate a better future for the firm and for future generations of humans.

Chapter Summary

Given the uncertainty of an external environment characterized by turbulence, complexity, discontinuity, and change, strategic managers engaged in sustainable strategic management must develop a systems-based environmental scanning culture within their organizations. This means that macro environmental scanning needs to be expanded to include the social and ecological sectors, and that traditional industry analysis needs to move toward a coevolutionary analysis of business ecosystems. Within the context of SSM, strategic managers will have to engage not only in adaptive learning as they respond to the demands of the marketplace, but they will also have to engage in generative (creative) learning, questioning the fundamental assumptions and values on which their decisions are based. Strategic managers will have to work to rewrite industry rules and create opportunities beyond existing industry boundaries to include the larger society and ecosystem. This will not only allow them to focus on "what is" within their industries; it will also allow them to think in terms of "what can be" within and beyond their industries. Successful formulation of sustainable strategic management requires that strategic managers be able to create the future for their organizations and society by thinking and learning outside the box of traditional industry analysis, and scenario analysis provides an excellent tool for such generative processes.

Case Vignette 3

A Brief Environmental History
of the Chemical Industry

Rachel Carson's 1962 book, *Silent Spring*, was largely responsible for shaping the worldview of the chemical industry as the global economy was dawning over 50 years ago. Unfortunately for the industry, that reputation was one of a deadly industry in need of complete reformation. She referred to synthetic chemicals—especially pesticides—as "elixirs of death" (Carson 1962, 15), and she portrayed them as imminent threats to the survival of the Earth's entire biological system. Early in her book, she created an eerie image of an Earth saturated by dangerous chemicals, saying (p. 2), "A strange blight crept over the area and everything began to change. . . . There was a strange stillness. The birds . . . where had they gone?" Her book includes a litany of chemicals—DDT, ADP, ATP, BHC, heptachlor, chlordane, acetylocholine, aldrin, aminotriazole, arsenic, and numerous others—which she describes as carcinogenic or otherwise poisonous to humans and nature. Ironically, Carson died of breast cancer two years after *Silent Spring* was published (Lear 1998).

The chemical industry's reputation was further rocked in the 1970s and 1980s by high-profile chemical disasters. One of those was the highly publicized disaster that occurred when toxic chemical wastes inundated the homes and schools of a Niagara Falls, New York, neighborhood known as Love Canal. Hooker Chemical Company legally buried 21,000 tons of toxic chemical wastes in the 1940s and 1950s on approximately 36 square blocks of vacant land it owned in Niagara Falls. In the 1950s Hooker sold the land for one dollar to the Niagara Falls School Board. Even though Hooker explicitly warned the school board before the sale that dangerous chemicals were buried on the property, Love Canal quickly grew into a popular bedroom community with homes and schools and parks. Then, in August 1978, the wastes buried under Love Canal by Hooker began bubbling up from their underground tombs (rusted-out 55 gallon drums) and into the homes and schools of Love Canal, openly exposing virtually all of the residents to cancer, disease, and birth-defect causing toxins. The community was eventually rendered uninhabitable and demolished (Hoffman 1999).

The most prominent chemical disaster of the 1980s occurred at the Bhopal, India, plant of Union Carbide. In December 1984, an explosion at the plant released methyl isocyanate, a highly poisonous gas. Like many of the factories in India, a very large shanty community housing thousands of urban poor had grown up around the Union Carbide plant over the years. The explosion and resultant methyl isocyanate leakage wreaked havoc on this shanty neighborhood, exposing a half million people to the deadly gas. Over 2,000 people died during the explosion, and at least 8,000 died later because of exposure to the poison gas. Union Carbide CEO Warren Anderson was arrested when he attempted to visit the plant after the disaster, and seven Union Carbide employees were convicted of the deaths caused by the leak and sentenced to two years in prison.

These and other highly publicized incidents and issues, such as spraying Agent Orange in Vietnam, illegally dumping toxic wastes (known as "midnight dumping"), prominent oil spills, research tying chemical exposure to various forms of cancer, and so forth, led to a quagmire of complex, expensive, innovation-stifling, command-and-control environmental regulations affecting the chemical industry. In the United States alone these included the Comprehensive Environmental Response, Compensation, and Liability Act (the Superfund law), the Toxic Substances Control Act, the Resource Conversation and Recovery Act, the Clean Water Act, the Clean Air Act, and numerous others.

The negative reputations suffered by all firms in the chemical industry because of the above incidents and the resultant oppressive regulatory environment became imminent environmental threats to the industry in the 1980s. In a talk he gave at the University of Michigan in 1994, David Buzzelli, CEO of Dow Chemical Canada during the days of Bhopal, said (Buzzelli 1994) that public relations surveys taken after the Bhopal disaster concluded that the reputations of every firm in the industry had suffered because of the accident. He realized after seeing the survey data that the firms in the chemical industry were either going to live or die together. He said in his talk that the industry's reputational damage and the resulting excessive costs of regulatory compliance were causing a crisis that could be solved only if all the firms in the industry worked together. Understanding this, Dow Canada and other Canadian chemical companies worked together under the auspices of the Canadian Chemical Producers Association to establish the original Responsible Care® program in 1984.

Since its inception, Responsible Care® has shifted the culture of the entire chemical industry from one of disaster management and regulatory compliance to one of voluntary ecological and social responsibility (Hoffman 1999). From its Canadian roots, Responsible Care® has expanded across the globe. It is now prevalent in 60 nations that produce 90 percent of the world's chemicals (American Chemistry Council 2012). The emergence of Responsible Care® served to improve the image of the chemical industry during some of its darkest days, and it encouraged firms to create value rather than just spend money on improved ecological and social performance.

The fact that 90 percent of all the chemicals produced in the world are now being manufactured under the Responsible Care® guidelines speaks volumes regarding the significant sustainability-centered changes that the chemical industry has undergone since Rachel Carson declared it the evil culprit of the "silent spring." Despite the fact that some still want to depict the chemical industry as society's worst nightmare, as Annie Leonard (2007) does in her popular Internet video, "The Story of Stuff," today's chemical companies are in fact continuing to improve their sustainability performance. Besides their commitment to ever-tightening Responsible Care® guidelines, they are now focusing increased attention on working with customers and other stakeholders to provide sustainably advantaged products and services that provide sustainable solutions to customers in a wide variety of global markets ranging from affluent developed markets to markets at the base of the economic pyramid.

4

SSM Resource Assessment

Two sets of data are required when formulating an effective strategy: data from the environmental scan concerning the opportunities and threats facing the firm (as discussed in the previous chapter) and internal data concerning the firm's resources and capabilities. In this chapter, the strategic focus shifts to the internal interface between the strategy and the firm's resources and capabilities. The sustainable strategic management (SSM) resource assessment process takes place at the functional levels of the firm across the firm's open-system value chain, as depicted in Figure 4.1. The process of SSM resource assessment includes: (1) an audit of the firm's resources and capabilities utilizing various data-gathering processes; (2) a thorough analysis and evaluation of the firm's resources and capabilities; and (3) a determination of the firm's core competencies, the cornerstones on which the firm builds its competitive strategies. It is through the exploitation of core competencies via the firm's competitive strategies that sustained competitive advantages are created. The stages of resource assessment are coevolutionary in nature where identifying, analyzing, and evaluating resources is a spiraling, reciprocally adaptive process representing the collective wisdom of the firm.

The Resources of the Firm

According to the **resource-based view (RBV)** of the firm (Barney 1986, 1991; Barney and Hesterly 2010; Wernerfelt 1984), organizational competitive advantages are achieved through the effective management of internal resources, where profit differentials result from the heterogeneity of the firms rather than the structure of the industry. Whereas the industry is considered the fundamental unit of analysis when formulating competitive strategy in the industry-based view discussed in the previous chapter, the RBV approach considers the firm as the primary unit of analysis for strategy formulation. Thus, firm performance is a function of the types of resources developed and

Figure 4.1   **Resource Assessment**

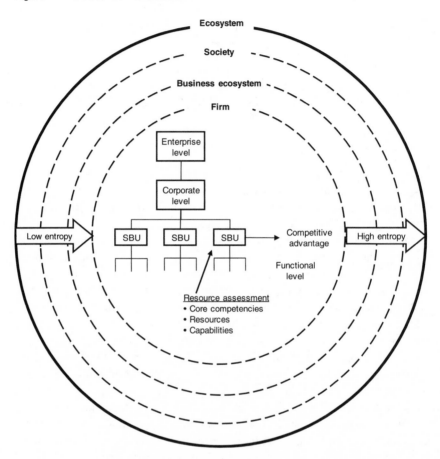

exploited by managers through functional and competitive level strategies that build competitive advantages. Resources are factors that allow a company to create more value for customers than do its competitors. Thus, the concept of **value creation** lies at the heart of the firm's resource assessment process that yields competitive advantages. The following section discusses how perceived value creation has coevolved over time.

Coevolving Capital Sources

Resources can be defined as available wealth-generating capital (Merriam-Webster Dictionary 2012). There are various forms of capital, and the relative importance of them has shifted over time. For many decades, the term **capital,**

along with **labor**, were considered two of the primary factors of production and referred to exclusively as a firm's material wealth—its physical and financial assets that were used to produce more material wealth. However, as the financial markets grew, alternative uses of capital became more common, so the term **financial capital** was created to distinguish the asset of money from the physical capital of land, plant, equipment, and so forth. Thus, firms began to consider both their physical and financial capital in value creation (Tymon and Stumpf 2003).

Stimulated by the growth of the service economy, another type of capital emerged—**human capital**. Initially this term was simply a euphemism for labor, but its meaning has expanded over time. Human capital is now viewed as instrumentally valuable in achieving organizational goals, thus requiring firms to invest in it. Over time, other forms of capital have emerged, including **intellectual capital** and **knowledge capital**, which are now measured and reported to stakeholders. Technologies, patents, copyrights, and so forth are considered intellectual capital, where *knowledge capital* consists of organizational learning based on skills that employees share with each other (Tymon and Stumpf 2003).

As the population of the Earth has expanded exponentially, placing stress on the planet's ability to provide the necessary resources for humankind, land has been redefined as **natural capital** in order to recognize the value of the ecosystem services it provides. In addition, as the economy has coevolved into the networked economy of business ecosystems, **social capital**, the value of relationships, has emerged as critical. Also, **reputational capital**, the stakeholders' moral perceptions of the firm's products and activities, has been identified as a primary benefit of sustainability (Kiron et al. 2013), and **spiritual capital**, the organization's higher purpose, has emerged as a means of achieving competitive advantages. As can be noted from the above discussion, these various forms of capital have emerged over time in response to the coevolutionary interactions among organizations and their competitive environments. Figure 4.2 depicts this spiraling coevolutionary view of capital, which will be further discussed later in the chapter.

In the RBV *resources* are also defined as "the tangible and intangible assets that a firm controls that it can use to conceive and implement its strategies" (Barney and Hesterly 2010, 66). **Tangible resources** include the firm's physical assets such as factories and inventories, and **intangible resources** include nonphysical entities such as the firm's brand and reputation. **Organizational capabilities** are a subset of organizational resources that enable the firm to take advantage of other resources, thus providing the ability to conceive and implement strategies. There are two critical assumptions about resources and capabilities underlying the RBV that strategic managers can control:

Figure 4.2   **Coevolution of Capital**

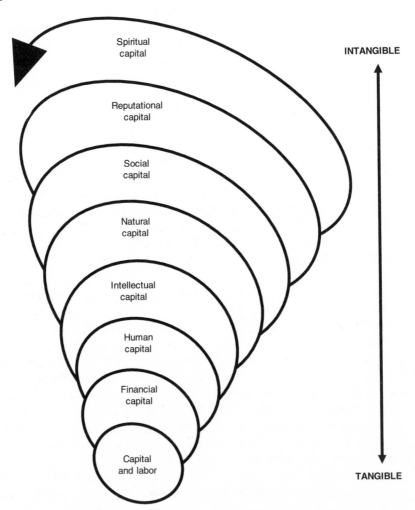

The first is the assumption of **resource heterogeneity**, which says that firms may possess different bundles of resources even if they are competing in the same markets, implying that some firms may be more skilled than other firms in accomplishing an activity. Second is the assumption of **resource immobility**, which says that the resource and capability differences among firms may be long lasting because it is costly for other firms without certain resources and capabilities to develop or acquire them (Barney and Hesterly 2010). For example, Apple continues to be more skilled in product design than its competitors, and Harley-Davidson's reputation for big, loud motorcycles separates it from its competitors. The following sections more fully describe the resources and capabilities available to firms for creating more value for customers than their competitors do, thereby building competitive advantages for the firm.

Tangible Resources

Tangible resources are the easiest to identify and evaluate because they are accounted for on the firm's financial statements. **Physical assets** are typically defined to include buildings, plant, equipment, inventory, and land. Physical assets shown on financial statements can be either under- or overevalued since historic cost valuation often provides little indication of market value, especially in today's environment where social and ecological value are directly linked to market value. For example, land is natural capital that is usually undervalued on financial statements because its value in nature as a watershed, a species habitat, and so forth is not accounted for on financial statements.

Natural capital is composed of nature's goods (abiotic resources) and nature's services (biotic resources). Nature's goods include land, water, minerals, fossil fuels, solar energy, and so forth; and nature's services include renewable resources, ecosystem services, waste-absorption services, and so forth. The entropy law imposes absolute scarcity on natural capital by placing limits on factor substitution, meaning that reproducible man-made capital is seldom a proper substitute for natural capital. Financially treating man-made and natural capital as if they are substitutable improperly equates land and other natural assets, which embody life, with the nonliving assets of the firm, such as buildings and equipment (Daly 1977; Daly and Farley 2004). Thus, the SSM resource assessment process expands the view of land to include the value of the natural capital that embodies and sustains life.

The market is relied upon to reflect the full cost of products and services. If the market gives society poor information by not recognizing the full value of natural capital, then poor decisions are made in the allocation of these scarce resources. A key issue in including the value of natural capital in the cost of products and services is the common practice of discounting the value of assets and liabilities in the future. Discounting means that when managers make investment decisions, they weigh future benefits and costs as less valuable than present ones. While sound for short-term financial decisions, when applied to natural capital, discounting distorts the ecological costs and benefits of decisions. Further, the choice of the discount rate can determine the quality of life for future generations. For example, using a discount rate of 6 percent, one study recommended that we not spend $300 million today to prevent $30 trillion of ecological damage from climate change in 200 years. However, using a discount rate of 2 percent, another study indicated that we should make substantial investments now to reduce the impacts of global warming (Daly and Farley 2004).

Nicholas Stern (2006), the former chief economist at the World Bank, says that the gap between the climate change costs and the market prices for fossil fuels is huge. He says that including the costs of climate change in the market price of gasoline would add approximately US$12 per gallon to the price at the pump. In other words, the market is grossly undervaluing the price of gas by failing to fully account for the environmental costs of burning fossil fuels (Brown 2008). Further, a study of firms in the fast-moving consumer goods market segment concludes that these firms may experience a decline in earnings up to 47 percent by 2018 unless they develop strategies that mitigate their risks posed by environmental pressures. The study concludes with this advice to strategic managers, "if you are not internalizing the externalities proactively in the present, you will be dragged into action by downward pressure to the bottom line" (Laszlo and Zhexembayeva 2011, 120). Thus, the SSM resource assessment process includes an expanded view of physical resources that includes the evaluation of externalities associated with natural capital.

Financial capital is a tangible resource that represents the firm's cash, cash equivalents, capacity to raise equity, and capacity to borrow, where **market capital** represents the current stock price of the firm and the outstanding number of shares. Market capitalization has emerged as a type of capital that is used to value companies. However, market capitalization is an incomplete and sometimes misleading index of value since it is only when a firm is sold in its entirety that its true market value can be determined (Tymon and Stumpf 2003). **Intellectual capital** includes the value of the firm's trade secrets, patents, copyrights, and innovative production processes.

Intangible Resources

Executives responding to the Kiron et al. (2013) survey said that the difficulty they have measuring the intangible benefits of sustainability-related strategies is a major obstacle to implementing sustainability in their organizations. Intangible resources, such as brand loyalty, reputation, organizational culture, and so forth add significant value to firms, and yet they generally remain invisible on firms' financial statements (Grant 2008). Also intangible human capital, such as employee commitment, skills, expertise, effort, and trust, has value for the firm and its stakeholders that is not fully evident in the firm's financial statements. Even so, it can afford the firm major competitive advantages. **Knowledge capital**, a subset of human capital, is an intangible resource comprising the information and skills of a company's employees, their experience with business processes, group work, and on-the-job learning. Knowledge capital is based on organizational learning, where employees share skills with each other in order to improve efficiencies. Thus, the process of increasing knowledge capital within organizations involves investing in developing human potential in the workplace. Human capital investment can also be both socially responsible and economically profitable for the firm (Benn and Probert 2006; Spirig 2006), and having employees with skills and knowledge capital enhances firm competitiveness.

Research indicates that the most important corporate resource over the next 20 years will be the **human capital** of the firm, talented employees who are smart, technologically skilled, globally astute, and operationally agile. The battle for talented employees is dramatically intensifying, and attracting and retaining talent is a business imperative for economic survival. Research reveals that in the United States 75 percent of workforce entrants consider environmental and social criteria when selecting employers. Firms with progressive human resource policies and strategies based on an inspiring vision such as sustainability have been shown to have a competitive edge in attracting and retaining high-quality employees (Nidumolu, Prahalad, and Rangaswami 2009). The vision of sustainability engages employees' desires to feel that they are part of a larger purpose, and managers find that their investments in human capital lead to greater productivity and profitability as well as a means of fulfilling their social responsibilities.

Investing in sustainability can also add value by enhancing reputation and brand recognition. General Electric, Starbucks, and Unilever have all established world-class brand recognition by investing in sustainability. However, the sustainability reputation of a brand can be easily damaged if organizations do not practice vigilant product stewardship. According to Stuart Hart, "It's becoming increasingly clear that companies that fail to live by a set of principles that optimize results for all stakeholders might get away with it for awhile. But in the end, the negative feedback loops get you and it's going to bring you down" (as quoted in *MIT Sloan Management Review* and BCG 2011, 10). BP's Gulf of Mexico oil spill in 2010 and Toyota's massive product recall in 2009 make this fact abundantly clear.

Because of the impact of such incidents on financial performance, it has been recommended that the risks to intangible **reputational capital** be integrated into the firm's enterprise risk management system (Young and Hasler 2010). Though it is not simple, examining the gap between the firm's market value and book value can give an idea of its reputational value. Essentially, when market value exceeds book value, it is a sign that stakeholders hold the firm's reputation in high value (Dess, Lumpkin, and Eisner 2008). In other words, reputational capital is the financial value of the firm's intangibles (Fombrun, Gardberg, and Barnett 2000). Indeed research indicates that 91 percent of people claim that their purchasing decisions are influenced, at least in part, by how much they trust the firm and its reputation (Waddock and McIntosh 2011).

Social capital is an intangible resource that refers to the connections among individuals—social networks, the norms established by reciprocal relationships, and the trustworthiness that arises from them (Putnam 2000). Because business ecosystems are relationship-based structures, building positive social capital is critical for their survival. The idea that social capital is a means of economic value creation is relatively new in managerial thinking. "Whereas economic capital is in people's bank accounts and human capital is inside their heads, social capital inheres in the structure of their relationships" (Portes 1998, 7). Social capital includes the institutions, relationships, standards, values, and so forth that underpin and shape a society (Grootaert and van Bastelaer 2001).

Thus, social capital comprises both the network and the assets that may be mobilized through that network. Social capital knits a community's social fabric by enabling people to build communities and to commit to one another. High levels of social capital increase the potential for collective action to address local concerns (Smith 2000). Governments, citizen sector organizations (CSOs), nongovernmental organizations (NGOs), business organizations, and others can create social capital in isolation. However, more and more clusters are forming in which these organizations are working in concert with one another to create social change. This is resulting in social capital creation in both the network and the resources mobilized within the network.

As the previous chapter discusses, these networks may coevolve into business ecosystems unified by a shared strategic vision around creating social change. The social capital garnered from the shared values and social norms that compose an ecosystem's culture result in relationships built on trust among diverse business ecosystem members. These trusting relationships, this creation of social capital, may provide **ecosystemic competencies** for the business ecosystem that may result in such advantages as lower transaction costs and economies of scale. As this occurs, the ecosystem as a whole can achieve more than any single ecosystem member acting alone (Dyer and Singh 1998; Gueguen, Pellegrin-Boucher, and Torres 2006; Kanter 1994; Nahapiet and Ghoshal 1998). The ecosystemic competencies that result from the social capital creation process can enhance diverse ecosystem members' abilities to work together and integrate their specific skills into a viable ecosystem strategy, especially for those firms who have embraced the core value of sustainability (*MIT Sloan Management Review* and BCG 2011). The platforms offered by the keystone firms, the ecosystem leaders, to ecosystem members enhance the collaboration so necessary for building social capital. The resulting social networks help to build the "we" mentality that is so necessary for moving toward a shared vision of sustainability.

Human capital serves as the foundation for **spiritual capital** within the firm or business ecosystem. Spiritual capital is a kind of intangible wealth earned by acting out of the human need to serve a higher purpose. This type of wealth helps to create a sustainability-based culture that is nourishing and sustaining for the human spirit. High levels of spiritual capital allow for disruptive change and generative (creative) learning within organizational cultures without causing them to fracture. It enhances the organization's ability to meet the real needs of society rather than just meeting material needs. In essence it exists in the soul of a firm or business ecosystem, and it defines its fundamental core values and larger purpose (Zohar and Marshall 2004). This provides a sound foundation for implementing an organizational vision of sustainability.

Capabilities

Capabilities are "tangible and intangible assets that enable a firm to take full advantage of the other resources it controls" (Barney and Hesterly 2010, 66). Capabilities are specific skill sets that can be creatively composed in various and sundry ways to build unique core competencies that provide the firm with sustainable competitive advantages. Examples of organizational capabilities include outstanding customer service, exceptional innovation processes, and superb product development processes. The more complex the integration of capabilities, the harder it is to imitate the competencies and the longer the competitive advantage can be sustained (Prahalad and Hamel 1990). Thus, capabilities are process-focused.

Dynamic capabilities are critical success factors in today's turbulent environment where strategic managers must continuously scan the external environment and strategically fit the firm's internal resources to the dynamic external environment (Eisenhardt and Martin 2000). Specifically, strategic managers must have the ability to change the firm's resource base and activity system as the external environment changes. Thus, dynamic capabilities are essential in order to gain and sustain competitive advantages. Not only do dynamic capabilities allow firms to adapt to changing market conditions, they enable firms to create market changes and explore new market space.

Apple, as discussed in Chapter 3, utilizes its dynamic product development capabilities to create new market space and redefine its business ecosystem's position. The introduction of the iPod generated environmental changes to which Sony and others had to respond. With its iPhone, Apple redefined the market for smartphones, again creating environmental changes to which RIM, HP, Nokia, and others tried to respond. More recently, Apple's introduction of the iPad has again redefined the media space, forcing competitors to respond (Rothaermel 2013). This dynamic capability is the cornerstone of Apple's competitive advantage in product differentiation. Thus, competitive advantage does not result from a static resource base, but rather from the ability to leverage a dynamic reconfiguration of the firm's resource base. Since the advantage lies in the firm's ability to change the resource base, dynamic capabilities are considered an intangible resource.

As the external environment becomes more infused with increasing demands from multiple stakeholder groups, dynamic sustainability capabilities are becoming a competitive necessity. Whereas the tangible capabilities may together provide firms with cost-saving and revenue-generating benefits, without also having intangible sustainability capabilities, firms are unlikely to support the development of the "disruptive innovations" necessary for long-term survival during the sustainability revolution. The ability to build an organizational culture based on the shared vision of sustainability, the ability to create spiritual and social capital resulting in positive economic, social, and ecological business ecosystem relationships, and the ability to build an ethical system grounded in sustainability are some examples of intangible sustainability capabilities. These tangible and intangible sustainability-based capabilities range from scientific to technological to organizational to spiritual (Laszlo and Zhexembayeva 2011). Developing these internal capabilities will lead to the transformational changes required for a shared vision of sustainability creating long-term competitive advantages for the firm.

In sum, research supports the idea that resource assessment should be expanded to include ecological and societal resources, which means natural, social, human, and spiritual capital must be considered in the process. Hart (1995) and Russo and Fouts (1997) have found that resource assessment should be expanded to include natural resources as sources of sustained cost and differentiation competitive advantages. They discovered that natural resource capabilities improve both organizational performance and profitability. Further, Richard (2000) found that racial, cultural, and social diversity in organizations can be valuable social resources that add to firms' long-term competitive advantages. According to Laszlo and Zhexembayeva (2011, 28–29), "Never before have the boundaries of the corporation been so clearly under siege. Tomorrow's business solutions and competencies lie outside the organization's walls." Therefore, the SSM resource assessment process expands the analysis of resources and capabilities to include the greater society and ecosystem, even though data gathering, measurement, and evaluation of these resources and capabilities may be difficult.

SSM Resource Assessment Data-Gathering Tools

The first stage in this coevolutionary, spiraling resource assessment process is the data-gathering phase where organizational resources (tangible and intangible resources and capabilities) are profiled to determine what resources and capabilities the organization currently has and which of those resources will provide the firm with potential strengths and weaknesses. As the sustainability movement has gained more global momentum, leading to increasing demands for more sustainable organizational performance, the tools utilized for profiling organizational resources have expanded to include the greater society and ecosystem. The discussion below examines some of these key tools.

Value Chain Analysis

Value chain analysis (VCA), popularized by Michael Porter (1985), is the most popular strategic management tool used in resource assessment (see Figure 4.3). An implicit assumption underlying VCA is that it operates within a closed economic system that does not include the greater society and ecosystem. VCA is utilized to disaggregate the firm's activities and allocate costs according to their value-creating functions so that the relevant resource or capability can be analyzed for its potential as a cost or differentiation strategic driver. Porter (1985) argues that each of a firm's activities—from physical creation through manufacture to the consumer—can be analyzed in order to better understand the firm's sources of **costs** and market **differentiation**, which are the generic bases of competitive advantage. A competitive advantage can be achieved only if the firm performs its value-creating activities at a cost less than its competitors or in such a way that its products and/or services are so unique that consumers are willing to pay a premium price for them.

The value chain includes **primary activities**, which represent the physical creation of the product or service; these include the value-creating functions directly related to the design, production, and delivery of the product, including its marketing and after-sales service. **Support activities**, on the other hand, provide inputs so that the primary activities can take place. Support activities include infrastructure activities, such as information systems, planning systems, finance, and legal services. Infrastructure represents the overall context in which all the value-creating activities take place, including the organization's structure, culture, and control systems. Because strategic managers exert considerable influence in shaping these aspects of a firm, stra-

Figure 4.3   **Closed-System Value Chain**

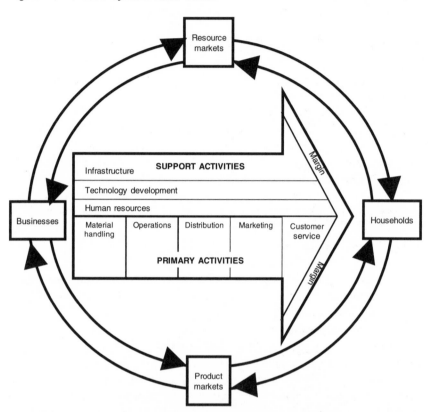

Source: Adapted from Michael E. Porter (1985)'s Value Chain Model.

tegic leaders are considered a part of the firm's infrastructure. In fact, effective strategic leadership (discussed in Chapter 8), influences both the context and the performance of all other value-creating activities. Other support activities include human resource management and technology development.

Disaggregating the activities of the firm into value-creating activities provides managers with insights into how to effectively deploy resources via **functional level strategies** to develop competitive advantages. Functional level strategies in such areas as operations, marketing, human resources, or finance, may be implemented to improve efficiency, quality, innovation, and customer responsiveness across the value chain. For example, Southwest Airlines has implemented operational functional strategies that increase efficiency and reduce costs in their primary value-creating activities, while concurrently implementing human resource strategies to support these operational strategies. Operationally, Southwest flies only a single type of plane (Boeing 737), flies into smaller airports, has avoided complicated hub-and-spoke route systems, and instead, flies a point-to-point system; all these operational strategies are focused on increasing efficiency and lowering costs. On the people side, despite being highly unionized, Southwest has been able to develop a sense of commitment and loyalty within its workforce. Employee productivity at Southwest is higher than most airlines; the average turnaround time at Southwest is around 18 minutes compared to the 45 minutes of the average airline. By being on the ground less time and in the air more time than competitors, Southwest reduces its costs by hundreds of millions of dollars every year (Barney and Hesterly 2010). Thus, by using VCA and implementing operational and human resource functional strategies, Southwest has developed the capability to deliver air travel at a cost less than competitors.

VCA encourages top managers to engage in strategic thinking rather than just performing an audit of the functional levels of the firm. However, the traditional value chain as seen in Figure 4.3 is an outdated approach to value creation for four reasons. First of all, the stakeholder relationships implied in the model are too narrow, consisting solely of the relationships between the firm, its suppliers, and its customers. This narrow perspective excludes stakeholders such as CSOs, social entrepreneurs, NGOs, and competitor networks, which are necessary for social value creation (Drayton and Budinich 2010; Freeman and Liedtka 1997; Mahon and McGowan 1998). Second, the primary activities of the firm do not account for natural capital, the value of resources in nature, and the value of wastes after consumption, thus ignoring the entropy law. Third, traditional VCA fails to account for social and human capital as sources of competitive advantage. Fourth, the support activities in the traditional value chain are not generally structured to support SSM. For example, human resource policies that will enhance the value of human capital, full-cost accounting systems that can account for natural and social capital over time, and design processes based on sustainability are all necessary for SSM.

Porter and Kramer (2011) agree that the traditional value chain provides too narrow a focus on short-term financial performance while ignoring broader societal, ecological, and customer needs that are critical for long-term success. Therefore, they have developed an expanded view of value creation that includes the greater society and ecosystem. Their expanded view of the value chain is based on the principle of **shared value**, "which involves creating economic value in a way that *also* creates value for society by addressing its needs and challenges" (Porter and Kramer 2011, 64).

Drayton and Budinich (2010) agree that the traditional value chain is too narrow for SSM purposes. They conceptualize replacing it with a **hybrid**

value chain that depicts collaboration between corporations and social entrepreneurs, CSOs, and NGOs that creates economic value, social value, and ecological value. The multiorganizational perspective of the hybrid value chain is especially appropriate for framing value creation in business ecosystems. Laszlo and Zhexembayeva (2011), have called for businesses to create **sustainable value**, "a dynamic state that occurs when a company creates ongoing value for its shareholders and stakeholders—a natural outcome of the new external environment" (p. 42). Thus, sustainable value represents a single integrated value-creation space where value is created for multiple stakeholders. The discovery of this value-creation space is the essence of SSM resource assessment.

Life Cycle Analysis

Life cycle analysis (LCA) allows firms to expand the scope of traditional VCA to include the ecosystem services and natural capital. LCA is a total systems approach that provides an appraisal of the ecological impacts of the firm's products and processes all along its value chain, from cradle to grave (Svoboda 2008), making it "one of the most useful tools for measuring the [firm's] footprint" (Esty and Winston 2008, 169).

A cradle-to-grave LCA process involves analyzing resources, emissions, energy, and environmental impacts of every value chain activity. LCA-based tools such as eco-tracking, which utilizes relative and absolute metrics to capture data at multiple organizational levels across the full spectrum of the value chain, have been instrumental for firms such as GE, Dow, DuPont, IBM, and Bayer, as they work to respond proactively to the rising ecological consciousness across the globe (Esty and Winston 2008; Hawken 2007). LCA is a tool that can give organizations solid data regarding how to improve environmental performance and reduce resource intensity, and it can help them to extend the life of their products, thus making them more competitive by being more sustainable. LCA is seen as a sustainability driver in innovative firms where sources of waste throughout the value chain are identified and eliminated or reduced, cutting costs, enhancing environmental and economic performance, and providing data for entrepreneurial thinking within the firm (Nidumolu, Prahalad, and Rangaswami 2009). Figure 4.4 depicts the open-system value chain where the true value of natural capital is recognized.

Footprint Analysis

Whereas VCA and LCA provide data that help firms improve their economic and ecological value added, **footprint analysis** expands the analysis to include

Figure 4.4 **Open-System Value Chain**

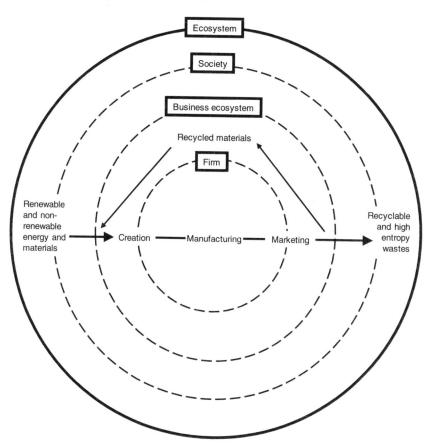

social value-added data, which are critical for creating value for stakeholders in all three sustainability arenas. A complete organizational footprint analysis must go beyond the limited economic and ecological scope of VCA and LCA to determine the true impact of the organization's footprint (Lazlo 2008).

In the first stage of footprint analysis, the types and amounts of raw materials and energy needed by the firm are determined, and the ecological and social impacts of acquiring and using these raw materials and energy are analyzed. In the second stage, the ecological and social impacts of the manufacturing process are assessed. This includes examining the materials and energy used in component manufacturing processes, final product manufacturing processes, and product assembly processes; it includes examining the impact of the firm's operations on the communities in which it operates; and it includes examining the firm's impact on the human capital of the firm (such as employees), includ ing issues such as child labor and human rights. Third, the transportation and distribution systems related to delivering the product to market are analyzed in terms of distribution modes, distances, energy consumption, carbon emissions, and impacts on social and human capital. Fourth, the environmental and social consequences of how the product is used are analyzed, including assessments of product durability, energy requirements, polluting potential, and impacts on the health and safety of consumers and community members. Fifth, the product's potential for reuse and/or recyclability are analyzed. The sixth stage of footprint analysis is to examine the product's ultimate disposal in terms of its toxicity, volume, biodegradability, and impacts on community health and safety (Laszlo 2008).

It is important to understand that footprint analysis is an extremely complex concept in the early stages of development. Thus, it is difficult to implement, its outcomes can be easily skewed by the assumptions of those doing the analysis, and it does not always provide clear-cut answers concerning the environmental and social benefits and challenges of products and processes. Footprint analysis can also be very information-intensive due to the required stakeholder engagement and dialogue processes. It is, therefore, potentially cost-intensive depending on how many factors are assessed and the extent of upstream or downstream activities within its scope. Nonetheless, footprint analysis is essential if firms want to work to include the absolute entropic limits of the planet and the welfare of its people in their product design, creation, and distribution processes. Thus, even though footprint analysis is a complex, imperfect process that cannot currently give organizations all the answers they need concerning the impacts of their products and services on society and the planet, forging ahead with its development and improvement is absolutely essential for building dynamic capabilities for firms.

Stakeholder Analysis

Stakeholder analysis provides additional data on stakeholder impacts and thus a greater understanding of the organization's footprint as Figure 4.5 demonstrates. Stakeholder analysis entails determining who the stakeholders are, how they are changing, what their power and stakes in the organization are, what their expectations and interests are, and what their values are (Freeman 1984). These data are gathered across the full spectrum of the open-system value chain and compared to organizational and stakeholder goals, which leads to the identification of performance gaps. This type of analysis provides triple-bottom-line data for stakeholder value creation.

A recent survey identified senior managers, customers, industry associa-

Figure 4.5 **Coevolution of Eco- and Socio-Effectiveness**

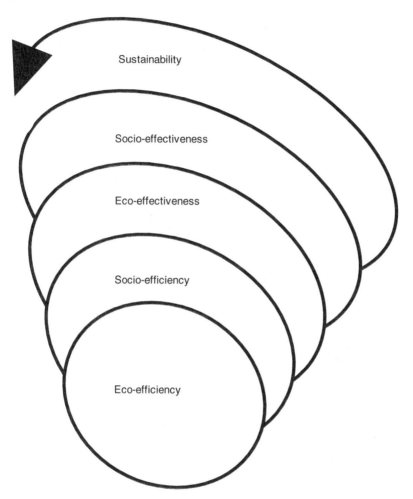

Sustainability

Socio-effectiveness

Eco-effectiveness

Socio-efficiency

Eco-efficiency

tions, value-chain partners, local communities, investors, NGOs, and con-
tractors as the key stakeholders in firms' sustainability agendas (Kiron et al.
2013). Given that this broad array of stakeholders is currently demanding
more sustainable business practices, stakeholder analysis today naturally
encourages managers to broaden their strategic processes to include societal
and ecological concerns. Doing so means that the Earth and its people are
assigned stakeholder status in the organization. Recognizing the significance
of the Earth and the broader society as stakeholders is critical in integrating
sustainability into the ethical core of organizations, allowing managers to

recognize that the long-term survival of business and the long-term survival of the human species and its quality of life are intricately interconnected coevolutionary processes. After all, the Earth includes and supports all of humankind within its sphere, it is the geographical location of all business activity, it is the source of the resources and energy necessary to make the economic engine purr, it is the sink into which the wastes of economic activity are poured, and it is humankind's home (Gladwin, Kennelly, and Krause 1995; Post 1991; Shrivastava 1995; Starik 1995). From this perspective, the Earth and its people are the ultimate stakeholders of business organizations.

Of course, the planet and its 6 billion plus inhabitants cannot all be active stakeholders, sitting on boards of directors or attending shareholder meetings of the world's global corporations. Many exist on the fringe of the organization and have little traditional stakeholder power (Hart and Sharma 2004). However, the Earth and its inhabitants have a growing cadre of friends in the world's communities, boardrooms, executive suites, retail stores, financial markets, courtrooms, media, halls of government, and factory floors that are representing the interests of society and the natural environment. These include environmentally and socially conscious consumers, investors, employees, legislators, regulators, litigators, interest groups, lenders, insurers, and industry standards setters, among others (Edwards 2005; Hawken 2007; Starik 1995; Stead and Stead 2000). The worldwide growth in the influence of these sustainability conscious stakeholders will ensure that they will be increasingly significant players in the coevolution to SSM in the global economy.

Many of the socially and environmentally motivated stakeholders, such as the poor, physically weak, isolated, and many nonhumans, remain on the periphery of traditional corporate stakeholder power circles despite their pervasiveness in both numbers and interests represented. Finding productive ways of communicating with them is no easy task. Hart and Sharma (2004) and Gregory (2000) encourage the development of value-based, open dialogue processes that allow the voices of these hard to identify and reach stakeholders to be heard and accounted for in managerial decisions. Hart and Sharma (2004) believe that if such processes are put into place, these "fringe" stakeholders will provide real sources of imaginative new capabilities for corporations doing business in the undeveloped and developing markets of the world. One of these open-dialogue stakeholder engagement processes is appreciative inquiry (AI), which we will explore further in Chapter 7.

Consultants from Ernst and Young (2011) found that shareholders are quite worried about the financial risks from damaged reputational capital if a firm is perceived to be a poor steward of society and the planet. Because of this, they recommend that boards take a more active role in engaging all stakeholders on sustainability issues. If strategic managers will carefully listen to their stakeholders and view them as sources of information and resources rather than problems to be managed, they can enhance the dynamic capabilities of their firms to embrace and manage change because the stakeholders themselves are important agents of change. Further, reframing stakeholder analysis to include the Earth as the ultimate stakeholder of business organizations and recognizing the maze of stakeholders in the business environment that represent the Earth's social and ecological systems can provide strategic managers with the motivation to discover and take advantage of their triple-bottom-line opportunities.

Analyzing and Evaluating Resources and Capabilities to Build Core Competencies

After gathering data on the resources and capabilities of the firm across the open-system value chain, the next stage of SSM resource assessment involves analyzing and evaluating resources in order to provide insight to potential strengths, weaknesses, competitive parity, and core competencies. This process begins with an evaluation of the firm's resources that compares current performance with historical performance and internal quality standards. This analysis will yield performance **trends**, which are helpful in ascertaining whether a resource or capability is a potential strength or weakness. For example, a decline in CO_2 emissions for several years could be a potential strength, an increase of the debt/equity ratio over time could be a potential weakness, or the increase in the number of worker injuries could be a potential weakness. Therefore, a **strength** is a potential resource or capability that could provide a unique pillar on which to build a strategy, while a **weakness** is the potential lack of a resource, skill, or capability that could impede strategy implementation. The analysis of triple-bottom-line data compared over time with internal standards provides insights about future trends.

After comparing resources and capabilities with internal standards and historical data of firm performance to identify potential trends, the analysis expands to include external data gathered from the firm's competitors, macro environment, footprint, and stakeholders. These data provide the critical information for strategic managers to evaluate and identify those resources and capabilities having the potential to be developed into **core competencies**, unique strengths that are valuable, rare, difficult to imitate, and organized to capture value (Barney 1991). These unique strengths allow the firm to more effectively differentiate its products and/or achieve substantially lower costs than competitors. As Figure 4.1 depicts, core competencies must be strategically combined and deployed by functional level strategies so as to build **sustained competitive advantages** through the exploitation of the core competencies in the market via the firm's competitive strategies (Barney and Hesterly 2010). If numerous competitors possess the valuable resource, it becomes a basic business requirement, which is a resource or capability that the firm is required to possess to compete in the industry. A basic business requirement provides a firm with **competitive parity** but no unique competitive advantages.

In order for a resource to be a core competence it must be valuable, rare, and costly to imitate. These are the characteristics that distinguish core competencies from other resources, and it is core competencies that provide the basis for competitive advantage. A resource is considered **valuable** if it can be utilized to exploit an external opportunity or neutralize a potential threat. A resource is considered **rare** when there are few competitors in the industry that possess it (Barney 1986, 1991). Thus, a resource that is valuable and rare has the potential to be a competitive advantage. However, environmental turbulence may make a competitive advantage transitory as competitors respond.

For example, initially, Toyota's flexible, lean manufacturing system was both a rare and valuable resource in the automobile industry because it was the first automaker to resolve the trade-off of how to lower production costs and maintain high quality. Toyota was therefore able to capture a temporary competitive advantage. However, as the knowledge of lean manufacturing diffused throughout the industry, high quality and low cost became an industry standard. And over time, Toyota's capability was no longer a competitive advantage, but a necessary requirement for doing business within the industry that led to competitive parity (Rothaermel 2013).

To be considered a core competence, a resource must also be **costly for competitors to imitate**. A resource is costly to imitate when firms that do not possess the resource or capability face a cost disadvantage in obtaining or developing it compared to firms that already possess it (Barney 1986, 1991). Thus, the inimitability of a resource is a key factor in determining core competencies. Further, by examining resources through the lens of complexity theory, resources can be examined in terms of complex systems, such as business ecosystems, that allow for a more holistic, less reductive evaluation of resources. This includes evaluating the resource's inimitability in terms of causal ambiguity, social complexity, and system level resources (Colbert 2004).

Causal ambiguity occurs when competitors do not fully understand how the firm is using its capabilities as foundations to build a competitive advantage. Causal ambiguity has its base in bounded rationality, the idea that the ability to make rational decisions is limited because of imperfect information. As the term causal ambiguity suggests, the cause–effect nature of situations is obfuscated, making them hard to understand and evaluate rationally. Causal ambiguity exists because problems, ideas, processes, and so forth are ill defined and complicated. According to Reed and DeFillippi (1990), causal ambiguity is a legitimate barrier to imitating sustainable core competencies.

Social complexity relates to complex social phenomena such as interpersonal relationships, trust, friendships among managers, and a firm's reputation with suppliers and customers. Social complexity generally refers to the fact that human relationships are highly complex phenomena that are difficult to understand and systematically manage with any real certainty. As examples of socially complex factors in business organizations, Barney and Hesterly (2010) give interpersonal relationships among managers, the dynamics of an organization's culture, and the reputation of a firm with its customers.

System level resources are holistic in nature and are difficult to imitate. As we have previously discussed, the business ecosystem structure provides sources of collaboration through platforms that can create the trusting relationships that hold the ecosystem together. **Ecosystemic competencies** resulting from the social capital built over time in the development of a business ecosystem afford the ecosystem a competitive advantage because the relationships within the network are causally ambiguous, socially complex, and holistic in nature. Thus, from a complex adaptive systems perspective, the more causally ambiguous, socially complex, and holistic the resources are, the more difficult it is for competitors to imitate them, thus offering a potential sustained competitive advantage to the firm (Barney 1986, 1991; Colbert 2004; Grant 1991; Reed and DeFillippi 1990; Schoemaker 1990).

Take Croc Shoes, for example, the maker of the plastic clog, launched in 2002 as a spa shoe. Croc experienced explosive growth, with its shoes being worn by people in every age group. Croc protected its unique design with several patents and revenue grew to over $800 million by 2008. However, numerous other cheap imitations copied the colorful, comfortable plastic shoe, and competitors cut into Croc's profits. Competitors easily imitated the shape, look, and feel of the original shoe, demonstrating that competitive advantage cannot be sustained if the underlying resource can be replicated and thus be directly imitated. Where Croc Shoes is more or less a one-hit-wonder, Nike, on the other hand, has the dynamic capability to continuously innovate and build brand recognition leading to a sustained competitive advantage that is difficult to imitate (Rothaermel 2013).

And finally, an assessment of **organizational capabilities** must be made to determine whether the firm has the capabilities to support the exploitation of resources that are valuable, rare, and costly to imitate in order to create a core competence on which to build the firm's competitive strategy (Barney and Hesterly 2010). In other words, is the firm organized to capture value?

Given the sustainability-infused external environment, developing dynamic capabilities and the ability to reconfigure the resource base to be dynamically responsive to changing stakeholder demands must be assessed. The firm's ability not only to adapt to market changes but also to create and explore new market space must be evaluated.

For example, Google's core competence is in developing proprietary search algorithms. This dynamic capability provides a competitive advantage for Google in that its competitors have not been able to imitate this search capability. Google has an 88.8 percent share of the global search engine market, with Bing, its closest competitor, holding only 4.4 percent of the market (Karma Snack 2012). Google's applications of this core competence have resulted in products such as Gmail, Google Maps/Earth, AdWords, Google Books, Google Scholar, and so forth. On the other hand, Apple has built its business ecosystem around its dynamic capability of leveraging product design to integrate hardware and software in innovative mobile devices that produce highly differentiated products with high levels of customer loyalty. Applications from this dynamic capability have resulted in products such as iTunes, iMac, iPod, iPhone, and iPad. Thus, the Apple and Google business ecosystems are structured around quite different ecosystemic core competencies, resulting in competitive advantages that competitors have had difficulty imitating. As the ecosystem leaders, Google and Apple have demonstrated that the more complex the integration of capabilities, the harder it is to imitate the competencies and the longer the competitive advantage can be sustained (Prahalad and Hamel 1990).

Research indicates that intangible resources such as spiritual capabilities and social capital are more valuable than tangible resources in building sustainability-based competitive advantages. A survey of 3,000 business executives around the world representing every major industry revealed their belief that sustainability performance has become a source of sustained competitive advantage where the evaluation and measurement of intangible resources is emphasized. Leading firms such as Johnson and Johnson, Proctor and Gamble, and New Belgium Brewing all place a very high value on sustainability-based intangibles (*MIT Sloan Management Review* and BCG 2011).

The companies that have embraced sustainability as a core value spend more time and effort quantifying the impact that their businesses have on brand, reputation, employee productivity, and the ability to attract top talent than do firms that see sustainability merely as an add-on to their strategies. These firms have deep values for the conservation of natural resources, and they strongly believe that valuing such intangibles improves their long-run effectiveness. They have developed ways to measure intangibles, even though such measurements are generally fraught with problems that render their accuracy suspect. However, despite any potential scalar inaccuracies, these firms want to show that they place a high value on these important intangibles (*MIT Sloan Management Review* and BCG 2011).

In sum, firms generally have numerous resources (tangible and intangible) and capabilities that can be strategically deployed and combined via functional level strategies into a system of a few core competencies that are valuable, rare, and costly to imitate. If the firm is organized to capture value, these core competencies provide the building blocks for competitive strategies that will create multiple stakeholder value.

Creating Stakeholder Value via Eco- and Socio-Efficiency

Triple-bottom-line firms are committed to economic success that both en-hances and is enhanced by their concerns for the greater social and ecological contexts in which they exist (Sharma and Vredenburg 1998). Gathering data across the open-system value chain allows managers to more clearly focus their organizational initiatives at those points where economic success, social responsibility, and/or ecological health intersect. This framework, as Figure 4.4 depicts, allows strategic managers to expand their view of the value-creation process to an open-system value chain where natural, social, human, and economic capital are synergistic, value-creating resources and capabilities within the firm and business ecosystem. By utilizing the data gathered and analyzed via VCA, LCA, stakeholder analysis, and footprint analysis, strategic managers can cocreate value with multiple stakeholders and create long-term competitive advantages.

Eco-Efficiency and Stakeholder Value Added

Eco-efficiency involves developing both cost and differentiation competi-tive advantages by eliminating or reducing resource depletion, materials use, energy consumption, emissions, and effluents. Eco-efficiency is an effective adaptive learning process that seeks improved sustainability performance in present operations. Eco-efficiency techniques include things such as: redesign-ing pollution and waste control systems, redesigning production processes to be more environmentally sensitive, using recycled materials from production processes and/or outside sources, using renewable energy sources, increasing the durability and service intensity of goods and services, and so forth. Envi-ronmental value added is created because eco-efficiency techniques provide the capabilities for firms to enhance both their economic and environmental performance. Innovation is the strategic driver in improving eco-efficiency, and significant data demonstrate a direct relationship between eco-efficiency, competitiveness, and financial performance (Esty and Winston 2008; Laszlo 2008; Stanwick and Stanwick 2005).

At least four processes are common to eco-efficiency efforts in organizations: (1) dematerialization—designing products that use fewer and safer materials; (2) closing production loops—creating minimal/zero wastes in manufacturing processes, (3) extending service—customizing responses to customer demand and offering customers the choice of either leasing or buying goods; and (4) extending function—developing products that are smarter with enhanced functionality and durability (Holliday, Schmidheiny, and Watts 2002).

Johnson and Johnson found that eco-efficiency directly contributes to their profitability. Between the years 2004 to 2009, the firm invested US$187 million in more than 60 energy reduction projects that have reduced carbon emissions by 129,000 metric tons annually. The projects have generated about 247,000 megawatt hours of cumulative energy savings a year, while generating an internal rate of return of almost 19 percent. Also, during the same period hazardous and nonhazardous wastes were reduced by 32 percent. According to Johnson and Johnson's senior director for worldwide health and safety, "Waste is a cost to the corporation . . . and, of course, the less waste you send out of your gates, the less expensive it is to make your product" (as quoted in *MIT Sloan Management Review* and BCG 2011, 8).

Socio-Efficiency and Stakeholder Value Added

The open-system value chain expands value-creation processes to include the stakeholder influences of employees, ecosystem members, and the community, all of which have symbiotic coevolutionary relationships with the firm. From a stakeholder perspective, social performance can be defined as the social impacts the firm has on its stakeholders: the fewer the negative social impacts and the more the positive social impacts, the better the firm's social performance (Spirig 2006). The Global Reporting Initiative (GRI) groups social performance into four categories: labor practices, working conditions, human rights, and product responsibility. The ability to enhance both social and human capital while contributing to the organization's economic sustainability is referred to as **socio-efficiency**, which is an adaptive learning process that seeks to improve sustainability performance in current strategies and operations (Dyllick and Hockerts 2002; Figge and Hahn 2004, 2005, 2006; Hockerts 1999). Socio-efficiency involves creating stakeholder value by connecting the investments in social and human capital to the firm's core business strategy (Holliday, Schmidheiny, and Watts 2002).

Socio-efficiency entails viewing human capital as an important instrumental asset in the value-creation process. Innovative human resource practices that focus on the long-term capabilities of the workforce are used to develop human capital. This is encouraged because it leads to higher levels of performance in organizations, increasing social value added at each stage of the value chain. Jobs are designed to be economically, intellectually, and socially fulfilling, enhancing both the personal development of employees and the economic sustainability of the firm.

For example, Google's founders Larry Page and Sergey Brin, along with the human resources director and the leadership team, have literally crafted every professional job and workplace element so that all employees are working on interesting projects, learning continuously, constantly being challenged to do more, and feeling that they are adding value. This earned Google the top spot on *Fortune Magazine*'s Best Companies to Work For list. The key element of Google's human resource strategy is to change the nature of work so that the work itself becomes a critical attraction, retention force, and driver of innovation and motivation. Google calls this "20 percent work." It essentially means that the firm's professional employees work the equivalent of one day a week on their own, researching individually selected projects that the company funds and supports. Both the Google Groups and Google News products are reported to have started as a result of "20 percent work" projects. The program has been a phenomenal recruiting tool, and it has kept their attrition rate at almost zero. But its greatest value added is that this investment in human capital by Google drives innovation and creativity throughout the firm, demonstrating how the investment in human capital can be a competitive advantage for the organization (Iyer and Davenport 2008).

Socio-efficiency also entails viewing the social capital of the firm, of the business ecosystem, and of the community as instrumental in value creation. As discussed above, organizational culture, reputation, and trusting stakeholder relationships are intangible resources that can afford the firm competitive advantages. The open-system view extends the value chain to community stakeholders—governments, activists, interest groups, and others—that can influence the firm's economic sustainability. Being a good corporate citizen in the communities in which the firm or business ecosystem operates helps to build social and reputational capital both internally and externally, and it contributes to the profitability of the firm.

For example, Target has made substantial contributions to K–12 education in the United States through its "Take Charge of Education" program. The firm has contributed to 95 percent of K–12 schools, it has given 5,000 field trip grants and 1,800 early childhood reading grants, it has renovated 188 school libraries, and it has instituted Target's "Meals for Minds" program in 72 schools (Target Corporation 2011). These educational investments enhance

Target's brand and reputational capital in the communities in which it operates, influencing its long-run profitability.

Thus, eco- and socio-efficiency represent the intersection of economic, social, and ecological value-creating functions that can be exploited to create value for multiple stakeholders. The development of eco-efficient capabilities currently is more highly developed and more prominent in firms than the development of socio-efficient capabilities. The primary reason for this discrepancy is that the economic value created by eco-efficiency is for the most part more easily and precisely measured, and thus it is more tangible than the value created by socio-efficiency, which consists largely of intangible resources and capabilities (Esty and Winston 2008).

Measuring the Value Added from Eco- and Socio-Efficiency

Measuring social and environmental value added requires calculating the organization's economic, social, and environmental stakeholder impacts and aggregating them into an organizational footprint. Once complete, the firm can compare its current footprint with its past efforts, competitors, government standards, and industry standards, and from this analysis determine whether performance gaps exist. Industry standards, such as those established by the Global Environmental Management Initiative (GEMI), the Sustainable Forestry Initiative (SFI), and the American Chemical Council's Responsible Care program, have become particularly popular as benchmarks in this process. Other external indicators, including the GRI, the UN Global Compact, the Dow Jones Sustainability Index (DJSI), and metrics developed by socially responsible investment (SRI) rating agencies such as Innovest, IW Financial, and KLD are also used extensively as sustainability performance benchmarks (Laszlo 2008; Rosinski 2006). The leading edge sustainability companies use extensive measurement processes that allow them to establish performance baselines, even in measuring intangibles where the metrics are not perfectly accurate, and they track their sustainability performance. These types of metrics help make intangibles more tangible. They serve as powerful organizational signposts indicating that sustainability performance is important, and they help tie sustainable value to a firm's financials (*MIT Sloan Management Review* and BCG 2011).

The data from the competitor analysis, as we discussed in Chapter 3, provide important, comparative information for strategic managers that is essential in determining firm and ecosystemic core competencies. Thus, by carefully benchmarking the organization's and business ecosystem's current footprint in relation to established standards for stakeholder well-being and in relation to their competitors' footprints, strategic managers can better determine their effectiveness regarding their ability to cocreate eco- and socio-stakeholder value. This type of analysis provides a shift from a cost-based to a value-based assessment of environmental and social performance (Figge and Hahn 2004, 2005, 2006), thus enhancing shared stakeholder value (Porter and Kramer 2011).

Beyond Eco- and Socio-Efficiency: Eco- and Socio-Effectiveness

Where eco- and socio-efficiency are directly tied to the short-run economic sustainability of the firm, eco- and socio-effectiveness have posterity as the planning horizon in the value-creation process. The essence of eco- and socio-effectiveness lies in viewing the firm as an agent of social change with a higher-level purpose, as Figure 4.5 depicts. The ability to generate an understanding of the aesthetic value of nature and humankind that cannot be touched or displayed is essential in moving toward eco- and socio-effectiveness. Only by viewing the firm as a holistic part of the spiraling, coevolutionary process of sustainability can the spirit be stirred, which is the essence of eco- and socio-effectiveness. Eco- and socio-effectiveness require viewing the organization's role in society quite differently. A shift from viewing the value chain as a firm-specific, cradle-to-grave process to an ecosystemic-based, cradle-to-cradle mental model is required, where human, social, and spiritual capital become the defining competitive advantages. Only by creating a business ecosystem committed to the higher purpose of sustainability can the soul be stirred to think beyond traditional boundaries and to create and explore new market space for the benefit of future generations.

Specifically, **eco-effectiveness** refers to transforming renewable energy and resources into products whose wastes in turn serve as inputs for other biological and/or industrial cycles with the goal of total materials recycling. William McDonough and Michael Braungart (2002) said that the key to making the shift from cradle-to-grave to cradle-to-cradle lies in redesigning industrial systems in ways that mimic natural metabolic processes, many of which are not so much efficient as effective. Many of nature's processes have built-in inefficiencies, but whatever wastes are generated are always absorbed and reused in the natural environment. No wastes are left as wastes. To accomplish this, McDonough and Braungart suggest that products be designed around two types of materials: **biological nutrients**, materials that biodegrade and can be returned to the biological cycle, and **technical nutrients**, materials that do not biodegrade but can be circulated continuously through the industrial cycle. In other words, the key to eco-effectiveness lies in design. Figure 4.6 depicts eco-effectiveness, providing a vision for ecological sustainability.

Figure 4.6   **Eco- and Socio-Effectiveness**

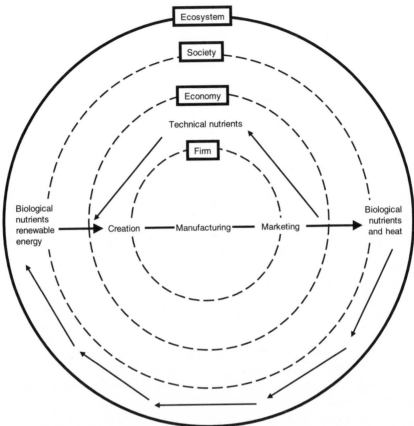

General Mills's oat milling facility in Minnesota was designed with eco-effectiveness in mind. Its biomass unit uses leftover oat hulls as the energy source to generate 90 percent of the steam used to heat the plant and to produce the flour. The remaining oat hulls are burned to generate electricity to power 17,000 homes located within its business ecosystem (Business Roundtable 2011). Closed-loop processes such as this are keys to moving toward eco-effectiveness.

A cradle-to-cradle process also requires accounting for the responsibility of organizations to develop and sustain a just and equitable workplace, thus investing in human capital and making positive contributions to building social capital in the business ecosystem and community. This is referred to as **socio-effectiveness** (Benn and Probert 2006; Dyllick and Hockerts 2002; Hockerts 1999). Socio-effectiveness means that employees, the human capital of the firm, are no longer viewed as merely instrumental in value creation. They are considered to have intrinsic value in and of themselves. Their personal visions are purposively tied to the organization's vision (Senge 1990), and they are treated as ends rather than means to ends (Freeman and Liedtka 1997). It also means that fringe stakeholders such as the poor, weak, and disenfranchised are accounted for in the organization's stakeholder network (Hart and Sharma 2004). Via socio-effectiveness, global corporations can be agents of positive social change, where they become part of the solution to many of the world's problems (Bies et al. 2007). These social change initiatives include addressing issues such as child labor, human rights, economic justice, disease, poverty, overconsumption, and preservation of indigenous cultures. Socio-effectiveness provides a vision of the role of the business enterprise in society's sustainable future.

Unlike eco- and socio-efficiency, which can be directly tied to short-term profitability, the business case for socio-effectiveness is mixed because posterity is the planning horizon. However, the increased number of organizations acting as agents of social change reflects that many strategic managers perceive that these initiatives are adding to stakeholder value by making long-run, positive contributions to a sustainable society for posterity. Examples of firms engaged in socio-effective initiatives abound. The Coca-Cola Company has formed an alliance with the U.S. Food and Nutrition Research Institute of the Department of Science and Technology and the Philippine Ministries of Education and Health to develop a product, NutriJuice, to directly address the high prevalence of iron-deficiency anemia in elementary schoolchildren. The vitamin and mineral fortified drink is provided to the school children of the Philippines free of charge.

Accenture's "Skills to Succeed" initiative is about helping people develop skills so they can get jobs, build businesses, and improve their communities with a goal to equip 250,000 people worldwide by 2015. Currently Accenture has 80 separate initiatives and has committed more than US$100 million to support these initiatives (Business Roundtable 2011). Such examples demonstrate how organizations are strengthening their reputational and social capital by being agents of social change and making long-run positive contributions to society while creating value for multiple stakeholders and future generations. This is the essence of socio-effectiveness.

This emerging, cradle-to-cradle view of the value chain can be conceptualized as virtual and capability focused rather than physical and product focused within the business ecosystem structure. In this view, value is created through a community of partnerships and alliances focused on innovative ideas for sustainability that often require firms to span multiple stakeholders and industries. Working together, the community creates value and shapes its own future. Thus, the SSM view of the value chain is as a system of value-creating capabilities that provide a unique value mix based on sustainability for the ecosystem members.

Chapter Summary

The focus in this chapter is on the interface between the firm's strategy and its internal resources. We have examined the coevolutionary process of resource assessment in SSM that entails profiling the resources and capabilities of the firm using the open-system value chain as the basic framework, evaluating resources using internal and external data, and determining which resources or capabilities could be core competencies and potential competitive advantages for the firm. Given that the open-system value chain is the conceptual base for the SSM resource assessment process, data on economic, natural, human, and social capital are gathered via VCA, LCA, stakeholder analysis, and footprint analysis. These data are combined with the competitors' footprint data gathered during the environmental analysis process (Chapter 3) to determine which of the resources or capabilities profiled are valuable, rare, and not easily imitated by competitors.

In the SSM resource assessment process traditional VCA has expanded to an open system that includes eco- and socio-efficiency with their value-creating capabilities for multiple stakeholders. The open-system value chain also enables the examination of the role of organizational eco- and socio-effectiveness in making positive contributions to future generations, laying the foundation for strategic managers and their organizations to become agents of social change. Further, these provide the processes and data necessary for formulating effective functional level strategies to develop core competencies that exploit opportunities that add socio- and eco-efficient value added. They help to reduce the environmental impacts, social impacts, and resource intensity of firms' products and services, and by doing so they help organizations create competitive cost and differentiation competitive advantages in the marketplace.

However, we believe that a sustained competitive advantage has become more a matter of the ability to change and coevolve and less a matter of location or market position. As the spiraling coevolution of the concept of capital indicates, future competitive advantage lies in a higher-level organizational purpose such as sustainability and the intangible resources required to achieve it. The resources and dynamic capabilities to think outside traditional industry boundaries, to manage the creative tension of cooperative and competitive relationships with multiple stakeholder networks, and to rewrite industry rules will be the necessary capabilities for organizational survival in the twenty-first century.

Case Vignette 4

Eco-Efficiency at Eastman Chemical Company

It is no secret that the chemical industry is ecologically intense. Chemical firms convert vast amounts of energy and resources into products and wastes all along their value chains, and as the industry painfully learned from early disasters like Love Canal and Bhopal, these products and wastes can be hazardous to both human and ecosystem health if not managed responsibly. Therefore, developing and continuously honing eco-efficiency capabilities is now and will be for the foreseeable future a central strategic requirement for firms in the chemical industry. This is no doubt a primary reason why chemical firms have been pioneers in developing eco-efficiency tools and processes like pollution prevention and total quality environmental management.

Eastman Chemical Company understands the critical importance of effective eco-efficiency strategies very well. That is why it has put so much effort into improving its energy efficiency, resource efficiency, product safety, waste management systems, and so forth. As CEO Jim Rogers pointed out (see Case Vignette 1), such efforts are both economical for the firm and the right thing to do for the environment and society. For example, even with burgeoning sales from 2001 to 2010, Eastman was able to reduce its hazardous waste generation 37 percent. Also, from 2005 to 2010 Eastman reduced volatile organic compound emissions 32 percent, sulfur dioxide emissions 10 percent, nitrous oxide emissions 20 percent, and Toxic Release Inventory (TRI) emissions 22 percent.

Continuously improving energy efficiency is a primary eco-efficiency focus for Eastman. The firm gets 50 percent of its energy from natural gas and 50 percent from coal (a local, affordable resource). The firm is aware that traditional power generation from coal is very inefficient, so it has embarked on a concerted effort to improve the efficiency of the coal it uses. Eastman has built highly efficient cogeneration systems at its largest manufacturing facilities. This is ideal for Eastman because cogeneration produces electrical power and steam, both of which are required to produce Eastman's chemical products. Essentially, cogeneration systems capture energy normally lost when converting coal to electrical power and use it to generate steam. This allows 70 percent of the coal's energy to be converted to usable energy (up from 50 percent for traditional power generation). Further, cogeneration has led to a significant reduction in greenhouse gas emissions at Eastman. Cogeneration at just one of its manufacturing plants keeps the equivalent of about 131,000 cars worth of greenhouse gases out of the atmosphere each year.

Eastman's focus on energy efficiency has led it to a position as energy leader in the chemical industry. It has won numerous energy efficiency awards over the years, including recognition for superior energy efficiency by the American Chemistry Council for 18 consecutive years. Also, as mentioned in Case Vignette 1, Eastman was recognized as an Energy Star® Partner of the Year by the Environmental Protection Agency in 2012 and 2013, becoming the only chemical company to win this recognition twice. Energy Star® is a 20-year-old incentive-based EPA program designed to encourage firms to help reduce greenhouse gas emissions by improving their energy efficiency. Among other things, Eastman was recognized for developing integrative manufacturing systems that use excess heat from one chemical process to fuel the next, reducing greenhouse gas emissions by 357 million pounds, establishing a steam-leak repair initiative, forming an energy assessment process, budgeting $8 million for energy improvements, and involving employees in its Energy Star® efforts.

At the heart of Eastman's eco-efficiency efforts is the firm's commitment to full value-chain life cycle assessment (LCA), which the firm defines as "holistic evaluations of products' entire existence, from raw material sourcing and manufacturing processes through distribution, usage and disposal." Eastman began its LCA efforts by assessing the cradle-to-gate life cycles of its current products, and to date it has completed these assessments on 60 percent of its current product lines, which account for 80 percent of its revenues. Also, Eastman has a goal of having preliminary life cycle assessment data available on all of its new product launches by 2015.

Eastman is now focusing its LCA efforts downstream from its gates, collaborating with its customers to improve the ecological footprints of both the firm and its customers. For example, one of the most comprehensive LCAs at Eastman was performed when a customer requested LCA data on Eastman's rosin resins, which are made primarily from the gum of living pine trees. These resins contain 90 percent renewable content, and are used in products ranging from paint coatings to chewing gum. The life cycle assessment of Eastman's resin rosins revealed that the dense canopies of live pine trees tapped for their resins were very effective for sequestering carbon dioxide, meaning that the firm's rosin resin production actually contributes to the reduction of greenhouse gases in the atmosphere.

5

SSM Competitive Level Strategies

Chapter 3 examines the external environment and provides frameworks for analyzing opportunities and threats, while Chapter 4 discusses how a firm develops core competencies to achieve competitive advantages through developing and implementing functional level strategies. The focus of this chapter is on the various strategies a firm can adopt to achieve a competitive advantage and profitability in an industry or product/market segment. We will explore how strategic managers can utilize these two coevolving data sets of external and internal information to build various strategies to gain a competitive advantage within target market segments. In addition, we will examine how to choose the appropriate strategies dependent on the firm's competitive position and type of market in which its strategic managers have chosen to compete.

The Nature of Competitive Level Strategies

Positioning the firm against its competitors in its chosen market in order to achieve a competitive advantage is the essence of **competitive** or **business level strategies**. These strategies explain how the firm will use its core competencies to build strategies that gain a competitive advantage over rivals. The building blocks of competitive strategy come from the choices made in defining the business (as we discussed in Chapter 1); these are strategic choices about **customer needs** (what is being satisfied), **customer groups** (who is being satisfied), and **core competencies** (how customer needs within specific customer groups are being satisfied) (Abell 1980). Strategic managers formulate strategies that **differentiate** their products and services to meet unique customer needs. The determination of customer needs provides the data for **market segmentation** according to customer groups. Then specific strategies are formulated, based on the core competencies determined via the resource assessment process (Chapter 4), to meet customer needs within

Figure 5.1   **Foundations of Competitive Strategy**

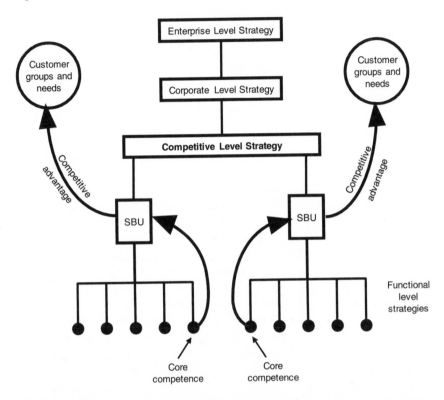

specific market segments. These decisions determine how strategic managers will organize and combine core competencies to gain competitive advantage via a firm's competitive strategy. This is the foundation of competitive strategy, as Figure 5.1 demonstrates.

When Gap was founded in 1969, its targeted customers were younger generations (hence its chosen name, which refers to the generation gap of the time). Gap originally sold signature blue jeans and white cotton T-shirts, but later expanded to include clothing for men, women, and children. Gap, one of the world's best-known brands, has very successfully segmented its markets according to customer needs. The Gap brand that includes Gap, GapKids, babyGap, GapMaternity, and GapBody is clearly designed to appeal to a broad demographic of customers desiring an American iconic style, while its Banana Republic stores try to convey a more sophisticated image for an upscale customer seeking accessible luxury. The Old Navy chain, on the other hand, is designed to appeal to families and younger customers by emphasizing fashion for value. In addition, the Athleta brand focuses on performance apparel for women, while Piperlime, a unique online boutique, was designed to target online customer needs. Thus, Gap tailors its stores and brands to appeal to unique customer groups by developing multiple formats and designs (their core competence) to meet the customer needs of each market segment (Gap 2012). This is the essence of building a successful competitive level strategy.

As discussed in Chapter 4, the two generic sources of competitive advantage for the firm result from performing the value-creating activities at a cost less than competitors or performing them in such a way that customers perceive the product or service as unique, thus commanding a premium price. Each of Michael Porter's (1985) generic competitive strategies of **cost, differentiation**, and **focus** requires strategic managers to make consistent decisions with respect to product/service, market, and core competence in order to achieve competitive advantages through the firm's value-creating functions. The following section covers Porter's (1985) generic competitive strategies.

Cost-Leadership Strategies

Managers pursuing a **cost-leadership strategy** have the goal to produce goods and services at a cost less than competitors, setting the market's price floor as the low-cost producer (Porter 1985), thus achieving a low-cost competitive advantage. The product choice for a cost-leadership strategy is typically one of low differentiation, a commodity type product that achieves economies of scale by spreading fixed costs over a larger output. The cost-leadership strategy is, therefore, characterized by a standardized product offered to a mass market with low market segmentation. In order to keep unit costs low, the strategy must focus on operational efficiency through deploying resources to build **core competencies in operations and logistics**. Customers targeted by this strategy are price-sensitive, with no brand loyalty.

Core competencies of the cost-leader focus on lowering costs across the firm's value chain activities. Cost drivers are **learning curve effects**, where learning by doing can drive down cost. Individuals and teams engaged repeatedly in an activity learn from their cumulative experience. **Experience curves** capture both learning effects and economies of scale, where economies of scale allow the firm to reduce unit costs by moving down a given learning curve. A firm can gain a competitive cost advantage if it can move further down its learning curve than its competitors. Taken together, leveraging experience based on learning and economies of scale allows the firm to leapfrog to a steeper learning curve, thereby further reducing its unit costs (Rothaermel 2013). These competencies need to be supported by a formalized, mechanistic organizational structure with close supervision of employees and tight cost controls designed to keep unit costs low. The primary risk to this strategy is the erosion of the firm's cost position arising from competitors' ability to imitate operations or to develop new technologies to produce at a lower cost (Porter 1985).

Choosing to implement a cost-leadership strategy requires strategic managers to focus on reducing the overall costs of the product or service, while maintaining the quality that will meet customer needs. Walmart implements an effective cost-leadership strategy in the discount retailing market. From early on, Walmart has pursued low product differentiation, targeting the average customer by providing the fewest products desired by the greatest number of customers, thereby achieving economies of scale (Hill and Jones 2009). Walmart's cost-leadership strategy is supported by its ecologically based core competencies in its functional levels of logistics (i.e., sustainable packaging), operations (i.e., eco-efficiency techniques), and information technologies (i.e., environmental performance reporting). Unit costs are kept low through the platform that Walmart provides to its ecosystem members (as discussed in Chapter 3). Thus, by making consistent strategic decisions in terms of low product differentiation that target a mass market and by building ecologically based functional level core competencies, Walmart has been able to implement a cost-leadership strategy that has achieved higher than average returns due at least in part to its improved environmental performance.

Differentiation Strategies

The goal of the generic **differentiation strategy** is to perform the value-creating functions in such a way as to create a product or service that customers perceive as unique, thus commanding a premium price in the market. Customers pay the above-average price because they believe the product's unique qualities are worth the difference; therefore, the price is based on what the customer is willing to pay (Porter 1985). The strategic choices concerning product/service, market, and core competencies determine the effectiveness of a differentiation strategy, where the product/service differentiation is high with high market segmentation according to uniqueness.

The core competencies of product development, research and development, sales, and marketing, when exploited through a strategy of new product/service introductions targeted toward unique customer needs, create competitive advantages for the firm. The organic, flexible organization structure supports the strategy by encouraging cross-functional, interdisciplinary interactions fostering dialogue and learning. An organizational culture that encourages innovation and provides the amenities to attract talented people is critical in implementing a differentiation strategy. Quality, innovative features, and/or customer responsiveness may differentiate products and services. Firms should attempt to differentiate their offerings across as many of these dimensions as possible (Hill and Jones 2009).

The bases for differentiation are endless. Luxury automobiles and fine jewelry differentiate themselves by appealing to customers' psychological desire for prestige and luxury. Other customers perceive that exceptional service is a source of product differentiation worth higher prices. Also, in today's high-tech market, innovation is a critical source of differentiation. In fact, the more dimensions on which a firm can differentiate its products, the greater its competitive advantages. For example, Apple differentiates its products on innovative design, cutting-edge features, high-quality operation, and exceptional customer service in its stores. This strategy is supported by an organizational culture that fosters innovation, dialogue, and creative thinking. Thus, Apple differentiates itself across multiple dimensions, making it harder for competitors to imitate what Apple does (Hill and Jones 2009). Sustainability is another differentiation dimension that can provide competitive advantages that are difficult for competitors to duplicate. We will discuss this basis for differentiation later in the chapter.

Integrating Cost-Leadership and Differentiation Strategies

Successful implementation of a generic strategy requires that strategic managers ensure that their choices of product, market, and core competence are consistent with at least one of the firm's competitive strategies. If these choices are not strategically consistent, then firms will likely become **stuck in the middle** because they have made strategic choices that cannot exploit their core competencies in ways that achieve or sustain a competitive advantage (Porter 1985). There are many paths to getting stuck in the middle; consider Kmart's position in discount retailing, where it is stuck between Walmart, the cost-leader, and Target, the differentiator, resulting in Kmart's below-average returns and reorganizational bankruptcy.

However, competitive conditions may demand that firms develop competencies that both lower costs and add to uniqueness. This may be especially true in global markets where the firm has to compete with firms in countries with lower wage rates, but at the same time must add special features to appeal to local preferences and conditions. Thus, in some competitive situations, strategic managers are required to integrate both strategic positions, **differentiation** and **low cost**, which is a complex strategy to implement due to the conflicting requirements of each strategic position (Rothaermel 2013).

Traditionally, the view has been that differentiation can be achieved only by high costs because firms had to customize products for specific markets, resulting in shorter production runs and higher manufacturing costs. The differentiator also typically had higher marketing costs due to servicing many market segments while the cost-leader produced standardized products for mass markets. However, the development of new flexible-manufacturing technologies has made it easier for strategic managers to obtain the advantages of both strategies. Flexible-manufacturing technologies allow firms to pursue a differentiation strategy at lower costs because they significantly reduce the costs of retooling the production line and making small production runs. Because strategic managers can charge a higher price for their products compared to the cost leader, and because they have lower unit costs than the pure differentiator, they have the potential to achieve a higher level of profit than firms pursuing just one of the generic strategies (Hill and Jones 2009).

The integration of cost and differentiation, however, is a complex strategy to execute due to the conflicting requirements of each strategy. The ability to reconcile the trade-offs between cost and differentiation is difficult because they are distinct strategic positions that require that strategic managers effectively manage value chain activities that are fundamentally different. Cost-leaders structure value chains around operational efficiency with a research and development focus around process technologies to improve efficiency, where a differentiator spends its research and development dollars on product technologies that add uniqueness (Rothaermel 2013).

IKEA is one firm that has been able to effectively managing two value chains in order to successfully implement a unique strategy that reconciles the tension between differentiation and cost leadership. The complexity of the strategy entails designing beautiful furniture that is inexpensive and functional. IKEA differentiates its products via innovation in design, engineering, and store format that offers customers furniture that is stylish, functional, and designed for easy assembly. IKEA reduces its costs by displaying its furniture in a warehouse setting, and by having customers serve themselves and transport their new furniture to their homes in flat packs for assembly. Thus, IKEA is simultaneously leveraging innovation to increase the perceived value of its furniture, while lowering its costs through operational efficiency (Rothaermel 2013).

Focus Strategies

The third generic strategy identified by Michael Porter (1985) is the **focus strategy**, which is directed toward a **market niche** (a small group of customers). Unlike the other two generic strategies, the focus strategy is not a source of competitive advantage in and of itself. Rather its competitive advantage comes from the firm's ability to specialize while serving a specific market segment's needs. Thus, market segmentation is low and product differentiation may range from high (uniqueness) to low (price). The market segment can be defined by geographic uniqueness, by specialized requirements in using the product, or by special product attributes that appeal only to niche members. Companies often choose focus strategies in order to better serve the needs of a narrower market segment than their competitors (Hill and Jones 2009).

Thus, focus strategies can provide competitive advantages based on either cost-leadership or product differentiation. A focused cost-leadership strategy is one that serves a small market niche of customers by operating at a lower unit cost, thus providing a lower price than competitors. For example, Southwest Airlines entered the airline industry with a focused cost-leadership strategy of being the low-cost carrier in the southwestern region of the United States by providing a no-frills airline with exceptional operational efficiencies. A focused differentiation strategy, on the other hand, serves a small market niche with products that are designed to appeal to the unique preferences and needs of the well-defined group of buyers. For example, manufacturers such as Ferrari, Aston Martin, and Lamborghini use a focused-differentiation strategy to compete in the small supercar market segment of automobiles costing US$150,000–600,000. Companies that use such focused-differentiation strategies often enjoy high customer loyalty that discourages other firms from competing with them directly. The primary risks of focus strategies arise from a focus that becomes too narrow to satisfy customer needs, the erosion of cost advantages, new competition, competitors' ability to imitate the offering, and the disappearance of the niche due to technological changes, changing customer preferences, and so forth (Dess, Lumpkin, and Eisner 2008).

Focusing a company's entire competitive effort on a narrow market segment is very adequate for small and medium-sized companies that lack the resources to serve a large market. This strategy provides opportunities for strategic managers to find a gap in the market (a niche) and to develop innovative products or services for customers within that niche. A focused company can take many avenues to create competitive advantages, which explains why there are many more small firms than large ones (Hill and Jones 2009).

Competitive Dynamics and Strategic Positioning

Strategic positions change over time as the external environment changes. As discussed in Chapter 3, a competitor analysis is a prerequisite in the formulation of the firm's competitive strategy because only by truly understanding how competitors think can competitive moves and countermoves be anticipated. Thus, **competitive dynamics** refers to the moves and countermoves of the competitors within an industry (Hitt, Ireland, and Hoskisson 2009). **Preemp-**

tive strategic moves create **first-mover** advantages that achieve competitive advantages for firms. By investing in product development, innovation, and research and development, firms can preempt their competitors by being first to market, securing a superior competitive position along with customer loyalty. Of course, the preemptive firm assumes the risks of uncertain market demands since it is testing the market, and even if it is successful, the advantageous market position may only be short-lived as competitors follow. A **second mover** is a firm that responds to a competitor's preemptive first move, learning from its mistakes and attempting to imitate its innovative offering in a more efficient manner. A **late mover** usually achieves much less success than first and second movers, earning only average returns (Hitt, Ireland, and Hoskisson 2009).

Since strategic managers must adjust the timing and content of the markets in which they compete, strategic positioning involves complex strategic decisions. The organizational ability to create new market space in a preemptive move or to anticipate and effectively respond to competitive countermoves requires both generative learning capabilities and environmental analysis capabilities. Together these dynamic capabilities can create the culture and structure that fosters the dialogue, innovation, and learning that enable strategic managers to make the decisions concerning how to strategically position their firms in order to achieve competitive advantages. The key is for strategic managers to understand and reflect upon the coevolving relationships between their firm, its external environment, and its value chain members, leveraging the learning from its stakeholder engagement processes for competitive advantage through astute competitive market timing and positioning.

Consider the strategic timing of General Electric's (GE) preemptive strategy of **reverse innovation** (discussed later in the chapter) with the purpose of expanding the firm's markets in China and India to include lower price-point products for the lower income markets. According to GE CEO Jeffrey Immelt, being first to these markets will preempt local companies from India and China from creating products for their local markets and then using them to "disrupt" GE's market share in its developed markets (Immelt, Govindarajan, and Trimble 2009, 56). Product innovation is linked across undeveloped, developing, and developed markets, providing the potential for the innovations in undeveloped and developing markets of the world to drive attacker strategies against established firms like GE in developed markets. In fact, "entrepreneurs in emerging markets start 25 percent more companies than their U.S. counterparts do, and their firms have a higher survival rate" (Habiby and Cole 2010, 77). Given this, Immelt firmly believes that GE's future will be in these undeveloped and developing markets. The firm's strategic intent is to cocreate products and services with multiple stakeholder groups that meet the unique customer needs of the undeveloped and developing markets, thus preempting local competitors from their ability to grow into emerging giants with the intent of entering GE's established developed markets (Immelt, Govindarajan, and Trimble 2009).

SSM Competitive Level Strategies

A coevolutionary view of market analysis within the business ecosystem structure, as Chapter 3 discusses, is required in formulating SSM strategies. SSM competitive strategies expand the scope of Porter's (1985) generic competitive strategies to ones that create **shared value** for both the firm and the greater society and ecosystem (Porter and Kramer 2011). As discussed in the previous chapter, shared value is created through the dynamic capabilities that make triple-bottom-line performance possible. SSM strategies are what organizations that "stand for sustainability" do (Stead and Stead 2000, 324). It is through these strategies that the philosophies and ethics of SSM become tangible, because SSM strategies are designed as vehicles for operationally integrating the ecosystem and the greater society into strategic decision-making processes. SSM strategies vary in content depending on their scope, markets, customer needs, and purpose. SSM strategies exist in a hierarchy (see Figure 5.2) similar to the hierarchy of strategies discussed in Chapter 1. SSM strategies are typically characterized as multisector strategies requiring broad collaboration with stakeholders that create shared value within the business ecosystem at each level in the hierarchy. Thus, SSM strategies provide valuable avenues for bringing to life the ecological, social, and economic dimensions of an organization's strategic vision of a sustainable world.

The coevolutionary nature of SSM strategies is reflected in the progression of the strategies over time up the hierarchy of strategies. There has already been a coevolution from eco-efficiency-based competitive level strategies such as pollution prevention that provide cost reductions and the preservation of natural and economic capital, to the broader-based socio-efficiency strategies that facilitate the creation of social and human capital, including investments in community, human resources, and partnerships. Both eco- and socio-efficiency are sources of potential competitive advantages based on sustainability-based core competencies that generally create relatively short-term sustainability and economic value added.

Today, however, many organizations are beginning to implement higher-level, eco- and socio-effectiveness corporate strategies (discussed in depth in the next chapter). These are designed to enable organizations to become social and ecological change agents that make positive contributions to a sustainable world that will pay off economically for them in the long term (Stead and

Figure 5.2   **Hierarchy of SSM Strategies**

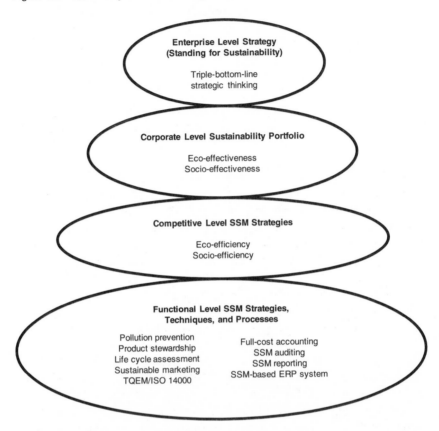

Stead 2009). Figure 5.3 reflects the coevolutionary, spiraling progression of SSM strategies over time. In the section below we will expand our current discussion of competitive level strategies to include how SSM strategies based on eco- and socio-efficient capabilities can provide the generic competitive advantages of cost and differentiation (Porter 1985).

Generic Competitive Level SSM Strategies

Market opportunities for environmentally and socially sensitive products and services can directly link the organization's economic sustainability with its environmental and social sustainability, affording competitive advantages associated with cost reduction and market differentiation (Porter 1985). Since the metrics are much more difficult for measuring social performance than for

Figure 5.3   **Coevolution of SSM Strategies**

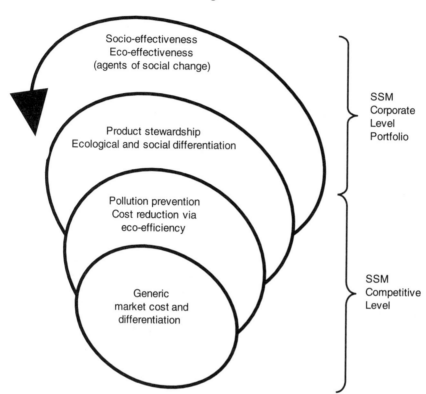

measuring ecological performance, the social dimension of SSM competitive strategies has been slower to coevolve than the ecological dimension.

Eco-efficiency–Based Pollution Prevention Strategies

Eco-efficiency, discussed in the previous chapter, is rapidly transforming from a unique competitive advantage enjoyed by a few cutting-edge organizations into a basic business requirement necessary for the survival of virtually all industrial firms. Due to the dynamics of coevolutionary competitive adaptation, the emergence of eco-efficiency as a basic business requirement means that those organizations that do not expand their value-creating processes to include natural capital may eventually become unable to successfully adapt to the sustainability-infused business environment.

SSM strategies that are designed to provide firms with cost advantages and risk reduction through improved eco-efficient capabilities are generally referred to as **pollution prevention** strategies (Christmann 2000; Hart 1995, 1997; Senge et al. 2008; Stead and Stead 1995). Recall from Chapter 4 that eco-efficiency involves developing cost-competitive advantages by eliminating or reducing resource depletion, materials use, energy consumption, emissions, and effluents. These strategies were the first win–win strategies to be based on eco-efficient capabilities. In a true biophysical sense, eco-efficiency slows the entropic flow through the economy. As with Porter's (1985) cost-leadership strategy, core competencies in pollution prevention strategies are in operational eco-efficiencies that include redesigning pollution and waste control systems, redesigning production processes to be more environmentally sensitive, using recycled materials from other production processes and/or outside sources, and renewing renewable energy sources. Further, eco-efficient pollution prevention strategies provide firms with opportunities to establish social legitimacy in the greater community, which means that these strategies can provide firms with socio-efficient as well as eco-efficient value added.

3M is generally given credit for being the first mover and leader in eco-efficiency and pollution prevention. 3M introduced its now famous Pollution Prevention Pays (3P) program in 1975, demonstrating that preventing pollution before it occurs can create greater economic and ecological value added. In 1975 this was the innovative, first-mover thinking that secured 3M a competitive cost position. To date, 3M has completed more than 9,300 3P projects designed to slow the entropic flow of energy and resources through the firm. These projects have included such things as product reformulation, process modification, equipment redesign, and recycling and reuse of waste materials. Collectively, they have resulted in the elimination of more than 3.5 billion pounds of pollution at a savings for 3M of nearly US$1.5 billion. The firm makes it clear that the fourth P, people, is critical to the success of the 3P program because it relies completely on voluntary employee participation (3M 2012).

Operations and logistics are critical functions in creating the cost advantages afforded by eco-efficiency. In the biophysical sense, it is via their operations and logistics systems that organizations transform low-entropy natural resources into high-entropy goods and services. Thus, these systems offer organizations the best opportunities to slow down their entropic flow. The greatest financial, physical, and human capital expenditures that organizations generally must make in eco-efficiency are in new and improved operations and logistics systems. FedEx, for example, has improved the eco-efficiency of its logistics system by investing in Boeing 777s, which have increased the firm's carrying capacity by 20 percent and cut its daily fuel use by 36 percent. FedEx has also developed a set of 30 software programs that optimize aircraft schedules, and it is replacing 25 percent of its fleet of vans with hybrids that are 42 percent more fuel efficient than conventional trucks. A by-product of FedEx's sustainability investments is the organizational learning it acquired in the process; it has even turned its energy saving expertise into a stand-alone consulting business (Nidumolu, Prahalad, and Rangaswami 2009).

Total Quality Environmental Management and ISO 14000

Total quality environmental management (TQEM) is a tool that uses the firm's continuous improvement processes to enhance its eco-efficiency. TQEM was pioneered in the late 1980s by firms in the Global Environmental Management Initiative (GEMI), and it has become a standard process for improving eco-efficiency in most manufacturing organizations. TQEM incorporates the conservation and preservation of natural capital into the total quality management formula, improving firms' capabilities to prevent waste and pollution while reducing costs. A shortcoming of TQEM efforts is that their scope has been limited to improving the eco-efficiency of internal throughput processes. To overcome this limitation, it has been recommended that TQEM be expanded to TQSM, total quality sustainability management, making it a useful tool for building both ecological and social responsibility into products/services.

TQEM alliancing is one way this can be done (O'Dea and Pratt 2006). Essentially, TQEM alliancing involves using TQEM as a framework for forming industrial ecologies with other firms. These reduce waste and pollution while creating social capital within a business ecosystem. Alliances such as these create advantages that one firm cannot achieve alone, thus demonstrating the creative potential of investing in the development of social capital to build ecosystems that reduce the entropic flow. The importance of alliance management capabilities is discussed further in Chapter 6.

The International Standards Organization (ISO) 14000 family of standards has also become widely used by organizations wishing to improve their environmental management. The ISO 14000 requirements are an integral part of the European Management and Audit Scheme (EMAS) structure. As with the ISO 9000 quality standards, the ISO 14000 standards pertain to the processes of how products are produced rather than what the products are. TQEM and ISO 14000 provide firms with frameworks that help them account for the ecological impacts of their products and processes all along the open-system value chain.

Sustainability-Based Supplier Relationships

Sustainability-based supplier relationships create social capital and are critical in minimizing the ecological, social, and economic costs of the firm's resource acquisition. A recent study found that vendors consume as much as 80 percent of the energy, water, and other resources used in a supply chain, which makes it imperative that sustainability become a priority in supplier relationships. Efficient supply chains are being developed with shorter distances and more efficient, less polluting modes of transportation. In fact, many firms are mandating more sustainable practices from their suppliers. Staples has a goal that all of its paper products come from sustainable forests; Unilever has declared that it will buy tea and palm oil only from sustainable sources by 2015; and Walmart has given a directive to its Chinese suppliers to reduce waste and emissions, cut packaging costs by 5 percent, and increase product energy efficiency by 25 percent by 2012 (Nidumolu, Prahalad, and Rangaswami 2009). Other firms require suppliers to secure ISO 14001 certification and to adopt pollution prevention policies. Not only does Toyota require ISO 14001 certification for its suppliers, it also requires them to eliminate toxic substances from their manufacturing processes. Other firms such as Royal Dutch Shell regularly audit the child labor practices of their suppliers.

Regardless of the position of a firm in its value chain, there is pressure on it to find eco-efficiency solutions that slow the entropic flow of energy and resources. For example, the Sustainable Packaging Coalition (SPC) is an industry working group dedicated to a more robust environmental vision for packaging. SPC is a project of GreenBlue, a nongovernmental organization (NGO) that provides businesses with the science and resources to make more sustainable decisions. SPC promotes supply-chain collaboration that builds packaging systems that encourage the creation of economic value through a sustainable flow of materials. SPC has created a curriculum of the essentials of sustainable packaging and a software package to calculate the product's environmental life cycle impacts to assist its members in moving toward more sustainable solutions in their packaging. Starbucks, an SPC member, shared at an SPC meeting that it has begun a trial process in its Chicago stores where it will recycle cups into napkins for further use in its stores. Starbucks hopes to institute this closed-loop resource recycling process throughout its stores in the United States by working with individual communities and their varying recycling infrastructures (SPC 2012).

In today's business environment of unpredictable energy and materials costs, worldwide pressures to reduce greenhouse gas emissions, and the incessant pressures from competitors and customers to improve efficiency, organizations are showing a willingness to make significant investments in eco-efficiency. Production facilities in most industries are being built or redesigned to use minimal energy and to generate minimal emissions and wastes. For example, many large manufacturers (such as Eastman Chemical

Company—see Case Vignette 4) are using energy cogeneration whereby heat formerly wasted in production processes is now captured and used to produce steam power. This captured energy can be used by the organization that generates it, or it can be passed to industrial ecology partners, business ecosystem partners, utilities, and so forth. Firms expanding their eco-efficiency operations beyond their boundaries in this way are coevolving from a strategic position of eco-efficiency to one of eco-effectiveness.

Consider Subaru's plant in Indiana. Subaru designed this plant's operations around eco-and socio-effectiveness; it produces zero wastes and has had zero layoffs and zero pay cuts, all in a state that has lost 46,000 automobile jobs in the past decade. The firm has saved $5.3 million due to its eco-effective design, and it produces enough energy at its waste-to-fuel operation to sell power back to the grid (Farzad 2011). Stakeholders demand that strategic mangers take full stewardship of their value chain from cradle to cradle, thus eco- and socio-effective operational designs like Subaru's that slow entropic flow and save money are the future of operations management (McDonough and Braungart 2002).

Product Stewardship Strategies:
Ecological and Social Differentiation

Strategies designed to provide a firm with competitive advantages by allowing it to ecologically and socially differentiate its products and services from its competitors in the marketplace are referred to as **product stewardship strategies** (Hart 1995, 1997; Reinhardt 1999; Stead and Stead 1995). Product stewardship strategies focus on improving an organization's ecological and social footprints by offering products/services that are safer, more socially responsible, less materials and energy intense, more recyclable, more biodegradable, more durable, less wasteful, and so forth. Product stewardship strategies require capabilities for gathering and assessing the environmental and social impacts of a firm's products and services across the open-system value chain, thus these strategies are based on core competencies such as innovation, product development, sales, and marketing.

Stuart Hart (1995) described product stewardship as a logical strategic step for firms that have achieved eco-efficiency. Essentially, he said that once firms establish production processes that reduce costs by better managing and protecting the earth's rare, nonsubstitutable, nonduplicable natural resources, they are in a position to differentiate their products/services in the marketplace based on their sustainability features. Thus, he said that product stewardship strategies provide firms with both cost-leadership and differentiation competitive advantages that can be sustained over a long period of time.

As discussed in Chapter 4, product stewardship strategies can lead to improvements in the firm's reputation, perceived legitimacy, and brand equity, all of which are intangible resources that are difficult for competitors to imitate. Also, product stewardship efforts are more effective if all of the firm's stakeholders are involved in the firm's product/service development processes from the beginning. This allows the firm to build a wide variety of stakeholder perspectives into its products/services.

According to Xerox CEO Ursula Burns, product stewardship is at the heart of her firm's innovations. She said, "We approach sustainability from a life cycle perspective because we recognize that the biggest opportunity for us to make an impact is by addressing all aspects of our actions, products, and services" (Business Roundtable 2011, 115). Product stewardship goals have motivated Xerox to form an alliance with the Nature Conservancy to promote sustainable forestry and to protect biodiversity. Xerox has also developed a solid ink technology that reduces waste by 90 percent, uses 9 percent less energy, reduces greenhouse emissions 10 percent, uses no water, and is designed to print pages that are easier to recycle. The firm also created the industry's first Sustainability Calculator to help customers evaluate their environmental footprint (Business Roundtable 2011). Thus, Xerox uses its product stewardship lens to examine both internal processes and external market dynamics.

The effectiveness of product stewardship strategies can potentially be enhanced by participation in eco-labeling and social labeling programs. An **eco-** or **social label** designates that the firm has exercised ecological or social stewardship over its products and services across its value chain. Participating in such programs allows firms to more easily inform consumers about the sustainability features of their products and services, and it provides outside verification that products and services meet certain sustainability standards. Research indicates that approximately 28 percent of consumers look to certification labels to determine the credibility of product claims (Ottman 2011). An eco-label designates to consumers that the firm has had ecological stewardship over its value chain in the production of its products. The Forest Stewardship Council's FSC certification program, the U.S. Department of Agriculture's organic food label, and the Green Building Initiative's Leadership in Energy and Environmental Design (LEED) certification program are important eco-labeling initiatives today. The Ethical Trade Initiative, Fairtrade International (FLO), and the Clean Clothes Campaign are important social labeling initiatives that provide consumers with assurance about the social and ethical impacts across the firm's value chain concerning such issues as working conditions, fair wages, human rights, and child labor (Ottman 2011). Eco- and social labels reflect the consumer pull for business to be fully transparent in terms of its triple-bottom-line performance and the consumers' willingness to pay a premium price for full product stewardship of the products and services they buy.

As discussed in Chapter 3, Starbucks leads a business ecosystem based on a shared vision of sustainability and has successfully used both eco-labels and social labels to effectively leverage its brand by social and ecological differentiation. By actively listening to, interacting with, and acting on the expectations of its customers who are socially and environmentally conscious, Starbucks has effectively incorporated eco- and socio-efficiency into their operations and tells its story of ecological and social responsibility right on its packages and cups. The key to its success is its ability to leverage the learning attained from the 50 million customers it sees in its stores every week who give their ideas about how Starbucks can be more ecologically and socially sensitive. By listening to its customers, Starbucks, for example, developed its own set of stringent guidelines (Coffee and Farmer Equity Practices, CAFÉ) to ensure that coffee purchases are ethically sourced, with a goal of having 100 percent of its coffee purchases responsibly grown and ethically traded by 2015 (Ottman 2011). By connecting coffee producers and consumers, Starbucks works directly to promote fairer trading conditions, fair wages, and sustainability so workers in undeveloped and developing markets can invest in a better future for themselves and their communities. Starbucks customers pay a premium price for a cup of fair-trade coffee, demonstrating the relationship between socio-efficiency, social labeling, and competitive advantage.

By offering sustainable products in a highly segmented market aimed at environmentally and socially conscious consumers, and by building its strategy on the core competencies of eco- and socio-efficiency, Starbucks has been able to effectively differentiate itself, thus achieving a competitive advantage in the gourmet coffee market. In sum, by making consistent strategic choices concerning product, market, and core competencies, Starbucks has successfully created the dynamic product stewardship capabilities to implement an effective strategy of social and ecological differentiation.

Sustainability and Competitive Dynamics

As previously discussed, the key to strategic positioning is to competitively position products and services into carefully segmented markets, anticipating competitive attacks and counterattacks. One key to successful ecological and social differentiation is astute market timing. As previously discussed, eco-efficient strategies are often the preemptive entry point, the first move firms make into sustainability. Because the business case for not producing wastes and for reducing resource use is so strong, these strategies have become a basic business requirement in most industries. Therefore, they no longer afford firms a competitive advantage. Firms that do not account for natural capital in their operational strategies are lagging behind most of their competitors and are late in reaping the benefits afforded by eco-efficiency.

The competitive responses to the increased demand for triple-bottom-line performance by stakeholders vary depending on the perception of strategic managers in terms of the opportunities afforded by sustainability. A global survey of 3,000 business executives conducted by BCG and the *MIT Sloan Management Review* (2011), found two categories of strategic moves demonstrated by the firms surveyed. The **casual adopters** were those firms that were late into the sustainability market and invested only in short-run, eco-efficient strategies (which do not afford much of a competitive advantage today, as discussed above). The **embracers**, on the other hand, were those strategic managers who preemptively put sustainability at the top of their strategic agendas because they believed that sustainability was important to their firm's competitiveness.

These different perceptions of sustainability among business executives result in spiraling competitive moves and countermoves. Embracers typically preempt their competitors with socially or environmentally positioned products or services to achieve advantageous market positions. "First movers who value innovate alternatives to fossil fuels, distributed electricity generation, cellulosic plastic, and *in vitro* meat substitutes have the possibility to create new, profitable, and uncontested market space for years to come" (Lazlo and Zhexembayeva 2011, 85). However, these first-mover strategies may provide only short-run advantages if competitors follow suit (Reinhardt 2008). The key, of course, is to have another competitive countermove in place when, for example, differentiation is lost due to imitation by competitors.

Executives from Clorox believe that embracing sustainability can enhance their firm's brand position by allowing them to penetrate the sustainability-based segments within their markets. Clorox has repositioned its Brita water pitchers and filter lines, has introduced a new natural cleaning product line called Green Works, and has acquired and expanded the Burt's Bees line of natural personal care products. Their market research indicates that 15 percent of customers take sustainability and health into account when purchasing, and 25–30 percent take environmental benefits into consideration. By carefully segmenting their market and offering a product such as Green Works, Clorox is able to charge a premium price of 15–20 percent above conventional cleaners. A multisector marketing agreement with the Sierra Club for their endorsement created a more differentiated brand for Clorox, and a partnership with Walmart and Safeway made sure that consumers could easily find the new product entry. Clorox achieved first-mover advantages, securing a 40 percent share of this $200 million market by the end of 2008, and the Sierra Club received $500,000 as its share of revenue (*MIT Sloan Management Review* and BCG 2011). Thus, Clorox developed a small business ecosystem around its new sustainable product introduction, creating shared value for the whole system.

Strategies Dependent on Relative Competitive Position and Market Type

Although markets are often characterized by their geographical location (i.e., the undeveloped markets of Africa or the developing market of India), they are more accurately portrayed in terms of their specific demographics and varying socioeconomic factors. As Chapter 3 discusses, the United States, a highly developed market, also consists of the undeveloped market segments of urban slums, the rural poor, and regions like Southern Appalachia. These coevolving undeveloped, developing, and developed markets of the world offer major opportunities and challenges for businesses that have an SSM portfolio of strategies tailored for each of these market segments. The choice of the content of the SSM competitive strategy depends on the commitment to sustainability at the top management level, the specific characteristics of markets that reflect unique consumer needs, and the firm's position within its business ecosystem. Figure 5.4 reflects a portfolio of strategic choices depending on the context of the situation.

Strategies Dependent on the Firm's Relative Competitive Position

A firm's competitive position within its target market will shape its competitive strategy regardless of whether or not it is operating in a structured business ecosystem. The decisions of strategic managers of **dominant market share** firms involve the balance between how to best harvest what has been achieved and how to maintain or improve upon the present competitive position. One strategic option is to keep the offensive in order to continue to outperform competitors by exercising the initiative, preempting competitors with new product/service introductions and increased marketing efforts. Another option is to hold and maintain the present competitive position by erecting barriers to entry such as new patents, the introduction of more brands, and so forth. Strategic managers must be careful not to get complacent when implementing a hold-and-maintain strategy. Keeping prices competitive, maintaining quality, and preserving a high level of customer service are critical elements for success. Strategic managers may also implement a confrontational strategy to work in conjunction with either a strategy of keep the offensive or a strategy

Figure 5.4   **Corporate Portfolio of SSM Competitive Strategies**

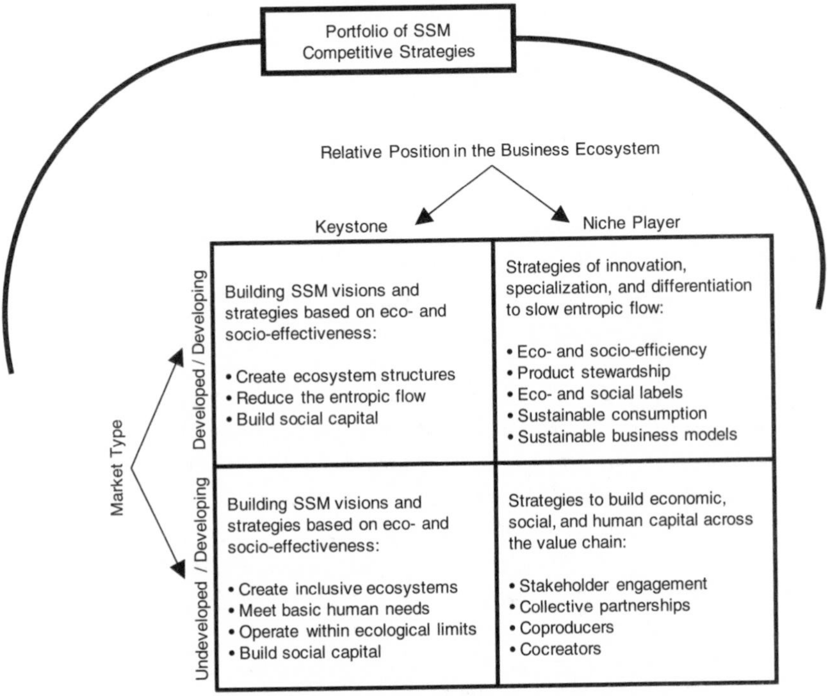

of hold and maintain. These are concerted strategic efforts designed to make it hard for smaller, aggressive-minded firms to grow and prosper.

For a **small share** firm, the general strategic prescription is to use a focused differentiation strategy based on disruptive change and generative learning in carefully segmented markets. The available strategic options include avoiding head-on competition with the dominant share leader by identifying and competing in market segment gaps or by creating new market space altogether. The strategic intent is on specialization and profits rather than diversification, sales growth, and increased market share. Strategic managers should dare to be different by focusing on building core competencies in research and development, technical capabilities, and new product/service development, thus managing for innovation as the route to growth.

Ecosystem Leadership Strategies

Keystone firms, the ecosystem leaders, will be responsible for shaping the vision and structuring the business ecosystem based on eco- and socio-effectiveness by providing platforms that solve fundamental problems, thus providing sustainable solutions for its niche ecosystem members. The ecosystem leader's leverage over niche players is determined by the nature of the relationships represented by the **degree of coupling** with the niche players (Iansiti and Levien 2004a, 2004b). The ecosystem leader is responsible for shaping a sustainability-based vision and a supportive business ecosystem structure regardless of whether the ecosystem is operating in developed, developing, or undeveloped markets.

Business ecosystem analysis focuses on the critical interactions between the leader's capabilities and those of its network of business ecosystem partners. The SSM strategies formulated and implemented by ecosystem members will depend heavily upon their relative ecosystem position. Three ecosystem positions are identified in the literature: the ecosystem leader, the niche player, and the dominator (Iansiti and Levien 2004b). Of these, only the ecosystem leader position and niche player position have significant value for creating the type of inclusive, collaborative, trusting relationships required to build effective sustainability-based business ecosystems. On the contrary, the dominator position would likely impede building such relationships because ecosystem dominators typically seek maximum short-run benefits for themselves instead of long-term shared value for all ecosystem members. For example, Enron was a dominator that created value only for the top managers of the firm and destroyed value for all of its other stakeholders. Thus, dominators negatively affect the overall health and eventual survival of business ecosystems because they extract more value than they contribute (Iansiti and Levien 2004b). Thus, it is critical that business ecosystems guard against including firms that exhibit dominator behaviors due to their lack of value creation and destructive behavioral patterns. For the remainder of this discussion we will focus on healthy business ecosystems in which ecosystem leaders and niche players work together to cocreate their common futures (Iansiti and Levien 2004b; Moore 2006).

Given the complexity and coevolutionary nature of innovating across a multitude of complementary contributors within a business ecosystem, effective ecosystem leadership is essential. As discussed above, ecosystem leaders are responsible for shaping the vision, core values, boundaries, platforms, and relationships of the business ecosystem, and they are responsible for the ecosystem's overall health. Healthy business ecosystems have leader firms that can translate their shared visions into platforms that provide ecosystem members with the operating leverage that comes with the ecosystem's collective actions and community-based learning structures (Iansiti and Levien 2004b).

Ecosystem leaders essentially serve as a hub in a network of ecosystem member interactions. In this role, leader firms serve to enhance the robustness, the efficiency, and the stability of the ecosystem, opening space for value-sharing opportunities among the niche players and providing sustained competitive advantages for their own firms. As previously discussed, ecosystem leaders also establish the nature and coupling strength of the relationships in the ecosystem. Coupling strength determines the switching costs of moving between ecosystems for the niche players, and it is an important measure of ecosystem stability (Iansiti and Levien 2004b). Thus, it is up to the ecosystem leader to find a healthy balance of coupling strength within the business ecosystem. Starbucks, Apple, Google, Amazon, Microsoft, and Walmart are all examples of keystone firms, ecosystem leaders of healthy business ecosystems.

Ecosystem Niche Player Strategies

Niche players make up the majority of the members in the ecosystem, and they are responsible for formulating specific strategies based on **innovation**, **specialization**, and **differentiation** designed to address customer needs that are unique in their particular markets. For example, niche players operating in developed markets will likely focus their strategies more on reducing the entropic flow of physical throughputs, and niche players operating in undeveloped and developing markets will likely focus their strategies more on serving basic human needs within ecological limits.

Niche players often use focused-differentiation strategies based on innovative, disruptive change aimed at carefully segmented target markets. Thus, sustainable innovation with respect to products, services, business models, and markets is a basic business requirement for ecosystem membership. As Chapter 3 discusses, the entrepreneurial niche players are self-contained modules that coevolve around a keystone firm that provides them with a common platform creating shared sustainable value. This modularity defines the contributions of each ecosystem member and is developed somewhat independently. The entrepreneurial niche strategy is one of specialization through taking explicit advantage of the opportunities provided by the ecosystem while mitigating the challenges posed by such a business environment. By selecting a specialization that is truly unique and investing in unique capabilities, niche players can create competitive advantages. Risks, however, arise when a niche firm's tight coupling with the ecosystem leader results in a lack of mobility between ecosystems and the vulnerability to technological change (Iansiti and Levien 2004b).

Healthy business ecosystems will often support a large number of niche players for a sustained period of time. The huge and always changing software business ecosystem has historically supported numerous niche players that have created a variety of product innovations (Iansiti and Levien 2004b). Intuit is one such niche player. The firm has specialized in integrating technology components provided by Microsoft, the ecosystem leader. For over 25 years, Intuit has coevolved within its ecosystem by developing innovative business and financial management products for small and midsized businesses, consumers, and accounting professionals (i.e., QuickBooks, Quicken, and TurboTax). In 2007, Intuit added sustainability to its vision, creating Intuit Green, in order to formalize the sustainability efforts in its core business operations (Intuit 2011). Intuit's movement over the years to a sustainability-focused differentiation strategy demonstrates the coevolutionary nature of a successful niche strategy, where competitive strategies can create shared value within the ecosystem by taking advantage of the opportunities provided by business ecosystem platforms for innovation, specialization, and sustainability.

SSM Strategies for Developed Markets

Remember that the current global market involves coevolving developed, developing, and undeveloped markets. The developed markets of the world currently house the richest 25 percent of the world's population and control 75 percent of the world's income and purchasing power (Milanovic 2002). These markets are the world's largest producers and consumers of goods and services, and they have controlled the global marketplace for most of its history. The human footprint in the developed and developing markets is very large. Corporations in many of the resource-intensive industries in these markets, such as chemicals and energy, have large ecological footprints and use older technologies with limited ecological performance improvement potential (Hart 2005).

Recall from Chapter 2 that the planet has available 1.9 hectares per person of biologically productive land, yet the average person on Earth already uses 2.3 hectares, and these are not equitably distributed. For example, average Americans live on 9.7 hectares worth of energy and resources, while average Mozambicans live on .47 hectares worth (Worldwatch Institute 2011). Therefore, it is critical for the survival of future generations that strategic managers in developed and developing markets formulate strategies based on innovative business models that provide consumer value while slowing the entropic flow of resources through their organizations.

Climate Change Strategies

Simply stated, climate change is a central ecological issue that will affect the economy, the society, and the planet for years to come (Barrett 2012). New business models are desperately needed that can decouple carbon emissions from economic growth, especially in the developing and developed markets of the world where carbon emissions are the highest. As Chapter 3 discusses, the United States has less than 5 percent of the global population, and yet it uses about a quarter of the world's fossil fuel resources (25 percent of the coal, 26 percent of the oil, and 27 percent of the natural gas) (Worldwatch Institute 2011). It is critical that the high carbon emissions in markets like the United States be brought into balance with a human-friendly carbon cycle.

Climate change and the resultant increase in natural disasters have put carbon emissions much higher on the agendas of organizational stakeholders around the world. They are demanding indicators of firms' carbon emissions, and the result has been a significant increase of carbon disclosure in corporate reporting. The most popular means for a firm to disclose its carbon footprint is through its sustainability report, its SEC (Securities and Exchange Commission) filings in the United States, or the Carbon Disclosure Project, a multisector partnership formed to assist the international community in carbon emissions reduction (Pinkse and Kolk 2009). Executives across a broad range of sectors have started to recognize that climate change is a business reality— whether they believe in the science or not. McKinsey and Company has long believed that a low-carbon global economy is a pending reality, and business organizations must get ready for it, especially those in transport, energy, and other heavy industries that are the heart of today's carbon-intensive economy (Enkvist, Nauclér, and Oppenheim 2008).

Due to the emergence of carbon emission trading, typically in the form of cap-and-trade systems, the strategic relevance of climate change for business has increased in importance. In these systems, firms get limited allowances to emit greenhouse gases and they are allowed to trade these with other market participants. Through this process, carbon can actually be assigned a price. The total value of emission rights in the EU Emissions Trading Scheme is about €40 billion a year. Only a fraction of that value is traded now, but it is a growing fraction. This provides opportunities for firms to capture profit in the carbon-trading market via many roles, including buying or selling for speculative purposes or creating low-carbon projects that would help companies outside the system reduce emissions at low costs and then profitably sell their emission rights in the market. Thus, these systems can help strategic managers to translate their firms' impact on global climate change into financial figures that they can use to account for climate change in business investment decisions (Hoffman 2007).

Since emission trading is market based, it does not stipulate what means firms may use to stay within the regulatory limits. This enhances strategic managers' ability to innovate and incorporate carbon management issues within their firm's overall business strategy. Since carbon is so closely tied to other commodity products, such as coal, oil, and natural gas, carbon emissions impact strategic decisions related to sourcing energy, the engine that drives the firm and the economy. Thus, trading emissions has created a whole new financial market, where carbon has a price, providing opportunities for firms to capture profit in the carbon-trading market (Pinkse and Kolk 2009). McKinsey and Company believes that carbon markets will grow in number and will be attractive in coming years (Enkvist, Nauclér, and Oppenheim 2008).

Climate change strategies have coevolved over time. As global climatic disasters have increased, the carbon market has emerged and the sustainability movement has grown. Typically, the initial climate change strategy implemented by firms is to make efforts to optimize their carbon efficiency through strategies to improve the efficiency of their infrastructure (buildings, factories, data centers), supply chains, and finished goods (automobiles, flat-screen TVs, computers). Often, these strategies involve not only eco-efficiency measures but also a shift to less carbon-intensive sources of power such as wind, solar, or geothermal. Therefore, incremental improvements in carbon efficiency are usually the first step firms make in implementing a climate strategy (Enkvist, Nauclér, and Oppenheim 2008).

However, as the low-hanging fruit of eco-efficiency is picked, new business models are necessary that create radically more effective low-carbon solutions that reward suppliers and end users for consuming less energy. Value chains that disrupt existing industries and create new ones will necessarily spring up. In forestry and bioenergy, for example, a major new value chain seems likely to appear around the large-scale supply of biomass to power plants and other resource-intensive industries. Or a value chain may emerge that is built on cellulosic ethanol, which could significantly change the supply patterns of transportation fuels if its cost comes down as quickly as many predict (Enkvist, Nauclér, and Oppenheim 2008). Slowing the flow of low entropy energy through the value-creating activities of the business ecosystem will slow emissions growth, but will it be enough, soon enough? The reality is that a new generation of strategies that question the underlying assumptions of the current business model must emerge to fundamentally decouple economic growth from carbon emissions growth. This will require building continuous organizational learning and innovation capabilities to learn how climate change issues affect core activities and which strategic adjustments are necessary to manage these impacts (Pinkse and Kolk 2009).

The French specialty chemical company Rhodia, with one-third of its sales in sustainability-leveraged products, has a committed climate change strategy that has led to increased earnings from low-carbon projects and participation in the carbon-trading market. These low-carbon projects reduced the firm's emissions of greenhouse gases by 2 million tons a year, which had significant economic value for the firm (Enkvist, Nauclér, and Oppenheim 2008). Inspired by the French and Brazilian governments' collaborative positions on reducing climate change, Rhodia has also partnered with Brazilian counterparts to target a reduction in greenhouse gases by: (1) combating deforestation, which is the main source of greenhouse gas emissions in Brazil; (2) developing cleaner and more sustainable production processes by using clean technologies and biomass as raw material for industrial chemistry; (3) developing carbon capture and storage technologies and cogeneration technologies; and (4) developing renewable energy sources, with priority given to biomass and wind energy, which are still underexploited in both countries (Rhodia Group 2009). Collaborative industry relationships such as these have allowed Rhodia to implement a climate change strategy that continues to coevolve as new value chains are discovered and organizational learning takes place.

Emerging Business Models for Developed Markets

As previously discussed, consumers in developed markets are becoming increasingly socially conscious, infusing significant green consumer pull into these markets (Ottman, 2011). In fact, specialty chemical companies that are typically located in the middle of value chains, such as Eastman Chemical and Rhodia, say that their consumers are the driving factor in their increasingly sustainability-leveraged portfolio of products. Thus, the primary sustainability challenge in today's developed markets is to provide a stream of innovative products and services that are designed, produced, marketed, delivered, consumed, and disposed of in sustainable ways that significantly reduce the firm's high-entropy corporate and consumer footprints. Eco-efficiency strategies along with product stewardship strategies, discussed above, are effective in reducing costs and providing a means for ecological and social differentiation that enables firms to capitalize on the green consumer pull in many segments of developed markets.

Achieving sustainability will, however require that organizations in developed markets create and implement innovative SSM strategies that deliver long-term consumer value in creative ways that protect and enhance the planet's ecological and social systems, and encourage sustainable consumption patterns that are in balance with the carrying capacity of the Earth. For this reason, more eco- and socio-effective business models are being developed that go beyond the short-run gains achieved by eco- and socio-efficiency (Stead and Stead 2009).

One such model suggests that firms can create value for consumers while minimizing environmental and social impacts by emphasizing bundling services, selling end-use value, and ensuring cradle-to-cradle product steward-ship. Hawken, Lovins, and Lovins (1999, 146) say, "In the . . . model, value is delivered [to consumers] as a flow of services—providing illumination, for example, rather than selling light bulbs." Customers get the same level of performance from products, but with reduced environmental impacts through minimizing entropic throughput. The late Ray Anderson of Interface pioneered the idea of leasing carpet instead of selling it to consumers, and Cengage, a leader in the textbook industry, is moving toward book leasing and electronic publishing (Ottman 2011).

Innovative products that slow the entropic flow of resources while still providing consumer value will require a rethinking of product design and de-velopment models. According to Jacquelyn Ottman (2011), merely redesigning existing products based on eco-efficiency will no longer afford competitive advantages, because firms are basically left with the same product concept in markets where eco-efficiency has become a basic business requirement. Rather, she views "eco or functional innovation" as the next stage of the in-novation process. She says, "develop[ing] new product concepts that perform the same function as existing products but with significantly less impacts starts with questioning fundamental assumptions" (Ottman 2011, 90). Ques-tioning the basic assumptions of the business model moves product/service development from a cradle-to-grave to a cradle-to-cradle mentality where product design mimics nature based on the principles of eco-effectiveness. Eco-effective product design requires an organizational culture supported by entrepreneurial, generative learning.

Ottman (2011) uses the redesign of a simple toothbrush to demonstrate generative eco-effective thinking. A toothbrush can be made more eco-effi-ciently by producing it with recycled and recyclable materials, and so forth, but it is still the same product concept—a toothbrush that must eventually be disposed of. However, thinking eco-effectively may lead to a very differ-ent type of solution. Questioning the underlying assumption that a brush is required for cleaning teeth may well trigger new products such as specially treated chewing gums or food additives that prevent plaque buildup without a brush, paste, water, and packaging.

Sustainable Marketing Strategies

Sustainability marketing puts an organization's product stewardship commit-ment at the center of its marketing efforts, which is an essential prerequisite for transforming the consumer society into a sustainable society (Kirchgeorg and Winn 2006). According to Ottman (2011, 45), the idea of product steward-ship has led to the emergence of a whole new marketing paradigm that views people not "as mere customers with insatiable appetites for material goods, but as human beings looking to lead full, healthy lives." This constitutes a shift from a socio-efficiency to a socio-effectiveness perspective of who and what customers are.

This shifting perspective makes it clear why stakeholder engagement processes with customers are important vehicles for developing consumer learning, which is a basic element of sustainability marketing. Consumer learning allows strategic managers to attend to the consumption end of the value chain by engaging consumers in dialogue about sustainable consumption practices and so forth. Consumers have the capacity and willingness to learn, and it is the role of sustainable marketing to help them learn how to use and dispose of products and packaging responsibly. If organizations provide consumers with useful information such as life cycle and footprint data, they can facilitate more sustainable consumption. That is why organizations such as Proctor and Gamble, Clorox, and Unilever educate their customers about how to safely use and dispose of their products (*MIT Sloan Management Review* and BCG 2011).

Progressive business organizations are no doubt making efforts to broaden their strategic intent to address the global outcry for more sustainable business practices. Results of a recent survey of 3,000 global executives indicate that almost 70 percent expected their organizations to increase their investments in sustainability-related projects during the recent economic downturn, unlike previous economic downturns when sustainability was put on the corporate back burner (*MIT Sloan Management Review* and BCG 2011). As mentioned earlier, sustainability is clearly becoming more strategically important as "the sustainability movement nears a tipping point" (Kiron et al. 2012, 69). As consumers and other stakeholders increase demands for sustainable solutions to the environmental and social problems generated by the human footprint in the developed and developing markets, more and more opportunities will emerge for business to be part of the solution through collaborative action as a leading social change agent. Thus, SSM strategies for developed markets include dynamic, strategic initiatives that create shared stakeholder value (Porter and Kramer 2011) by reducing the entropic flow of energy and natural resources, and by creating innovative, sustainable products and services, both of which meet current stakeholder demands and enhance the triple-bottom-line performance of the firm and its business ecosystem.

SSM Strategies for Undeveloped and Developing Markets

The **base of the pyramid (BoP)** is a market of approximately 4.6 billion people who live on less than US$4 per day (Hart 2005). About 1.4 billion of them live below the international poverty line of US$1.25 per day (World Bank 2008). The BoP is a fragmented market consisting of many segments based on the individual characteristics of regions, countries, and industry sectors that are not fully integrated into the formal market economy. Entering the BoP market is difficult because of this inability to scale operations. Within the informal economy there are few channels of distribution, few formal regulations, and few means of financing. Living at the base of the pyramid makes people highly susceptible to isolation, disease, illiteracy, crime, environmental degradation, exponential population growth, and so forth. As desperate as this sounds (and is), these issues offer numerous win–win strategic opportunities to create long-term economic benefits by helping to improve the lives of the poor in these undeveloped markets through eco- and socio-effective BoP strategies (Hart 2005; London and Hart 2011; Prahalad 2006; Prahalad and Hart 2002).

As mentioned previously, even highly developed markets like the United States have BoP market segments that are in desperate need of economic, human, and social capital creation. Panera Bread cofounder and chairman Ron Shaich believed that Panera had many capabilities valuable for addressing food insecurity in these depressed U.S. communities. Based on this belief, the Panera Bread Foundation has opened Panera Cares Cafés in economically stressed urban areas such as Dearborn, Michigan. In the cafés anyone who needs a meal gets one. Panera Cares Cafés encourage people to take what they need and donate what they can. There is a donation box near the counter with a suggested donation amount posted. So far, about 20 percent of the customers have left more than the suggested donation, 60 percent have left the suggested amount, and 20 percent have left less. All of the Panera Cares Cafés have reported revenues in excess of their costs, and the extra money is used to train at-risk youth from the communities to become Panera employees (Kavner 2011). This is an example how a BoP socio-effectiveness strategy in an economically depressed market segment can serve the needs of the poor while building the firm's brand and reputational capital, both of which provide competitive advantages for the firm.

The Coevolution of BoP Strategies

BoP strategies specifically target the low-income demographic in order to generate revenues by "selling goods to and sourcing products from the BoP" (London and Hart 2011, 9). As more and more firms have discovered the BoP market space, two generic strategies have coevolved: one focuses on **serving BoP consumers** and the other focuses on **serving BoP producers**. Given the coevolutionary nature of BoP market space, the firm may employ either strategy or both strategies to compete in the BoP market. Typically, organizations implement market strategies that focus on the poor as consumers for the goods and services of their corporations (Boyle and Boguslaw 2007; Kirchgeorg and Winn 2006). These strategies are designed to provide low-cost products and services that address the basic needs of the poor, such as education, health care, sanitation, and clean water (Boyle and Boguslaw 2007; Hart and Christensen 2002).

The **poor as consumers** is generally the initial perception strategic managers have when they enter the BoP market space. These strategies are usually designed to merely sell an organization's standard products at lower prices to the masses or to generate rapid sales, often without regard to environmental responsibility or social welfare. Typically, these strategies take products created for developed markets, make some adjustments in them for local conditions, and then distribute them in the BoP markets. Such strategies can prove risky because they are often not well designed to serve the needs of those at the base of the pyramid. Rather they merely extract wealth from them in the form of consumer spending (Immelt, Govindarajan, and Trimble 2009). Such **fortune-finding strategies** are often viewed as a new form of corporate imperialism (Hart 2008).

The second generic type of BoP strategy shifts to **fortune-creating strategies**, which shift the focus from just extracting wealth from BoP customers to cocreating economic opportunities with them (London and Hart 2011). These strategies view the **poor as coproducers** within an inclusive business ecosystem of value-creating activities. The effectiveness of fortune-creating BoP strategies is that they have the potential to build economic capacity and generate jobs and income by creating economic opportunities within the local community.

Both types of generic BoP strategies span the informal and formal economies. The challenge is to link the productive assets of both sectors together to cocreate shared stakeholder value. Therefore, successful BoP strategies attempt to combine both the resources and technology found in the formal economy with the indigenous knowledge found in the local community (London and Hart 2011). BoP strategies involve collaborating and partnering with stakeholders spanning different sectors. Thus, a successful BoP strategy requires building an **inclusive business ecosystem** by partnering with social entrepreneurs, NGOs, citizen service organizations, governmental entities, competitors, and development agencies (Jenkins and Ishikawa 2010). The inclusive ecosystem is structured to develop wealth asset builders among the poor themselves. By enabling them to build "sustainable livelihood businesses" (Kirchgeorg and Winn 2006, 172) via an inclusive, collaborative ecosystem, the poor become coproducers in the value chain. This helps to reduce production costs, distribution costs, and the overall footprint of the business ecosystem while generating jobs, income, and creating local microenterprises.

Ultimately, successful BoP ventures must be able to recover their operating costs and become economically self-sustaining. In order to do this, they must reach economies of scale in the fragmented BoP market, which is a difficult task to achieve. Allen Hammond (2011) suggests that successful scaling strategies for the BoP market should be both global (top-down) and local (bottom-up), where capital and technology can be sourced while paying attention to local challenges and needs. He also notes the critical importance of building an inclusive ecosystem with multisector stakeholders that provide critical knowledge and multiple sources of solutions.

Such partnerships and alliances with local BoP stakeholders are designed to cocreate "entirely new businesses that generate mutual value" (Hart 2008, xi). Partnering with local social entrepreneurs can assist businesses in unlocking the potential in these BoP markets by providing linkages with local stakeholders that facilitate an understanding of local cost structures, local consumer behavior, and so forth (Drayton and Budinich 2010). These partnerships and alliances serve as mechanisms for deep dialogue with BoP stakeholders, leading to the development of capabilities and strategies that truly serve the needs of the poor. Stuart Hart (2008) has developed a BoP protocol for such inclusive ecosystems, which he says is a "co-venturing process that . . . creatively marr[ies] companies' and communities' resources, capabilities, and energies [in order to] bring life to new business ideas and models that exceed what either partner could imagine or create on their own" (Hart 2008, xi). Successful development of these partnerships and alliances provides the social capital that is necessary for these inclusive ecosystems to socially embed their BoP strategies into the chosen undeveloped markets (Hart 2005; Kirchgeorg and Winn 2006; Sánchez, Ricart, and Rodríguez 2005).

Corporate perceptions of the BoP market and the resulting strategic initiatives have coevolved and matured since C. K. Prahalad and Stuart Hart (2002) first introduced the idea of the BoP market space. Originally, the BoP was viewed simply as a huge market of economically restricted consumers ripe for exploitation, but today it is viewed more as a complex market of economic partners who cocreate value across the ecosystem along with helping their communities to meet their basic needs (Gradl and Jenkins 2011; Jenkins and Ishikawa 2010; Kirchgeorg and Winn 2006; London and Hart 2011). According to Prahalad (2011, xxx), "The process must start with respect for the Bottom of the Pyramid consumers as individuals." Successful BoP strategies convert poverty into an opportunity for all ecosystem members. For example, Unilever's Project Novella in Tanzania, which seeks to develop a sustainable supply of Allanblackia (AB) nuts and oil for margarine, has built an ecosystem including an AB Board, farmers associations, rural banks, and agricultural institutes. The ecosystem helps to create economic opportunity through building human and social capital within the BoP market (Jenkins 2007).

BoP Strategy Implementation

As mentioned above, the critical success factor in implementing a BoP strategy is the ability to construct an inclusive business ecosystem that achieves a scale of operations that covers operational costs. However, there are many barriers to accomplishing this. BoP markets are constrained by systemic challenges ranging from lack of infrastructure to low levels of worker knowledge and skills to limited access to finance among low-income consumers and producers (Jenkins and Ishikawa 2010). Creating an inclusive ecosystem to overcome these constraints requires entrepreneurial learning regarding navigating the uncharted waters of the BoP market. Thus, the stakeholder engagement dialogue with BoP ecosystem members provides vital input in the implementation process. This stakeholder input is critical in deciding how the inclusive business ecosystem will be framed, funded, supported, and structured (i.e., separate strategic business units, internal venture funds, cross-functional teams, spin-offs, etc.).

Stimulating entrepreneurship among BoP ecosystem members is essential in scaling operations in the BoP market. **Microfinancing** plays a critical role in creating and supporting local entrepreneurs at the base of the pyramid. Microloans allow the poor to break the cycle of poverty by building small businesses that provide them with a sustainable livelihood. Grameen Bank, established in the early 1970s by Nobel Peace Prize winner Muhammad Yunus, was founded on the principle that access to credit is a fundamental human right (Yunus 2003). Grameen Bank has loaned billions of dollars to millions of BoP entrepreneurs, mostly women, and there are now hundreds of microfinancing institutions across the globe using the Grameen methodology to serve both the urban and rural poor. Citibank has been involved in microfinance for over 40 years, offering savings, insurance, loan guarantees, and other financial services to the BoP market (Jenkins 2007). There can be, however, a dark side to microfinancing, and that is the possibility of lenders charging usurious interest rates to the poor.

General Electric's **reverse innovation strategy**, previously discussed as a preemptive strategy, has been successful in engaging BoP stakeholders in cocreating innovative products to address the needs of the BoP market. GE's strategy is to develop an inclusive business ecosystem in the target BoP market. GE utilizes long-term growth teams (LGTs) to actively engage in dialogue and collaboration with local stakeholders to facilitate the cocreation of products and services that satisfy unique customer needs at the base of the pyramid. It is called a reverse innovation strategy because innovations are developed at the base of the pyramid and flow to the top of the pyramid rather than the traditional top-to-base flow. For example, in 2009 Jeff Immelt, GE's CEO, announced a six-year goal to cocreate 100 low-cost health-care innovations in collaboration with customers in BoP markets via the LGT process (Immelt, Govindarajan, and Trimble 2009). Figure 5.5 demonstrates this strategic thinking.

GE implements a two-pronged development and market strategy with a focus on building infrastructure and upgrading technical capabilities at government hospitals and rural clinics. Initially, GE identifies a target country and then develops deep partnerships with its Ministry of Health. GE managers then work together with the LGTs to identify the best technological solutions for the target health-care provider. By partnering with Engineering World Health, an NGO whose mission is to improve the quality of health care in hospitals that serve BoP consumers, GE is able to train local health employees to maintain and repair the new technology. Meanwhile, the company reaps benefits in the form of design feedback, brand recognition, and reputational capital (Cleveland 2011). Thus, by constructing an inclusive ecosystem using deep dialogue in its target BoP market, GE serves the health-care needs of those at the base of the pyramid, creating human capital, social capital, and economic capital in the BoP communities where it operates. Further, these innovative products and solutions will likely flow from the base to the top of the pyramid as health-care costs continue to rise rapidly in developed markets like the United States. Thus, GE's reverse innovation strategy is a BoP strategy that encompasses the **whole pyramid**, providing sustainable solutions for both the undeveloped and developed markets served by GE's portfolio of businesses.

Strategies Dependent on Stage of Industry/Ecosystem Coevolution

The **stage of industry/business ecosystem coevolution** is a strategic environmental factor influencing the formulation of SSM competitive strategies since each stage of coevolution provides different opportunities and threats. As Chapter 3 discusses, industries and business ecosystems move through the stages of business ecosystem coevolution: the embryonic and pioneering stage, the establishment and growth stage, the maturity stage, and the decline stage (Moore 1996, 2006). The emphasis on generic and functional level strategies, the value-creating activities, and the overall objectives vary depending on the stage of coevolution, thus influencing the strategy formulation process (Dess, Lumpkin, and Eisner 2008).

Figure 5.5   **Whole-Pyramid Strategic Thinking**

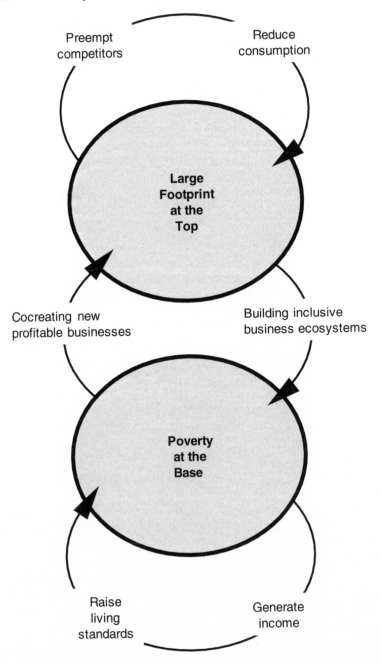

Source: Adapted from Stuart L. Hart 2011.

In the **embryonic, pioneering stage** where products are unfamiliar to consumers, markets are not well defined, and product features are not clearly specified, a successful strategy requires an emphasis on research and development and marketing activities to create consumer awareness. It is during this stage when early pioneers appear who explore a new market/opportunity space, creating first-mover advantages. Pioneering firms begin to structure a business ecosystem around their platforms.

After the new space is discovered, ecosystem settlers move in to establish the foundations that let the ecosystem expand, moving into the coevolutionary **stages of establishment and growth**. It is during this stage that pioneering firms seek to establish their platform as the dominant technology and to begin to build advantageous relationships with ecosystem settlers who are in the firm's value chain. Success requires rapidly improving product quality and performance, building a strong brand, creating selective demand for the firm's products, and forecasting future competing ecosystems. The potential for strong sales and profits attracts other competitors, increasing the intensity of competition (Dess, Lumpkin, and Eisner 2008). Recall from Chapter 3 that Apple's Steve Jobs introduced iTunes and the iPod family of products in the pioneering phase, creating new market space while establishing the iTunes platform as the dominant technology, and structuring the Apple ecosystem around this platform.

During the **maturity stage** of business ecosystem coevolution, relationships between ecosystem members are well defined and there is clear modularity in terms of each member's interface with the business ecosystem. With saturated markets, slowing demand, and more intense competition, weak firms exit the industry. Advantages associated with more efficient operations and process engineering become more important as customers become more price-sensitive. Thus, in a mature market it becomes harder and more costly to differentiate products and services, which results in the need to move more toward a cost-leadership posture. However, careful repositioning to identify, create, and exploit growth segments can provide growth opportunities during this stage. Using strategies such as **reverse positioning**, where products are offered with fewer product attributes and lower price points, or **breakaway positioning**, where products are created that are perceived as totally unique by customers, firms can effectively change consumer preferences and increase demand (Dess, Lumpkin, and Eisner 2008).

Consider the launch of the Swatch brand watch in 1983 when Swiss watches were marketed as expensive, serious jewelry to last a lifetime. Swatch changed all that by redefining the watch as a playful, fashionable accessory with bold new styling and design at a much lower price. Consumers were inspired to impulse buy, often purchasing half a dozen in different designs.

Swatch redesigned the quartz watch for manufacturing efficiency and fewer parts. This breakaway positioning strategy of Swatch combined marketing and manufacturing expertise and restored Switzerland as a major player in the world wristwatch market (Dess, Lumpkin, and Eisner 2008). It is during the maturity phase that business ecosystem leaders recruit new, innovative niche players that are using such strategies as reverse positioning or breakaway positioning to explore new market space. This ensures the health and robustness of the business ecosystem.

Decisions during the **decline** stage are particularly difficult because hard choices must be made. Demand growth becomes negative, sales and profits fall, while competition stiffens due to excess capacity within the industry (Hill and Jones 2009). Fundamental strategic choices to either exit or stay in the industry must be made. There are several basic strategic options available to a business ecosystem in the decline stage. These choices include hold and maintain, harvesting, divesting, or horizontal integration. The focus of a **hold-and-maintain strategy** (discussed briefly earlier in the chapter) is to maintain the present market position without significant reduction in marketing, technology, and other investments in hopes that competitors will eventually leave the market. If the firm remains in the market and others exit, there may still be potential for revenues and profits. On the other hand, strategic managers may choose to implement a **harvesting strategy** that involves obtaining as much profit as possible while quickly reducing costs. The objective is to wring out as much cash as possible. Divestiture strategies (discussed further in the next chapter) involve eliminating the business from the firm's product portfolio, while horizontal integration strategies (also discussed further in the next chapter), involve the firm's acquiring at a reasonable price the best of the surviving firms left in the business, thus consolidating its competitive position (Dess, Lumpkin, and Eisner 2008). Therefore, those firms who are able to hold and maintain their position and survive market shakeout will be able to take advantage of the opportunities posed by the market dynamics of the decline stage.

Chapter Summary

Strategic managers must make critical decisions regarding how to strategically position their firms in their chosen market segments in ways that provide them with cost and/or differentiation competitive advantages. They must choose some combination of cost-leadership, product differentiation, and focus strategies, and they must choose to implement them preemptively, as second movers, or as late movers. In SSM, strategic managers seek to improve their firms' competitiveness by implementing pollution prevention and other cost-saving eco-efficiency strategies, establishing TQEM and/or ISO 14000 processes, and practicing product stewardship in order to achieve eco- and socio-differentiation of their firms products/services. Research indicates that firms that raise sustainability to the top of their strategic agendas, develop competitive level SSM strategies, and implement those strategies assertively and preemptively can improve their competitive position relative to more timid, less committed, later moving firms.

The effectiveness of SSM strategies is dependent on the market type and relative market position of the firm. In developed markets where economic wealth and natural resource depletion are both high, organizations will have to focus their strategic efforts on improving their eco-efficiency, reducing their carbon footprint, and developing ecologically and/or socially responsible products and services. In developing and undeveloped markets, strategies should be designed to meet basic consumer needs while creating economic, social, and human capital within the ecological limits imposed by the entropic flow of energy and resources. In these markets, multisector, multistakeholder inclusive ecosystems have successfully implemented various SSM strategies that have created shared value for the business ecosystems, the people, and the planet.

Case Vignette 5

Product Stewardship at Eastman Chemical Company

A central belief at Eastman is that sustainability and innovation are synergistically interconnected routes to both current product improvements and future product developments. This belief lays a strong cultural foundation for establishing product stewardship as a centerpiece of Eastman's SSM efforts, allowing Eastman to successfully ecologically and socially differentiate many of its products. One such product is Perennial Wood™, mentioned in Case Vignette 1, which was officially introduced in the winter of 2012. Perennial Wood™ is Eastman's first product sold directly to the end-use customer, demonstrating Jim Rogers's strategic intent to move downstream in Eastman's value chain. Perennial Wood™ is a natural, renewable, highly durable wood product used for the construction of windows, trim, decking, siding, and so forth. It is manufactured from abundant, renewable, locally available southern pine, using Eastman's proprietary TruLast™ acetylation technology, with vinegar as the only by-product of the production process. The acetylation technology permanently expands the cell walls of the wood to a fixed position that will not shrink, swell, bow, cup, or warp for decades. Thus, Perennial Wood™ has a much higher level of performance and is more ecologically sustainable than its competitors' pressure-treated wood and Trex, recycled plastic. Unlike Perennial Wood™, neither of these competitive products can be recycled at the end of life. In addition Perennial Wood™ maintains its natural beauty throughout its long life. Eastman's Perennial Wood™ group is a member of the U.S. Green Building Council and the National Association of Homebuilders-Leading Suppliers Council, both of which are committed to environmentally and socially conscious building. Thus, the first end-use product introduced by Eastman is an ecologically differentiated product offered to compete in the expanding sustainable building materials segment of the market.

Tritan™ copolyester, also mentioned earlier, is another ecologically differentiated product made by Eastman. Unlike Perennial Wood™, Tritan™ is not sold to end-use customers, but is used for the manufacture of food and drink containers, cosmetic containers, sports bottles, durable housewares, medical devices and equipment, and medical packaging. CamelBak water bottle manufacturer and Estee Lauder cosmetics manufacturer are Eastman customers using Tritan™ in their water bottles and cosmetics containers. Tritan™ has received a great deal of market attention because it is a nonpolycarbonate plastic that contains no bisphenol A (BPA), a suspected endocrine disruptor considered potentially hazardous to fetuses, newborns, and young children. Being BPA free makes Tritan™ the preferred material in the manufacture of baby bottles. In addition, Tritan™ is free of other endocrine disruptors, contains no halogens, sulfur, nitrogen, lead, mercury, cadmium, or chromium, is very durable, has a long product life cycle, and is produced with low levels of energy, wastes, and greenhouse gases, demonstrating stewardship across its value chain.

The HydroPack™, mentioned in Case Vignette 1, is an ecologically and socially differentiated product of Eastman Chemical Company. The HydroPack™ uses Eastman's cellulose acetate technology in HTI's forward osmosis membrane system that enables virtually any water to be transformed into a clean, nutrient-enriched source of hydration. The HydroPack™ has multimarket potential, including disaster victims in all market segments, the rural poor who lack clean water in undeveloped and developing markets, and affluent hikers and campers in developed markets.

Of course, product stewardship begins with sustainable resources, so it is interesting that Eastman Chemical was founded in 1920 to secure a dependable source of cellulose needed to produce photographic film. Cellulose is the structural component of the cell walls of plants, and it is the most common organic compound found on Earth. Thirty-three percent of all plant matter (40–50 percent of trees) is cellulose. To this day Eastman Chemical uses cellulose from sustainably managed forests to produce several of its products, including some of its sustainably advantaged products, such as cellulose esters, which are used to make specialty films for tapes, labels, and LCD and LED flat panel displays, Estron™ acetate yarn, which is used to make medical tape, coat linings, women's fine knits and formal wear, graduation robes, window treatments, and upholstery trim, and Foralyn™ hydrogenated rosin esters used in sealants, cosmetics, and packaging.

Eastman has a goal to continue to build its stable of sustainably advantaged products. It wants two-thirds of its new product introductions to be sustainably advantaged by 2015. In addition to the products mentioned above, Eastman offers several other sustainably advantaged products, including: GEM™ 2-ethylhexyl palmitate used in face creams, body creams, and cosmetics; Solus™ 2300 performance additives used in automobile paints and other coatings; 168™ nonphthalate plasticizers used in bottle caps, wall coverings, toys, medical devices, and childcare products; and Benzoflex™ benzoate plasticizers used in coatings, adhesives, caulks, sealants, and flooring.

6

SSM Corporate Level Strategy

Corporate strategy is the overall plan for a diversified organization. The tasks of **corporate strategy** focus on managing the mix, scope, and emphasis of a firm's portfolio of strategic business units (SBUs), exploiting the synergies among its SBUs, and deploying capital to each SBU in order to achieve competitive advantages. The strategic decisions at the corporate level concern the **scope of the firm's operations** and determine the boundaries of the firm along three dimensions: the value chain, the mix of the products and services offered by the firm, and the geographic scope of operations (Rothaermel 2013). The firm's boundaries create the space in which strategic managers must position their firms for competitive advantage. As discussed previously, space is defined as new market domains that exist in the minds of strategic managers. Thus, decisions concerning scope are perceptions of what the boundaries of the firm will be and should be. Capital allocation decisions are also made at the corporate level. By deploying resources to SBUs in accordance with strategy, the corporate level serves as an internal market for the distribution of capital to the firm's lines of businesses, as seen in Figure 6.1. Thus, corporate strategy is a way for a corporation to create value through the configuration of its SBUs, the coordination of its multimarket activities, the exploitation of the synergy between its SBUs, and effective allocation of capital. An effective corporate level strategy creates value across all the firm's SBUs by achieving above-average returns for triple-bottom-line performance, thus the portfolio creates more value together than if each SBU stood alone (Campbell, Goold, and Alexander 1995).

For example, General Electric has a diversified portfolio of businesses that spans many global industries and markets. The recession of 2008–9 hit GE especially hard since more than half of its profits came from GE Capital. GE's share price fell 84 percent resulting in a loss of shareholder value of US$378 billion. GE also lost its AAA credit rating and had to ask for a US$15 billion liquidity injection from well-known investor Warren Buffett. The dramatic

Figure 6.1 **Corporate Strategy Capital Allocation**

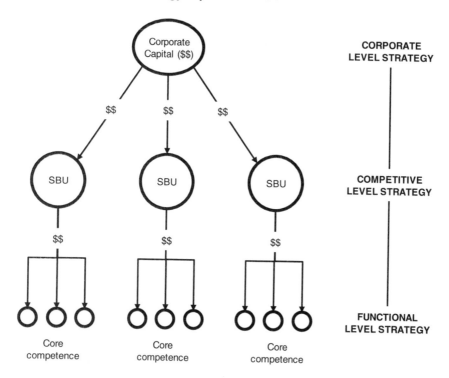

changes in GE's external environment made it very clear to Jeffrey Immelt, GE CEO, that a change in the corporate portfolio was needed (Rothaermel 2013).

In 2009, GE's portfolio of five SBUs (Capital Finance, Technology Infrastructure, Energy Infrastructure, Consumer and Industrial, and NBC Universal) brought in US$157 billion in annual revenues. Immelt decided to refocus GE's portfolio of SBUs in order to reduce its exposure to capital markets and to achieve more reliable growth by leveraging its core competencies in industrial engineering. GE sold a majority stake in NBC Universal to Comcast, sold its century-old appliance SBU, and identified the green economy and health care as major growth opportunities. Immelt then refocused the portfolio by launching two strategic initiatives. The first, known as Ecomagination, leverages GE's clean technology to provide sustainable solutions for future generations. GE has invested billions in clean technology, and the Ecomagination initiative contributes roughly US$25 billion in annual revenues for GE. The second is the Healthymagination initiative, which has a goal of reducing the cost of health care while increasing the quality of and access to health care. GE will invest US$6 billion in this initiative by 2016 (Rothaermel 2013). As discussed in the preceding chapter, by using a reverse innovation strategy to assist in product development, GE is better able to develop products that target the growing health-care market in undeveloped and developing markets. Immelt refocused GE's portfolio in light of dramatic changes in the external environment by changing the scope, mix, and emphasis of the firm's portfolio of SBUs in order to minimize external threats in the capital markets and to take advantage of emerging opportunities in the green economy and health-care markets. This demonstrates the essence of corporate strategy.

Strategic managers have several options at the corporate level in choosing which industries a firm should compete in to maximize its triple-bottom-line performance. Strategic managers can choose to compete in only one industry via a **concentrated growth strategy** focusing on the competitive strategies discussed in the preceding chapter that improve the firm's competitive position in one particular industry. A **horizontal integration strategy** can be used to expand the firm's competitive position in a specific industry by the acquisition of industry competitors. Strategic managers may decide to enter adjacent stages across the firm's value chain by implementing a strategy of **vertical integration**, where the firm begins to make its own inputs and/or sell its own products. Strategic managers can also choose to enter new industries that may or may not be related to the firm's core business by pursuing a strategy of **diversification**. Also, as discussed in Chapter 3, industries today are more global and interconnected, which increases environmental turbulence and the need for strategic managers to consider **strategies for global markets** and **alliance strategies** in implementing their integration and diversification decisions. Finally, strategic managers may decide to exit existing businesses and industries via **retrenchment strategies** by refocusing their portfolios, as Jeffrey Immelt did at GE, or they may decide to shrink the boundaries of their firms via strategies that restructure or downsize current operations. In this chapter, we discuss the strategic alternatives available to firms regarding where to compete, how to adapt the firm's scope to its turbulent external environment, and how to redefine the firm's portfolio and boundaries to create new market space. The following section discusses the strategic alternatives available to expand the firm's scope of operations.

Corporate Expansion Strategies

Strategic managers have several strategies available to them related to how to expand their firms' scope and improve their performance. Below we examine some of these corporate expansion strategies.

Concentration on a Single Industry

For many firms concentrating on one industry is an appropriate corporate level expansion strategy. This allows firms to concentrate all of their resources and capabilities on building their competitive position within a confined market segment (much like Porter's focus strategy discussed in the previous chapter). Advantages of this strategy are that strategic managers can focus all of their efforts on understanding their customer base, thus enhancing customer loyalty and repeat business. This allows firms to "stick to the knitting" (Peters and Waterman 1982), to focus on what they know best, and avoid entering new businesses they know little about and/or where they can create little value.

Concentrated growth strategies are particularly effective in growth markets that make heavy demands on a firm's resources and capabilities, but they also offer opportunities for long-term growth and profitability, if the firm can sustain its competitive advantage. Starbucks, discussed in the previous chapter, has employed a concentrated growth strategy in the expanding premium coffee-shop market, where finding new ways to compete successfully is important in sustaining their competitive position. Other firms, such as Neiman Marcus in luxury retailing, Target and Walmart in discount retailing, and McDonald's in the fast-food market, utilize concentrated growth strategies. When domestic markets become saturated, firms using concentrated growth strategies typically expand into global markets, whose downside is their inflexibility. By focusing on just one industry, a firm may miss opportunities in other industries where it could create more value, or it may face the risk of the industry's being subject to changes in consumer preferences and/or technology (Hill and Jones 2009).

Horizontal Integration Strategies

Horizontal integration strategies are among the most popular strategies employed at the corporate level to better position a firm within its chosen industry. Horizontal integration involves acquiring a competitor within the industry that enhances the firm's competitive position by increasing its market power and market share through the exploitation of cost-based and revenue-based synergies. These competitive advantages result from economies of scale. Research indicates that these strategies work best when the combining companies have similar characteristics (Hitt, Ireland, and Hoskisson 2009). The widespread popularity of horizontal integration and the resulting industry consolidation can be seen in the banking, pharmaceutical, telecommunications, transportation, and energy industries, to name but a few.

Strategic managers who pursue a horizontal integration strategy have made the decision that investing the firm's resources in purchasing a competitor (or competitors) is the best way to increase long-run profitability. Profitability is enhanced when horizontal integration lowers operating costs as a result of economies of scale and/or when product differentiation boosts profitability by providing customers with a wider range of products. Horizontal integration opens new markets and distribution channels that also enhance profitability. In many cases, a strategy of product bundling can increase profitability by offering customers the opportunity to buy a complete range of products at a single, combined price (Hill and Jones 2009). The acquisition of competitors can also reduce the competitive intensity within an industry by consolidating the industry. Industry consolidation reduces the threat of potential competitors by strengthening barriers to entry, increases the bargaining power with suppliers and customers, and reduces the intensity of competition, thus making the industry potentially more profitable (Rothaermel 2013).

The primary costs/risks to the firm of a horizontal integration strategy are integration failure, reduced flexibility, and increased potential for legal repercussions (Rothaermel 2013). Integration failure results from problems associated with merging different corporate cultures, high management turnover, and an overestimation of the benefits of the integration of the two firms. For example, Carly Fiorina, the former CEO of Hewlett-Packard, overestimated the benefits of acquiring Compaq and underestimated the difficulty of integrating the two distinct cultures, resulting in her removal as CEO before any benefits of the acquisition were apparent.

The use of horizontal integration to become the dominant industry competitor may have a major social cost. The Federal Trade Commission (FTC) is in charge of making sure that dominant industry competitors do not use their market dominance to crush competitors through abusing their market power via anticompetitive behavior. However, the antiregulatory sentiment that began during the Reagan administration has led to the repeal of numerous laws, such as the Glass–Steagall Act in 1999 that removed the separation between investment banks and depository banks in the United States. Critics believe that this antiregulatory environment combined with the popularity of the horizontal integration strategy created an environment where institutions became too big to fail (Sorkin 2009). This term is now commonly used to describe financial institutions that have become so large and so interconnected that their failure would be disastrous to the economy. Therefore, they must be given taxpayer support when they face financial difficulties of their own making. The term has emerged as prominent in public discourse since the 2007–10 global financial crisis, considered by many economists to be the worst financial crisis since the Great Depression of the 1930s. It resulted in the collapse of large financial institutions, the bailout of banks by national governments and taxpayers, and downturns in stock markets around the world. This can be a problem if a company that benefits from governmental protective policies seeks to profit by them by taking high-risk, high-return positions, as they are able to leverage these risks based on the policy preferences they receive. Critics see this policy as counterproductive and believe that large banks and other institutions, and even sovereign nations such as Greece or Spain, should be left to fail if their risk management is not effective, regardless of the potential impact on the world economy. In response to the financial crisis, the FTC substantially revised the Horizontal Merger Guidelines in 2010 in an effort to reinvigorate dominant firm enforcement. This was the first revision of the guidelines since 1992 (DeMasi and Clarke 2011).

Vertical Integration Strategies

A key corporate level decision that must be made by strategic managers involves the degree of ownership of the firm's value chain. Deciding whether to make the various value chain activities within the firm or buy them in the marketplace involves the strategy of **vertical integration**. When a firm pursues a strategy of vertical integration, it either expands its operations backward (upstream) into industries that produce inputs for its core products (**backward vertical integration**) or forward (downstream) into industries that use, distribute, or sell its products (**forward vertical integration**). A firm's value added related to its vertical integration strategy is its percentage of sales generated within its boundaries (Rothaermel 2013). Thus, the scope of the firm's value-creating activities determines the degree of vertical integration and the boundaries of the firm. If the firm owns all of its value-creating functions, it is **fully integrated**.

Weyerhaeuser is a fully integrated firm that owns its forests, grows, cuts, and mills its timber, manufactures a wide product line of paper and construction products, and distributes them to retail outlets and other large customers. Thus, Weyerhaeuser competes in numerous industries with different competitors in each industry, and its value added is 100 percent. By comparison, Apple has implemented a forward integration strategy by establishing its Apple Stores to sell its products directly to the consumer, while IBM has integrated backward by manufacturing the major components that go into its computers. These examples demonstrate that when strategic managers decide the degree of vertical integration of their firms, they are determining the boundaries of the firm across value chain activities.

Both risks and benefits are associated with vertical integration strategies. These strategies can strengthen the competitive position of the core business by erecting barriers to entry, lowering costs, securing critical resource inputs or distribution channels, protecting product quality, facilitating investments in specialized assets, and improving scheduling (Hill and Jones 2009). However, vertical integration strategies have the potential to increase costs and/or compromise quality when the firm has to purchase from in-house suppliers despite the opportunity to purchase from lower-cost, higher-quality suppliers externally. Vertical integration also may reduce the firm's strategic flexibility in responding to the rapidly changing environments in global sectors such as technology (Rothaermel 2013).

Strategic outsourcing is an alternative to vertical integration where the firm contracts one or more internal value chain activities to outside firms in the value chain in order to reduce the risks of vertical integration. The expansion of global outsourcing has become one of the most significant trends in strategic management as firms seek to improve their competitive position both domestically and globally. There has been tremendous growth in offshore outsourcing, where the value chain functions take place outside of the home country. The global offshore market is estimated to be US$1.4 trillion with an expected growth rate of 15 percent. Banking, financial services, information technology, and health care are currently the most active outsourcing segments. For example, Infosys, located in Bangalore, India, is one of the world's largest technology firms, providing information technology services to many of the Fortune 100 companies (Rothaermel 2013). This trend demonstrates the interconnectedness of the global economy in which firms must operate.

Diversification Strategies

After strengthening the firm's core business and competitive position through integration strategies, strategic managers have the option to invest the firm's resources in new markets in order to enhance long-run profitability. **Diversification** is a process of entering markets that are distinctly different from the firm's core business in order to create value for multiple stakeholders. As previously discussed, diversified, multimarket firms establish strategic business units in two or more industries in order to effectively compete within each market segment. These SBUs may or may not be related. **Related** or **concentric diversification** is the expansion into industries that have a **strategic fit** or synergies with the firm's core business, while **unrelated** or **conglomerate diversification** is the expansion into industries that have no relation to the firm's value chain. Whereas resources can be shared and competencies transferred between SBUs in related diversification, this is not usually the case in unrelated diversification. Also, through related diversification the firm can achieve **economies of scope**, which are cost savings resulting from operational relatedness, transference of core competencies between SBUs, and market power. Since related diversification has the opportunity to create more value than unrelated diversification and is perceived as having fewer risks, most diversified firms have a preference for related diversification (Hitt, Ireland, and Hosskinson 2009).

Consider ExxonMobil's petroleum-based product portfolio that has been subject to increasing negative public sentiment, including calls for more carbon regulation. Strategic managers realized that unless the firm diversified its petroleum-based product portfolio into one that relies on more sustainable energy sources, it would not likely be able to sustain its superior financial performance over time. In order to adapt to the dynamic changes in its external environment, ExxonMobil initiated a strategy of product diversification into clean energy by acquiring natural gas companies like XTO Energy, which is known for its ability to extract natural gas from unconventional places, for example, shale rock. Huge deposits have been found in North Dakota and other states. ExxonMobil hopes to leverage its core competencies in the exploration and commercialization of petroleum energy sources into its new natural gas business. Natural gas is lower in carbon compared to petroleum, and it provides ExxonMobil with a more diversified product portfolio that will help the firm adapt to the worldwide sustainability movement (Rothaermel 2013).

Unrelated diversification can also create value, as was demonstrated in the earlier discussion of General Electric. GE is a conglomerate with an unrelated portfolio of businesses. Not surprisingly, each one of General Electric's SBUs has its own CEO with profit-and-loss responsibility. An even more diversified firm is the Indian Tata Group, whose product offerings include cars (Jaguar, Land Rover, and Nano), chemicals, luxury hotels, steel, coffee, tea, software, and consulting. Its product portfolio includes Asia's largest software company, India's largest steelmaker, and the famed Taj Hotels and Resorts (Rothaermel 2013).

Strategies for Global Markets

As discussed above, strategic managers make decisions concerning the degree of ownership of the value chain and the degree of diversification in their product portfolios. More and more of these decisions are made within the global context of coevolving developed, undeveloped, and developing markets that offer opportunities unique to each market segment. Thus, effective strategies for operating outside of the firm's domestic market can add value to its domestic operations by expanding its market share, gaining access to low-cost factors of production via strategic sourcing, leveraging current core competencies in new ways, and developing new core competencies (Barney and Hesterly 2010).

Competitive Pressures

Two conflicting types of competitive pressures are faced by firms choosing to move out of their domestic markets: the need to reduce costs, and the need to be responsive to local customer preferences, unique distribution channels, infrastructure, traditional practices, and local government demands (Hill and Jones 2009). These competitive pressures are difficult strategic challenges because being locally responsive tends to raise costs. Thus, the appropriateness of a strategy varies depending on the intensity of pressures for cost reduction and local responsiveness.

The **international strategy** is commonly used when there are relatively low pressures for local responsiveness and cost reduction. It is essentially a strategy of selling the same product in both domestic and foreign markets and is used by firms with relatively large domestic markets, recognized brands, and reputations. This is usually the first step firms make into foreign markets, and it can be effective in leveraging domestically based core competencies into global markets (Rothaermel 2013). A criticism is that international strategies are often not well designed to serve the needs of those in undeveloped and developing markets. Rather they are designed to merely sell an organization's standard products at lower prices to the masses or to generate rapid sales without regard to environmental responsibility or social welfare. Thus, strategies of taking products created for developed markets, making minor adjustments for local conditions, and then distributing them in undeveloped and developing markets is risky (Immelt, Govindarajan, and Trimble 2009).

On the other hand, the **localization** (or **multidomestic**) **strategy** focuses on increasing profitability by customizing goods and/or services to meet local tastes and preferences in specific market segments. This strategy attempts to maximize local responsiveness in hopes that consumers will perceive the firm as domestic (Rothaermel 2013). By doing this, the firm is able to increase the value for its products in the local market. Thus, the localization strategy works best when there are substantial differences in customer preferences across markets and when cost pressures are not too intense. The strategy creates a fragmented industry by decentralizing functional level activities such as production and marketing in order to address the needs of the local market. GE's strategy of reverse innovation, discussed in the previous chapter, is an example of a localization strategy targeted toward undeveloped markets.

The **global standardization strategy** is effective when the firm produces a commodity-type product that enables it to achieve economies of scale and location that reduce its unit costs. Unlike the localization strategy, the global standardization strategy allows for the centralization of functional level activities in a few favorable locations since customer preferences are homogeneous across markets, creating a more consolidated industry. Therefore, by producing and marketing a standard product on a worldwide basis, this strategy enables the firm to effectively compete across various market segments. For example, firms in the pharmaceutical and semiconductor industries use global standardization strategies since customers expect the same product regardless of local conditions (Hill and Jones 2009).

Strategic managers pursuing a **glocalization strategy** (or **transnational strategy**) (Friedman 1999, 2004) attempt to combine the benefits of the localization (local responsiveness) and global standardization (cost-reduction) strategies. By harnessing the economies of scale and location and combining them with global learning from local markets, the firm pursues a strategy of product/service differentiation at low cost (Rothaermel 2013). Due to the organizational complexities of working across cultures and trying to reduce costs at the same time, the glocalization strategy is rather difficult to implement because differentiating the product to respond to local demands raises costs. Automobile companies have found that the varying tastes of American, Japanese, and European customers have necessitated producing products customized for local markets. In response, Ford, Honda, and Toyota have established production facilities in each of these regions to better serve customer needs; however, this customization limits their ability to achieve economies of scale (Hill and Jones 2009).

Entry Modes

After the appropriate strategy for the market has been selected, strategic managers have several options of **entry modes** into foreign markets. Usually, firms will start on a small scale and then increase their involvement, investment, and risk as they gain greater experience in the new market. The options to entry vary in terms of risk, investment, and the degree of ownership/control. Options include: (1) exporting, with low investment, risk, and ownership; (2) licensing and franchising, which entails a contractual agreement with the firm receiving a fee or royalty in exchange for the right to use its trademark, brand, or technology; (3) strategic alliances and joint ventures (to be discussed in the next section); and (4) wholly owned subsidiaries characterized by high levels of risk, investment, and control (Dess, Lumpkin, and Eisner 2008). A strategic fit is essential between the firm's strategies, the characteristics of its target market, and the entry mode it chooses. Thus, strategic managers must carefully analyze both the benefits and risks of each entry mode, and they must carefully analyze the characteristics of the foreign market(s) that they plan to enter.

For example, in the late 1990s Walmart faced a saturated domestic market, so the decision was made to expand into Germany, the third largest economy in the world (after the United States and Japan). Given Walmart's cost-leadership position in the United States, executives decided on a global standardization strategy in response to the continued pressures for cost reductions in the retail industry. Thus, the plan was to achieve even greater economies of scale and location by expanding its market scope. The entry mode Walmart used was to acquire already-established retailers in the German market. Thus, Walmart decided to risk the high levels of involvement and investment associated with ownership in order to have more control. However, this global standardization strategy using wholly owned subsidiaries as the entry mode did not prove successful for Walmart. By 2006, Walmart had exited the German market after losing billions of U.S. dollars. This was a shock to an organization that was used to success (Rothaermel 2013).

Walmart's failure resulted from a lack of fit between its strategy, its entry mode, and the characteristics of the German market. Cultural differences impeded the implementation of personnel policies and were especially hampered when English was declared as the official in-house language. In addition, domestic competition was very intense in the discount-retailing segment. Walmart was not able to establish its usual economies of scale or its efficient distribution centers, and its labor costs were high due to wage rates and restrictive labor laws (Rothaermel 2013).

When entering foreign markets, it is important for strategic managers to understand that their firms are not competing with nations but with other firms doing business in these nations. Nations do not compete. Industries and industry segments are the competitors in the global market. The role of the nation is to serve as a supportive "home base" for firms. A supportive home base is one with a quality workforce, available technology and resources, and other competitors in the industry. Strategic managers need to carefully explore the home-base potential for markets they are considering entering (Porter 1990).

Collaborative Alliance Strategies

The blurring of industry boundaries and the need to explore the global market space has led to the rising popularity of strategies of collaboration that allow firms to create competitive advantages within partnerships. Eighty percent of Fortune 1000 CEOs have indicated that more than a quarter of their firms' revenues were generated through collaborative alliances and partnerships. Paradoxically, while the use of these **alliance strategies**—strategies in which two or more firms come together to do something neither firm could do alone— is rising, research indicates that such strategies are risky, with failure rates of 30–70 percent (Kale and Singh 2009). Thus, strategic managers pursuing SSM will likely have to participate in alliances as a means of enhancing their triple-bottom-line performance, even though doing so will likely add issues related to maintaining and getting value from these partnerships. This strategic challenge increases the need for firms to build alliance management capabilities that, as will be discussed later in the chapter, are critical for managing SSM at the corporate level.

The competitive advantages afforded by collaborative alliance strategies are often embedded within the relationships among partners that span the traditional boundaries of the firm, creating resource combinations that are rare, valuable, and difficult for competitors to imitate (Gulati, Nohria, and Zaheer 2000; Kanter 1994; Lavie 2006; Nahapiet and Ghoshal 1998; Reed and DeFillippi 1990). In order to effectively explain firm performance and the competitive advantages afforded by interconnected organizations, the traditional definition of industry and firm must be expanded to include the broader business ecosystem structure (Dyer and Singh 1998) discussed in Chapter 3. Recall that within this structure sources of competitive advantage are found in the relationships between partners in the alliance. The social capital created by such interconnected organizations leads to the development of ecosystemic competencies that profoundly influence firm conduct and performance (Gueguen, Pellegrin-Boucher, and Torres 2006; Gulati, Nohria, and Zaheer 2000). Business ecosystem members can develop strategies that protect and exploit these common competencies, and in doing so they can help to improve competitiveness throughout the ecosystem because of the improved relation-specific assets, knowledge sharing processes, complementary resources/capabilities, and shared governance mechanisms (Dyer and Singh 1998).

Firms are able to enhance performance via collaborative strategies in numerous ways. Alliances may be used to enter new market space where partners in host countries are able to provide useful local data on customer preferences, cultural norms, and legal matters. Alliances can also help strengthen a firm's competitive position, helping it to hedge against uncertainty and reduce costs across the value chain. Motivation to learn new capabilities, to share and create new knowledge and technologies, and to access complementary assets are other reasons that firms collaborate (Rothaermel 2013). As previously discussed, collaboration is a critical success factor for firms pursuing sustainability as a competitive advantage because it expands opportunities to learn and create new knowledge.

Strategic alliances are relationships involving voluntary agreements between organizations that create competitive advantages for the alliance partners. In essence, strategic alliances are relationships defined by the partners themselves, and they are shaped by a vision of what they want to create together in the future. The portfolio of strategic alliance strategies varies in terms of formalization, investment, governance, and risk (Rothaermel 2013). The keystone firms, the business ecosystem leaders, must effectively manage the portfolio of strategic alliances within the network. This is a complex task given the diversity of stakeholders within the business ecosystem, but it is a critical success factor in the effective implementation of SSM.

The most common strategic alliance strategies are **nonequity alliances** in which there is a contractual agreement between firms, such as a distribution agreement, supply agreement, or licensing agreement. In many cases these alliances are vertical in nature, connecting different parts of the value chain. Typically, explicit knowledge is exchanged between partners. Nonequity alliances are flexible and fast, but they do not usually create much social capital, which can result in a lack of trust and commitment within the alliance (Rothaermel 2013).

In **equity alliances**, one partner takes partial ownership in the other partner, requiring more investment and commitment than contractual nonequity alliances. These alliances allow not only for explicit knowledge sharing but also for tacit knowledge sharing in which process learning can take place. **Corporate venture capital (CVC)** investments are a type of equity alliance in which established firms make equity investments in entrepreneurial ventures that create options for accessing new, potentially disruptive technologies. Large organizations such as Dow, Siemens, and Johnson and Johnson have huge investments in CVCs. Equity alliances tend to generate more social capital and greater trust between partners than nonequity alliances because the stronger ownership relationship and increased financial investment generate a higher level of commitment to success (Rothaermel 2013).

Joint ventures are collaborative strategies in which the partners contribute equity to create a separate legal entity (Dess, Lumpkin, and Eisner 2008). These alliances entail significant investments and may be extremely time-consuming in terms of negotiating and managing the nature of the relationships among partners. In a joint-venture strategy, the scope of the vision is usually broader than other alliance strategies, with the exchange of both tacit and explicit knowledge among partners focused on the shared vision. Trust and commitment are fostered, which creates the social capital embedded in the relationships that may afford the firm potential competitive advantages. Dow Corning, a global leader in silicon-based technology and innovation, equally owned by Dow Chemical Company and Corning, is a joint venture that was established in 1943 specifically to explore the potential of silicones. The longevity of this joint venture indicates that Dow and Corning have developed effective alliance management capabilities, thus avoiding the usual risks of the misappropriation of shared knowledge and the conflicts over sharing rewards that lead to the high failure rates for strategic alliances (Rothaermel 2013). Thus, the key to successful alliances is the ability of strategic managers to manage the relationships within the partnership in ways that develop high levels of trust-creating alliance management capabilities (Kale and Singh 2009).

The Build or Buy Decision

As discussed above, strategic managers have various corporate alternatives that are available to expand their firm's scope in order to find new market space to achieve competitive advantages. The choice of the appropriate scope for the firm's operations is a critical challenge in corporate strategy. Corporate strategic options that expand the firm's scope discussed above include concentrating on a single industry, horizontally integrating, vertically integrating, diversifying the product/market mix, and/or collaborating with partners in alliance strategies. Once the expanded boundaries of the firm have been envisioned, strategic managers must then decide how to organize the expanded economic activity, deciding which activities should be done in-house and which activities should be bought in the external market. This **build or buy decision** is a strategic judgment that is influenced by many factors.

The **transaction costs** of performing the new activities within the firm compared to buying them in the external market are critical in influencing this decision (Williamson 1981). The costs of buying activities in the marketplace are associated with the market value of acquiring the asset necessary to perform the expanded activity as well as finding an economic agent with whom to contract, negotiate, monitor, and enforce the contract. The costs of building activities within the firm are associated with administrative costs such as providing salaries, benefits, and office space for personnel, establishing organizational processes, recruiting and training employees, and so forth. These transaction costs clearly influence the activities that a firm should build in-house and those it should buy in the market. The more efficient the firm is in organizing the expanded economic activity internally, the more likely it will perform the activities in-house at a lower cost.

There are other market factors that influence the build or buy decision. High barriers to entry and a mature industry life cycle make it more difficult for a firm to enter a new market, thus buying an established firm in the new product/market segment is usually favored. It is also preferable to buy when the product/market is unrelated to the firm's core business, since there is little potential in sharing resources or skills internally. On the other hand, building within—internal venturing—is favored when the desired product/market is in the embryonic or growth stage of its life cycle with low barriers to entry or when the new product has a strategic fit with the firm's core business. Internal venturing is riskier and more time-consuming than acquiring a firm already established in the new market segment. An estimated 88 percent of innovations never achieve adequate returns when accounting for the capital invested in development and commercialization (Hitt, Ireland, and Hoskisson 2009).

Mark Zuckerberg, founder and CEO of Facebook, believes in acquiring entrepreneurial firms that bring their talented people with them rather than trying to build talent within the firm for each new strategic venture. This philosophy is reflected in Facebook's recent acquisition of the popular photo-sharing app, Instagram, a two-year-old start-up at the time of acquisition. Zuckerberg paid US$1 billion in cash and stock for Instagram instead of risking the time and resources involved in developing Facebook's own photo-sharing capability internally. The acquisition of Instagram, one of the most widely downloaded apps for smartphones, provided Facebook with an established winner in the emerging segment of photo-sharing (Carlson 2012). Of course, many other factors influence strategic choice besides costs and market factors, such as intuition, judgment, values, and other qualitative factors.

Mergers and Acquisitions

Mergers and acquisitions (M&A) are a popular vehicle for expanding a firm's scope once the decision has been made to buy expanded economic activity in external markets. The scope of the economic activity may be expanded vertically across the firm's value chain, horizontally within the firm's industry, or into new products and markets through diversification strategies. Although the terms "merger" and "acquisition" are often used interchangeably, they are distinctly different concepts. When one company purchases another company's assets, either through a stock purchase, cash, or the issuance of debt, and clearly establishes itself as the new owner, the purchase is called an **acquisition**. From a legal point of view, the target company ceases to exist, the buyer "swallows" the business, and the buyer's stock continues to be traded. On the other hand, in the pure sense of the term, a **merger** happens when two firms, often of about the same size, agree to go forward as a single new company rather than remain separately owned and operated. This kind of action is more precisely referred to as a "merger of equals." Both companies' stocks are surrendered and new company stock is issued in its place. For example, both Daimler-Benz and Chrysler ceased to exist when the two firms merged, and a new company, DaimlerChrysler, was created (Hitt, Ireland, and Hoskisson 2009).

In practice, however, actual mergers of equals do not happen very often.

As was the case in the DaimlerChrysler merger, Daimler-Benz was clearly the dominant party, but Chrysler's managers would not let the business deal be completed unless it was termed a merger. Typically, as part of the deal's terms, the acquiring firm will simply allow the acquired firm to proclaim that the action is a merger of equals, even if it is technically an acquisition. Being bought out often carries negative connotations. Therefore, by describing the deal as a merger, top managers try to make the acquisition more palatable to stakeholders (Hitt, Ireland, and Hoskisson 2009).

During the 1970s and 1980s, corporate takeovers became a prominent feature of the American business landscape. The **takeover** strategy is a specialized acquisition strategy that is hostile in nature since the target firm does not solicit the acquiring firm's bid. A **hostile takeover** usually involves a **tender offer**—a public offer for a substantial percentage of the target firm's stock at a specific price, usually at a substantial premium over the prevailing market price, good for a limited period of time. Unlike a merger, which requires the approval of the target firm's board of directors as well as voting approval of the stockholders, a tender offer can provide voting control to the bidding firm without the approval of the target's management and directors. Securities and Exchange Commission laws require any corporation or individual acquiring 5 percent of a company to disclose information to the SEC, the target company, and the exchange (Dess, Lumpkin, and Eisner 2008).

In 2010, Kraft Foods bought its UK competitor, Cadbury PLC, for approximately US$20 billion in a hostile takeover. Unlike Kraft, a diversified food company, Cadbury was narrowly focused on candy and gum and was highly attractive to Kraft because of its market presence in the rapidly growing economies of Latin America, India, and Thailand. In the United States the acquisition opened up access to convenience stores, a new distribution channel for Kraft. Therefore, Kraft successfully used a hostile takeover strategy to expand through acquiring access to new markets and new distribution channels (Rothaermel 2013).

However, in some cases strategic managers resist takeovers because they believe that the target firm has hidden value, they believe resistance may increase the offer price, or they want to retain their positions. If the shareholders accept the offer to sell, then the top managers of the target firm will either lose their jobs or will be stripped of their power, so there are often incentives for **antitakeover tactics** at the corporate level to protect incumbent managers. Three common antitakeover tactics are greenmail, poison pill, and golden parachutes. **Greenmail** is an offer to buy back the acquiring firm's stock at a price higher than it paid for it, but the offer is not extended to other shareholders. **Poison pills** (shareholder rights provisions) give shareholders certain rights in the event of a hostile takeover. **Golden parachutes**, typically part of the CEOs compensation package, specify a significant severance package in the event of a hostile takeover, which protects executives' income in the face of job loss. When a firm puts antitakeover tactics in place, shareholders and other stakeholders should be aware that in many cases the motives may reflect more concern for top management interests than for shareholder interests, thus raising some potentially serious ethical issues (Dess, Lumpkin, and Eisner 2008).

Internal Venturing and Strategic Intrapreneurship

After considering transaction costs and other market factors, strategic managers may decide that it will be more effective to expand within the boundaries of the organization by internal venturing or engaging in **strategic intrapreneurship** within the firm (Pinchot 1986). The pursuit of new venture opportunities within a firm helps to create new sources of competitive advantage in new market space, thus renewing the firm's value propositions. The key to successful strategic intrapreneurship is to build the organizational capabilities necessary to generate the entrepreneurial spirit throughout the firm. Such capabilities arise from an organizational culture that allows for open questioning of fundamental values and assumptions and through continuously asking, "what can be?" This requires that top managers provide the leadership, the resources, the structures, and the organizational processes necessary for a culture that celebrates taking risks and exploring new market spaces. The corporate venture capital investments, discussed above, are vehicles that can enhance a firm's ability to stimulate innovation and intrapreneurship.

Via internal venturing, a firm can capture all the value generated by its own innovative activities. Developing stakeholder engagement processes and capabilities facilitates dialogue between the firm and its stakeholders within its target markets. Dialogue with stakeholders enhances the ability of organizations to discover and evaluate innovative opportunities to meet specific market needs. Alliance strategies with stakeholders are common in internal venturing where learning from partners enables innovative, out-of-the-box thinking that enhances the innovation process. Learning from consumers, suppliers, and other stakeholders has led to sustainable innovations such as Tide Coldwater and Starbucks recyclable coffee cups.

Building inclusive business ecosystems with multiple partners using high levels of alliance maintenance capabilities creates the environment for developing sustainable solutions to meet the needs of the world's growing population. Internal venturing is best able to create triple-bottom-line value when the capabilities are developed that allow the processes to move quickly from initial opportunity recognition to market introduction and competitive positioning (Gundry and Kickul 2007). GE's strategy of reverse innovation, as previously discussed, has been effective in utilizing stakeholder engagement processes in the development of health-care equipment with lower price points to address the health-care needs of low-income consumers in all markets.

Retrenchment and Restructuring Strategies

The corporate **retrenchment** or **restructuring strategy** takes its name from military warfare. When an army's initial trench line gets threatened, it will pull back and establish a secondary trench line, sacrificing ground in order to save lives and continue the fight. The same principle holds true for corporate retrenchment, with struggling corporations temporarily retreating to regroup for a later push back into markets. During corporate retrenchment, the corporation reduces the scope of its portfolio of activities or changes its financial structure. Such a reduction in scope may mean selling or divesting assets, discontinuing unsuccessful product lines, dismissing employees, restructuring debt, declaring bankruptcy, or even liquidating the firm. Corporate restructuring continues to be a global trend, and the strategic alternatives that reduce the boundaries of the firm may take on various forms.

Turnaround Strategies

A **turnaround** strategy is a strategic response by struggling firms to corporate decline indicated by conditions such as negative cash flow, declining profits, loss in market share, uncompetitive products or services, and ineffective strategic management. A turnaround strategy involves reversing these negative trends in firm performance by using an intentional proactive strategy. The inability of strategic managers to adapt their firms to external conditions, such as increased environmental turbulence, global competition, unfavorable economic cycles, and increased stakeholder demands, may result in the board of directors bringing in new strategic managers to lead the turnaround. This is often the first step in a turnaround strategy, as was the case when Apple brought back Steve Jobs to reinvent the company in light of its declining market share and profitability.

Downsizing is the immediate response to declining margins, market share, and cash flow. It is a strategy used to put a tourniquet around the firm's outflow of cash. This is often done by reducing costs through reducing the number of employees and/or the number of operating units (Hitt, Ireland, and Hoskisson 2009). Other turnaround strategies include divesting unproductive assets (discussed below) and improving operational efficiency. After dealing with a firm's initial cash-flow crisis, strategic managers will need to refocus the turnaround strategy onto the future by defining the firm's strategic vision for recovery and future profitability.

Divestment Strategies

Divestment involves a firm's selling or spinning off one or more of the businesses from its corporate portfolio in order to improve the market value of the firm's stock, to reduce debt, to increase cash, or to prune/refocus the firm's portfolio. A **spin-off** refers to separating a SBU from the corporate portfolio by creating an independent business that takes assets from the parent company and its shareholders; the shareholders receive equivalent shares in the new company as compensation for their loss of equity in the original stock. Sometimes referred to as **downscoping**, this strategy is used to refocus the firm around its core business by eliminating unrelated SBUs (Hitt, Ireland, and Hoskisson 2009). It is hoped that the influx of cash will secure a better future for the overall corporate portfolio.

Essentially, the purpose of divestment is to cut away the deadwood so the rest of the corporate tree can grow, which is exactly what Daimler AG did when it divested Chrysler after investing US$32 billion to acquire it. The merger failed primarily due to labor and health-care legacy cost differences between the partners, with the difference ranging from an average $1,500 per vehicle for Chrysler to an average $250 for Daimler. Daimler sold Chrysler to a private equity firm and changed its name to Daimler AG, where the only benefit of the sale for Daimler was the unloading of US$18 billion in pension and health-care liabilities (Hitt, Ireland, and Hoskisson 2009).

A **leveraged buyout (LBO)** is a restructuring strategy in which a party buys the assets of the firm and takes the firm private; the company's stock is no longer publicly traded. LBOs may be used to correct managerial mistakes, to restructure distressed assets, to act as an antitakeover defense, or to strategically reposition the firm. Significant amounts of high-risk debt are typically incurred to finance the buyout, leaving the firm extremely leveraged. To support debt payments, the new owner usually has to immediately sell off assets. **Private equity firms**, such as Kolberg, Kravis, and Roberts (KKR), facilitate the process of taking companies private. Usually, LBOs are used to restructure the firm so that it can be sold at a profit within five to eight years (Hitt, Ireland, and Hoskisson 2009).

The LBO of Harley-Davidson, the iconic motorcycle manufacturer, in 1981 is considered one of the most successful in history. At the time, Harley-Davidson was an SBU of AMF Corporation, and with an infusion of private equity, 13 executives bought the company for US$81.5 million. In five years, the new owners competitively repositioned Harley-Davidson within the market and relisted the stock as a public offering, known as a **reverse LBO**. The share price was 40 times higher than the price paid by the investors who took the firm private (Harley-Davidson Corporation 2012).

Reorganizational Bankruptcy

Reorganizational bankruptcy (Chapter 11 bankruptcy) also serves as a form of corporate retrenchment. During a **reorganizational bankruptcy**, creditors agree to give the firm time to reorganize, allowing the firm to restructure its debt obligations in order to increase cash flow. This type of bankruptcy buys the corporation time, providing a chance to engineer a new strategy to reclaim financial success. Corporations consider reorganizational bankruptcy only after divestment and other forms of turnaround have failed.

Eastman Kodak has utilized numerous retrenchment strategies over the past two decades. Kodak, which invented the digital camera nearly 40 years ago, failed to leverage this critical innovation because executives feared it would kill their cash-generating film business. Kodak executives were blinded by previous success and could not fathom a world without traditional film, so they felt little incentive to deviate from that strategy. This lack of adaptation to the new digital technology resulted in Kodak's being faced with a turnaround situation of declining sales, margins, and market share.

In 1994 George Fisher, former CEO of Motorola, was brought in to re-invent Kodak and to lead it in a turnaround strategy. Faced with a bloated cost structure, confused marketing, and a fierce competitor in Fuji, Fisher continued the downsizing strategy of his successor, cutting manufacturing costs and slashing administrative costs (which were 27 percent of sales at the time). This began a tough new era of employee layoffs for Kodak. Further, the cost-restructuring strategies implemented by the firm were not enough to stem the outflow of cash, so Fisher divested US$8.9 billion of noncore assets, including the spinning off of Eastman Chemical Company in 1994 (Smith and Symonds 1997).

Unable to reinvent Kodak, Fisher was replaced by Daniel Carp in 2000. Under his leadership Kodak finally made its move into the digital camera market. Unfortunately, Carp did not anticipate how quickly digital cameras would be commoditized by cell phones, smartphones, and tablets. In response, the Kodak board replaced Carp as CEO in 2005 with Antonio Perez, who began another turnaround strategy. He shifted Kodak's production activities from manufacturing everything in-house to strategically outsourcing its manufacturing, thus eliminating 27,000 jobs, and he refocused the strategy to reposition Kodak in the printing market. Despite these efforts as well as the turnaround and divestment strategies implemented by the three CEOs, Kodak could not stave off bankruptcy. On January 19, 2012, Kodak filed for Chapter 11 bankruptcy protection and obtained a US$950 million, 18-month line of credit from Citigroup to enable it to continue operations. Under the terms of its bankruptcy, Kodak was given a deadline to produce a reorganization plan that will reposition Kodak in the market so that it can capitalize on its iconic brand name (*Economist* 2012).

Liquidation Bankruptcy

No corporation wants to face liquidation. The most drastic form of corporate retrenchment, **liquidation bankruptcy** (Chapter 7 bankruptcy), involves selling all the assets and closing the entire corporation to recover whatever funds remain to pay creditors. The firm ceases to exist, with all employees fired and all products and services discontinued. Corporate strategists see liquidation bankruptcy as a last resort and will do anything possible to try to avoid taking that final step.

Unable to sell the business or restructure its debt, Circuit City fell victim to the financial crisis of 2007, and in 2009 declared the exit strategy of last resort, liquidation bankruptcy. Circuit City's failed turnaround efforts included replacing higher-paid commission-based employees with salaried employees, opening smaller concept stores, seeking potential buyers, changing management, and closing stores. After all of these turnaround efforts failed, Circuit City liquidated its inventory, shut down its remaining 567 U.S. stores, and laid off 34,000 employees (Felberbaum and Tong 2009).

SSM Corporate Portfolio

As we discussed in Chapter 3, taking a coevolutionary view of the world's developed, developing, and undeveloped markets within a sustainability-based business ecosystem structure is an effective approach for creating an SSM corporate portfolio that extends an organization's planning horizons to include future generations. Within this context, the SSM corporate portfolio takes a **whole-pyramid** approach (as Chapter 5 discusses), where corporate strategic decisions (the decisions of scope) are made within the context of addressing the unique needs to create triple-bottom-line performance in all three types of markets in the global economic pyramid—developed, developing, and undeveloped (Jenkins and Ishikawa 2010) (see Figure 5.5). The specific content of these strategies varies according to top management commitment, the unique needs of the market segment, and the firm's position within its business ecosystem. These strategies were discussed in the previous chapter and are demonstrated in the portfolio of SSM competitive strategies (Figure 5.4).

The real value of focusing an organization's SSM portfolio on the whole pyramid lies in the fact that such a portfolio will by definition reflect a deep organizational commitment to making a positive contribution to a sustainable world. In such a portfolio a firm's vision, mission, goals, strategies, capabilities, structures, and processes will all in some way embody a commitment to serving the needs of the greater society and ecosystem for generations to come. Thus, establishing a whole-pyramid perspective can provide an organization and its members with a sense of meaning and higher purpose that eclipses the firm's economic success. The firm is not just earning a profit, it is doing so in ways that benefit fellow humans and nature now and in the future. Therefore, infusing a commitment to the whole pyramid in an organization's SSM portfolio provides a deep foundation for the organization's continuous transformation to a more sustainable entity.

The **purpose** of the SSM corporate portfolio is to build capabilities that enhance the firm's ability to effectively manage its configuration of multimarket strategies so that triple-bottom-line value is created across the whole pyramid. An SSM corporate portfolio provides a framework that allows strategic managers to continually examine and, if necessary, change organizational values, assumptions, and strategies in light of eco- and socio-effectiveness. Doing this requires firms to move beyond strategies for eco- and socio-efficiency that allow them to readily calculate the direct economic, social, and ecological costs and benefits of their strategies. Shifting to socio- and eco-effectiveness strategies requires taking a long-term intergenerational perspective that can blur these direct links between actions and outcomes. Thus, an SSM corporate, whole-pyramid portfolio requires developing corporate level capabilities that allow the firm to sustain itself by making positive long-term contributions to the planet and its people by becoming an agent of social change.

Taking a whole-pyramid approach at the corporate level requires **balancing** cash flow among the firm's various lines of SBUs. This may mean using the cash flow from economically successful business lines to fund businesses created to address the opportunities arising from the expanded social and ecological scope of the portfolio. Thus, as Figure 5.5 demonstrates, taking a whole-pyramid perspective may lead firms to use profits from core businesses in developed markets to pursue new market opportunities in developing and undeveloped markets (Hart 2005). Research in the telecommunications industry conducted by the Harvard Kennedy School found that by conceptualizing the corporate portfolio as a whole pyramid, companies were able to balance their portfolios over time to create positive triple-bottom-line performance. These firms entered developed markets at the top of the pyramid to establish revenue streams and recoup infrastructure investments. This put them in a financial position to provide products and distribution channels for lower-income developing and undeveloped markets with lower average returns per customer. Thus, the whole-pyramid portfolio approach increased these firms' capabilities to meet consumer needs in their developed, developing, and undeveloped markets (Jenkins and Ishikawa 2010).

To fulfill the purpose of the SSM portfolio, strategic managers will need to establish **inclusive business ecosystems** of multisector stakeholder partners that expand the **scope** of the firm's operations. The decisions in terms of who is included in the value chain (suppliers, distributors, franchisees, retailers, and/or customers) determine the degree of inclusiveness of the business ecosystem. Inclusive business ecosystems are structured to create value throughout the whole pyramid. In order to create a whole-pyramid portfolio, the scope of operations must expand to include the poor as a segment within a much broader overall portfolio, where both local and global partnerships create triple-bottom-line performance across the entire portfolio (Gradl and Jenkins 2011). This entails implementing a top-down initiative in which the ecosystem leader creates a platform that supports economies of scope and helps to develop ecosystem niche strategies that capture the bottom-up, entrepreneurial learning from local partnerships that enable the ecosystem to develop sustainable solutions to meet consumer needs (Hammond 2011).

Multisector stakeholder ecosystems are excellent vehicles for establishing effective dialogue that provides for all voices to be heard and for collective stakeholder wisdom to be tapped. These networks provide a neutral space for safe discussion and partnering in order to solve global issues ranging from economic opportunity to climate change to poverty. Thus, structuring the ecosystem with a high degree of stakeholder inclusiveness allows strategic managers to integrate the complex issues of how to care for future generations, how to care for their organizations, and how to care for the Earth.

In 2009, Coca-Cola structured an inclusive business ecosystem based on its newly developed sustainability platform. The vision underlying this platform is "to create a positive difference in the world" (Coca-Cola Company 2011, 4). The platform establishes specific goals in key areas such as sustainable packaging, healthy living, water stewardship, and climate protection. Progress is measured and reported based on the firm's triple-bottom-line performance across the whole value chain. Coca-Cola's sustainability platform underlies the design of its whole-pyramid portfolio of strategies targeted toward developed, undeveloped, and developing markets. Being the world's most recognized brand and largest nonalcoholic beverage company, with a portfolio of over 300 beverage brands and more than 3,300 different products, Coca-Cola has the resources to move toward a sustainability-balanced portfolio. The firm is leveraging its portfolio so cash generated from businesses in developed and developing markets can be invested in socio- and eco-effective strategies targeted toward undeveloped markets (Coca-Cola Company 2011).

For example, Coke has established a socio-effective strategy targeting poverty reduction in Zambia and El Salvador. Both countries are major sugar producers, and sugar is Coke's primary agricultural ingredient. Thus, Zambia and El Salvador are integral players in Coke's supply chain. Both countries are undeveloped markets with high poverty levels. Coke has partnered with its largest bottler, SABMiller, and the highly respected NGO Oxfam America, to engage in dialogue with poor communities in Zambia and El Salvador to develop strategies for poverty reduction. This process encourages full visibility and inclusion of Coke's value chain, from sugar growers to sugar producers to bottlers to local customers (Coca-Cola Company 2011).

Ecosystem members have engaged the Salvadoran government, the Salvadoran Sugar Association, and other stakeholders on ending child labor in sugarcane harvesting. Although the ecosystem value chains support thousands of jobs, these are characterized by seasonal availability, low wages, and no benefits. Thus, Coca-Cola hires third-party audit firms and NGOs to assess partner workplaces to ensure that they uphold the company's workplace and environmental standards. The distribution and sale of Coco-Cola products support vital self-employment opportunities, providing income these workers urgently need. Using strategies focused on building human, economic, and social capital, the Coca-Cola business ecosystem provides technical assistance and credit programs to build triple-bottom-line capacity at strategic points in the value chain (Coca-Cola Company 2011).

SSM Capabilities

Inclusive business ecosystems require corporate capabilities that enable strategic managers to manage the complexity of relationships arising from alliances with partners within the whole pyramid. We envision an SSM corporate portfolio as a set of integrative processes that build the SSM capabilities needed to create an organizational culture that supports the generative, entrepreneurial learning, the dialogue, and the transformational change processes required for SSM. These processes provide the vehicles for strategic managers to question the underlying assumptions of their corporate portfolios, to develop innovative approaches for sustainable product and service introductions, and to create economic opportunity through building human and social capital across their value chain activities. The SSM portfolio reflects a strong strategic commitment to the ecosystem leader's sustainability vision based on eco- and socio-effectiveness, and it reflects a strong strategic commitment to meaningful innovation and multimarket, stakeholder partnerships with other business ecosystem members. Thus, an SSM corporate portfolio within a business ecosystem structure can provide organizations with multiple synergistic avenues for contributing to global sustainability that are not available to organizations operating independently of one another.

Recall from Chapter 1 that corporations wishing to develop SSM strategic portfolios must begin by viewing themselves as parts of a living system (see Figure 1.2). This mental model provides the appropriate foundation for SSM thinking and decision making. It provides strategic managers with a framework that allows them to view their employees, customers, shareholders, communities, and other stakeholders as human capital with intrinsic as well as instrumental worth, and it allows them to view their relationships with ecosystem members and communities as valuable, rare, and nonimitable. Building SSM capabilities at the corporate level on this framework serves to legitimize an organization's pursuit of higher-purpose goals that tie the economic success of their organizations to the improved social and ecological health of the planet. Thus, within this framework strategic managers are better able to integrate the complex issues of sustainability into their strategic decision-making processes. Creating SSM capabilities at the corporate level allows strategic managers to expand the scope, purpose, and balance of their portfolios.

Collaboration and dialogue with multiple partners within an inclusive business ecosystem create entrepreneurial learning that can lead to the development of disruptive technologies. As discussed in Chapter 1, these are innovative technologies that create dramatic technological shifts that can transform entire industries, economies, societies, and/or ecosystems, leading to **creative destruction**, which is the economic disequilibrium caused by disruptive technologies (Schumpeter 1950). When these technologies appear, they create new entrepreneurial opportunities for business ecosystem members. Strategies based on creative destruction hold the promise of providing both socio- and eco-effective means for developing products and services that can make positive contributions to economic, social, and natural capital across the firm's value chain (Hart and Milstein 1999; Holliday, Schmidheiny, and Watts 2002). Building SSM capabilities of generative entrepreneurial learning, collaboration, and dialogue can create a culture that will facilitate this type of transformational change, creating the potential to bring to development and commercialization "green leap" technologies aimed at "leapfrogging today's unsustainable practices" (Hart 2011, 81).

Cell phone and satellite technologies are examples of disruptive technologies. They have changed the global telecommunications industry, and they now provide nations that lack the resources to build expensive landline-based telecommunications systems with the opportunity to build much less-expensive cell- and satellite-based networks that connect them with the entire globe. Ecologically, disruptive clean-energy and zero-pollution technologies are critical for achieving global sustainability. Thus, fostering a climate of disruptive change at the corporate level creates SSM capabilities that support transformational change that may lead to SSM portfolio opportunities now and in the foreseeable future (Hart 2008).

Building SSM Capabilities Through Alliance Management

As previously discussed, within the whole-pyramid portfolio approach, strategic intent can vary according to the unique needs of markets, thus requiring alliances with multisector stakeholder partners based on a vision of sustainability. Research indicates that successful alliances have high levels of **alliance management capability** at the corporate level—the ability to manage the configuration of the portfolio of alliances to achieve a shared vision (Kale and Singh 2009). Given the complexity of building alliances with multisector stakeholder partners that are required to build sustainability-based, whole-pyramid portfolios, alliance management capability is an essential component of SSM capabilities.

Alliance management capability requires the research and selection of alliance partners that are compatible and share a common vision. Also, careful design of the appropriate governance mechanisms that fit the alliance partners' needs is essential for successful alliance management. As discussed earlier in this chapter, strategic managers have three options of alliance governance mechanisms: nonequity contractual agreements, equity alliances, and joint venture strategies. The choice of governance mechanism defines the level of investment and the degree of formalization of the partners' relationships, so it must be carefully designed and selected.

Once the choice is made, the business ecosystem leader must begin to build interorganizational trust among alliance partners in the postformation alliance stage (Rothaermel 2013; Zaheer, McEvily, and Perrone 1998). In effective postformation alliance management, trust among the ecosystem members will undergird the inclusive ecosystem's creative and innovative core, and it will give the ecosystem members the ability to build and maintain the relationships that constitute the social capital of the ecosystem. These trust-based interorganizational relationships are important sources of competitive advantage for the alliance by reducing transaction costs and conflicts (Dyer and Singh 1998; Luo 2002). Traditional alliances that have expanded their scope to include partnering with citizen sector organizations (CSOs) and individuals who share a common vision of "doing well by doing good" have increased in popularity. Kale and Singh (2009) refer to these as a new class of alliance strategies with increased managerial complexity.

The managerial complexity increases as the business ecosystem becomes more inclusive, making it more difficult to create the trust necessary for effective alliance management capability. Many times, difficulty in the management of alliances arises because partners vary significantly in terms of profit-seeking objectives, skills, resources, and organizational culture. Incentive problems and the risk of self-serving behavior from opportunism arise from these differences in orientation and needs among ecosystem members may prevent alliance partners from fully participating in the ecosystem. Incentive problems result when ecosystem members lack trust due to the absence of credible information and effective governance mechanisms, thus discouraging them from entering what may have been mutually beneficial transactions. Ecosystem members will not put their assets at risk unless they can trust others to hold up their ends of the bargain.

Given that ecosystem members need to share resources and experience to create common goods, without trust the prospect that others will free ride discourages them from contributing their share (Gradl and Jenkins 2011). Therefore, alliance management capability requires developing a high level of trust and creating structures appropriate for resolving the resource and capability constraints associated with incentive problems. Such trust helps ensure the survival of the ecosystem and the achievement of the vision by facilitating decision making and creating reputational capital (Rothaermel 2013).

Consider the complexity and the alliance management capability required in such alliances as the Sustainable Food Lab, a multisector, stakeholder inclusive ecosystem started by Unilever and its partners Oxfam and the Kellogg Foundation. The ecosystem is based on a shared vision of bringing sustainability to the global food system by accelerating the shift of sustainable food from niche to mainstream. It is an alliance of businesses, nonprofit, and public organizations working together to promote sustainable agriculture, distribution, and consumption. The Sustainable Food Lab facilitates market-based solutions to key issues such as climate, soil, poverty, and water that are necessary for a healthy and sustainable food system to feed a growing world population. The Sustainable Food Lab uses collaborative learning to incubate innovation at every stage along the supply chain from producing to distributing and selling food (Sustainable Food Laboratory 2012). Thus, by building an inclusive ecosystem, the partners are able to "undertake radical changes in their established ways of operating, including creating alternative products, processes, and business models" (Senge 2007, 26).

Accountability alliances are additional types of complex, multistakeholder, strategic networks. These industry-led coalitions focus on improving social and/ or environmental accountability where there are market failures or governance gaps. For example, the Alliance for a Healthier Generation in the United States brought together the American Heart Association, the Clinton Foundation, Coca-Cola, PepsiCo, and Cadbury Schweppes with the goal to reduce the prevalence of childhood obesity by 2015, and to empower kids nationwide to make healthy lifestyle choices (Alliance for a Healthier Generation 2012).

A sustainability-based inclusive business ecosystem can implement three complementary strategies to achieve high levels of alliance management capability: strategies for developing human and social capital; strategies for building institutional capacity within the ecosystem; and strategies for managing the "rules of the game" (Jenkins 2007, 4). These strategies are complementary and reinforcing. For example, providing training and assistance for entrepreneurs and microbusinesses in the value chain, as Coca-Cola did, builds human capital while increasing the economic development impact of a local procurement program (an inclusive ecosystem). By expanding the pool and capacity of entrepreneurs who can qualify for it, this leads to a healthier community (social and economic capital) (Jenkins 2007). The role of the ecosystem leader is to effectively manage this alliance of multisector stakeholders that share the vision of a more sustainable world for future generations.

The whole-pyramid approach increases the complexity of managing the SSM corporate portfolio of multisector stakeholder alliances, creating the need for greater alliance management capability. Effective alliance management requires an expansion of the management functions of the business ecosystem leader to include configuring the whole-pyramid portfolio to create a set of complete, complementary, and noncompetitive alliances, along with creating knowledge-sharing routines that lead to dialogue, entrepreneurial learning, and innovation (Kale and Singh 2009). Using these processes, the ecosystem leader can embed in the business ecosystem capabilities necessary for earning profits in ways that contribute to a higher quality of life for current and future generations. Among other things, such capabilities ingrain higher levels of meaning and purpose into the core of an inclusive business ecosystem, and they empower the creation of structures that foster and maintain high levels of trust among ecosystem members. This enhances the corporate SSM capability to create shared value by balancing multisector alliances according to the unique needs of the various markets and stakeholders within the whole pyramid, as Figure 6.2 depicts.

Achieving Balance in the SSM Corporate Portfolio

As discussed earlier, balancing cash flow among the firm's various lines of SBUs is a crucial task of corporate strategy, and in the SSM portfolio this may mean using the cash from economically successful business lines to fund businesses created to address the opportunities arising from the expanded

Figure 6.2   **Whole-Pyramid Portfolio**

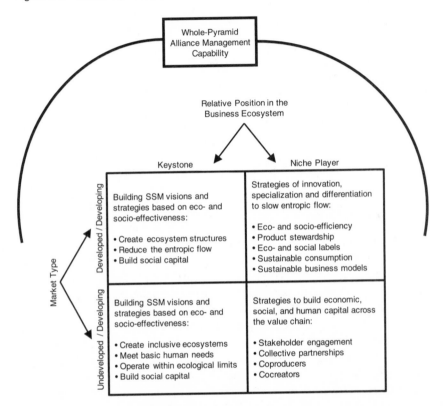

social and ecological scope of the whole-pyramid portfolio. Thus, some firms may choose to use profits from core businesses in developed markets to pursue new market opportunities in developing and undeveloped markets (Hart 2005). However, other firms may choose to integrate sustainability-advantaged products throughout their portfolio rather than having discrete SBUs focusing on eco- and socio-effectiveness. As the Case Vignette 6 discusses, Jim Rogers at Eastman Chemical utilizes this integrative portfolio management strategy in crafting his portfolio toward his vision of creating a high performing, specialty chemicals company focused on providing sustainable solutions to its customers. Regardless of the strategic approach taken in constructing the SSM corporate portfolio, it is crucial for strategic managers to effectively manage and balance the firm's cash flow.

A traditional tool that is useful in analyzing the cash-generation and cash-use relationships among the SBUs in a corporate portfolio is the **Boston Consulting Group (BCG)** growth share matrix, originally developed in 1968

Figure 6.3 **BCG Growth Share Matrix**

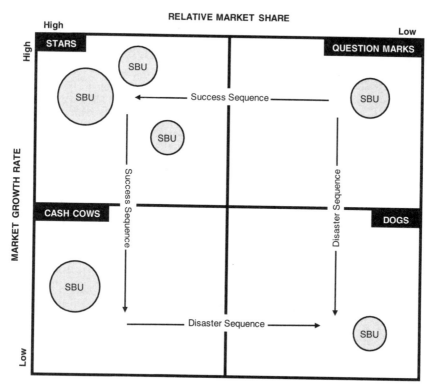

(Figure 6.3). In the matrix, corporate SBUs are represented graphically in terms of their relative market share (horizontal axis) and their relative market growth rate (vertical axis). SBUs are plotted into four categories: stars, cash cows, dogs, and question marks. The use of cash is appropriate because it is typically proportional to the rate of growth of SBUs, and the generation of cash is a function of market share because of the experience-curve effect (Henderson 1973).

Stars (in the upper-left quadrant) hold a high market share in a fast-growing market. They grow rapidly, so they use large amounts of cash. However, since they are market leaders, they also generate large amounts of cash. Stars normally generate a balance in terms of net cash flow. Over time the industry growth rate of stars slows. If they hold their market share during this slower growth period, they will become cash cows (a success sequence), but if they fail to hold market share, they become dogs (a disaster sequence). **Cash cows** (in the lower-left quadrant) compete in a low-growth market, but hold a considerable market share. Since growth is slow, cash use is low. However, market share is high and therefore comparative cash generation is also high. Cash cows generate more cash than what they need to hold and maintain their competitive position, and their excess cash is often used to assist other SBUs to grow, to pay dividends, to pay the interest on debt, or to cover the corporate overhead. Care must be taken, however, to invest enough to hold and maintain market share, or the cash cow may turn into a dog, a disaster. **Dogs** (in the lower-right quadrant) hold a small market share in a low-growth market. Dogs often report a profit even though they are net cash users, but they are essentially worthless cash traps that should either be divested or harvested. **Question marks** (located in the upper-right quadrant) are the real cash traps and the real gambles. Their cash needs are greatest because of their high growth potential. Yet their cash generation is very low because their market share is low. Strategic managers invest in question marks in hopes of increasing market share and becoming a star and eventually a cash cow when market growth slows (a success sequence). However, if the market growth rate slows, and question marks have not increased their market share, they can easily become dogs, a disaster sequence (Henderson 1973).

Though it has its limitations and should never be relied on as the sole source of data in corporate strategic decision making (Henderson 1973), the BCG matrix is a well-established framework for analyzing the strategic positions and strategic options among the SBUs in a corporate portfolio, especially as it relates to cash flow and resource allocation. We suggest that the value of the BCG matrix can be extended to the analysis of the cash-generation, cash-use relationships among the partners in a whole-pyramid SSM portfolio. Doing so would generate important data for building a picture of the strategic relationships among the for-profit and not-for-profit partners in an inclusive business ecosystem.

The SSM Portfolio and Social Change

Inclusive business ecosystems that combine the resources and efforts of business, government, and civil society provide alliances that can affect transformational change toward sustainability across the globe. The essence of the SSM corporate level portfolio is to develop spiritual-capability-based processes that enable firms to become agents of transformational social change (Bies et al. 2007). We believe that business organizations implementing an SSM, whole-pyramid portfolio, embedded in an inclusive business ecosystem that is built upon the spiritually based capabilities of dialogue and entrepreneurial learning are the keys to the transformational change necessary to move toward a more sustainable world. Dunphy, Griffiths, and Benn (2007, 4) say,

"Corporations have contributed to the problems . . . and they must therefore be part of the answer."

If business organizations across the globe were to universally move toward a whole-pyramid SSM portfolio, this would infuse a huge force for change into the sustainability revolution. CSOs, NGOs, and other groups working hard to move the world toward sustainability would be joined in the movement by millions of business organizations seeking ways to make social and environmental responsibility more and more a part of doing business. The addition of these organizations would create the critical mass of people and organizations across the planet necessary to create a more sustainable world. Also, it would infuse into the movement desperately needed financial resources critical for turning the good ideas of creative people into actions that lead to real change. That is why we say that the time is now for business organizations to expand their responsibilities and strategies beyond the economic to include the social and ecological dimensions. If the assessments of Hawken (2007), Edwards (2005), Speth (2008), and others are correct, then this is the ideal time for organizations to contribute to a planet that is fiscally, socially, and ecologically welcoming for all human beings now and in the future.

Chapter Summary

Corporate strategy is the overall plan for a diversified organization. It focuses on managing the mix, scope, and emphasis of a firm's strategic business units (SBUs), exploiting the synergies among them and deploying capital to them in order to achieve advantages over competitors. The choice of the appropriate scope for a firm's operations is a critical challenge in corporate strategy. Corporate strategic options designed to expand the firm's scope include growing within a single industry, horizontally integrating, vertically integrating, diversifying the product/market mix, and/or collaborating with partners in alliance strategies.

Once the expanded boundaries of the firm have been envisioned, strategic managers must then decide how to organize the expanded economic activity, deciding which activities should be done in-house versus which activities should be bought in the external market. This build-or-buy option is a strategic decision that is influenced by many factors. Mergers and acquisitions are methods of expanding via the external market, and internal venturing/intrapreneurship is a means for encouraging expansion in-house.

Of course sometimes retrenchment rather than expansion is called for. During retrenchment a corporation is faced with reducing the scope of its portfolio and/or changing its financial structure. This may mean selling or divesting assets, discontinuing unsuccessful product lines, dismissing employees, restructuring debt, declaring reorganizational bankruptcy, or even declaring liquidation bankruptcy. Corporate restructuring continues to be a global trend, and it can take on various forms, including takeovers, turnarounds, divestments, leveraged buyouts, and bankruptcies.

We advocate a whole-pyramid approach to sustainable strategic management in this chapter. In this approach, corporate strategic decisions are structured to address the unique sustainability needs in all three coevolutionary markets in the global economic pyramid—developed, developing, and undeveloped. Establishing a whole-pyramid perspective can provide an organization with a sense of higher purpose that eclipses the firm's economic success. The firm is not just earning a profit; it is doing so in ways that benefit fellow humans and nature. Therefore, a whole-pyramid-focused SSM portfolio provides a solid foundation for the organization's sustainability journey. Thus, building SSM capabilities at the corporate level with the whole-pyramid framework serves to legitimize an organization's pursuit of higher-purpose goals that tie its economic success to the improved social and ecological health of the planet.

The whole-pyramid design for business ecosystems does increase the complexity of managing an SSM corporate portfolio. This is because a whole-pyramid design increases the number and types of multisector stakeholder alliances in the ecosystem. Thus, the business ecosystem leader must configure the whole-pyramid portfolio so as to create a set of complete, complementary alliances structured for knowledge sharing, dialogue, entrepreneurial learning, and innovation. Therefore, high levels of alliance management capability are required in effectively managing an SSM corporate portfolio.

Case Vignette 6

Corporate Strategy at Eastman Chemical Company

Having served as chief financial officer of Eastman Chemical Company for the previous ten years, Jim Rogers was thoroughly familiar with the culture of the firm when he was appointed CEO during the global financial crisis in 2009. His primary role when he took over as Eastman CEO was to serve as the leading change agent for a firm that was operating at 42 percent capacity (50 percent below the industry average), had seen its stock price fall from $38 per share to $17 per share, and had a bloated management structure.

As he got started, Rogers drew on his education at the University of Virginia and Wharton to develop his strategy for the turnaround situation the firm faced. An immediate tourniquet was applied to stop the bleeding of cash and the ballooning of costs. He used one of his core values, "the highest paid are the most at risk," as the foundation for his decision to lay off none of the hourly operational workers during the retrenchment. Rogers also believed that the Eastman culture would support a pay cut as long as all employees were included, so he implemented an indefinite 5 percent across-the-board pay cut with a promise to reinstate the pay when the economic outlook improved. The pay was reinstated eight months later, and because Eastman had not laid off any operational employees during that time, it had the people it needed to effectively respond to the economic upturn, whereas its competitors that had reduced the number of hourly workers were much slower to respond.

Even though no hourly operational employees were let go, 24 percent of the officers and 16 percent of the directors were laid off, several high-level positions were reclassified at lower levels, and those who remained in executive positions had their compensation more closely aligned with Eastman's strategic intent. Rogers stressed two factors in particular in restructuring executive compensation: relative total shareholder returns and the return on capital over the cost of capital.

After dealing with the immediate crisis, Rogers then considered the strategic repositioning of Eastman's portfolio toward more growth opportunities. Case Exhibit 6.1 shows Eastman's portfolio of businesses when Rogers took over in 2009. The portfolio consisted of some underperforming acquisitions made during the previous CEO's tenure, so Rogers's first decision was to divest a couple of the favorite projects of previous management, the gasification expansion project in Beaumont, Texas, and the PET business, which had become commoditized and cyclical over time. The divestitures of these low-margin businesses totaled US$3.5 billion, which freed up the cash Rogers needed to take advantage of some opportunities to reposition Eastman's portfolio of businesses toward higher-end specialty markets.

Interestingly, even though these divestitures provided much needed cash for Eastman at a critical time, the failure of these two acquisitions initially made Rogers uncomfortable with using acquisitions as a growth strategy. However, after some time, Rogers realized that an acquisition strategy would help the firm meet its growth goals, so he initiated a series of small acquisitions in Estonia, Texas, and China that were related to his goal of becoming a top-tier specialty chemical company offering sustainable solutions to customer needs.

Rogers views the firm's portfolio of businesses as "four buckets of strategic cash," with two buckets being for growth opportunities and two for increased shareholder equity and decreased debt. He describes his corporate strategy as "a simple strategy of cash flow," although it is in

Case Exhibit 6.1   **Eastman Product Portfolio 2009**

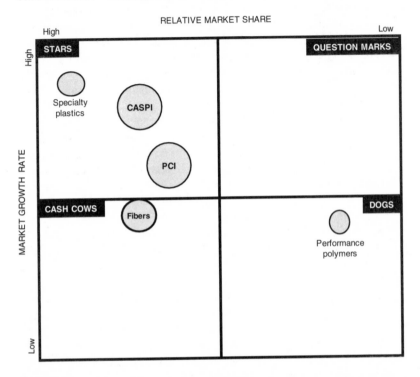

fact quite complex to execute. The strategy maximizes the cash flow from Eastman's core businesses, two-thirds of which have leading positions in their markets. Differentiation is achieved by using the revenues from the core businesses to pursue organic growth opportunities, merger and acquisition opportunities, and returns to shareholders. Eastman's allocation of resources complements its strategic intent to become a top-tier specialty chemical company offering sustainable solutions to customers. Thus, Rogers's portfolio philosophy of cash flow provides Eastman with the capability to capitalize upon opportunities to expand its portfolio of businesses when they arise.

Such an opportunity arose in 2011 in the $4.7 billion acquisition of Solutia, a specialty chemicals company with a strong strategic fit with Eastman's portfolio. According to Rogers, "The addition of Solutia will broaden our geographic reach into emerging geographies, particularly Asia Pacific, establish a powerful combined platform with extensive organic growth opportunities, and expand our portfolio of sustainable products, all of which are consistent with our growth strategy." Now the challenge is to integrate the decentralized culture of Solutia into the

Case Exhibit 6.2   **Eastman Product Portfolio 2012**

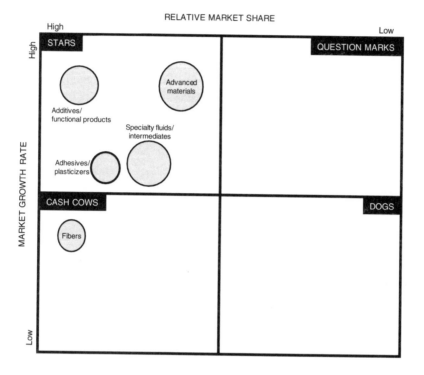

Eastman culture. For the first time, the members of Rogers's top management team are not located at corporate headquarters in Kingsport, Tennessee, but are scattered from St. Louis to the Netherlands. Rogers, however, is extremely committed to the successful integration of Solutia into the Eastman corporate portfolio because the memories of the painful divestitures he was required to make when he first became CEO are still fresh in his mind.

Thus, through the corporate strategies of turnaround, divestiture, and acquisitions, Rogers has successfully repositioned Eastman's portfolio as a top-tier specialty chemical company that provides sustainable solutions for its customers. The new portfolio of businesses has resulted in increased market value for the firm with an increase in its share price from $17 when Rogers became CEO to over $66 at the end of 2012, including a two-for-one stock split and an 11 percent increase in the quarterly dividend to shareholders. Case Exhibit 6.2 demonstrates Eastman's strategically repositioned, sustainability-advantaged portfolio of businesses since Rogers became CEO.

7

Choosing and Implementing
SSM Strategies

In this chapter, we will focus on key strategic management processes and practices required for successfully choosing and implementing sustainable strategic management (SSM) strategies in business organizations. As we begin, it is important to understand that strategic managers have **strategic choice**, which is the power and responsibility to choose the environments in which their firms compete, the strategies their firms pursue, the performance criteria their firms use, and the structures their firms establish for achieving these performance criteria (Child 1972). Lewin and Volberda (2003b, 575) say, "The strategic choice perspective assumes that organizations have the discretion and the strategic capacity to select, enact, and shape their environments." Miles and Snow (1978) explain that there are a wide variety of ways for firms to prosper in a particular environment, and it is the job of strategic managers to make the choices that will successfully align their firms' strategies, structures, and processes to take advantage of those ways to prosper.

Choosing Portfolios of SSM Strategies

Strategic choice in SSM begins with strategic managers choosing viable strategies that will allow their firms to achieve their triple-bottom-line performance goals in today's sustainability-rich business environment. Specifically, strategic managers are responsible for identifying, analyzing, and choosing among alternative SSM strategies at all three strategic levels—functional, competitive, and corporate.

Strategic Choice at the Functional Level

We discussed several functional level strategies related to improving the triple-bottom-line performance of the primary value-chain activities in operations and marketing in Chapters 4 and 5. These functional level strategies related to the primary activities of the value chain include eco-efficiency, total quality environmental management, life cycle analysis, pollution prevention, product stewardship, sustainable marketing, and so forth. In this section we will focus on some functional level, value-chain support strategies that will provide strategic managers with the triple-bottom-line data critical for SSM decision making. It is important for SSM implementation to incorporate sustainability into the scope of the firm's functional level support systems. Doing so will give strategic managers quality data they need on economic, social, and environmental performance, allowing them to make effective triple-bottom-line decisions. Below we discuss some important SSM support systems that organizations should develop for the implementation of SSM.

Enterprise Resource Planning Systems

Enterprise resource planning (ERP) systems have coevolved from customized software applications for specific functions, such as materials requirement planning, into complex standardized systems that are applicable for all organizational value-chain activities. ERP integrates internal and external management information systems across the entire value chain, embracing finance, accounting, manufacturing, sales and service, customer relationship management, supply chain management, reporting, and human resources. Its purpose is to facilitate the flow of information between all business functions inside the boundaries of the organization and to manage its connections to outside stakeholders. In addition to providing information for managerial decisions, ERP systems have been shown to enhance the intellectual and social capital creation process (Lengnick-Hall, Lengnick-Hall, and Abdinnour-Helm 2004).

As stakeholder pressures for sustainability grow, firms are turning to ERP systems to help implement and track the success of sustainability initiatives and to provide a communication channel with stakeholders. For example, carbon is now surfacing as a critical resource that companies must manage for their stakeholders. Organizations are now required to provide increasingly accurate reports on carbon footprints, carbon trades, and information to support product carbon labeling. The Environmental Protection Agency (EPA) Greenhouse Reporting Program, for example, requires manufacturers producing at least 25,000 or more metric tons of carbon emissions per year to measure and report those emissions (Moad 2010). This requires expanding the scope of the ERP systems to include carbon data.

Transparency in the ERP system is critical. The leading-edge sustainability companies communicate to their stakeholders not only their successes but also their challenges. Firms like Nike and Gap discovered this in the mid-2000s after noncompliance with labor, environmental, health, and safety standards in their supply chain was encountered (*MIT Sloan Management Review* and BCG 2011). Thus, it is critical that modern ERP systems be robust and accurate enough to meet continuously increasing stakeholder demands for expanded triple-bottom-line data.

There are, however, many hurdles to incorporating the full costs of the firm's value-creating functions into ERP systems (Wright 2009). Integrating sustainability into the firm's ERP system is more than just an add-on function. Since sustainability requires new ways of thinking, redesigning ERP systems to include sustainability performance may be expensive, intrusive, and disruptive, requiring radical as well as incremental change in the system (Sommer 2009). Although incorporating sustainability is an innovative challenge to the ERP providers, both SAP and Oracle, the market share leaders in ERP systems, have recently introduced carbon emission management tools because of increased consumer and regulatory demands (Moad 2010). Although difficult, the integration of sustainability data into ERP systems will be critical in formulating and implementing SSM. Functioning within an open-systems value chain requires generating and communicating sustainability data so managers will have relevant sustainability-based information on which to base their triple-bottom-line decisions.

Full-Cost Accounting Systems

Having accurate, timely financial data that reflect the true economic, social, and environmental costs of producing, delivering, consuming, and disposing of products is essential for effective SSM. According to Joshi and Krishnan (2010), strategic decisions requiring timely sustainability-based financial data include: regulatory compliance decisions, cost reduction decisions, risk management decisions, product mix and pricing decisions, green marketing and labeling/certification decisions, and product design decisions. Butler, Henderson, and Raiborn (2011) point out that implementing SSM requires a broad array of financial data on sustainability performance all along the value chain. They recommend what they call a "balanced scorecard" approach, which involves gathering data on 20 sustainability activities along five value-chain stages—inputs, supply, production, consumption, and disposal.

Unfortunately, traditional accounting methods are inadequate for SSM. At the heart of this inadequacy is that the discounting methods used in traditional financial accounting are virtually useless for providing the long-term financial perspectives necessary for SSM. Thus, traditional financial accounting is incapable of providing answers to numerous important SSM questions. For example: What is the economic value of clean air? How much is the aesthetic beauty of the land worth? How much is a mountaintop worth? How much are good community relations worth? What monetary amount can be placed on the psychological costs of human displacement due to environmental or social upheaval? How can value be assigned to future generations of human beings? How much value can be assigned to other species, now and in the future?

The inadequacy of traditional financial accounting methods for SSM has led to the development of "full-cost accounting" systems, which are financial accounting systems capable of accounting for both the short-term and long-term economic, social, and environmental costs of doing business (Bebbington et al. 2001). These systems work to fully integrate economic, social, and environmental criteria, assign fundamental rather than secondary importance to social and environmental concerns, account for all internal and external costs now and in the future, and reflect long-term financial performance (Sherman, Steingard, and Fitzgibbons 2002).

One group committed to both research and development of full-cost accounting is the Association of Chartered Certified Accountants (ACCA) (Bebbington et al. 2001). The ACCA is an association of professional accountants in the United Kingdom that has been a proponent of full-cost accounting for over two decades. The ACCA helps organizations to: (1) integrate sustainability into their core business strategies; (2) develop measurement protocols for carbon and greenhouse emissions; (3) develop portfolios of social and environmental accounting techniques that more accurately account for negative sustainability impacts in the short term and long term; (4) develop sustainability reporting tools designed to increase firm transparency and credibility; and (5) improve the accuracy and usefulness of individual firm footprint analysis (Chambers and Lewis 2001).

SSM Reporting

Accurately and fully reporting a firm's social and environmental performance to its stakeholders is critical for effectively engaging stakeholders and contributing to the firm's legitimacy within society as it pursues improved triple-bottom-line performance via SSM. The ACCA recommends that sustainability reports should meet several criteria, including: (1) covering the information in ways that are readily comprehensible; (2) responding to stakeholder inquiries and concerns; (3) ensuring both continuity and comparability of data over time; (4) fully describing all activities, products, processes, policies, programs, and performance targets related to implementing the firm's SSM strategies; and (5) reporting on both normal operations and unusual events or incidents.

Some sustainability reports are mandatory, such as the U.S. EPA's Toxic Release Inventory (TRI) report that gives the public access to vast amounts of environmental performance data. However, many corporations today are taking a more proactive approach to reporting their SSM activities and results. In addition to the traditional shareholder reports that focus on the economic performance of firms, organizations are now creating detailed social and environmental performance reports. These reports are generally distributed widely to employees, shareholders, financial institutions, customers, local communities, interest groups, the media, regulators, and the public at large via the firm's Web site and social media sites.

A common practice (and in some cases a requirement) in reporting is to use external sustainability indices such as the Dow Jones Sustainability Index and the chemical industry's Responsible Care Guidelines to benchmark sustainability performance and to determine performance gaps in SSM strategies. One very extensive sustainability reporting effort is the Global Reporting Initiative (GRI). The focus of the GRI is to develop environmental, social, and economic reporting guidelines that help advance global comprehensiveness and consistency in SSM reporting. GRI released its G3 (third generation) guidelines in 2006. The G3 guidelines include 79 "core" and "additional performance" indicators, covering economic outcomes, labor practices, human rights, decent work, environment, society, and product responsibility. The G3 guidelines not only include separate criteria for environmental, social, and economic performance data but also ask organizations to report on the interactions among these three (GRI 2012a). The G3 guidelines were updated with the G3.1 guidelines in 2011. These more thoroughly cover human rights, local community impacts, and gender issues (GRI 2012b).

Employing external indices such as these is one of six major trends in sustainability reporting. The second trend is that more organizations are reporting sustainability activities than ever before, and the number is still rising. One survey found that 76 percent of U.S.-based firms currently report their sustainability activity, and that within five years that number will increase to 93 percent. Third, the roles of chief financial officers (CFOs) in sustainability reporting are growing. Fourth, sustainability-reporting processes in organizations are involving more participative employee engagement processes such as green teams. Fifth, the reporting of greenhouse gas emissions is rising sharply, even among firms not required by regulation to report these statistics. Sixth, there is a trend toward reporting the social and ecological risks of "invisible ingredients" in products—dangerous hidden ingredients that have the potential for causing ecological or social harm (Goodman 2012).

SSM Auditing

The purpose of SSM auditing is to regularly evaluate a firm's economic, social, and environmental performance all along its value chain, thus providing useful data for closing a firm's sustainability performance gaps. Social auditing began as a field in the 1970s, but it really began to gain attention in the late 1990s. Waddock (2000) refers to it as "responsibility auditing," which she says involves using external benchmarks (such as GRI's G3.1 guidelines) along with internal performance data to determine how organizational practices impact stakeholders. Responsibility audits are generally undertaken to improve sustainability performance. For example, a responsibility audit may assess employee practices, community relations, environmental performance, and quality performance. The performance in these areas is then compared to the firm's stated vision, values, and mission to determine the performance gaps where stakeholder value can be added (Waddock 2000, 2007). Thus, responsibility auditing is very valuable in evaluating and improving sustainability performance.

In sum, designing sustainability into the functional level support systems is critical in providing strategic managers with the important triple-bottom-line data they need for SSM decision making. Incorporating sustainability into support level activities, such as enterprise resource planning (ERP), full-cost accounting systems, full-cost financial models, sustainability auditing, and sustainability reporting, presents challenges in implementation because it requires managers not only to do things differently but also to view things differently.

Strategic Choice at the Competitive Level

Recall that managers at the competitive level focus on how to compete within specific product/market segments, thus they need the dynamic capabilities to match the coevolving opportunities and threats in their market segments with the strategic business unit's (SBU's) resources. These dynamic capabilities make up the **core competencies** that are at the cornerstone of the SBU's competitive strategy. With them the SBU has the ability to identify the **strategic fits** between the SBU's **strengths** and **weaknesses** and the **opportunities** and **threats (SWOT)** in its market segment. Finding a strategic fit is the most important ingredient in formulating an effective strategy. Thus, in order to have the triple-bottom-line data to effectively choose a successful competitive level strategy, SBU managers must develop the sustainability-based processes and dynamic capabilities that enable them to identify and manage the strategic fit between external and internal variables. Figure 7.1, a **SWOT analysis**, is a static representation of this capability.

Figure 7.1   **Competitive Level Strategic Choice**

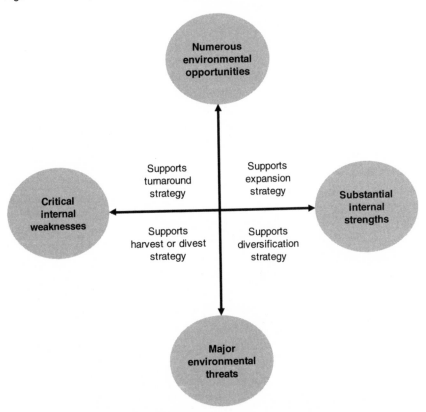

Strategic Choice at the Corporate Level

As discussed in Chapter 6, corporate level strategy consists of managing the mix, scope, and emphasis of a firm's SBUs. Therefore, corporate level decision making requires that strategic managers configure their portfolio of SBUs to create more value than if each stood alone. A conceptual portfolio management tool developed by Hamel and Prahalad (1994) to assist managers in making strategic choices focuses on opportunities to create value by building and leveraging core competencies across the firm's portfolio of SBUs. Whereas traditional portfolio management tools such as the BCG (Boston Consulting Group) matrix (discussed in Chapter 6) treat lines of businesses as separate and independent, Hamel and Prahalad (1994) recognize the interdependencies among SBUs, and thus they analyze firms as portfolios of core competencies rather than actual businesses.

Figure 7.2 **Corporate Portfolio of Core Competencies**

Industry

	Existing	New
New	Opportunity to develop new competencies to improve competitive position in existing industries	Opportunity to develop new competencies for future markets—to discover and explore market space beyond existing borders
Existing	Opportunity to improve competitive position in existing markets by leveraging existing core competencies	Opportunity to fill market gaps by redeploying or recombining core competencies

(**Competence**)

Source: Adapted from Hamel and Prahalad 1994.

Recall from Chapter 4 that **core competencies** are central value-creation capabilities of organizations. They are core skills, so identifying them is the first step firms should take in deciding which opportunities to pursue. Once firms have identified their core competencies, a matrix similar to Figure 7.2 can be used to establish an agenda for building and leveraging these core competencies in order to create new business opportunities. Hamel and Prahalad (1994) distinguish between existing and new competencies and existing and new industries in the matrix, with each quadrant having a distinct strategic implication.

Hamel and Prahalad (1994) argue that where a company is going is more important than where it is coming from. Strategic choice should therefore focus on building new competencies to compete in the industries of the future and on creating new products and services by redeploying or recombining current competencies to address gaps in traditional markets. In other words, strategic choice should be based on generative learning where fundamental assumptions are questioned, new market space is created, and gaps within existing markets identified. Note that although creating the future does not necessarily mean abandoning the past, it does require identifying what from the past has current strategic value and ejecting the rest as excess baggage.

Strategic managers too often look at the future through the narrow context of existing served markets. Hamel and Prahalad (1994) contend that to really compete in the future, strategic managers must enlarge their opportunity horizon, and thus strategic analysis should move away from just analyzing current products in existing industries to developing current and future capabilities that will position the firm to create new market space. To see the future, strategic managers must be capable of escaping the narrow view of "What business are we in?" and "What is our product or service?" and moving to the strategic goal of occupying the high ground in tomorrow's business world. The Hamel and Prahalad framework is designed to aid organizations in doing this, helping them to create new market space by assisting strategic managers in reconceptualizing their companies' core competencies and lines of business in order to create the desired future. The successes of 3M in creating new opportunities and market space have come from its innovative capabilities to apply its core competencies in adhesives to create new opportunities from Scotch Tape to Post-it Notes (Hamel and Prahalad 1994). Just imagine the new opportunities and market space that would unfold from the effective alliance management of the portfolio of core competencies of the members of an inclusive business ecosystem formed around the shared vision of sustainability.

In sum, strategic decision making at the corporate level ultimately determines the success or the failure of the organization. Corporate level decisions determine where the organization will compete and the scope and boundaries of its operations, thus influencing the firm's ability to create its own future. Strategic choice involves objectively evaluating alternative strategies and deciding which ones the firm should pursue in order to achieve its goals. Thus, it is critical for strategic managers to clearly analyze the quantitative external and internal data available to them when choosing what strategies to implement and how to implement them.

Instilling SSM Value Systems

A key point from the above discussion is that rational quantitative analysis is critical for effective strategic choice. Of course, interpreting and using these data effectively entails mental processes such as judgment and intuition, and these are heavily influenced by values. Thus, given that strategic choices are invariably influenced by the values of strategic managers, implementing successful SSM strategic initiatives should begin with the establishment of a sustainability-centered value system. This means deeply seeding sustainability into the core value system of an organization where it can grow and provide solid roots for the firm's sustainability efforts. Given the importance of such deep cultural integration, strategic managers guiding their organizations toward SSM may want to begin their journey by examining their firms' core value systems to ensure that they will support their organizations' drive for improved triple-bottom-line performance.

Values are enduring, emotionally charged abstractions about matters that are important to people. Understanding values is no simple matter. Some have conceptualized values as existing in hierarchies; that is, a person ranks his/her values based on their importance to him/her. Others say that the importance of any individual value varies. They say that the real key to understanding how important values are in influencing decisions is to discern how important an individual's total system of values is to her or him. This approach views values from a holistic perspective in which the values people employ are influenced by the situation. When people actually apply their values to their decisions, both of these frameworks are likely to come into play to one degree or another. No doubt, some values are more important to people than other values; at the same time, the total strength of people's value systems and the situations in which they find themselves are also important (Liedtka 1989; Rokeach 1968).

Specifically, the values of strategic managers influence their decisions at two points. First, values serve as data filters, influencing what information strategic managers attend to and how they interpret it. Second, they serve as decision shapers, providing frameworks upon which final decisions are based (Schwenk 1988). Thus, sustainability-centered values are necessary for identifying and understanding SSM opportunities, and they are necessary for creating and implementing SSM strategies that capitalize on these opportunities.

A firm's values are deeply rooted in its culture. An **organization's culture** is composed of artifacts (i.e., logos, products, and icons), norms, values, beliefs, and assumptions shared by its members. Of these, the artifacts and norms are more surface-level while the values, beliefs, and assumptions are more deeply planted in the firm's foundation (Schein 1985). This is important to understand because, as discussed briefly in Chapter 1, organizational change efforts targeted at the shallower levels of an organization's culture are generally adaptive, incremental, and focused on improving what the organization is currently doing. However, change efforts that focus on the deeper levels of an organization's culture are generally transformational, employing deep dialogue processes that allow the organization to closely examine and redefine who it is and what it does.

Values are generally arranged in systems. These systems are complex webs of related values centered on core values. **Core values** (intrinsic values) define the essence of a value system. They are considered good in and of themselves, they are typically few in number, they are very enduring and difficult to change, and they express the overarching ideals of the organization. Core values are made operational via **instrumental values** (extrinsic values) that facilitate their implementation. For example, a core value of democracy is made operational when citizens choose to apply a wide range of related instrumental values such as voting, staying informed, and so forth.

Although many perceive that managing with values is a soft approach, nothing could be further from the truth. Values represent what is important to people. They are roadmaps for how organizations view their world and how they behave in it. Values can be contradictory and messy, and managing them requires a willingness to encourage a continuous open dialogue on all organizational levels around the firm's purpose and values (Freeman, Harrison, and Wicks 2007). Thus, organizations wishing to survive over the long term in today's upwardly spiraling sustainability-centered business environment will need to ingrain sustainability deeply into their core values and purpose. Also, they will need to surround this core value with relevant instrumental values, such as open dialogue, community prosperity, quality, posterity, and others, that allow firms to pursue a sustainability path to their economic success.

Enterprise strategy is an overarching values-based strategic framework that allows a firm to answer its most fundamental ethical question: "What do we stand for?" (Freeman 1984, 90). Answering this question requires examining how the firm is serving its stakeholders (Freeman, Harrison, and Wicks 2007), which in turn focuses attention directly on what the firm "should be doing." Thus, enterprise strategy explicitly addresses the value systems of managers and stakeholders in concrete terms.

A firm's enterprise strategy reflects the interactions among three components. The first component is the organization's value system, composed of its core and related instrumental values. The second component includes the myriad social and ecological issues facing the organization. The third component involves the values and needs of the firm's stakeholders (Ansoff 1979; Freeman 1984; Freeman and Gilbert 1988; Freeman, Harrison, and Wicks 2007; Hosmer 1994; Stead and Stead 2000).

In an enterprise-strategy context, strategic managers guiding their firms toward SSM need to: (1) facilitate the development and implementation of a network of instrumental values centered on a core value of sustainability (as discussed above); (2) analyze how social and environmental issues (such as those discussed in Chapter 2) relate to their firms' inputs, operations, products, services, and other activities; and (3) account for the rapidly growing social

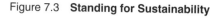
Figure 7.3 **Standing for Sustainability**

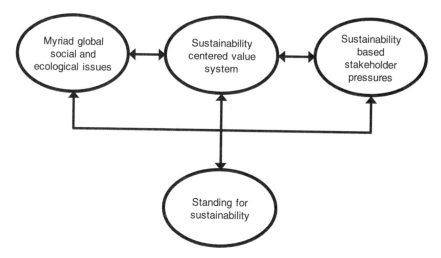

and environmental concerns of their stakeholders, including suppliers, customers, investors, employees, regulators, insurers, lenders, nongovernmental organizations (NGOs), citizen sector organizations, and so forth. As Figure 7.3 depicts, a firm with a sustainability-based value system, an understanding of how social and environmental issues relate to the firm's activities, and a sustainability-centered perspective on its relationships with stakeholders can be said to "stand for sustainability" (Stead and Stead 2000).

Creating Meaning Beyond Profit

We have clearly established throughout the book that successful implementation of SSM is a multidimensional process that requires deeply seeded organizational commitments not only to profits but also to people and the planet. Thus, organizations on SSM journeys are required to look beyond their economic profitability and factor their efforts to contribute to the greater social and ecological good into their formulas for corporate success. Of course, this is much more likely to occur in organizations where strategic managers hold sustainability as one of their deep personal values—where they truly stand for sustainability. In those situations, strategic managers are more likely to work to create the necessary sustainability-centered value systems in their organizations (Bansal and Roth 2000; Egri and Herman 2000; Middlebrooks and Noghiu 2010). Such systems bring both deeper and broader meaning to organizations by tying their economic success to their ability to serve the greater society and ecosystem (Middlebrooks and Noghiu 2010).

Spiritual Foundations of SSM

In the pursuit of SSM, strategic managers establish a higher purpose and deeper meaning that transcends their economic accomplishments. The term **spiritual fulfillment** generally refers to people's search for higher purpose and deeper meaning in their lives (Driver 2007; Gull and Doh 2004; Zohar and Marshall 2004). This search is a higher-level aspiration that is unique to human beings (Schumacher 1977; Wilber 1996, 2000). When people speak of seeking spiritual meaning in their lives, they are generally expressing their search for joy, purpose, happiness, love, peace, creativity, achievement, beauty, caring, compassion, divinity, service, and so forth. Pruzan and Mikkelsen (2007) interviewed 31 executives and found that spiritual factors like these were powerful motivators for these executives and their organizations.

Patricia Aburdene (2005) describes the rising sustainability consciousness as a spiritual phenomenon. Over sixty years ago, naturalist and conservationist Aldo Leopold (1949) said that adopting a **land ethic**, giving nature moral standing in humankind's ethical system, would require people to take a more spiritual view of their relationships with each other and with nature. Pioneer ecological economist E. F. Schumacher (1973, 1977) echoed this sentiment, saying that a societal shift toward sustainability represents a shift to a higher level of human consciousness that is more organic, more inwardly focused, more heartfelt, and more spiritual. In the same vein, leading ecological economist Herman Daly (1977) has said that pursuing sustainability requires realizing that a belief in a high quality of life for posterity is the highest of humankind's ethical and spiritual aspirations (its "ultimate ends"). SSM can bring greater social and ecological meaning to organizations, thus enhancing organizational commitment to posterity.

Of course, organizations pursuing SSM will need to develop sustainability-based spiritual capabilities that allow them to develop and implement strategies that bring greater meaning to organizational members and stakeholders. The development of **spiritual capabilities** involves the development of both **spiritual intelligence** and **spiritual capital**. Howard Gardner (1993) said that human intelligence is multifaceted, with each person having different intelligences that coexist and develop relatively independently of one another. Most common among these human intelligences is rational intelligence, generally referred to as **intelligence quotient (IQ)**. Theoretically, a high IQ reflects a high ability to solve logical problems. Goleman (1996) demonstrated that **emotional intelligence (EQ)** is as important as IQ. EQ is a measure of people's awareness of other people's feelings as well as their own. As such, it is the source of human compassion, empathy, and motivation. EQ has been shown to be especially important within the business context. For example,

Walter, Cole, and Humphrey (2011) found a strong tie between EQ and effective strategic leadership attitudes and behaviors.

In the past decade or so, **spiritual intelligence (SQ)** (Zohar and Marshall 2000, 2004) has gained attention. This is the intelligence that humans use to solve problems of value and meaning. It is a means of integrating internal and external experiences, which facilitates problem solving (Hyde 2004; Vaughan 2002) and enables humans to adapt to coevolving life conditions (Beck and Cowan 1996; Wilber 2000). SQ helps put human behaviors and lives within a larger context of meaning, and thus it serves as the foundation of both IQ and EQ. Unlike other species, human beings search for meaning and value in what they do because they are driven by questions regarding why they exist and what their lives mean. Humans have a longing to feel a part of a larger purpose, something toward which they can aspire throughout their lives.

SQ allows humans to be creative, to use their imaginations, and to change their rules. It allows them to think outside of the box and to play with the boundaries of their existence. It is this transformative characteristic that distinguishes SQ from IQ and EQ. Whereas both IQ and EQ work within the boundaries of the situation, SQ allows individuals to question whether or not they want to be in the situation in the first place. SQ facilitates the dialogue between reason and emotion, between mind and body. It provides the ability to integrate all the intelligences. Thus, it is a transcendent intelligence that enables people and organizations to serve higher purposes (Beck and Cowan 1996; Graves 1970, Sisk and Torrance 2001; Wilber 2000).

SQ equips strategic managers to lead the transformation of the organization to SSM. Using their SQ, they can guide their firms through transformational processes that create spiritual capital. Recall that in Chapter 4 (Figure 4.2) we identified **spiritual capital** as a higher-level, intangible form of capital, a higher-level purpose that serves fundamental human needs beyond the organization. In SSM, spiritual capital is the by-product of the transformational, organizational processes led by a top management team with high levels of spiritual intelligence. Zohar and Marshall (2004, 27) define spiritual capital as "the amount of spiritual knowledge and expertise available to an individual or organization." Research on spiritual capital indicates that: (1) building it usually begins with the personal disposition of top managers to commit their organizations to a larger purpose, and (2) this top-management commitment must permeate an organization's culture (its systems, norms, and values) before spiritual capital can provide real value (Middlebrooks and Noghiu 2010). Doing so facilitates the creation of shared value, building an organizational culture that serves both organizational and societal needs (Middlebrooks and Noghiu 2010; Porter and Kramer 2011).

Spiritual Capabilities and Sustained Competitive Advantage

As managers begin to create spiritual capital through transformational change processes, they develop the strategic capabilities to nurture, renew, and sustain the transcendent purpose of their organizations. These **spiritual capabilities** become the glue—the cultural foundation—that binds all business ecosystem members and stakeholders together. They provide ecosystem members with an ethos—a **spirit**—that transcends, sustains, and enriches both the material capital and social capital of all members. In other words, they embed the organizational culture with spiritual meaning (Zohar and Marshall 2004). This enhances strategic managers' understanding and commitment to a core value of sustainability, and it gives them the deeper insights they need to understand why contributing to humanity's efforts to meet the needs of present and future generations is critical for their ecosystems' and organizations' long-term survival.

Thus, a key to effectively implementing SSM is to develop the spiritual capabilities that result when leaders with spiritual intelligence are leading transformational change processes that create spiritual capital within and between ecosystem members that support and enhance their ability to create triple-bottom-line competitive advantages. The resource-based view of the firm (RBV) provides an excellent framework for examining the competitive nature of spiritual capabilities. Recall from Chapter 4 that, according to the RBV, organizational performance is a function of the types of resources (tangible and intangible resources and capabilities) developed and exploited by managers through strategies that accomplish organizational goals. For these resources to provide competitive advantages to the firm, they must be valuable, rare, and difficult to imitate, and they must be strategically combined and deployed (Barney 1986, 1991; Wernerfelt 1984).

Spiritual capabilities exhibit these attributes and are extremely hard to imitate due to being causally ambiguous, socially complex, and holistic. In turn this offers a sustained competitive advantage to the firm (Barney 1986, 1991; Colbert 2004; Grant 1991; Reed and DeFillippi 1990; Schoemaker 1990). Thus, the foundation of SSM leadership is the spiritual capital created by spiritually led transformation processes that instill the spirit within the ecosystem and its members. The vision of sustainability and its higher-level purpose embeds the business ecosystem with the spiritual capabilities that support sustainability. Although they are complex and intangible capabilities and are difficult to build, they have the potential to afford a sustained competitive advantage. The aesthetic value of nature and humankind cannot be touched or displayed. However, it can certainly be experienced, and it can certainly stir the spirit when it is. Leading firms in the sustainability revolution discussed earlier—Unilever, Johnson and Johnson, New Belgium Brewing, and Proctor and Gamble—place a very high value on these sustainability-based intangibles, which they believe enhance their competitiveness.

Designing Self-Renewing Learning Structures

In addition to creating a sustainability-centered value system and building spiritual capabilities around it, it is also necessary for strategic managers implementing SSM to design organizational structures that will support shaping the organization's sustainability-centered strategic capabilities into viable strategies that improve the firm's triple-bottom-line performance. Peter Senge (1990, 2011) says that self-renewing structures, which he calls "learning organizations," are ideal for integrating sustainability into the strategic core of business organizations. Senge defines learning organizations as organizations capable of using adaptive and generative learning to create and re-create themselves in order to survive and thrive in their coevolutionary dance with their turbulent environments. He says that learning organizations provide "a more sacred view of work" (Senge 1990, 5). They encourage a more intrinsic, spiritual view of organizational life and organizational purpose. Because of this, they are capable of operating directly out of their essence—their basic purposes, identities, and relationships (Beckhard and Pritchard 1992).

Principles of Self-Renewing Structures

Organizational structures come in a wide variety of shapes and sizes. There is general agreement among management scholars that organizational structures exist along a continuum, ranging from mechanistic rule-driven organizations designed for more stable environments to organic knowledge-driven organizations designed for more turbulent environments. Mintzberg (1979) identified four organizational forms along this continuum, ranging from highly mechanistic "machine bureaucracies" to less mechanistic "professional bureaucracies" to more organic "divisional structures" to highly organic "adhocracies."

As should be clear from these descriptions, as structures progress from the mechanistic end of the continuum to the organic end of the continuum, they become more adaptive and more self-renewing. Today's rapidly changing co-evolutionary selection-adaptation cycles require that firms adopt self-renewing organizational structures that are flexible and adaptable to new entrepreneurial ventures, shifting competitive pressures, disruptive technologies, and so forth (Flier, Van Den Bosch, and Volberda 2003; Hart and Milstein 1999; Lampel and Shamsie 2003; Lewin and Volberda 1999, 2003a, 2003b; Porter 2006; Rodrigues and Child 2003; Schumpeter 1950; Volberda and Lewin 2003).

The management literature is replete with formulas for creating self-renewing organizational structures. Volberda and Lewin (2003) examined many of these and discovered among them three common principles for creating and maintaining self-renewing organizations. The first is "**the principle of managing internal rates of change**" (Volberda and Lewin 2003, 2126), which says that internal organizational change-management structures and routines should function at rates of change equal to or greater than the rates of change in the external environment.

The second is "**the principle of optimizing self-organization**" (Volberda and Lewin 2003, 2126), which says that managers should eschew the use of bureaucratic outcome control mechanisms in favor of self-organizing principles that stress self-responsibility and self-control, and they should push decision making down to the lowest level possible in the organization. In these self-organizing systems, "managers function as stewards of the evolutionary process and focus their managerial role on devising and articulating critical values and on establishing boundary conditions that enable and guide decision making at lower levels of the organization" (Volberda and Lewin 2003, 2126).

Third is "**the principle of synchronizing concurrent exploration and exploitation**" (Volberda and Lewin 2003, 2127), which means that strategic managers should seek to balance their organizations' efforts to enhance their current competitive capabilities via product and process improvements (called exploitation) with their efforts to find new ideas and innovations that will improve their competitiveness in the future (called exploration). Essentially, exploitation is about maintaining the viability of present market space, and exploration is about identifying and developing new market space. Overemphasis on exploitation creates the potential for the "competence trap" in which organizations protect short-term gains but fall behind their competitors with regard to innovations. Overemphasis on exploration creates the potential for the "renewal trap" in which organizations expend energy and resources on future innovations, but in doing so lose their current identity in the market. Thus, it is all in the balancing of the core competencies within the corporate portfolio (Hamel and Prahalad 1994).

Structuring for Innovation

When 2600 executives were asked what the primary immediate business challenge is for their firms (Kiron et al. 2013), their number one response (48 percent) was developing innovations that can differentiate their firms from their competitors. Self-renewing, learning structures are ideal frameworks for fostering organizational innovation. Such structures allow strategic managers to employ adaptive and generative learning processes so that their organizations can both exploit current sustainability-based opportunities and explore for new ones beyond traditional industry boundaries. Via adaptive learning processes, firms can seek incremental innovations via eco- and socio-efficiency designed to improve their triple-bottom-line performance in present operations. Via generative learning processes, firms can seek radical innovations and disruptive technologies via eco- and socio-effectiveness that have the potential to make positive contributions to the greater society and ecosystem.

Sixty-seven percent of the executives surveyed by Kiron et al. (2013) identified innovation as the best route to sustainability-based profits, and 29 percent identified such innovations as the most important benefit their organizations are deriving from their sustainability efforts. As discussed in Chapter 4, one key to finding such innovations is for the organization to establish stakeholder engagement processes designed to allow all stakeholders to be aware of, reflect on, inquire about, discuss, and make suggestions regarding an organization's sustainability performance. In this way stakeholders are involved in cocreating innovative new sustainability-based products and market opportunities. Open dialogue mechanisms such as appreciative inquiry (discussed later in the chapter) can provide the means for organizational members and stakeholders to continuously examine two key questions regarding their innovative efforts: "What is?" and "What can be?"

We have discussed disruptive technologies in some depth in previous chapters. Recall that these are essentially new technologies that create dramatic technological paradigm shifts that transform entire industries, economies, societies, and/or ecosystems. Because of their potential for creating new market space (or blue oceans), innovations tied to disruptive technologies are considered by many to be at the heart of moving toward global sustainability. Disruptive technologies hold the promise of providing both socio- and eco-effective means for developing products and services that can serve billions of untapped customers in emerging markets in sustainable ways, thus making positive contributions to the economic, social, and natural capital of those markets (Hart and Christensen 2002).

For example, Health Point Services saw a latent demand for health care in the undeveloped and developing markets of the world, creating new market space. Through an alliance with NGOs, Health Point utilizes electronic medical records and video technology to overcome the barrier of lack of transportation for potential consumers. It has established E Health Points, clinics where consultations cost only a dollar, and many diagnostic tests are less than fifty cents. The clinics sell clean water for five cents and provide health education on-site. Thus, by thinking outside of the box and assuming that low-income consumers are willing to pay what they can for quality health-care, Health Point is able to access previously underserved markets. Currently, it has plans to enter the Southeast Asian and Latin American markets. This is an innovative business model resulting from questioning some fundamental assumptions about low-income consumers (Drayton and Budinich 2010). This is the kind of multistakeholder, entrepreneurial, generative-learning capability that forms the basis of SSM.

One key to successful sustainability-based innovation is to use nature as a model for products and processes. Systems that mimic nature consider waste as lost profit and create economic, social, and ecological value by design. Nature uses feedback loops that trigger adaptations that lessen the physical constraints on species. Design efforts structured around a model of nature provide for the same sort of systems thinking processes in organizations, and they also encourage organizations to view the ecological and social limits of economic growth as opportunities for new product development, innovation, and entrepreneurial learning. These nature-based design efforts can motivate managers to rethink their business models and to generate innovative new approaches for sustainable product and service introductions in order to take advantage of these opportunities, often in heretofore underserved developing and undeveloped markets.

Establishing Transformational Change Processes

Recall from Chapter 1 that transformational change is designed to lead organizations to entirely different qualitative states. It requires dialogue-based change processes that allow organizations to reveal and change the underlying core values upon which their decisions and actions are rooted. As we have emphasized numerous times, changing these core value systems constitutes a generative shift in how organizations think about the world and their role in it. Transformational change has been a common theme throughout this book because, as we have said many times, implementing SSM will require that most organizations transform their value systems and their strategies in ways that reflect a deep abiding belief in the sacredness of people and nature. Transformational change processes are required for strategic managers and their organizations to become agents for social change.

In fact, strategic managers implementing SSM can choose to take one of two roads in their quest for improved triple-bottom-line performance. The first is the adaptive, incremental road, which is likely the more traveled of the two these days. On this road, managers instill changes in an orderly linear fashion. Whereas incremental change processes are effective in helping organizations do things differently, they are less effective in helping organizations view things differently. For that, organizations must take the least traveled road: transformational change.

Organizations that choose the incremental road may be capable of implementing the basic practices of SSM, but developing such proficiencies will not necessarily lead them to a fundamental transformation to a sustainability-centered value system. They may be quite capable of doing things in more sustainable ways, but they may still lack the capability to view things in more sustainable ways. Therefore, without a guiding sustainability-based value system in place, organizations are more likely to eventually lose their way in their search for improved sustainability performance, and this threatens their potential to continuously adapt to the increasing sustainability demands in the environment.

On the other hand, organizations that choose the transformational road start their environmental adaptation journeys by examining and changing the fundamental values that guide what they do. This provides them with the underlying cognitive foundations necessary for thinking in terms of sustainability, and thinking in terms of sustainability makes acting in terms of sustainability a more natural, logical process. When this happens, organizations' roads to SSM become clearer and more navigable, and this increases their chances of successfully adapting to the changing sustainability-rich business environment. Thus, the transformational change road—the road least traveled because the changes it brings are so fundamental—is the best route to the long-term adoption and implementation of SSM where the firm becomes an agent of social change.

A very effective transformational change process that has gained popularity in recent years is **appreciative inquiry (AI)**, which "involves a systematic discovery of what gives life to an organization or a community when it is most effective and most capable in economic, ecological, and human terms" (Cooperrider and Whitney 2005, 8). AI seeks to reveal, expand, and exploit the positive core of an organization or community. It always focuses on the positive—inquiry, imagination, and innovation—rather than on the negative—problem solving, criticism, and blame. AI explores "unconditionally positive questions that strengthen a system's capacity to apprehend, anticipate, and heighten positive potential" (Cooperrider and Whitney 2005, 8). AI interventions essentially follow a four-stage process of discovering what is good about the organization, dreaming about a positive future for it, designing ways to make those dreams come true, and empowering organizational members to employ these ways to pursue the organization's destiny. By using AI along with other organizational change processes, the top management team can shepherd the vision of becoming an agent for social change.

Chapter Summary

SSM implementation begins with strategic managers making key choices regarding what strategies to implement and how to implement them in order to improve their firms' triple-bottom-line performance. This involves choosing a portfolio of SSM strategies that are integrated at all three levels of the strategic hierarchy—functional, competitive, and corporate. Functionally, firms can implement strategies that enhance the triple-bottom-line performance of both their primary and supporting value-chain activities, contributing valuable data for SSM decision making. Competitively, firms can seek both cost-based and differentiation-based SSM competitive advantages by managing the strategic fit between internal and external variables, choosing strategies that enhance this fit. At the corporate level, strategic managers must make strategic choices regarding how to configure their firms' whole-pyramid portfolios into a system in which sustainability-centered synergies between SBUs can be identified and exploited to create sustainable, shared value for multiple stakeholders.

Given that the strategic choices are highly influenced by the values of the managers that make them, a core value of sustainability is clearly critical for effectively implementing SSM. By adopting such a value, a firm's enterprise strategy—its highest-order strategy that defines who and what it is—becomes based on a deep commitment to "standing for sustainability." As such, an organization that stands for sustainability has an excellent chance of finding meaning beyond profit for itself and its stakeholders, creating spiritual capabilities that reinforce its vision of sustainability, thus creating sustained competitive advantage. It has a chance to find a larger purpose that ties its financial gains to how well it serves humankind and the planet.

Implementing SSM also requires developing flexible, knowledge-based self-renewing structures that empower employees to exercise their self-responsibility and self-control in order to continuously create current product improvements and new product innovations that are responsive to the rapidly increasing sustainability demands in their environments. Implementing SSM also requires having transformational change processes, such as appreciative inquiry, in place that will allow organizations to continuously explore what they are and what they want to be with regard to their role as agents for social change.

One final note on the idea of strategic choice before we close this chapter. Strategic choice has broad implications for strategic managers pursuing an SSM path. With strategic choice, strategic managers clearly have the power to shape their organizations into forces for change for a more sustainable world. Collectively then, strategic managers truly have the power to make social and environmental responsibility a part of doing business all across the globe, and in doing so they have a chance to leave a legacy of economic, social, and environmental justice and well-being for generations to come.

Case Vignette 7

Strategies, Structures, and Processes for Implementing SSM at Eastman Chemical Company

Eastman Chemical has gone a long way toward establishing itself as a firm that "stands for sustainability." Sustainability has become a centerpiece of the firm's culture, and it is now a key lens through which Eastman establishes its goals, structures itself, develops its new products, improves its old products, forms and maintains its external partnerships, determines the efficacy of its future acquisitions, hires and trains its employees, and measures its contribution to the greater world. Eastman executives view sustainability as a key strategic driver of economic growth for years to come, and they have begun the journey of implementing corporate, competitive, and functional level strategies, structures, and processes to bring that to fruition.

In discussing Eastman's strategic choice to focus its future success on sustainability, CEO Jim Rogers said, "Sustainability . . . represents our culture of continuous improvement, innovation, and responsibility." In fact (as mentioned in Case Vignette 5), the belief that sustainability and innovation are synergistically interconnected pathways to future organizational success lies at the center of Eastman's current culture. Based on this belief, Eastman is pressing ahead on its sustainability journey by applying its "core values" (teamwork, quality, responsibility, and safety) and "brand beliefs" (experience, insight, creativity, adaptability, collaboration, and commitment to doing things right) to finding creative new products that connect sustainability and innovation.

Further, when Eastman executives discuss the success of the firm's sustainability efforts, they point out that they mean success that goes beyond just serving the firm's own financial gain. As we discussed earlier, both CEO Jim Rogers and chief sustainability officer (CSO) Godefroy Motte described sustainability at Eastman as coming from both the head and the heart: it is the right thing to do for the firm, and it is the right thing to do for humankind and the planet. As Jim Rogers said, "Eastman's continued growth and future success depend on the intelligent way in which we integrate sustainability across everything we do, from product development and manufacturing processes to strategic acquisitions and our continued protection of the earth's valuable resources."

Appointing Godefroy Motte as CSO in December 2010 was a loud structural shout from the top of Eastman to all of its internal and external stakeholders that sustainability is now central to who Eastman is and what Eastman does. This appointment gave sustainability an official voice on the Eastman executive team, and it put structural teeth in CEO Jim Rogers's long-standing commitment to sustainability. "Naming a chief sustainability officer—Godefroy Motte—is an important milestone on our sustainability journey and for our business," Rogers said.

A year before the appointment of Motte as CSO, Eastman established another sustainability-centered top-management structural mechanism— its Innovation and Sustainability (I&S) Council, which is charged with linking the firm's sustainability goals, initiatives, and strategies directly to its overall growth strategies. The I&S Council is currently chaired by Godefroy Motte, and it includes seven high-level executives from areas such as innovation, legal, technology, and marketing. This group is described as "overseeing the development of the foundation necessary to embed sustainability across Eastman." Among other functions, it sets and prioritizes corporate sustainability goals, provides guidance on innovation platforms and R&D investments for sustainability, endorses sustainability as a lens to view all corporate decisions, and expands the firm's sustainability reporting transparency.

In 2010 a structural companion to the I&C Council called the Sustainability Ambassador Team was formed in Eastman's Europe, Middle East, and Africa (EMEA) Region. This team, composed of "18 employee leaders representing various functions and business units," essentially does the job of the I&C Council in the EMEA Region. It "provides strategic direction on internal and external sustainability . . . , helps embed sustainability into daily decision making . . . , and plays a key role in reinforcing a corporate culture that proactively identifies and acts on sustainability opportunities."

The Corporate Sustainability Group, a small, five-person team with varying educational backgrounds, business experiences, and tenure with the company, was created at Eastman in 2008. According to group member and chemical engineer Dr. William Heise, "Our role has evolved and changed as sustainability has evolved and changed at Eastman." Indeed, just as a focus on compliance was the initial stage of Eastman's sustainability journey (see Case Vignette 1), compliance was the initial focus of the Corporate Sustainability Group. Again quoting Heise: "During the first few years of existence, the corporate sustainability group reported through Eastman's Legal Department. The initial focus was one of compliance and consideration of pending regulations and/or legislation with respect to carbon usage."

As Eastman's sustainability journey progressed, the focus of the Corporate Sustainability Group shifted to more external communications, such as development of the sustainability reports, which highlight the sustainability attributes of specific products, establish the short- and long-term sustainability goals and the execution of life cycle assessments. During this phase, the group reported to the vice president of Innovation and Sustainability. When Eastman named Godefroy Motte CSO, the group was placed under his direct leadership. The current responsibilities of the Corporate Sustainability Group include: (1) inform corporate leaders of sustainability trends; (2) prepare the corporate sustainability report; (3) report corporate data to the Global Reporting Initiative; (4) track all corporate sustainability goals and measures; (5) assess the sustainability of current products and projects; (6) assist business and marketing leaders with certifications and marketing communications; (7) create employee awareness and engagement regarding sustainability; (8) manage programs for external engagement with key stakeholders and influencers in the value chain; (9) conduct product assessments using life cycle analysis (LCA) and other sustainability tools.

Eastman has not restricted its sustainability-centered structure to internal organizational mechanisms. It has, as a part of its Responsible Care® efforts, established Community Advisory Panels (CAPs) in communities where it has operations. These CAPs are responsible for "forging meaningful relationships within our local communities." They are composed of citizens and community leaders who advise Eastman on its plant issues, employment issues, community impacts, educational issues, and so forth.

Another important structural mechanism for supporting sustainability at Eastman is its Code of Ethics, which formally establishes sustainability as an ethical responsibility of Eastman personnel. The code says, "Eastman will carry out its worldwide business in a manner consistent with sound health, safety, environmental, and security practices and applicable laws, regulations, and Responsible Care® principles." The inclusion of the phrase "Responsible Care® principles" in the code is especially important because by including it, Eastman is putting at the center of its ethical core a commitment to an industry-wide sustainability journey that involves reducing its energy use and toxic releases, improving its materials, manufacturing, and transportation efficiency, increasing its recycling and reuse processes, improving its employee, product, process, and community safety, improving its community transparency, educating its employees and value-chain partners about sustainability, and so forth.

Eastman is looking to increase the number and scope of its voluntary sustainability efforts in the organization. One of its stated structural goals is to create a sustainability-centered culture that encourages and supports the emergence of voluntary green teams by 2015. Open, voluntary, naturally participatory teams like these are important conduits of information, sources of ideas, mechanisms for actions, and vehicles for empowering employees to make a difference in their organization and in their world. Eastman also has in place a voluntary intranet-based "Energy Wise" program that encourages its employees to suggest energy-saving measures.

Clearly, Eastman has established the top management commitment, values, beliefs, and structural mechanisms to effectively choose and implement SSM strategies. Eastman is in fact pursuing numerous functional, competitive, and corporate SSM strategies. For example, at the functional level, Eastman has strategies for reducing energy use, greenhouse gas emissions, and volatile organic compound emissions, and it has a goal that all new product launches be accompanied by LCA data. At the competitive level, Eastman has introduced sustainability-advantaged products such as the HydroPack, Tritan™, and Perennial Wood™, and it has a goal of generating two-thirds of its future revenues from new product launches of sustainability-advantaged products by 2015. At the corporate level, Eastman has acquired Solutia, which has allowed it to expand into emerging markets and to expand its sustainability-advantaged product portfolio. Also, it has a goal of developing new businesses that use sustainable, renewable feedstocks by 2020. Other SSM strategic initiatives at Eastman include becoming an active voice by sharing leading sustainability practices throughout its value chain; expanding its value-chain engagements to focus on strategic sustainability issues with key influencers such as designers, academicians, the government, and NGOs; and expanding sustainability awareness education for employees and local stakeholders.

8

Organizational Governance and Strategic Leadership in SSM

We now turn our attention to organizational governance and strategic leadership in this age of sustainability. Strategic leaders are top managers who are generally responsible for the long-term direction of their firms, including chief executive officers, chief operating officers, chief financial officers, chief sustainability officers, boards of directors, and so forth. These are the executives who are responsible for choosing and implementing portfolios of strategies, instilling value systems, building spiritual capital, creating organizational designs, developing support systems, and developing transformational change processes that support a high level of triple-bottom-line performance. The environment they operate in is rife with growing demands for improved economic, ecological, and social performance, and they are being asked to exercise leadership not only in their own firms but also in complex strategic alliances and business ecosystems where they are being called on to be agents for social change. Given this context, effective governance mechanisms and strategic leadership processes are critical success factors for firms implementing sustainable strategic management (SSM).

Establishing Effective Corporate Governance Mechanisms for SSM

Corporate governance is a set of mechanisms designed to manage the relationships among stakeholders in determining the strategic direction, control, and performance of the firm. These mechanisms must at a minimum focus on managing the relationships among three key internal stakeholders: (1) the **shareholders,** the owners of the firm, (2) the **board of directors**, which has been elected by the shareholders to represent their interests, and (3) the **chief executive officer**, who is typically paid handsomely to create value for the firm.

Governance mechanisms must also focus on external forces in the market that can contribute to or threaten firm survival, such as external investors seeking to acquire undervalued firms and turning them around by replacing the top management teams (Hitt, Ireland, and Hoskisson 2009). Thus, corporate governance involves implementing strategic evaluation and control mechanisms that help to ensure that the decisions and actions of strategic leaders contribute positively to the firm's triple-bottom-line performance.

Corporate governance addresses the **principal–agent** issue, which arises when an agent performs activities on behalf of a principal. In publicly traded companies there is a separation between the owners (the shareholders) and the agents (professional managers), where the shareholders give authority to professional managers to make decisions on their behalf (Eisenhardt 1989). A conflict arises when strategic managers and boards of directors (the agents) pursue their own personal interests that are at odds with the principals' (the shareholders) interests of maximizing their total returns. In situations like this, managerial self-interest and opportunism can put at risk the long-run competitiveness of the firm and the interests of shareholders. When this occurs, it is referred to as an agency problem.

Agency problems occur when asymmetric information exists, in which the agents are more informed than the principals. Separation of ownership and managerial control is the primary cause of asymmetric information (Rothaermel 2013). Indeed, strategic managers typically have access to more information than do other stakeholders, such as investors and shareholders. Without a monitoring system, the agents are free to act in their own self-interests. When this occurs, a potential **moral hazard** exists (Eisenhardt 1989). Given that there is no perfect system for monitoring and controlling moral hazards, and if there were, it would likely be prohibitively expensive, there will always be opportunities for agents to behave unobserved. Thus, the firm's enterprise strategy (discussed in the previous chapter), its underlying value system and spiritual capabilities that define what it stands for, will be a major factor determining the degree of the agent's exploitation of asymmetric information to achieve personal gain.

Consider the case of the British bank Barclays, which agreed to pay US$453 million to settle a manipulation charge brought by U.S. and U.K. bank regulators and law enforcement officials. The bank admitted participating in a scheme to fix two key lending rates, including Libor, which affects as much as US$350 trillion in loans and derivatives. The Libor rate is used to calculate trillions of dollars in consumer and business loans, and it is used to set interest rates on mortgages, loans, and contracts around the world. Barclays has admitted that it manipulated the Libor rate to benefit its own economic bottom line. According to Marcus Agius, the former chairman of the board of directors who resigned in the face of the scandal, "I am confident we can and will repair the reputational damage done to our business in [the customers'] eyes and those of all our stakeholders. . . . We continue to address the operational and control issues . . . [and], as a consequence of recent events, the board of directors is now focused on identifying and recruiting a new chief executive as well as a chairman of the board" (Smith 2012, 1).

Effective corporate governance mechanisms were obviously not in place at Barclays and the firm was unable to avoid moral hazard. Notice that both the chairman of the board of directors and the CEO resigned their positions because of their lack of management oversight and control. To overcome agency problems such as this, organizations may utilize several governance mechanisms for strategic control. However, the best control mechanism is the firm's sustainability-based value system, the organizational spirit, which forms the foundation of organizational decision making.

Boards of Directors

Boards of directors, as discussed above, are elected representatives of the shareholders, and they are charged with ensuring that the interests and motives of management are congruent with those of the shareholders. This is the fiduciary responsibility of boards of directors, and it is the centerpiece of corporate governance (Rothaermel 2013). This responsibility entails overseeing the strategic management processes of formulation and implementation of the firm's vision, mission, goals, and strategies, thus setting the strategic direction of the firm. A recent survey of boards of directors found that 72 percent identified strategic planning and oversight as their first priority (McPherson 2012). Board composition is a key to its ability to function effectively. **Inside directors** generally come from the firm's senior management team, a governance arrangement that provides valuable internal information not available to those on the outside. Inside directors' interests, however, usually align more with the CEO and less with the shareholders, especially when the CEO serves as the board chair, which is often the case in the United States. **Outside directors**, on the other hand, are not employees of the firm. Typically, they are senior executives from other firms and organizations. Their independence makes them more likely to watch out for shareholder interests (Rothaermel 2013). Thus, a balanced mix of both inside and outside directors is generally desirable for fulfilling the board's full range of governance responsibilities.

Boards of directors have responsibilities for **five governance functions** (Hitt, Ireland, and Hoskisson 2009): (1) As discussed above, they are responsible for overseeing the strategic direction of the firm. (2) They are responsible for auditing the financial performance of their firms, including being responsible for ensuring that the audited financial statements represent a true and accurate picture of the firm. This is essentially their watchdog role. (3) They are responsible for the selection and succession of CEOs as well as the determination of CEO pay. If the CEO loses their confidence, they are responsible for replacing him/her. (4) They are responsible for assessing risks and developing strategies that mitigate risks. (5) They are responsible for ensuring the ethics and legality of the firms' activities, thus building and preserving reputational capital (Rothaermel 2013).

When boards fail to exercise these responsibilities, serious problems can arise. For example, JPMorgan Chase's CEO Jamie Dimon and his board of directors did not effectively manage the risks from trading credit derivatives, resulting in a loss of US$30 billion or more. After the loss was reported, JP-Morgan Chase's reputation fell to the lowest level on record, and the board of directors and CEO were held directly accountable for a decline in both stock value and reputational capital (Bradford 2012).

Many critics wonder where the oversight of the board of directors was at Merrill Lynch (now a part of Bank of America) during the financial crisis. Former CEO John Thain spent $1.2 million of shareholder funds redecorating his office while he demanded cost cutting on the part of employees. He also allegedly demanded a bonus in the range of $10–30 million in 2009 despite the fact that Merrill Lynch had lost billions of dollars that year, losing its ability to operate independently (Rothaermel 2013). Unfortunately, there are many more such examples where boards of directors have not put strategic control mechanisms in place to guard against the moral hazard of pursuing personal self-interest at the expense of the shareholders. As mentioned above, a clear enterprise strategy that defines what the firm stands for must be a part of these strategic control mechanisms. Thus, for organizations pursuing SSM, "standing for sustainability" is not just the essence of their visions; it is the moral foundation of their strategic control system.

Bringing Sustainability to Boards

As we have pointed out throughout the book, the importance of integrating sustainability into corporate governance is dramatically increasing. A 2010 study of 800 CEOs conducted by Accenture found that 96 percent believed that sustainability should be integrated into the strategies and operations of their companies, and 93 percent believed that boards of directors should discuss and act on sustainability issues. Both of these results were 24 percent higher than they were when the same CEO survey was conducted in 2007 (United Nations 2012).

Of course, taking on sustainability means that boards must expand their responsibilities to include their firms' social and ecological as well as economic performance. In fact, it is increasingly becoming the legal view that boards have a fiduciary responsibility to oversee the pursuit of corporate sustainability (United Nations 2012). Adding social and ecological performance to the traditional economic oversight responsibilities of board members requires the creation of **learning boards of directors** capable of probing and questioning the fundamental assumptions that underlie their firms' strategic initiatives. The unique perspectives attainable from learning boards provide organizations with a greater capability to push their existing boundaries and create new triple-bottom-line opportunities. John Elkington (1997), architect of the triple-bottom-line concept, says that such boards are the best vehicles for incorporating sustainability into what he refers to as the DNA of firms.

In order to provide the plethora of learning perspectives required for SSM governance, boards need to be composed of members who have broad backgrounds that collectively represent the economic, social, and ecological interests of the firm. Generally, this requires going outside the traditional ranks of inside board members and outside senior executives in order to find knowledgeable board members who represent the interests of social and ecological stakeholders. The board members chosen to represent society and nature should be both prepared and allowed to voice their perspectives and have them incorporated into the strategic choices of the firm. Building these boards will likely require adding directors that represent nonshareholder interests, such as nongovernmental organizations (NGOs), citizen sector organizations (CSOs), and labor unions. If this cannot be achieved, then stakeholders' interests can be brought to the board via stakeholder engagement processes (such as those discussed in Chapter 4) (United Nations 2012).

Having the appropriate board structure is crucial in establishing a board that stands for sustainability. Board structures normally include standing and ad hoc committees that focus on governance functions such as risk management, compliance, auditing, and executive compensation. Boards of organizations pursuing SSM have a need for sustainability to be specifically integrated into these committees. In this way, boards will have the potential to fully explore the legal requirements and fiduciary responsibilities of their firms related to environmental and social performance in areas such as pollution prevention, human rights, worker safety, product safety, community safety, and so forth. Given the increasing pervasiveness of sustainability in the business environment, there is now a trend toward establishing a separate board committee, called the **sustainability committee** or **corporate responsibility committee**, to oversee the integration of sustainability into the operations of the firm (United Nations 2012). Also, more and more firms, such as Eastman

Chemical, are appointing **chief sustainability officers** to give sustainability a formal voice in corporate governance.

Board members today are more concerned than ever that they will be held legally liable for the actions of the corporation, risking their own assets (and possibly even imprisonment) for their actions on the board. For example, shareholders may sue boards for selling the company for too low a price. With regard to their fiduciary responsibility for their firms' sustainability performance, board members can be held legally accountable for developing nonrecyclable packaging in Germany, cutting hardwoods in Canada, importing ivory from Asia or East Africa, or polluting waterways in England. Thus, boards today have a strong self-interest in implementing a value system based on sustainability.

Executive Compensation

Executive compensation is a governance mechanism that seeks to align incentives of shareholders and management through strategic manager salaries, bonuses, and long-term incentive compensation. Boards typically use stock options as the basis of their long-term equity compensation packages for executives. **Stock options** give the recipient the right to buy a firm's stock at a predetermined price sometime in the future. If the stock price rises above the price of the stock on the day the compensation was negotiated, then the executive stands to reap significant gains (Rothaermel 2013). Theoretically stock-option plans address the agency problems by linking managerial compensation with the creation of shareholder wealth. However, major agency problems still exist with the use of stock-option incentives. For example, fraudulent behavior has been associated with the use of stock options, especially if the CEO holds the board chair position and board members also hold stock options (Hitt, Ireland, and Hoskisson 2009). Interestingly, in the United States it is common for the CEO to be chair of the board and for board members to hold stock, as was the case with John Thain of Merrill Lynch (discussed above).

CEO compensation is increasingly becoming a target for media, activist shareholders, and regulators. This stakeholder anger coalesces around two common issues: (1) the absolute size of the CEO compensation package compared to the average worker, and (2) the relationship between firm performance and CEO compensation. In the United States the ratio of CEO pay to the average worker pay is 300 to 1, up from 40 to 1 in 1980 (Rothaermel 2013). CEO pay in Britain in 2011 rose by more than five times that of ordinary workers, who have seen a decline in wages in real terms, leading to escalating anger from the public. Pressured by British public opinion, the business secretary recently announced that the government will legislate to give shareholders binding votes to block executive pay increases (Goodway 2012). The head of a typical U.S. public company made $9.6 million in 2011, according to an analysis by the Associated Press (AP). This was an increase of 6 percent, the highest since the AP began tracking executive compensation in 2006 (Rexrode and Condon 2012).

As Chapter 6 discusses, **golden parachutes** are typically part of the CEOs compensation package. Recall that these are contractual provisions that compensate executives in the event of a hostile takeover or termination without a cause. There has been growing public and shareholder outrage about executive pay packages for poorly performing CEOs. For example, while Bob Nardelli was Home Depot's CEO from 2000 to 2007, its stock value fell 12 percent while its major competitor, Lowe's, saw its stock price increase 173 percent. Under the terms of the separation agreement negotiated when Nardelli joined the company, Nardelli received about $210 million in cash and stock options, including a $20 million severance payment and retirement benefits of $32 million (Mui 2007). Thus, although he drove shareholder value down during his tenure, Nardelli was awarded multimillions of dollars when he left the firm.

In the wake of the 2008 financial crisis, the right to reclaim compensation from executives who engage in ethical or financial misdeeds is becoming a part of executive compensation packages. An astounding 86.5 percent of Fortune 100 companies have adopted **clawback** provisions that allow them to recover cash bonuses or stock from unethical and poorly performing executives (Olson 2012). The clawback was the first thing invoked by JPMorgan Chase's board to fend off criticism of its billions of dollars in trading losses discussed above. Similar to other corporations, JPMorgan Chase adopted a clawback policy to discourage the practice of rich rewards for short-term gains that later evaporate. Referred to sometimes as "If you didn't earn it, you must return it" provisions, these are typically reserved for serious misdeeds, such as accounting irregularities, before triggering the right to reclaim back compensation. The JPMorgan Chase board of directors used this policy to dock the pay of CEO Jamie Dimon and the other executives who oversaw the hedging and resulting losses from the firm's trading in 2012.

Strategic Evaluation and Control

Strategic evaluation and control processes are used to implicitly and explicitly evaluate whether or not a firm's strategy is achieving its intended results. This process should be embedded throughout the organization so that managers at all levels are continuously evaluating the firm's actual performance in comparison

Figure 8.1 **Performance Gap Analysis**

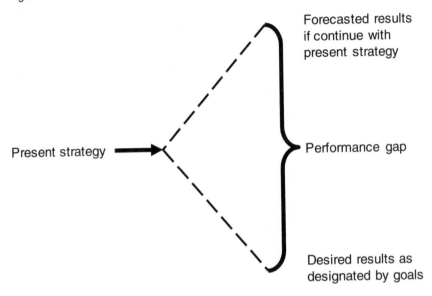

Forecasted results
if continue with
present strategy

Present strategy

Performance gap

Desired results as
designated by goals

to expected results. As discussed above, corporate governance is concerned with mechanisms that ensure that management's motives are consistent with stakeholder interests. SSM strategic evaluation and control provides additional mechanisms that enable strategic managers to determine **performance gaps**, the extent of change needed in current strategies in order to achieve their strategy's intended results, as Figure 8.1 demonstrates. The size of the performance gap determines the corrective actions that need to be made in present strategies. The larger the gap, the more strategic managers must reassess their present strategies in light of current goals. If facing a large performance gap, the strategic choice is either to change strategies or revise the firm's goals in order to the close the gap. In SSM, gap analysis is viewed as a continuous, coevolutionary process where collectively managers ask if their actions are achieving the goals that were formulated in the participative SSM planning process.

SSM corporate governance mechanisms are necessary to ensure the alignment of strategic managers and stakeholders' triple-bottom-line interests. The continuous process of evaluating and questioning results is necessary due to the coevolutionary relationship the firm has with its external environment, and it should take place at each stage of the SSM process. Environmental scanning capabilities continuously provide strategic managers with data on the dynamic changes in the firm's external environment. Using these data, strategic managers can make continuous alignments in internal resource deployments and strategies in order to adapt their firms to the changes in the environment,

Figure 8.2   **SSM Evaluation and Control**

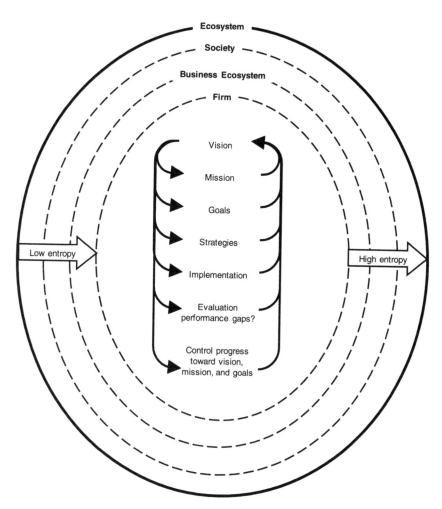

ensuring goal achievement (see Figure 8.2). These strategic evaluation and control mechanisms are like a compass is to a sailor, providing data so the firm can stay on course to its desired future.

Emerging Perspectives on Organizational Leadership

Leadership is historically one of the most prominent topics in management education, research, and practice. Leaders have generally been cast as bigger-than-life heroes who are stronger, smarter, more charismatic, and have more authority than their followers. Leadership theories have historically proposed that leaders who behave in appropriate ways at appropriate times and provide appropriate reinforcements can motivate their followers to perform effectively and efficiently, which Freeman et al. (2007) call Theory I leadership. The common thread here is that leadership theories have in the past focused on leader–follower relations, with the leaders typically being cast as all-knowing, all-powerful, out-front superiors, and the followers typically being cast as less informed, less powerful, willing-to-fall-in-line subordinates.

However, leadership thinking has made a dramatic shift in the past 25 years or so. Numerous models have emerged that portray strategic leadership very differently from the historical superior–subordinate perspective. For example, Peter Senge (1990) describes strategic leaders as thoughtful, knowledgeable vision shepherds who establish organizational systems and processes built on a fundamental respect for human beings and the belief that the best route to organizational success is to tie the personal visions of employees directly to the transcendent long-term visions of organizations. Strategic leaders in this model function as designers, stewards, and teachers, not all-knowing autocrats. As designers, strategic leaders reflect their organizations' most basic intentions, aspirations, and hopes. As stewards, strategic leaders commit to long-term visions of something larger and more important than themselves. As teachers, strategic leaders guide organizational members through deep dialogue processes that allow them to clearly define the current realities of the environment, examine current organizational practices, processes, values, and assumptions, and make changes when necessary.

Owens and Hekman (2012, 806) say that emerging ideas about leadership such as Senge's are looking at leaders as "human rather than superhuman." They say (2012, 788), "Researchers suggest that leaders should move away from the hero myth and the great-man perspective and show their humanness by being open about their knowledge and experience [and that of] their followers." The primary reason for this shift in leadership thinking is the increasing complexity and dynamics of the business environment and the resultant need to increase workplace complexity and adaptability. As we discussed in Chapter 7, this means that the authority-driven, mechanistic, rule-bound, monolithic bureaucracies of yesterday are giving way to self-renewing, value-controlled, organic, vision-driven networks of diverse organizations, and these new structures require a new type of leadership (Owens and Hekman 2012).

Practicing Humble Leadership

One of the most recent and most valuable models of leadership appropriate for modern network-based organizations is Owens and Hekman's (2012) portrayal of Humble Leadership. They point out that **humility is a core human virtue** that lies at the foundation of most of the world's philosophies and religions. As a core human virtue, humility spawns other key virtues, such as moral strength, wisdom, courage, compassion, and knowledge beyond self. The word "humility" is derived from the Latin word *humus*, which means "earth" or "ground." Thus **Humble Leadership** can be defined as "leadership from the earth," "leadership from the ground," or "bottom-up leadership." As such, the term connotes a completely opposite perspective from the old leader–follower models (Owens and Hekman 2012). Especially notable here are the implications these definitions hold for strategic leaders employing Humble Leadership to guide their organizations on an SSM journey. Together they say that Humble Leadership is grounded in the laws of nature, built on deeply held values for the sacredness of the earth and its people, and practiced from a position of service to others.

Owens and Hekman (2012) conducted in-depth interviews with 55 managers from multiple levels in manufacturing, financial services, retail, religion, and the military. They identified three characteristics of Humble Leadership from these interviews: (1) Humble Leaders acknowledge their own personal limits, weaknesses, mistakes, and so forth. Assuming that leaders are perceived to be competent, admitting their weaknesses will be seen as one of their strengths. Leaders perceived as competent will likely be viewed as being intelligent, resolute, and persuasive in addition to being humble. (2) Humble Leaders extol the strengths and contributions of their followers over their own. Assuming that this praise is honest, genuine, and substantive, this shines light on the efforts of others and motivates them to continue to contribute real value to organizations. (3) Humble Leaders are models of learning. They show openness to new ideas and information; they tend to listen before they speak; and they are open to feedback regarding their own ideas and inputs.

From their interviews, Owens and Hekman (2012) gleaned five outcomes of Humble Leadership: (1) Humble Leaders tend to increase the satisfaction with organizational relationships. Given that SSM is being played out in a world of complex relationships involving multiple stakeholders, networks of organizations, and so forth, this is critical. (2) Humble Leaders foster a high level of loyalty in organizations. By revealing their weaknesses, praising others, and showing a willingness to learn, Humble Leaders evoke commitment to the organization and its vision. (3) Humble Leaders foster a high level of trust (which we will discuss in more depth later in this chapter). (4) Humble Leaders help to legitimize the developmental journey of all employees by giving them the psychological freedom and organizational engagement opportunities to work creatively and bring their ideas to fruition. (5) Humble

Leaders legitimize uncertainty as an organizational state. They encourage people to work in a learning environment with open dialogue and organizational fluidity.

Practicing Ethical Leadership

Freeman et al. (2007) also say that modern leaders must go well beyond the leader–follower relationship. They say that leaders today must be able to release the human potential of all employees and stakeholders, they must be able to integrate their organizations into the larger community, they must embody and defend the values of the organization, and they must establish and live the vision of the organization, and (as discussed in Chapter 6), they must become agents of social change. This requires **Ethical Leadership**, which is defined as the ability of leaders to embed ethical expectations into the culture of the organization (Schaubroeck et al. 2012). Schaubroeck et al. (2012) describe the value-embedding process of ethical leadership as "cascading," meaning that the ethical values flow down through each organizational level from top to bottom.

Freeman et al. (2007) say that ethical leadership is absolutely required for managing at the enterprise strategy level (discussed in the previous chapter). They say, "Enterprise strategy must be executed in the spirit of Ethical Leadership. Given that there is . . . an increasingly demanding public that expects the worst from business, we must build ethics into the foundations of how value gets created. . . . We need a framework that expects them to be ethical leaders rather than stick with the current view of capitalists as a bunch of 'greedy little bastards' trying to do each other in" (pp. 13–14).

Freeman et al. (2007) say that Ethical Leadership incorporates six basic principles. According to these principles: (1) ethical leaders act for the benefit of all stakeholders; (2) ethical leaders view all constituents as stakeholders with a common vision; (3) ethical leaders connect organizational goals with stakeholders; (4) ethical leaders establish open dialogue with stakeholders; (5) ethical leaders use moral imagination to make tough ethical judgments; and (6) ethical leaders base all actions and purposes on a sound ethical framework.

Freeman et al. (2007) say that ethical leaders perform several important functions. First of all, ethical leaders articulate the purposes, values, and visions of their organizations. This begins with openly displaying what the organization is and what it stands for, but it also requires that leaders live their organizations' values in both private and public life. Also, like humble leaders, ethical leaders extol the successes of their organizations, not themselves. They celebrate the achievements of others, and they eschew stroking their own egos. Ethical leaders also recruit, select, and develop the best people they can find. This means going beyond simply identifying people with the knowledge, intelligence, abilities, and skills to do the job. It also means finding those with high principles of integrity, honesty, humility, and so forth. Further, ethical leaders encourage open conversations around ethics, values, and stakeholder value creation. Ethical leaders also create dissent mechanisms that allow for alternative views in order to neutralize any potential authority traps present in the system, and they work hard to understand and appreciate the values of their stakeholders, especially when they conflict with their own.

According to Freeman et al. (2007), one of the most difficult functions of ethical leaders is to be "ethically imaginative" in complex situations where stakeholders' interests and values may appear to conflict. For example, Mohammed Yunus's microloan program was a creative way to establish credit for the poor without the need for collateral (see Chapter 5). Ethical leaders also frame what they say and do in ethical terms, but they must learn to avoid appearing self-righteous. This can be done by showing a commitment to one's own values while remaining open to the values of others.

Practicing Spiritual Leadership

We discussed at some length in both Chapter 4 and Chapter 7 the importance of spiritual intelligence, spiritual capital, and spiritual capabilities for implementing SSM. Recall that research has clearly shown that the role of strategic leaders is critical in creating and maintaining spirituality in organizations (Fry 2003, 2009; Middlebrooks and Noghui 2010). Essentially, the research says there is little or no chance that sustainability-centered spiritual beliefs, values, norms, and systems can get a foothold in business organizations unless strategic leaders first demonstrate a deep, long-term personal commitment to the sacredness of nature and society. Thus, a key dimension of effective SSM strategic leadership is spiritual leadership.

Spiritual leadership reveals the organization's greater purpose, and it stirs the souls of its stakeholders. According to Fry (2003, 2009), spiritual leadership involves creating transcendent organizational visions, establishing organizational cultures on values such as altruism, inclusive membership, appreciation, and caring, building stakeholder relationships on service to others, and recognizing that organizational members and stakeholders have an inner life that is important to nurture. Fry says that spiritual leadership is required for building self-renewing, learning organizations such as those described by Senge (see Chapter 7) because the link between the personal visions of employees and the transcendent shared visions of organizations is inherently spiritual. After all, both visions focus directly on a greater purpose for the person and the firm.

Spiritual leaders focus on stimulating not only the minds and bodies but also the hearts and spirits of those they serve. Spiritual leadership reflects an honest effort to develop strategic initiatives that earn a profit by contributing to the greater good and making a difference in the larger community. Spiritual leadership has been shown to have a positive impact on strategic leader effectiveness, in terms of both relationships with employees and relationships with stakeholders outside the organization (Fry 2003; Nahavandi 2009). Given that transforming to a sustainability-based organization requires developing a transcendent vision for earning profits in ways that serve society and the planet, and given that such transformation requires basing an organization's culture on deeply held values for the sacredness of nature, humankind, and posterity, it should be clear why shifting to a sustainable organization requires effective spiritual leadership.

Practicing Servant Leadership

Humble leaders with their deep appreciation of others and their thirst for creativity and innovation, ethical leaders with their emphasis on establishing ethically centered relationships with all stakeholders based on mutual respect, strong convictions, and open dialogue, and spiritual leaders with their sense of greater purpose and greater value for humankind and nature represent the essence of modern leadership thinking. Those following these frameworks are viewed as highly competent, highly principled, very encouraging, trusting, charismatic leaders who treat everyone and everything with a deep and abiding respect and who are capable of tying together the diverse visions of their firms, employees, and stakeholders.

Yet as contemporary as these modern leadership frameworks are, all have elements of servant leadership as described by Robert Greenleaf (1977, 1996) over 30 years ago. In essence, servant leadership rests on a core value of stewardship, keeping things in trust for others. As stewards, **servant leaders** use their leadership capabilities to serve the needs of others. Servant leaders consciously choose to lead for reasons beyond ego satisfaction and wealth. That is, they are not leaders because they want to gain power or acquire material possessions for short-run personal gain. Rather, they truly desire to serve others over self. They believe that a good society is built upon caring relationships in which the more able and the less able serve each other's needs, and they believe that servant leaders who build and maintain caring relationships can tap the human spirit within their organizations and become agents for social change toward a more caring and just society (Greenleaf 1977, 1996).

Effective Business Ecosystem Leadership

As can be gleaned from the above discussion, leading business organizations as they make the transition to SSM in today's complex, ever-changing global economy is no simple task. Leaders are faced with guiding their organizations as they transform their visions, establish new cultures with new systems of values and beliefs, encourage continuous creativity and innovation, and in some cases redefine their very souls. Further, as if the modern leadership situation is not complicated enough, in today's world of expanding SSM-based business ecosystems (see Chapter 3) the roles of strategic leaders are by definition expanding from a single-organization perspective to a multi-organization perspective, where some of the organizations may not even be profit oriented.

Recall that SSM-based business ecosystems are networks composed of an ecosystem leader (keystone firm) and a variety of niche organizations (i.e., corporations, small entrepreneurs, NGOs, CSOs, or public agencies) that share platforms and information that allow them to pursue their triple-bottom-line goals under the umbrella of the ecosystem leader's transcendent sustainability-centered vision. Joining SSM-based business ecosystems is designed to provide organizations with opportunities to come together to do something for the planet and its people that they cannot do alone.

It is the responsibility of the ecosystem leader to make sure that this happens through effective **alliance management capability**, previously discussed in Chapter 6. Specifically, this requires that business ecosystem leaders: (1) provide the transcendent vision for the ecosystem; (2) build shared stewardship of the vision among ecosystem members; (3) provide the shared ecosystem platform; (4) define the boundaries of the ecosystem; (5) define and maintain the relationships among ecosystem members; (6) provide space in the ecosystem for value-sharing opportunities for the members; (7) build and maintain an innovative core; and (8) build community-based learning structures that allow the ecosystem members to translate their shared platforms and standards into coordinated collective actions.

Central to effective alliance management capability is building strong trusting relationships among ecosystem members—managing the collaboration, inclusion, diversity, and open dialogue processes necessary for sharing knowledge, structures, governance mechanisms, platforms, resources, capabilities, and risks among the ecosystem members. The firm's spiritual capabilities provide the foundation for effective alliance management capability that results in trusting relationships among ecosystem members.

Building Trusting Relationships

Freeman et al. (2007, 3) define a business as "a set of relationships among groups of [stakeholders]." They say, "To understand a business is to know how these relationships work. The executive's or entrepreneur's job is to manage and shape these relationships." We have stressed throughout this book that successfully implementing SSM requires that strategic managers create and maintain effective sustainability-centered relationships within their firms and among their interconnected plethora of stakeholders. This is certainly true for establishing and leading triple-bottom-line-anchored business ecosystems, for creating shared understanding of what firms stand for, for developing organizational cultures based on shared sustainability-centered value systems, and for molding transcendent capabilities into effective and efficient sustainability strategies.

In fact, all organizations are composed of networks of human relationships that emerge through systems of mutually beneficial interpersonal exchanges. These mutual benefits may be tangible (i.e., financial gain) or intangible (i.e., personal attraction), but in the long run organizations cannot exist without a strong system of mutually beneficial relationships among all parties involved, including strategic managers, employees, business ecosystem partners, investors, customers, and so forth.

This is important because, although entropy is a law of physical transformation, it has critical social implications as well. Just as entropy imposes limits on the value of physical capital, it also imposes limits on the value of **social capital**, which is composed of the relationships among organizational actors (Portes 1998). Relationships are entropic because developing and maintaining them requires a significant investment of human time and energy (Tymon and Stumpf 2003). Of course, human mortality places absolute entropic limits on human relationships, but aging and death are not required for entropy to diminish or destroy them. They will change, fade, and eventually disappear if the necessary human time and energy are not invested into them.

Many interrelated factors go into building and maintaining the complex human relationships required for doing things such as establishing healthy business ecosystems or implementing base-of-the-pyramid SSM strategies. Recall from Chapter 6, incentive problems and the risk of self-serving behavior from opportunism may arise from the differences in orientation and needs among ecosystem members, which in turn, may prevent partners from fully participating in the ecosystem. And recall, the essence of effective alliance management is building trust among ecosystem members, and these trust-based interorganizational relationships are important sources of competitive advantage for the business ecosystem (Dyer and Singh 1998).

Thus, successful ecosystem leadership requires strategic leaders to have the spiritual intelligence to create spiritual capital among ecosystem members so that trust-based, interorganizational, spiritual capabilities become a source of competitive advantage for the business ecosystem.

Trust is reliance or dependence on the ability, character, strength, or truth of others. According to Tymon and Stumpf (2003, 16), "When trust is developed the relationship takes on longer lasting qualities and thereby requires less maintenance." Thus, when there is trust, years can pass with minimal interaction while the relationship continues to grow strong. However, the opposite is true as well. Loss of trust is one of the quickest and easiest ways of choking off the flow of the human time and energy needed to maintain viable relationships, and once trust begins to deteriorate, the process is often irreversible. Therefore, trust is a key to slowing and arresting the entropic flow related to relationship building and maintenance (Prusak and Cohen 2001; Putnam 2000; Tymon and Stumpf 2003).

Because of the critical importance of trust in building and maintaining relationships, we offer an additional note. Being trustworthy is an essential characteristic for strategic managers. Their success or failure in building strong relationships with ecosystem partners and so forth is based on whether or not they are perceived as trustworthy by their partners and potential partners. Also, remember that being trusted is different from being liked. Whereas being liked results from personal attraction, being trusted results from one's ability and willingness to follow up with action. This is especially important in the business arena of coevolving business ecosystems where being liked is good, but being trusted is critical.

Chapter Summary

To effectively implement SSM in modern business organizations, strategic managers will need two key elements. First of all, they will need effective organizational governance mechanisms in place that will support the alignment of the triple-bottom-line goals of the organization with the interests of organizational stakeholders. This starts by embedding an enterprise strategy based on values that "stand for sustainability" across the organization. It also involves establishing a strategic evaluation and control system, executive review and compensation system, board of directors, and organizational units that are all aligned with SSM goals.

Strategic leadership skills are the second critical element for strategic managers working to implement SSM. Strategic leaders pursuing SSM must: (1) be personally committed to bold visions of their firms' earning profits in ways that benefit humankind and the planet; (2) guide their organizations through deep cultural shifts toward sustainability-centered systems, norms, values, and beliefs; (3) manage in ways that emphasize the ideas and accomplishments of others; (4) be both ethically grounded and ethically open in all interactions and transactions with stakeholders; (5) be continuously open to new ideas and new ways of thinking; (6) develop a multifirm business ecosystem perspective; and (7) be agents of social change willing to serve the needs of stakeholders, communities, and the world at large. At the heart of crafting and maintaining these governance systems and leadership processes is trust. Without it, the systems will crash and burn, but with it, they can soar to new coevolutionary heights.

Case Vignette 8

Strategic Leadership at Eastman Chemical Company

Jim Rogers, CEO of Eastman Chemical Company, believes that since values and beliefs heavily influence people's decisions, leaders must clearly understand their own core beliefs and what their companies stand for before they can make valuable strategic choices. In reflecting on the emergence of his leadership style, Rogers says his work experiences have shaped his leadership philosophy since his time as a lieutenant in the United States Navy. He said that as a naval aviator aboard the *USS Eisenhower,* he experienced the satisfaction of working in a highly trained professional team whose members always had each other's backs.

After completing his service in the navy and his MBA at Wharton, Rogers entered the world of finance, initially working at JPMorgan managing mergers, acquisitions, and leveraged buyouts. It was during these years in private equity that Rogers began to understand that knowledge and expertise are essential for good leadership. In later executive positions at GAF and International Specialty Products, Rogers discovered that effectively using one's formal position in the organizational hierarchy is also important for effective leadership. Since arriving as Eastman's CFO in 1999—a move he made because he wanted the opportunity to lead a team of people who were the best in the world at what they do—he has discovered that effective leaders are able to influence employees to follow them even when they do not have to follow.

So how does Rogers characterize his leadership style today? He says that he "leads from the other side of the table," where he works to see the points of view of others before formulating his own position. He refers to himself as a servant leader, and he notes that servant leaders are not associated with any single religion. Rather, they are motivated by a higher-level spiritual commitment to serve the needs of others. They are stewards holding their organizations in trust for those who follow. They engender a high level of trust and open dialogue among stakeholders. One way that Rogers creates such open dialogue and trust with stakeholders is to hold an annual breakfast for area clergy. At these breakfasts, Rogers shares his thoughts and concerns about the economic health of Eastman, the long-term health of Eastman's employees, and the plans for Eastman's future. At the 2013 breakfast, he asked the clergy in attendance to pray for Eastman's 13,500 employees because of the long hours, hard work, and in many cases personal uncertainty they were experiencing because of Eastman's acquisition of Solutia.

Thus, Eastman Chemical Company under the watchful eye of Jim Rogers demonstrates that sustainability and servant leadership are integrally linked. Rogers demonstrates the high levels of both emotional commitment and spiritual intelligence required of CEOs working to create and shepherd shared visions of sustainability throughout the business ecosystems in which they participate. Whether it is the decision to acquire Solutia for US\$4.7 billion because both firms stand for providing sustainable solutions to consumers, or the decision to join with a local university to provide desperately needed computers to local school children, the evidence is clear that Rogers and Eastman are committed to their sustainability journey. The philosophy of providing quality returns to their shareholders while learning how to serve as agents of social change is evident in Rogers's leadership style. He and his organization are proving that it is very possible to do well by doing good.

Bibliography

3M. 2012. "3P—Pollution prevention pays. We think it is better to prevent pollution than to clean it up later." http://solutions.3m.com/wps/portal/3M/en_US/3M-Sustainability/Global/Environment/3P/ (accessed July 18, 2012).

Abell, Derick. 1980. *Defining the Business: The Starting Point in Strategic Planning.* Englewood Cliffs, NJ: Prentice Hall.

Aburdene, Patricia. 2005. *Megatrends 2010: The Rise of Conscious Capitalism.* Charlottesville, VA: Hampton Roads.

Alliance for a Healthier Generation. 2012. "About Us." http://www.healthiergeneration.org/about.aspx (accessed July 16, 2012).

American Chemistry Council. 2012. Responsible Care. http://responsiblecare.americanchemistry.com/?gclid=CIeAwuey-7ACFdKR7QodKnew2A (accessed July 2, 2012).

Ansoff, Igor. 1979. "The Changing Shape of the Strategic Problem." In *Strategic Management,* ed. D. Schendel and C. Hofer, 30–44. Boston: Little Brown.

Argyris, Chris, and D. A. Schön. 1978. *Organizational Learning: A Theory of Action Perspective.* Reading, MA: Addison-Wesley.

Avert. 2012. "Sub-Saharan Africa HIV & AIDS Statistics." http://www.avert.org/africa-hiv-aids-statistics.htm (accessed December 19, 2012).

Ayres, Richard. 1989. "Industrial Metabolism." In *Technology and Environment,* ed. J. Ausubel and H. Sladovich, 23–49. Washington, DC: National Academy Press.

———. 1994. "Industrial Metabolism: Theory and Policy." In *The Greening of Industrial Ecosystems,* ed. B. Allenby and D. Richards, 23–37. Washington, DC: National Academy Press.

Bansal, Pratima, and Kendall Roth. 2000. "Why Companies Go Green: A Model of Ecological Responsiveness." *Academy of Management Journal* 43, no. 4, 717–736.

Barber, Benjamin. 1995. *Jihad Versus McWorld.* New York: Ballantine Books.

Barney, Jay. 1986. "Strategic Factor Markets: Expectations, Luck, and Business Strategy." *Management Science* 32, 1231–1241.

———. 1991. "Firm Resources and Sustained Competitive Advantage." *Journal of Management* 17, 99–120.

———. 2001. "Is the Resource-Based 'View' a Useful Perspective for Strategic Management Research? Yes." *Academy of Management Review* 27, no. 4, 339–358.

Barney, Jay, and William Hesterly. 2010. *Strategic Management and Competitive Advantage.* 3rd ed. Upper Saddle River, NJ: Prentice Hall.

Barrett, Paul. 2012. "It's Global Warming, Stupid." *Bloomberg Business Week*, November 1, 6–8.

Bebbington, Jan, Robert Gray, Chris Hibbitt, and Elizabeth Kirk. 2001. *Full Cost Accounting: An Agenda for Action*. London: Association of Chartered Certified Accountants.

Beck, Don E., and Christopher C. Cowan. 1996. *Spiral Dynamics: Mastering Values, Leadership and Change*. Oxford, UK: Blackwell.

Beckhard, Richard, and Walter Pritchard. 1992. *Changing the Essence*. San Francisco: Jossey-Bass.

Benn, Suzanne, and E. J. Probert. 2006. "Incremental Change Towards Sustainability: Integrating Human and Ecological Factors for Efficiency." In *Managing the Business Case for Sustainability*, ed. Stefan Schaltegger and Marcus Wagner, 542–552. Sheffield, UK: Greenleaf.

Bies, Robert J., Jean M. Bartunek, Timothy Fort, and Mayer Zald. 2007. "Corporations as Social Change Agents, Individual, Interpersonal, Institutional, and Environmental Dynamics." *Academy of Management Review* 32, no. 3, 788–793.

Bosker, Bianca, and Dino Grandoni. 2012. "Apple-Samsung Lawsuit: What You Need To Know About The Verdict." *Huffington Post*, August 25. http://www.huffingtonpost.com/2012/08/24/apple-samsung-lawsuit-verdict_n_1829268.html?1345857263&utm_hp_ref=technology (accessed September 15, 2012).

Boulding, Kenneth E. 1956. "General Systems Theory—The Skeleton of Science." *Management Science* 2, no. 3, 197–208.

———. 1966. "The Economics of the Coming Spaceship Earth." In *Environmental Quality in a Growing Economy*, ed. H. Jarrett, 3–14. Baltimore, MD: Johns-Hopkins Press.

Boykoff, Jules. 2011. "Why the Insurance Industry Gets Climate Change." *Guardian*, June 28. http://www.guardian.co.uk/commentisfree/cifamerica/2011/jun/28/climate-change-climate-change-scepticism (accessed September 17, 2012).

Boyle, Mary-Ellen, and Janet Boguslaw. 2007. "Business, Poverty and Corporate Citizenship: Naming the Issues and Framing the Solutions." *Journal of Corporate Citizenship* 26, 101–120.

Bradford, Harry. 2012. "JPMorgan Chase's Reputation Falls to Lowest Level on Record in Wake of $2B Loss." *Huffington Post*, May 23. http://www.huffingtonpost.com/2012/05/23/jpmorgan-chases-consumer-reputation-yougov_n_1540582.html (accessed August 17, 2012).

Brown, Lester R. 2008. *Plan B 3.0: Mobilizing to Save Civilization*. New York: Norton.

Bughin, Jacques, Michael Chui, and Brad Johnson. 2012. "The Next Step in Open Innovation." *McKinsey Quarterly*. https://www.mckinseyquarterly.com/Operations/Product_Development/next_step_in_open_innovation_2155 (accessed September 5, 2012).

Business Roundtable. 2011. *Innovating Sustainability: Report 2011*. Washington, DC.

Butler, Janet B., Sandra Cherie Henderson, and Cecily Raiborn. 2011. "Sustainability and the Balanced Scorecard: Integrating Green Measures into Business Reporting." *Management Accounting* 12, no. 2, 1–10.

Buzzelli, David. 1994. "Toward Sustainability Development: Beware of Environmental Pit Bulls." Nathan Lecture, University of Michigan, Ann Arbor, March 9.

Campbell, Andrew, Michael Goold, and Marcus Alexander. 1995. "Corporate Strategy: The Question for Parenting Advantage." *Harvard Business Review* 73, no. 2, 120–132.

Carlson, Nicholas. 2012. "An M&A Insider Explains Facebook's Game Plan for Massive Acquisitions." *Business Insider,* July 10. http://www.sfgate.com/technology/businessinsider/article/An-M-A-Insider-Explains-Facebook-s-Game-Plan-For-3696471.php (accessed July 12, 2012).

Carpenter, S., E. Bennett, and G. Peterson. 2006. "Scenarios for Ecosystem Services: An Overview." *Ecology and Society* 11, no. 1, 29. http://www.ecologyandsociety.org/vol11/iss1/art29/ (accessed September 17, 2012).

Carson, Rachel. 1962. *Silent Spring.* Boston: Houghton Mifflin.

Central Intelligence Agency (CIA). 2012. *The World Factbook.* Washington, DC. https://www.cia.gov/library/publications/the-world-factbook/geos/xx.html (accessed November 12, 2012).

Chambers, N., and K. Lewis. 2001. *Ecological Footprint Analysis: Towards a Sustainability Indicator for Business.* London: Association of Chartered Certified Accountants.

Chermack, T. J., and R. A. Swanson. 2008. "Scenario Planning: Human Resource Development's Strategic Learning Tool." *Advances in Developing Human Resources* 10, no. 2, 258–284.

Child, John. 1972. "Organization Structure, Environment and Performance. The Role of Strategic Choice." *Sociology*, 6, no. 1, 1–22.

Christmann, C. 2000. "Effects of Best Practices of Environmental Management on Cost Advantage: The Role of Complementary Assets." *Academy of Management Journal* 43, no. 4, 663–680.

Cleveland, Josh. 2011. "Advancing Healthcare with the BoP: To Emerging Markets and Back Again." *Next Billion,* February 23. http://www.nextbillion.net/blogpost.aspx?blogid=2163 (accessed August 6, 2012).

Coca-Cola Company. 2011. *Exploring the Links Between International Business and Poverty Reduction.* Report. http://www.thecocacolacompany.com/citizenship/pdf/poverty_footprint_report.pdf (accessed May 24, 2012).

Colbert, B. 2004. "The Complex Resource-Based View: Implications for Theory and Practice in Strategic Human Resource Management." *Academy of Management Review* 29 no. 3, 341–358.

Collins, Jim. 2001. *Good to Great.* New York: HarperBusiness.

Collins, Jim, and Jerry Porras. 1994. *Built to Last: Successful Habits of Visionary Companies.* New York: HarperBusiness.

Cooperrider, David L., and Diana Whitney. 2005. *Appreciative Inquiry.* San Francisco: Berrett-Koehler.

Corvalan, C., S. Hales, and A. McMichael. 2005. *Ecosystems and Human Well-being.* Geneva: World Health Organization.

Daly, Herman E. 1977. *Steady State Economics.* San Francisco: W. H. Freeman.

Daly, Herman E., and Joshua Farley. 2004. *Ecological Economics: Principles and Applications.* Washington, DC: Island Press.

Davies, James B., Susanna Sandström, Anthony Shorrocks, and Edward N. Wolff. 2008. *The World Distribution of Household Wealth.* United Nations University, World Institute for Development Economics Research, Discussion Paper no. 2008/03, February.

Dean, Thomas J., and Jeffrey S. McMullen. 2005. "Toward a Theory of Sustainable

Entrepreneurship: Reducing Environmental Degradation Through Entrepreneurial Action." *Journal of Business Venturing* 22, no. 1, 50–76.

Delgado, Alessandra. 2007. "Information Economy Thrives in Cities." *Vital Signs 2007–2008*, 114–115. New York: Norton.

de Kluyver, Cornelius, and John Pearce. 2012. *Strategy: A View from the Top*. 4th ed. Boston: Prentice Hall.

DeMasi, Karin, and Jonathan Clarke. 2011. "Top Five Antitrust Trends to Watch in 2011." Boardmember.com. http://www.cravath.com/files/Uploads/Documents/Publications/3255246_1.pdf (accessed July 12, 2012).

Del Nibletto, Paolo. 2010. "Microsoft and the Channel by the Numbers." Itbusiness. ca, July 16. http://www.itbusiness.ca/it/client/en/home/News.asp?id=58404&cid=6 (accessed September 15, 2012).

Dess, Gregory, G. T. Lumpkin, and Alan Eisner. 2008. *Strategic Management*. 4th ed. New York: McGraw-Hill.

Dinnick, Wilf. May 20, 2008. "Ethiopian Children Dying Daily from Starvation." CNN.com, May 21. http://www.cnn.com/2008/WORLD/africa/05/20/ethiopia. children/index.html (accessed May 20, 2008).

Doppelt, Bob. 2003. *Leading Change Toward Sustainability: A Change-Management Guide for Business, Government, and Civil Society*. Sheffield, UK: Greenleaf.

Drayton, B., and V. Budinich. 2010. "A New Alliance for Global Change." *Harvard Business Review*, September, 56–64.

Driver, Michaela: 2007. "A 'Spiritual Turn' in Organizational Studies: Meaning Making or Meaningless?" *Journal of Management, Spirituality and Religion* 4, no. 1, 56–86.

Dunphy, Dexter, Andrew Griffiths, and Suzanne Benn. 2007. *Organizational Change for Corporate Sustainability*. 2nd ed. London: Routledge.

Dyer, Jeff, and Harbir Singh. 1998. "The Relational View: Cooperative Strategy and the Sources of Interorganizational Advantage." *Academy of Management Review* 23, 600–679.

Dyllick, Thomas, and Kai Hockerts. 2002. "Beyond the Business Case for Corporate Sustainability." *Business Strategy and the Environment* 11, no. 2, 130–141.

Eastman Chemical Company. 2011. "Sustainability Goals." http://www.eastman.com/company/Sustainability/GoalsMeasures/Pages/Sustainable_Goals.aspx (accessed July 16, 2012).

Economist. 2012. "The Last Kodak Moment." January 14. www.economist.com/node/21542796 (accessed July 16, 2012).

Edwards, Andrés. 2005. *The Sustainability Revolution: Portrait of a Paradigm Shift*. Gabriola Island, BC: New Society.

Efrati, Amir. 2013. "Samsung Sparks Anxiety at Google." *Wall Street Journal*. http://online.wsj.com/article/SB10001424127887323699704578324220017879796.html (accessed March 24, 2013).

Egri, Carolyn P., and Susan Herman. 2000. "Leadership in the North American Environmental Sector: Values, Leadership Styles, and Contexts of Environmental Leaders and Their Organizations." *Academy of Management Journal* 43, no. 4, 571–604.

Ehrenreich, Barbara. 2001. *Nickel and Dimed: On (Not) Getting By in America*. New York: Henry Holt.

Ehrlich, Paul R. 1991. "Coevolution and Its Applicability to the Gaia Hypothesis."

In *Scientists on Gaia,* ed. Stephen H. Schneider and Penelope J. Boston, 19–22. Cambridge, MA: MIT Press.

Ehrlich, Paul R., and Ann H. Ehrlich. 1990. *The Population Explosion.* New York: Simon and Schuster.

Ehrlich, Paul R., and Peter H. Raven. 1964. "Butterflies and Plants: A Study in Co-evolution." *Evolution* 18, 586–608.

Eisenhardt, Kathleen. 1989. "Agency Theory: An Assessment and Review." *Academy of Management Review* 14, no. 1, 57–74.

Eisenhardt, K. M., and J. A. Martin. 2000. "Dynamic Capabilities: What Are They?" *Strategic Management Journal* 21, no. 10–11, 1105–1121.

Elkington, John. 1997. *Cannibals with Forks.* Oxford, UK: Capstone.

Engelman, Robert. 2011. "World Population Growth Slows Modestly, Still on Track for 7 Billion in Late 2011." *Vital Signs 2011,* 88–91. Washington, DC: Worldwatch Institute.

Enkvist, Anders, Tomas Nauclér, and Jeremy Oppenheim. 2008. "Business Strategies for Climate Change." *McKinsey Quarterly,* April. https://www.mckinsey-quarterly.com/Business_strategies_for_climate_change_2125 (accessed August 7, 2012).

Ernst and Young. 2011. *Shareholders Press Boards on Social and Environmental Risks.* New York.

Esty, D., and A. Winston. 2008. *Green to Gold: How Smart Companies Use Environmental Strategy to Innovate, Create Value, and Build Competitive Advantage.* New Haven, CT: Yale University Press.

Etherington, Darrell. 2013. "Google's Eric Schmidt Talks Apple Partnership, Samsung and Patent Problems." *TechCrunch.* http://techcrunch.com/2012/09/27/googles-eric-schmidt-talks-apple-partnership-samsung-and-patent-problems/ (accessed March 24, 2013).

Farzad, Roben. 2011. "Subaru of Indiana, America's Scrapiest Carmaker." *Bloomberg Business Week,* June 2. http://www.businessweek.com/magazine/content/11_24/b4232068147070.htm (accessed August 18, 2012).

Felberbaum, Michael, and Vinnee Tong. 2009. "Circuit City Liquidation: 567 US Stores Closing." *Huffington Post,* January 16. http://www.huffingtonpost.com/2009/01/16/circuit-city-liquidation_n_158474.html (accessed July 16, 2012).

Figge, Frank, and Tobias Hahn. 2004. "Sustainable Value Added—Measuring Corporate Contributions to Sustainability Beyond Eco-Efficiency." *Ecological Economics* 48, no. 2, 173–187.

———. 2005. "The Cost of Sustainability Capital and the Creation of Sustainable Value by Companies." *Journal of Industrial Ecology* 9, no. 4, 47–58.

———. 2006. "Sustainable Value Added: A New Approach to Measuring Corporate Sustainable Performance." In *Managing the Business Case for Sustainability,* ed. Stefan Schaltegger and Marcus Wagner, 146–164. Sheffield, UK: Greenleaf.

Flier, Bert, Frans A. J. Van Den Bosch, and Henk W. Volberda. 2003. "Co-evolution in Strategic Renewal Behaviour of British, Dutch and French Financial Incumbents: Institutional Effects and Managerial Intentionality." *Journal of Management Studies* 40, no. 8, 2163–2187.

Fombrun, Charles, Naomi A. Gardberg, and Michael Barnett. 2000. "Opportunity Platforms and Safety Nets: Corporate Citizenship and Reputational Risk." *Business and Society Review* 105, no. 1, 85–106.

Francis, David. 2012. "Breaking Down the Income Gap into Real Terms." *US*

News, January 4. http://money.usnews.com/money/business-economy/articles/2012/01/04/breaking-down-the-income-gap-into-real-terms (accessed November 3, 2012).

Freeman, R. Edward. 1984. *Strategic Management: A Stakeholder Approach.* Boston: Pitman.

Freeman, R. Edward, and Daniel R. Gilbert Jr. 1988. *Corporate Strategy and the Search for Ethics.* Englewood Cliffs, NJ: Prentice Hall.

Freeman, R. Edward, and Jean Liedtka. 1997. "Stakeholder Capitalism and the Value Chain." *European Management Journal* 15, no. 3, 289–299.

Freeman, R. Edward, Jeffrey S. Harrison, and Andrew C. Wicks. 2007. *Managing for Stakeholders.* New Haven, CT: Yale University Press.

Freeman, R. Edward, Jessica Pierce, and Richard H. Dodd. 2000. *Environmentalism and the New Logic of Business.* Oxford: Oxford University Press.

Friedman, Thomas L. 1999. *The Lexus and the Olive Tree.* New York: Anchor.

———. 2004. *The World Is Flat: A Brief History of the Twenty-First Century.* New York: Farrar, Straus and Giroux.

Fry, Louis W. 2003. "Toward a Theory of Spiritual Leadership." *Leadership Quarterly* 14, no. 6, 693–727.

———. 2009. "Spiritual Leadership as a Model for Student Inner Development." *Journal of Leadership Studies* 3, no. 3, 79–82.

Galindo, V., and A. Massena. 2011. "The Rise of Emerging Markets." *The Contributor,* Newsletter of the National Association of Government Defined Contribution Administrators, Inc.

Gap, Inc. 2012. "About Our Brands." http://www.gapinc.com/content/gapinc/html/aboutus/ourbrands.html (accessed July 17, 2012).

Gardner, Gary. 2011. "Global Output Stagnant." *Vital Signs 2011,* 74–76. Washington, DC: Worldwatch Institute.

Gardner, Howard. 1993. *Frames of Mind: The Theory of Multiple Intelligences.* London: Fontana.

Georgescu-Roegen, Nicholas. 1971. *The Entropy Law and the Economic Process.* Cambridge, MA: Harvard University Press.

Ghemawat, Pankaj. 2010. *Strategy and the Business Landscape.* 3rd ed. Boston: Prentice Hall.

Gladwin, Tom, James Kennelly, and T. Krause. 1995. "Shifting Paradigms for Sustainable Development: Implications for Management Theory and Research." *Academy of Management Review* 20, no. 4, 874–907.

Global Reporting Initiative (GRI). 2012a. "G3 Guidelines." https://www.globalreporting.org/reporting/latest-guidelines/g3-guidelines/Pages/default.aspx (accessed August 15, 2012).

———. 2012b. "G3.1 Guidelines." https://www.globalreporting.org/reporting/latest-guidelines/g3-1-guidelines/Pages/default.aspx (accessed August 15, 2012).

Goleman, Daniel. 1996. *Emotional Intelligence.* New York: Bantam Books.

———. 2009. "Wal-Mart Exposes the De-Value Chain." HBR Blog Network, July 17. http://blogs.hbr.org/leadinggreen/2009/07/walmarts-transparency-exposes.html (accessed September 15, 2012).

Goodman, Ann. 2012. "The 6 Biggest Trends in Sustainability Reporting." GreenBiz.com, January 30. http://www.greenbiz.com/blog/2012/01/30/6-biggest-trends-sustainability-reporting (accessed August 20, 2012).

Goodway, Nick. 2012. "What Recession? Top Bosses' Pay Rockets." *Independent,* August 18. http://www.independent.co.uk/news/business/news/what-recession-top-bosses-pay-rockets-8057359.html (accessed August 18, 2012).

Gradl, Christina, and Beth Jenkins. 2011. "Tackling Barriers to Scale: From Inclusive Business Models to Inclusive Business Ecosystems." Cambridge, MA: CSR Initiative at the Harvard Kennedy School.

Grant, Robert. 1991. "The Resource-Based Theory of Competitive Advantage." *California Management Review* 33, no. 3, 114–135.

———. 2008. *Contemporary Strategy Analysis.* 6th ed. Oxford, UK: Blackwell.

Graves, Clare W. 1970. "Levels of Existence: An Open System Theory of Values." *Journal of Humanistic Psychology* 10, no. 2, 131–154.

Graziano, Dan. 2013. "Google Exec Calls Motorola Acquisition an Insurance Policy Against Samsung." *BGR.* http://bgr.com/2013/02/26/google-samsung-relationship-android-344669/ (accessed March 24, 2013).

———. 1974. "Human Nature Prepares for a Momentous Leap." *Futurist,* April, 72–87.

Greenleaf, Robert K. 1977. *Servant Leadership: A Journey into the Nature of Legitimate Power and Greatness.* Mahwah, NJ: Paulist Press.

———. 1996. *On Becoming a Servant-Leader.* San Francisco: Jossey-Bass.

Gregory, R. 2000. "Using Stakeholder Values to Make Smarter Environmental Decisions." *Environment* 42, no. 5, 34–44.

Grootaert, Christiaan, and Thierry van Bastelaer. April 2001. "Understanding and Measuring Social Capital: A Synthesis of Findings and Recommendations From the Social Capital initiative." The World Bank Social Capital Initiative. Working Paper 24. http://siteresources.worldbank.org/INTRANETSOCIALDEVELOP-MENT/882042-1111750197177/20502279/SCI-WPS-24.pdf (accessed March 14, 2013).

Gueguen, Gael, Estelle Pellegrin-Boucher, and Oliver Torres. 2006. "Between Cooperation and Competition: The Benefits of Collective Strategies within Business Ecosystems." The Example of the Software Industry. EIASM, Second Workshop on Coopetition Strategy, Milan, Italy, September, 14–15.

Guillén, M. F., and S. L. Suárez. 2005. "Explaining the Global Digital Divide: Economic, Political and Sociological Drivers of Cross-National Internet Use." *Social Forces* 84, no. 2, 681–708.

Gulati, Ranjay, Nitin Nohria, and Akbar Zaheer. 2000. "Strategic Networks." *Strategic Management Journal* 21, 203–215.

Gull, Gregory A., and Jonathan Doh. 2004. "The 'Transmutation' of the Organization: Toward a More Spiritual Workplace." *Journal of Management Inquiry* 13, no.2, 128–139.

Gundry, Lisa, and Jill Kickul. 2007. *Entrepreneurship Strategy.* Thousand Oaks, CA: Sage.

Habiby, Anne, and Deirdre Cole. 2010. "The High Intensity Entrepreneur." *Harvard Business Review,* September, 74–78.

Halweil, Brian. 2004. *Eat Here: Homegrown Pleasures in a Global Supermarket.* New York: Norton.

———. 2007. "Ocean Pollution Worsens and Spreads." *Vital Signs 2007–2008,* 100–101. New York: Norton.

Hamel, Gary, and C. K. Prahalad. 1994. *Competing for the Future.* Cambridge, MA: Harvard Business School Press.

Hammond, Allen. 1998. *Which World? Scenarios for the 21st Century.* Washington, DC: Island Press.

———. 2011. "BoP Venture Formation for Scale." In *Next Generation Business Strategies for the Base of the Pyramid,* ed. T. London and S. Hart, 193–215. Upper Saddle River, NJ: Pearson Education.

Hardin, Garrett. 1974. "Lifeboat Ethics: The Case Against Helping the Poor." *Psychology Today,* September. http://www.garretthardinsociety.org/articles/art_lifeboat_ethics_case_against_helping_poor.html (accessed June 6 2008).

Harley-Davidson Corporation. 2012. "Get the Rest of the Story." http://www.harley-davidson.com/en_US/Content/Pages/HD_Museum/explore/hd-history.html (accessed July 16, 2012).

Hart, Stuart L. 1995. "A Natural Resource-Based View of the Firm." *Academy of Management Review* 20, no. 4: 986–1014.

———. 1997. "Beyond Greening: Strategies for a Sustainable World." *Harvard Business Review* 75, no. 1: 67–76.

———. 2005. *Capitalism at the Crossroads.* Upper Saddle River, NJ: Wharton School.

———. 2008. "Forward." In *Sustainability Challenges and Solutions at the Base of the Pyramid: Business, Technology, and the Poor,* ed. P. Kandachar and M. Halme, ix–xi. Sheffield, UK: Greenleaf.

———. 2011. "Taking the Green Leap to the Base of the Pyramid." In *Next Generation Business Strategies for the Base of the Pyramid,* ed. T. London and S. Hart, 79–102. Upper Saddle River, NJ: Pearson Education.

Hart, Stuart L., and Clayton M. Christensen. 2002. "The Great Leap: Driving Innovation from the Base of the Pyramid." *MIT Sloan Management Review* 44, no. 1, 51–56.

Hart, Stuart L., and Mark Milstein. 1999. "Global Sustainability and the Creative Destruction of Industries." *Sloan Management Review* (Fall), 23–33.

Hart, Stuart L., and Sanjay Sharma. 2004. "Engaging Fringe Stakeholders for Competitive Imagination." *Academy of Management Executive* 18, no. 1, 7–18.

Hawken, Paul. 2007. *Blessed Unrest.* New York: Viking.

Hawken, Paul, Amory Lovins, and L. Hunter Lovins. 1999. "A Road Map for Natural Capitalism." *Harvard Business Review* 77, no. 3, 145–157.

Henderson, Bruce. 1973. "The Experience Curve—Reviewed: IV. The Growth Share Matrix or The Product Portfolio." Reprint no. 135. Boston Consulting Group. http://www.bcg.com/documents/file13904.pdf (accessed August 15, 2012).

Hill, Charles, and Gareth Jones. 2009. *Essentials of Strategic Management.* 2nd ed. Mason, OH: South-Western/Cengage Learning.

Hitt, Michael, Duane Ireland, and Robert Hoskisson. 2009. *Strategic Management.* 8th ed. Mason, OH: South-Western/Cengage Learning.

Hockerts, Kai. 1999. "SustainAbility Radar." *Greener Management International* 25, 25–35.

Hoffman, Andrew J. 1999. "Institutional Evolution and Change: Environmentalism and the U.S. Chemical Industry." *Academy of Management Journal* 42, no. 4, 351–371.

———. 2007. "The Coming Market Shift: Climate Change and Business Strategy." In *Cut Carbon, Grow Profits: Business Strategies for Managing Climate Change and Sustainability,* ed. K. Tang and R. Yoeh, 101–118. London: Middlesex University Press.

Holliday, Charles, Stephen Schmidheiny, and Phillip Watts. 2002. *Walking the Talk: The Business Case for Sustainable Development.* Sheffield, UK: Greenleaf.

Hosmer, L. T. 1994. "Strategic Planning as if Ethics Mattered." *Strategic Management Journal* 15, 17–34.

Huff, Anne, Steven Floyd, Hugh Sherman, and Siri Terjesen. 2009. *Strategic Management.* Hoboken, NJ: Wiley.

Hunger, David, and Thomas Wheelen. 2011. *Essentials of Strategic Management.* Upper Saddle River, NJ: Prentice Hall.

Hyde, B. 2004. "The Plausibility of Spiritual Intelligence: Spiritual Experience, Problem Solving and Neural Sites." *International Journal of Children's Spirituality* 9, no. 1, 14–18.

Iansiti, Marco, and R. Levien. 2004a. "Strategy as Ecology." *Harvard Business Review,* March, 68–78.

———. 2004b. *The Keystone Advantage.* Boston: Harvard Business School Press.

Immelt, Jeffrey, Vijay Govindarajan, and Chris Trimble. 2009. "How GE Is Disrupting Itself." *Harvard Business Review* 87, no. 10: 56–65.

Interface Global. 2008. "Interface's Values Are Our Guiding Principles." http://www.interfaceglobal.com/Company/Mission-Vision.aspx (accessed July 16, 2012).

Internet World Stats. 2012. "World Internet Penetration Rates by Region." http://www.internetworldstats.com/stats.htm (accessed November 12, 2012).

Intuit Corporation. 2011. "Corporate Profile." http://about.intuit.com/about_intuit/profile/ (accessed July 11, 2011).

Isaacson, Walter. 2011. *Steve Jobs.* New York: Simon and Schuster.

Iyer, Bala, and Thomas Davenport. 2008. "Reverse Engineering Google's Innovation Machine." *Harvard Business Review,* April, 59–68.

Jenkins, Beth. 2007. "Expanding Economic Opportunity: The Role of Large Firms." Corporate Responsibility Initiative, Report no. 17. Cambridge, MA: Kennedy School of Government, Harvard University.

Jenkins, Beth, and E. Ishikawa. 2010. "Scaling Up Inclusive Business: Advancing the Knowledge and Action Agenda." Washington, DC: International Finance Corporation and the CSR Initiative at the Harvard University Kennedy School of Government.

Jordan, Lindsay Hower. 2007. "HIV/AIDS Continues Worldwide Climb." *Vital Signs 2007–2008,* 120–121. New York: Norton.

Jorgenson, Andrew, and James Rice. 2012. "Urban Slums and Children's Health in Less-Developed Countries." *Journal of World-Systems Research* 18, no. 1, 103–116. http://jwsr.ucr.edu/archive/vol18/Jorgenson_Rice-vol18n1.pdf (accessed November 12, 2012).

Joshi, Satish, and Ranjani Krishnan. 2010. "Sustainability Accounting Systems with a Managerial Decision Focus." *Cost Management* 24, no. 6, 20–30.

Kale, Prashant, and Harbir Singh. 2009. "Managing Strategic Alliances: What Do We Know Now, and Where Do We Go from Here?" *Academy of Management Perspective,* August, 45–62.

Kanter, Rosabeth Moss. 1994. "Collaborative Advantage." *Harvard Business Review,* July–August.

———. 2009. "Wal-Mart's Environmental Game-Changer." HBR Blog Network, July 16. http://blogs.hbr.org/kanter/2009/07/walmarts-environmental-gamecha.html (accessed September 15, 2012).

Karma Snack. 2012. "Oct. 2012-Updated//Search Engine Market Share." http://www.karmasnack.com/about/search-engine-market-share/ (accessed October 15, 2012).

Kavner, L. 2011. "Huffpost Greatest Person of the Day: Ron Shaich Lets Panera Bread Customers Pay What They Can." *Huffington Post,* June 15. http://www.huffingtonpost.com/2011/06/15/huffpost-greatest-person-ron-saich-panera-cares_n_877691.html (accessed June 15, 2011).

Kim, C., and R. Mauborgne. 2005. *Blue Ocean Strategy: How to Create Uncontested Market Space and Make the Competition Irrelevant.* Boston: Harvard Business School.

Kirchgeorg, M., and M. Winn. 2006. "Sustainability Marketing for the Poorest of the Poor." *Business Strategy and the Environment* 15, no. 3, 171–184.

Kiron, David, Nina Kruschwitz, Knut Haanaes, Ingrid Von Streng Velken. 2012. "Sustainability Nears a Tipping Point." *MIT Sloan Management Review* 53, no. 2, 69–74.

Kiron, David, Nina Kruschwitz, Knut Haanaes, Martin Reeves, Eugene Goh. 2013. "The Benefits of Sustainability-Driven Innovation." *MIT Sloan Management Review* 54, no. 2, 69–73.

Kitasei, Saya. 2011. "Global Coal Use Stagnates Despite Growing Chinese and Indian Markets." *Vital Signs 2011,* 12–15. Washington, DC: Worldwatch Institute.

Kiuchi, Tachi, and Bill Shireman. 2002. *What We Learned in the Rainforest: Business Lessons from Nature.* San Francisco: Berrett-Koehler.

Krebs, Valdis. 2011. "Ecosystem Wars." TNT—The Network Thinkers, May 11. http://www.thenetworkthinkers.com/2011/05/internet-ecosystem-warsapple-vs-google.html (accessed September 15, 2012).

Lampel, Joseph, and Jamal Shamsie. 2003. "Capabilities in Motion: New Organizational Forms and the Reshaping of the Hollywood Movie Industry." *Journal of Management Studies* 40, no. 8, 2190–2210.

Laszlo, Chris. 2008. *Sustainable Value: How the World's Leading Companies Are Doing Well by Doing Good.* Sheffield, UK: Greenleaf.

Laszlo, Chris, and Nadya Zhexembayeva. 2011. *Embedded Sustainability: The Next Big Competitive Advantage.* Sheffield, UK: Greenleaf.

Lavie, Dovev. 2006. "The Competitive Advantage of Interconnected Firms: An Extension of the Resource-based View." *Academy of Management Review* 31, 638–658.

Layton, Lindsay. 2012. "Is a Charter School Chain Called Rocketship Ready to Soar Across America?" *Washington Post,* July 29. http://articles.washingtonpost.com/2012-07-29/local/35486951_1_charter-school-achievement-gap-public-schools (accessed December 26, 2012).

Lear, Linda. 1998. "Rachel Carson's Biography." The Life and Legacy of Rachel Carson. http://www.rachelcarson.org/Biography.aspx#.UIwXj44RbzI (accessed October 26, 2012).

Legg, Sue Guinn. 2013. "'Heat or Eat' A Reality for Many in the Region. *Johnson City Press,* February 21, 1A, 10A.

Lengnick-Hall, C., M. Lengnick-Hall, and S. Abdinnour-Helm. 2004. "The Role of Social and Intellectual Capital in Achieving Competitive Advantage Through Enterprise Resource Planning (ERP) Systems." *Journal of Engineering and Technology Management* 21, no. 4, 307–330.

Leonard, Annie. 2007. "The Story of Stuff." http://www.youtube.com/watch?v=9GorqroigqM (accessed March 16, 2013).

Leopold, Aldo. 1949. *A Sand County Almanac*. New York: Random House.

Lewin, Arie Y., Chris P. Long, and Timothy N. Carroll. 1999. "Coevolution of New Organizational Forms." *Organization Science* 10, no. 5, 535–553.

Lewin, Arie Y., and Henk W. Volberda. 1999. "Prolegomena on Coevolution: A Framework for Research on Strategy and New Organizational Forms." *Organization Science* 10, no. 5, 519–534.

———. 2003a. "Beyond Adaptation and Selection Research: Organizing Self-Renewal in Co-evolving Environments." *Journal of Management Studies* 40, no. 8, 2109–2110.

———. 2003b. "The Future of Organization Studies: Beyond the Selection-Adaptation Debate." In *The Oxford Handbook of Organization Theory*, ed. Haridimos Tsoukas and Christian Knudsen, 568–595. New York: Oxford University Press.

Liedtka, Jean M. 1989. "Value Congruence: The Interplay of Individual and Organizational Value Systems." *Journal of Business Ethics* 8, 805–815.

Ligman, Eric. 2010. "The New Microsoft Partner Network Is Here!" Microsoft SMS&P Community Blog, November 1. http://blogs.msdn.com/b/mssmallbiz/archive/2010/11/01/the-new-microsoft-partner-network-is-here.aspx (accessed September 15, 2012).

London, Ted, and Stuart Hart. 2011. "Creating a Fortune with the Base of the Pyramid." In *Next Generation Business Strategies for the Base of the Pyramid*, ed. Ted London and Stuart Hart, 1–18. Upper Saddle River, NJ: Pearson Education.

Lovelock, James. 1979. *Gaia: A New Look at Life on Earth*. Oxford: Oxford University Press.

———. 1988. *The Ages of Gaia*. New York: Bantam Books.

Löw, Petra. 2010. "Devastating Natural Disasters Continue Steady Rise." *Vital Signs 2010*, 45–49. Washington, DC: Worldwatch Institute.

Luo, Y. 2002. "Contract, Cooperation, and Performance in International Joint Ventures." *Strategic Management Journal* 23, no. 10, 903–919.

Mahon, John, and R. McGowan. 1998. "Modeling Industry Political Dynamics." *Business and Society* 37, no. 4, 390–413.

McDonough, William, and Michael Braungart. 2002. *Cradle to Cradle*. New York: North Point Press.

McGahan, Anita M., and Michael E. Porter. 1997. "How Much Does Industry Matter, Really?" *Strategic Management Journal* 18, special issue, 15–30.

McKibben, Bill. 2007. *Deep Economy: The Wealth of Communities and the Durable Future*. New York: Times Books.

McPherson, Susan. 2012. "Why CSR's Future Matters to Your Company." HBR Blog Network, January 6. http://blogs.hbr.org/cs/2012/01/why_csrs_future_matters_to_you.html (accessed August 18, 2012).

Mead, Nick. 2012. "Developing Economies to Eclipse the West by 2060, OECD Forecasts." *Business Insider,* November 9. http://www.businessinsider.com/developing-world-will-pass-west-by-2060-2012-11#ixzz2BpqvK2is (accessed November 10, 2012).

Merriam-Webster Dictionary. 2012. Merriam-Webster Online. http://www.merriam-webster.com/dictionary/%20resources (accessed October 13, 2012).

Middlebrooks, Anthony, and Alain Noghiu. 2010. "Leadership and Spiritual Capital: Exploring the Link Between Individual Service Disposition and Organizational Value." *International Journal of Leadership Studies* 6, no. 1, 67–85.

Milanovic, B. 2002. "True World Income Distribution, 1988 and 1993: First Calculation Based on Household Surveys Alone." *Economic Journal* 112, no. 476, 51–92.

Miles, Raymond E., and Charles C. Snow. 1978. *Organizational Strategy, Structure, and Process.* New York: McGraw-Hill.

Mintzberg, Henry. 1979. *The Structuring of Organizations.* Englewood Cliffs, NJ: Prentice Hall.

Mintzberg, Henry, and James A. Waters. 1985. "Of Strategies, Deliberate and Emergent." *Strategic Management Journal* 6, no. 3, 257–272.

MIT Sloan Management Review and Boston Consulting Group (BCG). 2011. "Sustainability: The 'Embracers' Seize Advantage." *MIT Sloan Management Review* (Winter), 4–27.

Moad, Jeff. 2010. "SAP, Oracle Roll Out Carbon Emission Management Tools." ManagingAutomation, September 30. http://www.managingautomation.com/maonline/exclusive/read/SAP__Oracle_Roll_Out_Carbon_Emission_Management_Tools_27756431 (accessed June 15, 2011).

Moore, James F. 1993. "Predators and Prey: A New Ecology of Competition." *Harvard Business Review* 71, no. 3, 75–86.

———. 1996. *The Death of Competition: Leadership and Strategy in the Age of Business Ecosystems.* New York: Harper Business.

———. 2006. "Business Ecosystems and the View from the Firm." *Antitrust Bulletin* 51, 31–75.

Mui, Ylan Q. 2007. "Seeing Red over a Golden Parachute." *Washington Post,* January 4. http://www.washingtonpost.com/wp-dyn/content/article/2007/01/03/AR2007010300553.html (accessed August 18, 2012).

Mulrow, John. 2010. "Climate Change Proceeds Down Worrisome Path." *Vital Signs 2010,* 45–49. Washington, DC: Worldwatch Institute.

Nahapiet, J., and S. Ghoshal. 1998. "Social Capital, Intellectual Capital and the Organizational Advantage." *Academy of Management Review* 23, no. 2, 242–266.

Nahavandi, Afsaneh. 2009. *The Art and Science of Leadership.* 5th ed. Upper Saddle River, NJ: Pearson-Prentice Hall.

Nalebuff, Barry J., and Adam M. Brandenburger. 1996. *Co-opetition.* New York: HarperCollinsBusiness.

National Weather Service (NWS). 2011. "Meteorological Conditions and Ozone in the Polar Stratosphere." Web site, Climate Prediction Center. http://www.cpc.ncep.noaa.gov/products/stratosphere/polar/polar.shtml (accessed November 10, 2012).

Nidumolu, R., C. Prahalad, and M. Rangaswami. 2009. "Why Sustainability Is Now the Key Driver of Innovation." *Harvard Business Review,* September, 57–64.

Nierenberg, Danielle. 2007. "Farm Animal Diversity: Forgotten in Interlaken?" Worldwatch Institute, September 11. http://www.worldwatch.org/node/5343 (accessed March 19, 2008).

Normander, Bo. 2012. "World's Forests Continue to Fall as Demand for Food and Land Goes Up." *Vital Signs 2012,* 80–82. Washington, DC: Worldwatch Institute.

O'Dea, Katherine and Katherine Pratt. 2006. "Achieving Environmental Excellence

Through TQEM Strategic Alliances." *Environmental Quality Management*, 4, no. 3, 93–108.

Olson, Elizabeth G. 2012. "Executive Pay Clawbacks: Just a Shareholder Pacifier?" *Fortune,* August 16. http://management.fortune.cnn.com/2012/08/16/executive-pay-clawbacks/ (accessed August 18, 2012).

Ottman, Jacquelyn A. 2011. *The New Rules of Green Marketing.* Sheffield, UK: Greenleaf.

Owens, Bradley P., and David R. Hekman. 2012. "Modeling How to Grow: An Inductive Examination of Humble Leader Behaviors, Contingencies, and Outcomes." *Academy of Management Journal* 55, no. 4, 787–818.

Parker, Marjorie. 1990. *Creating Shared Vision: The Story of a Pioneering Approach to Organizational Revitalization.* Clarendon Hills, IL: Dialog International.

Peters, Thomas J., and Robert H. Waterman, Jr. 1982. *In Search of Excellence.* New York: Harper and Row.

Pfeffer, Jeffrey. 1993. "Barriers to the Advance of Organizational Science: Paradigm Development as a Dependent Variable." *Academy of Management Review* 18, no. 4, 599–620.

Pinchot, Gifford. 1986. *Intrapreneuring: Why You Don't Have to Leave the Corporation to Become an Entrepreneur.* New York: Harper and Row.

Pinkse, Jonatan, and Ans Kolk. 2009. *International Business and Global Climate Change.* London: Routledge.

Porter, Michael E. 1980. *Competitive Strategy: Techniques for Analyzing Industries and Competitors.* New York: Free Press.

———. 1985. *Competitive Advantage.* New York: Free Press.

———. 1990. *The Competitive Advantage of Nations.* New York: Free Press.

———. 1995. "The Competitive Advantage of the Inner City." *Harvard Business Review* 73, no. 3, 55–71

———. 1998. "Clusters and the New Economics of Competition." *Harvard Business Review* 76, no. 6, 77–90.

———. 2008. "The Five Competitive Forces that Shape Strategy." *Harvard Business Review,* January, 86–104.

Porter, Michael, and Mark R. Kramer. 2011. "Creating Shared Value." *Harvard Business Review,* January/February, 63–77.

Porter, Terry B. 2006. "Coevolution as a Research Framework for Organizations and the Natural Environment." *Organization and Environment* 19, no. 4, 1–26.

Portes, Alejandro. 1998. "Social Capital: Its Origins and Applications in Modern Sociology." *Annual Review of Sociology* 24, 1–24.

Post, James E. 1991. "Managing as if the Earth Mattered." *Business Horizons,* July/August, 32–38.

———. 2007. "Corporations and 21st Century Needs." Notes on an All Academy Symposium titled "Corporations and the 21st Century: How Do Today's Corporations Need to Change to Meet Tomorrow's Needs." Presented at the Academy of Management Annual Meeting, Philadelphia, PA, August, 16–20.

Post, James E., and Barbara Altman. 1992. "Models for Corporate Greening: How Corporate Social Policy and Organizational Learning Inform Leading-Edge Environmental Management." In *Research in Corporate Social Policy and Performance,* ed. James Post, 3–29. Greenwich, CT: JAI Press.

———. 1994. "Managing the Environmental Change Process: Barriers and Opportunities." *Journal of Organizational Change Management* 7, no. 4, 64–81.

Post, James E., Lee Preston, and Sybille Sachs. 2002a. "Managing the Extended Enterprise: The Stakeholder View." *California Management Review* 45, no. 1, 6–29.

———. 2002b. *Redefining the Corporation: Stakeholder Management and Organizational Wealth.* New York: Oxford University Press.

Prahalad, C. K. 2006. *The Fortune at the Bottom of the Pyramid: Eradicating Poverty Through Profits.* Upper Saddle River, NJ: Wharton School.

———. 2011. "The Big Picture." In *Next Generation Business Strategies for the Base of the Pyramid,* ed. T. London and S. Hart, xxvi–xxxii. Upper Saddle River, NJ: Pearson Education.

Prahalad C. K., and Gary Hamel.1990. "The Core Competence of the Organization." *Harvard Business Review,* May/June, 79–91.

Prahalad, C. K., and Stuart L. Hart. 2002. "The Fortune at the Bottom of the Pyramid." *Strategy+Business,* 26. http://www.cs.berkeley.edu/~brewer/ict4b/Fortune-BoP. pdf (accessed November 5, 2008).

Prusak, L., and D. Cohen. 2001. "How to Invest in Social Capital." *Harvard Business Review* 79, no. 6, 86–93.

Pruzan, Peter, and Kirsten Pruzan Mikkelsen. 2007. *Leading with Wisdom: Spiritual-based Leadership in Business.* Sheffield, UK: Greenleaf.

Putnam, Robert D. 2000. *Bowling Alone: The Collapse and Revival of American Community.* New York: Simon and Schuster.

Quah, Danny. 1997. "Empirical Growth and Distribution: Stratification, Polarization and Convergence Clubs." London School of Economics, Center for Economic Performance, Discussion Paper 324, 1–29.

Reed, R., and R. DeFillippi. 1990. "Causal Ambiguity, Barriers to Imitation, and Sustainable Competitive Advantage." *Academy of Management Review* 15, 88–102.

Reinhardt, Forest L. 1999. "Bringing the Environment Down to Earth." *Harvard Business Review* 77, no. 4, 149–157.

———. 2008. "Environmental Product Differentiation: Implications for Corporate Strategy." In *Environmental Management: Readings and Cases,* 2nd ed., ed. Michael V. Russo, 205–227. Los Angeles, CA: Sage.

Rexrode, Christina, and Bernard Condon. 2012. "Average CEO Pay 2011 Nearly $10 Million at Public Companies: AP Study." *Huffington Post,* May 25. http://www. huffingtonpost.com/2012/05/25/average-ceo-pay-2011_n_1545225.html (accessed August 18, 2012).

Rhodia Group. 2009. "French and Brazilian Company Chairmen Share Their Energy to Combat Climate Change." News release, December 8. http://www.rhodia.com/ en/news_center/news_releases/Brazil_France_high_level_group_081209.tcm (accessed August 9, 2012).

Richard, O. 2000. "Racial Diversity, Business Strategy, and Firm Performance: A Resource-Based View." *Academy of Management Journal* 43, no. 2, 164–177.

Rodrigues, Susanna, and John Child. 2003. "Coevolution in an Institutionalized Environment." *Journal of Management Studies* 40, no. 8, 2137–2162.

Rokeach, M. J. 1968. *Beliefs, Attitudes, and Values.* San Francisco: Jossey-Bass.

Rosinski, Niki. 2006. "Benchmarking Competitiveness and Management Quality with the Dow Jones Sustainability Index: The Case of the Automotive Industry and Climate Change." In *Managing the Business Case for Sustainability,* ed. Stefan Schaltegger and Marcus Wagner, 242–254. Sheffield, UK: Greenleaf.

Ross, Nancy. 2010. "World Water Quality Facts and Statistics." Pacific Institute.

http://www.pacinst.org/reports/water_quality/water_quality_facts_and_stats.pdf (accessed November 12, 2012).

Rothaermel, Frank T. 2013. *Strategic Management Concepts and Cases*. New York: McGraw-Hill.

Roudi-Fahimi, Farzaneh, Liz Creel, and Roger-Mark De Souza. 2002. "Finding the Balance: Population and Water Scarcity in the Middle East and North Africa." MENA Policy Brief, July. Washington, DC: Population Reference Bureau. http://www.prb.org/pdf/FindingTheBalance_Eng.pdf (accessed April 16, 2008).

Russo, Michael V., and Paul A. Fouts. 1997. "A Resource-Based Perspective on Corporate Environmental Performance and Profitability." *Academy of Management Journal* 40, no. 3, 534–559.

Sachs, Jeffrey. 2008. *Common Wealth: Economics for a Crowded Planet*. New York: Penguin.

Sánchez, Pablo, Joan Enric Ricart, and Miguel Angel Rodríguez. 2005. "Influential Factors in Becoming Socially Embedded in Low-Income Markets." *Greener Management International* 51, 19–38.

Satariano, Adam. 2012. "Apple's Latest IPhone Set to Become Best-Selling Gadget." *Bloomberg Business Week*, September 13. http://www.bloomberg.com/news/2012-09-13/apple-s-latest-iphone-poised-to-become-best-selling-gadget-tech.html (accessed September 15, 2012).

Schaubroeck, John M., Sean T. Hannah, Bruce J. Avollo, Steve W. Kozlowski, Robert G. Lord, Linda K. Treviño, Nicolaos Dimotakis, and Ann C. Peng. 2012. "Embedding Ethical Leadership Within and Across Organization Levels." *Academy of Management Journal* 55, no. 5, 1053–1078.

Schein, Edgar. 1985. *Organizational Culture and Leadership*. San Francisco: Jossey-Bass.

Schoemaker, P. J. H. 1990. "Strategy, Complexity and Economic Rent." *Management Science* 36, 1178–1192.

Schumacher, E. F. 1973. *Small Is Beautiful: Economics as if People Mattered*. New York: Harper and Row.

———. 1977. *A Guide for the Perplexed*. New York: Harper and Row.

———. 1979. *Good Work*. New York: Harper and Row.

Schumpeter, Joseph A. 1950. *Capitalism, Socialism, and Democracy*. New York: Harper.

Schwenk, Charles R. 1988. *The Essence of Strategic Decision Making*. Lexington, MA: Lexington Books.

Seeking Alpha. 2013. "Google-Samsung Partnership: When the Hunter Becomes the Hunted." http://seekingalpha.com/article/1268221-google-samsung-partnership-when-the-hunter-becomes-the-hunted (accessed March 24, 2013).

Senge, Peter M. 1990. *The Fifth Discipline: The Art and Practice of the Learning Organization*. New York: Doubleday/Currency.

———. 2007. "Waking the Sleeping Giant: Business as an Agent for Consumer Understanding and Responsible Choice." *Journal of Corporate Citizenship* 26, 25–27.

———. 2011. "Educating Leaders for a Sustainable Future." AACSB Sustainability Conference, Charlotte, NC, June 17.

Senge, Peter M., Bryan Smith, Nina Kruschwitz, Joe Laur, and Sara Schley. 2008. *The Necessary Revolution*. New York: Doubleday.

Shah, Anup. 2010. "Poverty Facts and Stats." Global Issues. http://www.globalissues.org/article/26/poverty-facts-and-stats#src7 (accessed November 12, 2012).

Sharma, Sanjay, and Harrie Vredenburg. 1998. "Proactive Corporate Environmental Strategy and the Development of Competitively Valuable Organizational Capabilities." *Strategic Management Journal* 19, 729–753.

Sherman, W., D. Steingard, and D. Fitzgibbons. 2002. "Sustainable Stakeholder Accounting: Beyond Complementarity and Towards Integration in Environmental Accounting." In *Research in Corporate Sustainability: The Evolving Theory and Practice of Organizations in the Natural Environment,* ed. S. Sharma and M. Starik, 257–294. Cheltenham, UK: Elgar.

Shrivastava, Paul. 1995. "Ecocentric Management in Industrial Ecosystems: Management Paradigm for a Risk Society." *Academy of Management Review* 20, no. 1, 118–137.

Sisk, D., and E. Torrance. 2001. *Spiritual Intelligence: Developing Higher Consciousness.* Buffalo, NY: Creative Foundation Education Press.

Smith, Aaron. 2012. "Barclays Apologizes for Libor Scandal." CNN Money, July 27. http://money.cnn.com/2012/07/27/investing/barclays-libor/index.htm (accessed August 17, 2012).

Smith, Geoffrey, and William Symonds. 1997. "Can George Fisher Fix Kodak?" *BusinessWeek,* October 20. http://www.businessweek.com/1997/42/b3549001.htm (accessed July 16, 2012).

Smith, Mark K. 2000. "Social Capital." *The Encyclopedia of Informal Education.* http://www.infed.org/biblio/social_capital.htm (accessed August 28, 2008).

Sommer, Brian B. 2009. "Sustainability: Hard for Business, Harder for ERP Vendors." ZDNet, October 22. http://www.zdnet.com/blog/sommer/sustainability-hard-for-business-harder-for-erp-vendors/681 (accessed August 20, 2012).

Sorkin, Andrew. 2009. *Too Big to Fail.* New York: Penguin Group.

Speth, James Gustave. 2008. *The Bridge at the Edge of the World.* New Haven, CT: Yale University Press.

Spirig, K. 2006. "Social Performance and Competitiveness: A Socio-Competitive Framework." In *Managing the Business Case for Sustainability,* ed. Stefan Schaltegger and Marcus Wagner, 82–106. Sheffield, UK: Greenleaf.

Stanwick, Peter A., and Sarah D. Stanwick. 2005. "The Relationship Between Environmental Sustainability, Environmental Violations and Financial Performance: An Empirical Study." In *New Horizons in Research on Sustainable Organizations,* ed. Mark Starik and Sanjay Sharma with Carolyn Egri and Rick Bunch, 79–98. Sheffield, UK: Greenleaf.

Starik, Mark. 1995. "Should Trees Have Managerial Standing? Toward Stakeholder Status for Non-Human Nature." *Journal of Business Ethics* 14, 207–217.

Starik, Mark, and Gordon Rands. 1995. "Weaving an Integrated Web: Multilevel and Multisystem Perspectives of Ecologically Sustainable Organizations." *Academy of Management Review* 20, no. 4, 908–935.

Stead, Jean Garner, and Edward Stead. 2000. "Eco-Enterprise Strategy: Standing for Sustainability." *Journal of Business Ethics* 24, no. 4, 313–329.

———. 2009. *Management for a Small Planet,* 3rd ed. Armonk, NY: M.E. Sharpe.

Stead, W. Edward, and Jean Garner Stead. 1994. "Can Humankind Change the Economic Myth? Paradigm Shifts Necessary for Ecologically Sustainable Business." *Journal of Organizational Change Management* 7, no. 4, 15–31.

———. 1995. "An Empirical Investigation of Sustainability Strategy Implementation in Industrial Organizations." In *Research in Corporate Performance and Policy,* ed. James E. Post, 43–66. Greenwich CT: JAI Press.

————. 1996. *Management for a Small Planet.* Thousand Oaks, CA: Sage.

Stead, W. Edward, Jean Garner Stead, and Don Shemwell. 2003. "Community Sustainability in the Southern Appalachian Region of the USA: The Case of Johnson County Tennessee." In *Research in Corporate Sustainability,* eds. Sanjay Sharma and Mark Starik, 61–84. North Hampton, MA: Edward Elgar.

Stern, Nicholas. 2006. *The Stern Review on the Economics of Climate Change.* London: HM Treasury.

Sustainable Food Laboratory. 2012. "A Global Network for Partnership and Innovation." http://www.sustainablefoodlab.org/about-us/about-us (accessed July 16, 2012).

Sustainable Packaging Coalition (SPC). 2012. Best Representation of the SPC Definition. http://www.sustainablepackaging.org/content/?type=&id=packaging-stewardship-video-challenge-submissions (accessed August 12, 2012).

Svoboda, Susan. 2008. Notes on Life Cycle Analysis. In *Environmental Management: Readings and Cases,* 2nd ed., ed. Michael V. Russo, 385–394. Los Angeles, CA: Sage.

Swartz, Peter. 1991. *The Art of the Long View.* New York: Doubleday.

Target Corporation. 2011. "Take Charge of Education." https://www-secure.target.com/redcard/tcoe/home (accessed June 15, 2011).

Thompson, Jonathon. 2011. "As Coal Use Declines in U.S., Coal Companies Focus on China." *Yale Environment 360,* December 8. http://e360.yale.edu/feature/as_coal_use_declines_in_us_coal_companies_focus_on_china/2474/ (accessed October 28, 2012).

Tickle, Phyllis. 2008. *The Great Emergence: How Christianity Is Changing and Why.* Grand Rapids, MI: Baker Books.

Tolle, Eckhart. 2005. *A New Earth: Awakening to Your Life's Purpose.* New York: Plume.

Tymon, W., and S. Stumpf. 2003. "Social Capital in the Success of Knowledge Workers." *Career Development International* 8, no. 1, 12–20.

United Nations (UN). 2004. "Population Size, Distribution and Growth." In *World Population Prospects: The 2004 Revision,* vol. 3: *Analytical Report.* New York: United Nations Department of Economic and Social Affairs/Population Division.

————. 2012. *A New Agenda for Board of Directors: Adoption and Oversight Corporate Sustainability.* UN Global Compact Report, January. http://www.unglobalcompact.org/docs/news_events/9.1_news_archives/2012_01_27/Lead-board-loresR.pdf (accessed August 18, 2012).

United Nations Environment Programme (UNEP). 2007. *Global Environment Outlook.* Valletta, Malta: Progress Press.

United Nations Development Programme (UNDP). 2007. *Human Development Report 2007/2008.* New York: Palgrave Macmillan.

U.S. Department of Energy. 2007. *International Energy Outlook.* DOE/EIA-0484, May.

University of Minnesota. 2012. "Why Urbanization?" GPS Alliance. http://global.umn.edu/spotlight/why_urban.html (accessed November 12, 2012).

Vaughan, F. 2002. "What Is Spiritual Intelligence?" *Journal of Humanistic Psychology* 42, no. 2, 16–18.

Volberda, Henk W., and Arie Y. Lewin. 2003. "Coevolutionary Dynamics Within and Between Firms: From Evolution to Coevolution." *Journal of Management Studies* 40, no. 8, 2111–2136.

Wack, P. 1985a. "Scenarios: Shooting the Rapids." *Harvard Business Review* 63, no. 6, 139–150.

———. 1985b. "Scenarios: Uncharted Waters." *Harvard Business Review* 63, no. 5, 73–89.

Waddock, Sandra. 2000. "The Multiple Bottom Lines of Corporate Citizenship: Social Investing, Reputation, and Responsibility Auditing." *Business and Society Review* 105, no. 3, 323–345.

———. 2007. "On Ceres, the GRI and Corporation 20/20: An Interview with Allen White." *Journal of Corporate Citizenship* 26, 38–42.

Waddock, Sandra, and Malcolm McIntosh. 2011. *SEE Change.* Sheffield, UK: Greenleaf.

Walter, F., M. Cole, and R. H. Humphrey. 2011. "Emotional Intelligence: Sine Qua Non of Leadership or Folderol?" *Academy of Management Perspectives* 25, no. 1, 45–59.

Weil, Richard. 2012. "World Grain Production Down in 2010, but Recovering." *Vital Signs 2012*, 62–64. Washington, DC: Worldwatch Institute.

Wernerfelt, B. 1984. "A Resource-Based View of the Firm." *Strategic Management Journal* 5, 171–180.

Wilber, Kenneth. 1996. *The Theory of Everything.* Boston: Shambhala.

———. 2000. *Integral Psychology: Consciousness, Spirit, Psychology, Therapy.* Boston: Shambhala.

Williamson, Oliver E. 1981. "The Economics of Organization: The Transaction Costs Approach." *American Journal of Sociology* 87, 548–577.

Winerip, Michael. 2007. "In Gaps at School, Weighing Family Life." *New York Times*, December 9. http://www.nytimes.com/2007/12/09/nyregion/nyregionspecial2/09Rparenting.html?_r=1&oref=slogin (accessed June 23, 2008).

World Bank. 2008. "New Data Show 1.4 Billion Live on Less Than US$1.25 a Day, but Progress Against Poverty Remains Strong." New release no. 2009/065/DEC, August 26. http://web.worldbank.org/WBSITE/EXTERNAL/TOPICS/EXTPOVERTY/0,,contentMDK:21881954~menuPK:336998~pagePK:64020865~piPK:149114~theSitePK:336992,00.html (accessed August 13, 2012).

World Commission on Environment and Development (WCED). 1987. *Our Common Future.* Oxford: Oxford University Press.

World Economic Forum. 2011. *Global Risks 2011.* 6th ed. New York: WEF. http://riskreport.weforum.org/ (accessed September 15, 2012).

———. 2012. *Global Risks 2012.* 7th ed. New York: WEF. http://www.weforum.org/reports/global-risks-2012-seventh-edition (accessed November 10, 2012).

Worldwatch Institute. 2011. "The State of Consumption Today." http://www.worldwatch.org/node/810 (accessed August 4, 2012).

Wright, Jonathon. 2009. "The Sustainable Future of ERP." *DC Velocity,* November 17. http://blogs.dcvelocity.com/sustainability/2009/11/the-sustainable-future-of-erp.html (accessed August 20, 2012).

Xinhua. 2012. "Urban Populations Expected to Grow in Asia, Africa: UN Report." April 5. http://news.xinhuanet.com/english/world/2012-04/06/c_131509732.htm (accessed November 12, 2012).

Young, G., and S. Hasler. 2010. "Managing Reputational Risks." *Strategic Finance,* November, 37–46.

Yunus, Muhammad. 2003. *Banker to the Poor: Micro-Lending and the Battle Against World Poverty.* New York: Public Affairs.

Zaheer, A., B. McEvily, and V. Perrone. 1998. "Does Trust Matter? Exploring the Effects of Interorganizational and Interpersonal Trust on Performance." *Organization Science* 9, no. 2, 141–159.

Zakaria, Fareed. 2008. *The Post American World.* New York: Norton.

Zohar, D., and I. Marshall. 2000. *Spiritual Intelligence: The Ultimate Intelligence.* New York: Bloomsbury.

———. 2004. *Spiritual Capital: Wealth We Can Live By.* San Francisco: Berrett-Koehler.

Index

Page numbers in *italics* indicate tables and figures

A

Abdinnour-Helm, S., 207
Abell, Derick, 20, 131
Aburdene, Patricia, 6, 68, 218
Accenture, 127, 234
Accountability alliances, 196-197
Accounting systems, 208-209
Acetylation technology, 167-168
Acquisitions, 184-186
Adaptability, in coevolutionary
    relationships, 12
Adaptive learning, 18
Affluent markets, *34*, 34, 35-37
Afghanistan, state failure in, 54
Africa. *See also* Undeveloped/developing
    markets
    HIV/AIDS epidemic in, 51
    literacy rate in, 52
    population growth in, 35
    water scarcity in, 39
African Wildlife Foundation, 83
Agent Orange, 6, 97
Agius, Marcus, 232-233
Air pollution, and climate change, 43-44
Alexander, Marcus, 170
Alliance for a Healthier Generation,
    196-197
Alliance management capability, 143,
    195-197, 245, 246
Alliance strategies, 172, 179, 180-183
Altman, Barbara, 14
Amazon, 84, 152
American Chemical Council, 5, 124
American Heart Association, 197
Anderson, Ray, 19, 157
Anderson, Warren, 97
Android platform, 86
Annan, Kofi, 93

Ansoff, Igor, 61, 62, 216
Antitakeover tactics, 185
Appalachian region, as undeveloped market
    segment, 52, 91, 149
Apple
    in business ecosystem, 84, 85, 86, 88,
        107-108, 152
    core competencies of, 102, 120
    differentiation strategy of, 135
    turnaround strategy of, 187
    vertical integration of, 175
Appreciative inquiry (AI), 116, 225
Arab Oil Embargo, 15, 60
Argyris, Chris, 18
Association of Chartered Certified
    Accountants (ACCA), 209
Audit, sustainability, 211
Automobile industry
    in China, 36
    eco-effective strategies of, 145
    glocalization strategy of, 179
    market segments of, 71, 137
    mergers and acquisitions in, 184-185
    mission statements in, 20-21
    strategic groups in, 74
Ayres, Richard, 32

B

Backward vertical integration, 175
Banana Republic, 132
Bank of America, 234
Bankruptcy, 189-190
Bansal, Pratima, 217
Barber, Benjamin, 36
Barclays bank, 232-233
Barnett, Michael, 106
Barney, Jay, 15, 16, 99, 101, 102, 107, 111,
    117, 118, 119, 177, 220
Barrett, Paul, 45, 153
Base of the pyramid (BoP) market, 90-91,
    158-159

Bebbington, Jan, 209
Beck, Don E., 13, 219
Beckhard, Richard, 14, 221
Benn, Suzanne, 14, 126, 200
Bennett, E., 94
Benzoflex benzoate plasticizers, 169
Bhopal disaster, 4–5, 6, 96–97, 129
Bies, Robert J., 78, 88, 127, 200
Bing, 120
Biological nutrients, as product material, 125
Biophysical barriers to sustainability, 54–55, 63
Birth control, 51
Bisphenol A (BPA), 168
Bloomberg Business Week, 45
Blue oceans, 81, 223
Board of directors, 231, 233–236
BoP (base of the pyramid), 90–91, 158–159
Bosker, Bianca, 87
Boston Consulting Group (BCG), growth share matrix of, 198–200, *199*, 212
Boulding, Kenneth E., 29, 31, 38
Boundary spanning, in coevolutionary relationships, 12
Boykoff, Jules, 67
Brandenburger, Adam M., 85
Brand recognition, 105, 146, 163
Braungart, Michael, 22, 125, 145
Brazil
climate change strategies of, 156
deforestation in, 40
as emerging market, 53
Breakaway positioning, 165, 166
Brin, Sergey, 123
Britain
corporate governance in, 232–233
executive compensation in, 236–237
food contamination in, 50
Brown, Lester R., 36, 39, 40, 43, 46, 47, 48, 49, 50, 51, 54, 104
Budinich, V., 69, 83, 91, 111–112, 161
Buffett, Warren, 170
Bughin, Jacques, 81
Build or buy decision, 183–184, 201
Burns, Ursula, 146
Business ecosystem
coevolution, 61–63, 163, 165–166
and collaborative alliances, 181
competitive dynamics in, 85–88, 147–149
defined, 78–80
dominators, 151
fundamentals of, 81–84, *82*
health and performance of, 84–85
inclusive, 160–161, 162–163, 192–193, 200

Business ecosystem *(continued)*
leaders, 78, 150–152, 195, 197, 245
niche players, 81, 84–85, 151, 152–153
structure of, 77–78
trusting relationships in, 246–247
Business environment analysis, 61–70, *64*
Business level strategies. *See* Competitive strategies
Business model, in developed markets, 156–157
Business Week, 62
Butler, Janet B., 208
Buzzelli, David, 97

C
Cadbury Schweppes, 185, 197
Calorie consumption, 50
Campbell, Andrew, 170
Canadian Chemical Producers Association, 97
Capabilities. *See also* Core competencies
assumptions about, 101–102
and competitive advantage, 15, 16, 117–121
corporate portfolio, 193–195
defined, 107
dynamic, 107–109, 211
spiritual, 218, 220–221
Cap-and-trade systems, 154
Capital. *See also* Human capital; Social capital
allocation, 170, *171*
coevolution of, 101, *102*
financial, 101, 104
forms of, 100–101, 103–107
knowledge, 101, 104–105
reputational, 101, 105–106, 123, 146, 163
spiritual, 101, *102*, 107, 120, 218, 219, 220
Carbon cycle, 44
Carbon Disclosure Project, 154
Carbon emissions
and climate change, 43–44, 154
and coal consumption, 41
management, 207, 208
trading, 154–155
Carlson, Nicholas, 184
Carp, Daniel, 189
Carpenter, S., 94
Carrying capacity, 33–35
Carson, Rachel, 6, 96, 98
Cash cows, in market share matrix, *199*, 199–200
Cash flow, balancing, 191, 197–200, *199*, 203–294
Casual adopters, 148
Causal ambiguity, 118–119
Cell phones, 194–195

Cellulose acetate technology, 168–169
Cengage, 157
Central Intelligence Agency (CIA), 54
Certification labels, 146
Chambers, N., 209
Change agents, 68–69, 83, 125, 127, 200, 224
Chapter 7 bankruptcy (liquidation), 190
Chemical industry. *See also* Eastman Chemical Company
  in environmental disasters, 4–5, 6, 96–97, 129
  environmental improvements in, 6
  environmental regulations affecting, 97
  Responsible Care program, 4, 5, 97–98, 210
  Silent Spring on, 6, 96
  sustainable products and services of, 156
Chermack, T.J., 95
Chief executive officer (CEO), 231, 234
  compensation of, 185–186, 236–237
Chief financial officers (CFOs), reporting role of, 210
Chief sustainability officers, 3, 227, 228, 236
Child, John, 206, 222
Children, health and educational inequities affecting, 51, 52
China
  carbon emissions of, 41, 44
  coal consumption of, 41
  consumption expenditure in, 35–36
  as emerging market, 53, 90
  hazardous wastes in, 43
  urbanization in, 53
  water scarcity in, 39
  wealth disparity in, 48
Christensen, Clayton M., 160, 223
Christmann, C., 142
Chrysler/Daimler-Benz merger, 184–185, 188
Chui, Michael, 81
Circuit City, liquidation bankruptcy of, 190
Citibank, 162
Citizen sector, 69, 83
Citizen sector organizations (CSOs), 83, 106, 195
Clarke, Jonathan, 175
Clawback provisions, 237
Clean Clothes Campaign, 146
Cleveland, Josh, 163
Climate change, 43–46, 104
Climate change strategies, 153–156
Climate events, extreme, 45, 49, 53, 155
Clinton Foundation, 197
Clorox, 148–149, 158
Closed circular flow economy, 7–8, *8*, 10

Coal consumption, 41
Coca-Cola Company, 127, 192–193, 197
Cocreation, 85
  distributed, 81
Code of Ethics, 229
Coevolution
  of business ecosystem, 61–63, 163, 165–166
  of capital, 101, *102*
  characteristics of, 12–14, *13*
  of competitive strategies, 139–140, *140*
  defined, 11–12
  in industry analysis, 75–76, *76*, 77, *79*, 80
  of macro environment, 63–79
  in market analysis, 88–91
  of undeveloped/developing market strategies, 159–161
Cogeneration systems, 129
Cohen, D., 247
Colbert, B., 118, 119, 220
Cole, Deirdre, 138
Cole, M., 219
Collaboration
  alliance strategies, 172, 180–183, 196
  in business ecosystem, 81, *82*
Collins, Jim, 19, 20
Community Advisory Panels (CAPs), 59, 229
Competencies. *See* Core competencies
Competitive advantage, 99, 108. *See also* Competitive strategies
  capability/competency building for, 15, 16, 117–121
  of collaborative alliances, 181
  cost, 133
  of eco- and socio-efficiency, 139, 140
  and focus strategy, 136, 137
  and spiritual capabilities, 220–221
  sustainability-based, 22
  sustained, 117–118, 128
  and value chain analysis, 109, 111
Competitive dynamics, 137–138, 147–149
Competitive forces, industrial analysis of, 72–74
Competitive intelligence, 75
Competitive parity, 118
Competitive strategies
  coevolution of, 139–140, *140*, 163, 165–166
  cost/differentiation integration, 135–136
  cost leadership, 133–134
  defined, 131
  for developed markets, 153–158
  differentiation, 134–135
  eco-efficient, 141–145, 147
  effectiveness of, 167
  focus, 136–137

Competitive strategies *(continued)*
foundation of, 131–132, *132*
marketing, 157–158
positioning, 137–139, 147–149, 165–166
product stewardship, 145–147, 157–158, 167–169
and relative competitive position, 149–153, *150*
social dimension of, 140–141
and strategic choice, 211–212, *212*
for undeveloped/developing market, 158–163
Competitive structure, industry, 74
Competitors
acquisition of, 174
co-opetition, 85–88
imitation, 118, 119
potential, 73
profile of, 74–75
Compliance, *4*, 4
Concentrated growth strategies, 172, 173
Concentric diversification, 176
Condon, Bernard, 237
Conglomerate diversification, 176
Congo, Republic of, state failure in, 54
Conservation International, 83
Consolidated industry, 74
Consumer class, 36
Consumers. *See* Consumption; Customers
Consumption
demographic factors in, 63
in developed markets, 36, 89–90
expenditure, 34, 35–37
of fossil fuels, 41, 49, 89
-production cycle, 7, *8*, 10
sustainable, 158
Cooperrider, David L., 225
Co-opetition, 85–88
Core competencies
and competitive advantage, 16, 22, 117–118
and competitive strategies, 131–132, *132*, 133–134, 211
defined, 22, 131
in resource assessment, 99, *100*, 117–121
in strategic choice, 213
Core values, 215–216, 226
Corporate culture, 22
Corporate governance. *See also* Leadership, strategic
agency problems in, 232–233
board of directors, 233–236
evaluation and control, 237–239, *238*, *239*
and executive compensation, 185–186, 236–237
functions of, 233–234
mechanisms of, 231–232

Corporate portfolio, SSM
and alliance management capability, 195–197
balance in, 197–200, 203–204
capability building, 193–195
at Eastman Chemical Company, 198, 203–205, *204*, *205*
and inclusive business ecosystem, 192–193
management tool, 212–213, *213*
purpose of, 191
and social change, 200–201
whole-pyramid approach to, 190–192, 195, 197, *198*, 202
Corporate responsibility committee, 234
Corporate strategies, 22
alliance, 172, 180–183
build or buy decision, 183–184, 201
expansion, 172–183
for global markets, 177–180
internal venturing/intrapreneurship, 186–187
mergers and acquisitions (M&A), 184–186, 203
options for, 172
retrenchment/restructuring, 187–190, 201–202, 203
scope of firm's operations, 170–172, 201
and strategic choice, 212–214
tasks of, 170
Corporate Sustainability Group, 228–229
Corporate venture capital (CVC), 182
Corvalen, C., 94
Cost-leadership strategy
characterized, 133–134
focused, 137
integration with differentiation strategy, 135–136
Costs
and differentiation, 135–136
and eco-efficiency, 139, 140, 142
transactions, 183
Coupling strength, 84–85, 151
Cowan, Christopher C., 13, 219
Cradle-to-cradle mentality, 157
Creative destruction, 194
Creel, Liz, 39
Croc Shoes, 119
Cropland, loss of, 49
Customers. *See also* Consumption
bargaining power of, 73
feedback, 85
groups, 131
learning, 158
and market segmentation, 131–133

D
Daimler-Benz/Chrysler merger, 184–185, 188

Daly, Herman E., 31, 32, 46, 48, 103, 104, 218
Danner, John, 69
Davenport, Thomas, 123
Davies, James B., 48
Dean, Thomas J., 91
Decline stage of business ecosystem coevolution, 166
Decline stage of industry coevolution, 75, 76
DeFillippi, R., 119, 220
Deforestation, 40
de Kluyver, Cornelius, 71
Delgado, Alessandra, 53
Del Nibletto, Paolo, 87
DeMasi, Karin, 175
Demographic factors, in business environment, 63, 65, 67–68
Desertification, 50
De Souza, Roger-Mark, 39
Dess, Gregory, 21, 74, 105, 137, 163, 165, 166, 179, 182, 185, 186
Developed markets
   climate change strategies in, 153–156
   emerging business models in, 156–157
   income/wealth inequity in, 52, 91, 149, 159
   natural resources consumption in, 89, 154
   sustainable growth in, 89–90
Developing markets. See Undeveloped/ developing markets
Diapers, eco-friendly, 5
Differentiation strategy
   characterized, 131, 134–135
   focused, 137
   integration with cost leadership, 135–136
   of niche player, 152, 153
Digital divide, 52
Dimon, Jamie, 234, 237
Dinnick, Wilf, 50
Discounting, 103–104
Diseases, 51, 53
Distributed cocreation, 81
Diversification strategies, 170–172, 176–177
Divestment strategies, 188–189
Dodd, Richard H., 14
Dogs, in market share matrix, 199, 200
Doh, Jonathan, 218
Dominance, market, 149, 174
Dominators, in business ecosystem, 151
Doppelt, Bob, 25
Dow Canada, 97
Dow Chemical, in joint venture, 182–183
Dow Jones Sustainability Index (DJSI), 124, 210
Downscoping, 188

Downsizing, 187–188
Drayton, B., 69, 83, 91, 111–112, 161
Driver, Michaela, 219
Dunphy, Dexter, 14, 200
Dyer, Jeff, 78, 106, 181, 195, 246
Dyllick, Thomas, 122, 126
Dynamic capabilities, 107–109, 211

E
Earth
   carrying capacity of, 33
   as closed system, 38
   ecosystem, 38–46
   and entropy, 31–32
   Gaia theory of, 30–31
   human footprint, 33–35, 89, 153
   as living system, 29–30
Earthwatch, 83
Eastman Chemical Company
   acquisition strategy of, 203–205
   commitment to sustainability, 3–4, 59, 227
   eco-efficiency initiatives of, 129–130
   goals of, 21, 229–230
   implementation of sustainability, 227–230
   leadership structure of, 3, 228–229
   leadership style of, 248–249
   portfolio management at, 198, 203–204, 204, 205
   product stewardship at, 167–169, 230
   retrenchment strategy of, 202–203
   spinning-off, 189
   stages of sustainable management, 4, 4, 5
   triple-bottom-line performance at, 58–59
Eastman Kodak, retrenchment strategies of, 189–190
Eco-effectiveness, 125–126, 126, 139
Eco-efficiency. See also Sustainability performance
   competitive advantage of, 139
   defined, 121–122, 142
   at Eastman Chemical Company, 129–130
   in labeling, 146–147
   measuring value added from, 124–125
   and pollution prevention, 141–143
   processes in, 122
   total quality environmental management (TQEM), 143
Eco-labels, 146–147
Ecological economy, 46
Ecological sector factors, 63, 65
Ecological sustainability
   and climate change, 43–46
   and pollution, 41–43
   and resource depletion, 38–41
Ecomagination, 171
Economic sector factors, 63, 64, 65
Economic value, 4

Economies of scale, 133
Economies of scope, 176–177
Economy
  closed circular flow, 7–8, *9*, 10, 23
  ecological, 46
  global, 53–54, 64, 65–68
  and glocalization, 70
  high-entropy, 32–33
  metabolic process in, 32–33
  open living system, 8–10, *9*, 16, 23–24
  unlimited growth, 7, 16, 36–37, 46, 56
Ecosystem. *See* Business ecosystem;
    Ecological sustainability
Ecosystemic competencies, business,
    78–79, 106, 119
Education
  literacy gap, 52
  revolutionary school model, 69
  social capital investment in, 123–124
Edwards, Andrés, 6, 26, 68, 116, 201
Effectiveness, eco-and socio, 125–128, *126*
Efficiency. *See* Eco-efficiency; Socio-
    efficiency
Efrati, Amir, 86
Egri, Carolyn P., 217
Ehrenreich, Barbara, 48
Ehrlich, Ann H., 34
Ehrlich, Paul R., 11–12, 30, 34
Eisenhardt, K.M., 107, 232
Eisner, Alan, 21, 74, 105, 137, 163, 165,
    166, 179, 182, 185, 186
Elkington, John, 10, 57
El Salvador, socio-effective strategy in, 193
Embracers, 148
Embryonic stage
  of business ecosystem coevolution, 165
  of industry coevolution, 75, *76*
Emergent strategies, 24, 156–157
Emotional intelligence (EQ), 218–219
Employees. *See also* Human capital
  downsizing, 187–188
  recruitment of, 105
  self-development, 58
Energy consumption, 40–41
Energy efficiency, 37, 129–130, 144–145
Energy Star Partner, 5
Engineering World Health, 163
Enkvist, Anders, 154, 155, 156
Enron, 151
Enterprise level strategy, 22
Enterprise resource planning (ERP)
    systems, 207–208
Enterprise-strategy context, 216–217
Entrepreneurial learning, 194, 197
Entrepreneurship, in base of the pyramid
    market, 162
Entropy law, 54–55, 63, 103, 246

Entropy process, 31–32, 33
Entry modes, to global markets, 179–180
Environmental analysis
  business environment, 61–70
  forecasting, 91–95
  industry, 70–88
  markets, 88–91
  of opportunities/threats, 60–61
Environmental disasters, 4–5, 6, 96–97, 129
Environmental performance. *See* Eco-
    efficiency
Environmental protection, in triple bottom
    line, *11*, 11
Environmental Protection Agency (EPA), 5,
    130, 207, 210
Environmental regulations, 97
Environmental stewardship, 4
Equity alliances, 182
Ernst and Young, 61–62, 116
Establishment/growth stage
  of business ecosystem coevolution, 165
  of industry coevolution, 75, *76*
Esty, D., 61, 62, 112, 122, 124
Ethical leadership, 242–243, 244
Ethical Trade Initiative, 146
Ethics, Code of, 229
Ethiopia, food insecurity in, 51
Ethrington, Darrell, 87
European Chemical Industry Council
    (CEFIC), Build Trust Program, 5
European Management and Audit Scheme
    (EMAS), 143
European Union Emissions Trading
    Scheme, 154
Executive compensation, 185–186, 236–237
Expansion strategies, corporate, 172–183
Experience curves, 133
Exploration and exploitation, synchronizing,
    222
ExxonMobil, diversification strategy of, 177

F
Facebook, 84, 184
Fairtrade International (FLO), 146
Farley, Joshua, 46, 48, 103, 104
Farm animal diversity, 40
Farzad, Robert, 145
Federal Trade Commission (FTC), 174, 175
Fed Ex, eco-efficiency of, 142–143
Felberbaum, Michael, 190
Figge, Frank, 122, 125
Financial capital, 101, 104
Financial institutions, deregulation of,
    174–175
Fiorina, Carly, 174
First-mover advantage, 138, 148–149
Fisher, George, 189

Fisheries, depletion of, 39
Fitzgibbons, D., 209
Five forces model, in industry analysis, 72, 72–74
Flier, Bert, 12, 221
Focus strategy, 136–137
Fombrun, Charles, 106
Food security, 49–51
Food system, alliance management in, 196
Footprint analysis, 112–114
Ford, Bill, 20
Ford, Henry, 20
Ford Motor Company, mission statement of, 20–21
Forecasting, environmental, 91–95
Foreign exchange reserves, 53
Foreign markets. See Global markets
Forests, and deforestation, 40
Forest Stewardship Council (FSC), 146
Fortress World scenario, 92–93
Fortune-creating strategies, 160
Fortune Magazine, 123
Forward vertical integration, 175
Fossil fuels, 41, 43, 44, 49, 89, 104, 154
Fouts, Paul A., 108
Fragmented industry, 74
Franchising, 179
Francis, David, 47
Freeman, R. Edward, 14, 22, 24, 111, 114, 216, 242, 243, 246
Friedman, Thomas L., 70, 179
Fry, Louis W., 243, 244
Full-cost accounting systems, 209
Fully integrated firm, 175
Functional level strategies, 22, 110–111

G
Gaia theory, 30–31, 45
Galindo, V., 67
Gap, Inc., 132–133, 208
Gardberg, Naomi A., 106
Gardner, Gary, 35
Gardner, Howard, 218
GEM 2-ethylhexyl palmitate, 169
Gender inequity, 51
General Electric (GE)
  brand recognition, 105
  diversification strategy of, 170–172, 177
  mission of, 21
  preemptive strategy of, 138–139
  reverse innovation strategy of, 162–163, 172, 187
  scenario analysis of, 92
General Mills, 125
Generative learning, 18, 213–214
Geographic scope, industry, 71
Georgescu-Roegen, Nicholas, 31, 32

German market, Walmart's entry into, 179–180
Ghemawat, Pankaj, 71
Ghoshal, S., 78, 106, 181
Gilbert, Daniel R., Jr., 22, 216
Gladwin, Tom, 14, 116
Glass-Steagall Act, 174
Global community, interconnected, 8–9
Global economy. See also Global markets
  and diffusion of power, 53–54
  low-carbon, 154
  political/legal environment of, 64
  risks in, 65–68, 66
Global Environmental Management Initiative (GEMI), 124, 143
Global markets. 172, 177. See also Developed markets; Undeveloped/developing markets
  competitive pressures in, 178
  entry modes into, 179–180
  outsourcing to, 176
  types of strategies, 178–179
Global Reporting Initiative (GRI), 122, 123, 210
Global standardization corporate strategy, 178–179
Global warming, and climate change, 43–46, 104
Glocalization corporate strategy, 70, 179
Goals (strategic objectives), 21–22
Golden parachutes, 185–186, 237
Goleman, Daniel, 80
Goodman, Ann, 210
Goodway, Nick, 237
Google
  in business ecosystem, 80–81, 84, 86–87, 88, 152
  core competencies of, 120
  human capital of, 123
Goold, Michael, 170
Govindarajan, Vijay, 138, 139, 160, 163, 178
Gradl, Christina, 161, 192, 196
Grain consumption, 50
Grain prices, 49
Grameen Bank, 162
Grandoni, Dino, 87
Grant, Robert, 71, 104, 119, 220
Graves, Clare W., 13, 219
Graziano, Dan, 87
GreenBlue, 144
Green Building Council, 168
Green Building Initiative, 146
Greenhouse gas emissions, 43, 44, 129, 210
Greenleaf, Robert, 244
Greenmail, 185
Green wave of concerns, 61–62

Gregory, R., 116
Griffiths, Andrew, 14, 200
Grootaert, Christiaan, 106
Gross domestic product (GDP), 7, 33, 34, 35
Groundwater contamination, 42
Gueguen, Gael, 78, 85, 86, 106, 181
Guillén, M.F., 52
Gulati, Ranjay, 181
Gull, Gregory A., 218
Gundry, Lisa, 187

H
Habiby, Anne, 138
Hahn, Tobias, 122, 125
Haiti, state failure in, 54
Hales, S., 94
Halweil, Brian, 42, 49
Hamel, Gary, 107, 120, 212, 213, 214, 222
Hammond, Allen, 92, 93, 161, 192
Hardin, Garrett, 50, 54
Harley-Davidson, 102–103, 188–189
Harrison, Jeffrey S., 216
Hart, Stuart L., 61, 77, 88, 89, 90, 91, 105, 108, 116, 127, 142, 145, 158, 159, 160, 161, 191, 194, 195, 221, 223
Harvard Kennedy School, 191
Hasler, S., 105
Hawken, Paul, 6, 26, 68, 112, 116, 157, 201
Hazardous waste disposal, 43, 129
Health
    infectious diseases, 51
    and poverty, 51
    urban, 53
Health care
    employee program, 58–59
    innovation, 223–224
    reverse innovation strategy, 163, 172
Health Point Services, 223–224
Healthymagination, 171
Heise, William, 228
Hekman, David R., 240, 241
Henderson, Bruce, 200
Henderson, Sandra Cherie, 208
Herman, Susan, 217
Hesterly, William, 99, 101, 102, 107, 111, 118, 119, 177
Hewlett-Packard, 174
High-speed change, in business environment, 62
Hill, Charles, 71, 74, 75, 134, 135, 136, 137, 166, 173, 174, 176, 178, 179
Hitt, Michael, 16, 20, 137, 138, 173, 177, 184, 185, 187, 188, 232, 233, 235
HIV/AIDS epidemic, 51
Hockerts, Kai, 122, 126
Hoffman, Andrew J., 6, 96, 154

Hold-and-maintain strategy, 149–150, 166
Holliday, Charles, 122, 194
Home Depot, 237
Honeybee extinction, 39–40
Hooker Chemical Company, 96
Horizontal integration strategies, 166, 172, 173–175
Horizontal scope, industry, 71
Hoskisson, Robert, 16, 20, 137, 138, 173, 177, 184, 185, 187, 188, 232, 233, 236
Hosmer, L.T., 216
Hostile takeover, 185
Huff, Anne, 62
Human capital
    and alliance strategies, 197
    defined, 101
    footprint analysis, 114
    as intangible resource, 104, 105
    in living system, 194
    and socio-effectiveness, 126–127
    and socio-efficiency, 122–123
Human footprint, 33–34, 89, 153
Humble leadership, 240–242, 244
Humphrey, R.H., 219
Hunger, David, 75
Hunger rate, child, 52
Hurricane Katrina, 39
Hurricanes, 45
Hurricane Sandy, 45
Hyde, B., 219
Hydration Technology Innovations, 5
HydroPack, 5, 168, 230

I
Iansiti, Marco, 78, 80, 81, 83, 84, 151, 152, 153
IBM, vertical integration of, 175
IKEA, competitive strategy of, 136
Immelt, Jeffrey, 138, 139, 160, 163, 171, 172, 178
Inclusive business ecosystem, 160–161, 192–193, 200
Income distribution, 46, 47–48, 51, 91. *See also* Poverty
India
    consumption expenditure in, 35–36
    as emerging market, 53, 90
    grain consumption in, 50
    hazardous waste disposal in, 43
    water scarcity in, 39
    wealth disparity in, 48
Industrial metabolism, 32–33
Industrial organizations (I/O) model, 16
Industrial Revolution, 7
Industry analysis
    business ecosystem, 77–88
    traditional, 70–76, 72, 77

Industry consolidation, 174
Industry/growth stage of industry
    coevolution, 75, *76*
Infant mortality, 51
Information technology, 60
Infosys, 176
Innovation
    and collaborative learning, 196
    nature-based, 224
    organizational, 222–224
    product, 89, 138, 152, 153, 162–163
    sustainable stage of, 4, 5
Innovation and Sustainability (I&S)
    Council, 228
Innovest, 124
Inside directors, 233
Instagram, 184
Instrumental values, 216
Intangible resources, 101, 104–197,
    120–121, 220
Intellectual capital, 101, 104
Intelligence quotient (IQ), 218, 219
Interface Global, 19–20, 157
Internal rates of change, managing, 222
Internal venturing, 186–187
International corporate strategy, 178
International Standards Organization (ISO),
    143
Internet
    access gap, 52
    and open innovation, 81
    stakeholder use of, 62
Intrapreneurship, strategic, 186–187
Intuit, 153
i-Pod family of products, 87, 108, 120, 165
Ireland, Duane, 16, 20, 137, 138, 173, 177,
    184, 185, 187, 188, 232, 233, 236
Isaacson, Walter, 86
Ishikawa, E., 160, 161, 162, 190, 192
IW Financial, 124
Iyer, Bala, 123

J
Jenkins, Beth, 160, 161, 162, 190, 192, 196,
    197
Jobs, Steve, 86, 87, 165, 187
Job training, 58
Johnson, Brad, 81
Johnson and Johnson, 120, 122, 182, 221
Joint ventures, 179, 182–183
Jones, Gareth, 71, 74, 75, 134, 135, 136,
    137, 166, 173, 174, 176, 178, 179
Jordan, Lindsay Hower, 51, 52
Jorgenson, Andrew, 53
Joshi, Satish, 208
JPMorgan Chase, 234, 237

K
Kale, Prashant, 181, 183, 195, 197
Kanter, Rosabeth Moss, 78, 80, 106, 181
Kavner, L., 159
Kellogg Foundation, 196
Kennelly, James, 14, 116
Keystone firm (ecosystem leader), 78,
    150–152, 195, 197, 245
Kickul, Jill, 187
Kim, C., 81
Kirchgeorg, M., 157, 160, 161
Kiron, David, 6, 7, 25, 26, 101, 104, 115,
    158, 222
Kitasei, Saya, 41
Kiuchi, Tachi, 10
KLD, 124
Kmart, 135
Knowledge capital, 101, 104–105
Kodak, retrenchment strategies of,
    189–190
Kolk, Ans, 154, 155
Kraft Foods, hostile takeover strategy of,
    185
Kramer, Mark R., 25, 111, 125, 139, 158,
    219
Krause, T., 14, 116
Krebs, Valdis, 88
Krishnan, Ranjani, 208

L
Labeling, eco-and-social, 146–147
Labor, as factor of production, 101
Lampel, Joseph, 12, 221–222
Land ethic, 218
Landfills, 43
Laszlo, Chris, 61, 62, 65, 81, 92, 104, 108,
    112, 113, 114, 122, 124, 148
Late mover advantage, 138
Latin America, wealth disparity in, 48
Lavie, Dovev, 181
Leadership in Energy and Environmental
    Design (LEED), 146
Leadership, strategic
    of business ecosystem, 78, 150–152, 195,
        197, 245
    compensation of, 185–186, 236–237
    defined, 231
    at Eastman Chemical, 248–249
    ethical, 242–243, 244
    functions of, 25–26
    humble, 240–242, 244
    management teams, 25
    servant, 244
    shift in perspective on, 239–240
    skills for, 247–248
    spiritual, 243–244
Lear, Linda, 96

Learning
  collaborative, 196
  entrepreneurial, 194, 197
  generative, 18, 213–214
  and knowledge capital, 104–105
Learning curve effect, 133
Learning structures, self-renewing, 221–224
Legg, Sue Guinn, 52
LEGO, 81, 85
Lengnick-Hall, C., 207
Lengnick-Hall, M., 207
Leonard, Annie, 98
Leopold, Aldo, 218
Leveraged buyout (LBO), 188–189
Levien, R., 78, 80, 81, 83, 84, 151, 152, 153
Lewin, Arie Y., 12, 77, 206, 222
Lewis, K., 209
Libor rate, 232
Licensing agreements, 179
Liedtka, Jean M., 111, 215
Life cycle analysis (LCA), 5, 112, *113*, 130
Life expectancy, 48
Ligman, Eric, 87
Liquidation bankruptcy (Chapter 7), 190
Literacy rate, 52
Living systems, 29–30, 31, 194
Localization corporate strategy, 178
London, Ted, 90, 159, 160, 161
Long-term growth teams (LGTs), 162–163
Love Canal, 6, 96, 129
Lovelock, James, 12, 30, 31, 45
Lovins, Amory, 157
Lovins, L. Hunter, 157
Lowe's, 237
Löw, Petra, 45
Lumpkin, G.T., 21, 74, 105, 137, 163, 165, 166, 179, 182, 185, 186

M

Macro environment, analysis of, 63–70
Mahon, John, 77, 111
Market analysis, 88–91
Market capital, 104
Market dominance, 149, 174
Marketing strategies, 157–158
Market niche, 136–137
Market segmentation, 131–133
Market share, dominant, 149
Market share matrix, 198–200, *199*
Market space, 81
Market World scenario, 92
Marshall, I., 107, 218, 219
Martin, J.A., 107
Massena, A., 67
Maturity stage of business ecosystem
  coevolution, 165–166
Mauborgne, R., 81

McDonald's, 173
McDonough, William, 22, 125, 145
McEvily, B., 195
McGahan, Anita M., 16
McGowan, R., 77, 111
McIntosh, Malcolm, 68, 83, 106
McKibben, Bill, 49, 50
McKinsey and Company, 154
McMichael, A., 94
McMullen, Jeffrey S., 91
McPherson, Susan, 233
Mead, Nick, 36
Mendes, Chico, 40
Mergers and acquisitions (M&A), 184–186, 203
Merrill Lynch, 234, 236
Microfinancing, 162
Microsoft, in business ecosystem, 84, 87–88, 152
Middlebrooks, Anthony, 217, 219, 243
Middle East, water scarcity in, 39
Mikkelsen, Kirsten Pruzan, 218
Milanovic, B., 89, 153
Miles, Raymond E., 206
Millennium Ecosystem Assessment (MA), 39, 93–94
Milstein, Mark, 194, 221
Mintzberg, Henry, 24, 221
Mission statement, 20–21
MIT Sloan Management Review, 105, 106, 120, 121, 122, 124, 148, 149, 158, 208
Moad, Jeff, 207, 208
Modularity, in business ecosystem, 79–80
Moore, James F., 70, 71, 77, 78, 80, 81, 83, 84, 151, 163
Moral hazards, 232
Motorola Mobility, 87
Motte, Godefroy, 3–4, 5, 58, 227, 228
Mui, Ylan Q., 237
Mulally, Alan, 20
Mulrow, John, 44
Multidomestic corporate strategy, 178
Multiple scenario analysis, 92–95, *94*

N

Nahapiet, J., 78, 106, 181
Nahavandi, Afsaneh, 25, 244
Nalebuff, Barry J., 85
Nardelli, Bob, 237
National Association of Homebuilders-
  Leading Suppliers Council, 168
Natural capital, 101, 103–104
Natural disasters, 45, 49, 53, 67, 154
Natural resources
  capabilities, 108
  demand for, 60, 89, 154
  depletion of, 38–41, 67

Nature, as model for innovation, 224
Nature Conservancy, 146
Nauclér, Tomas, 154, 155, 156
Neoclassical economics, 10
New Belgium Brewing, 120, 221
New consciousness, 14
Niche players, 81, 84–85, 151, 152–153
Nidumolu, R., 105, 112, 143, 144
Nieman Marcus, 173
Nierenberg, Danielle, 40
Nike, 208
Noghiu, Alain, 217, 219
Nohria, Nitin, 181
Nonequity alliances, 182
Nongovernmental organizations (NGOs), 83, 106
Normander, Bo, 40
Novel and discontinuous change, in business environment, 62
Nuclear waste, 43

O
Occupational Safety and Health Administration (OSHA), safety ratings of, 58
Ocean dumping, 42
Ocean warming, 45
O'Dea, Katherine, 143
Oil embargo, 60
Oil production, 40
Old Navy, 132
Olson, Elizabeth G., 237
Open innovation, 81
Open living system economy, 8–10, 9, 16
Open-system value chain, 99, 112, 113, 122, 123, 128, 208
Oppenheim, Jeremy, 154, 155, 156
Opportunities and threats, 60, 211
Organic food label, 146
Organic market, 89–90
Organizational capabilities, 119–120
Organizational change, 14
Organizational culture, 14, 215, 219, 220
Organizational structures, 221–224
Organizational survival, coevolutionary relationships in, 11–14, 13
Organizational sustainability. See Sustainable strategic management
Ottman, Jacquelyn A., 84, 89, 90, 146, 147, 156, 157–158
Outside directors, 233
Outsourcing, strategic, 176
Overpopulation, 35
Owens, Bradley P., 240, 241
Oxfam, 193, 196
Ozone depletion, 40

P
Packaging, sustainable, 144, 158
Page, Larry, 86, 87, 123
Panera Bread, socio-effectiveness strategy of, 159
Parker, Marjorie, 20
Pearce, John, 71
Pellegrin-Boucher, Estelle, 78, 85, 86, 106, 181
PepsiCo., 197
Perennial Wood, 5, 58, 167–168, 230
Perez, Antonio, 189
Performance. See also Sustainability performance
  benchmarks, 124
  criteria, 206
  gap analysis, 238, 238
  trends, 117
Permanence, in coevolutionary relationships, 12
Perrone, V., 195
Pesticide use, 42
Peters, Thomas J., 173
Peterson, G., 94
Pfeffer, Jeffrey, 12
Physical assets, 103
Pierce, Jessica, 14
Pinchot, Gifford, 186
Pinkse, Jonathan, 154, 155
Pioneering stage of business ecosystem coevolution, 165
Planned emergence, 24
Poison pills, 185
Political/legal sectors, in business environment, 64, 65
Pollution. See also Carbon emissions
  air, 43–44
  and hazardous waste disposal, 43, 129
  prevention/reduction strategies, 141–143, 195
  water, 41–42, 49
Poor as consumers, 160
Poor as coproducers, 160
Population, aging, 67–68
Population distribution, 46–47, 63, 65, 67
Population growth
  and business environment, 63, 65
  overpopulation, 35
  and resource depletion, 34, 34, 37, 47, 67
  slowing, 55
  urban, 53
Porras, Jerry, 19, 20
Porter, Michael E., 16, 25, 53, 70, 75, 91, 109, 111, 125, 158, 180, 219, 222
  five forces model of, 72–74
  generic competitive strategies of, 133–134, 135, 136, 139, 140, 142

Porter, Terry B., 12
Portes, Alejandro, 106, 246
Positioning strategies, 137–139, 147–149, 165–166
Post, James E., 14, 25–26, 78
Poultry industry, contamination in, 50
Poverty
   in developed countries, 91
   and disease patterns, 51
   and food insecurity, 50
   and literacy rate, 52
   and population growth, 46–47
   in undeveloped countries, 90–91, 159
   urban, 53, 91
   and wealth/income disparity, 47–48, 51
Prahalad, C.K., 90, 91, 105, 107, 112, 120, 143, 144, 159, 212, 213, 214, 222
Pratt, Katherine, 143
Preemptive strategic moves, 137–138
Preston, Lee, 78
Primary activities, in value chain analysis, 109
Principal-agent issue, 232–233
Pritchard, Walter, 14, 221
Private equity firms, 188
Probert, E.J., 126
Proctor and Gamble, 120, 158, 221
Product
   bundling, 174
   claims, 146
   development, 4
   differentiation, 131, 134–135
   innovation, 89, 138, 152, 153, 162–163
   redesign, 157, 165–166
   stewardship, *4*, 4, 5, 145–147, 157–158, 166–169, 230
   substitutes, 73–74
Production-consumption cycle, 7, *8*, 10
Productivity, of business ecosystem, 84
Profitability, 10–11, *11*, 174, 217
Prusak, L., 247
Pruzan, Peter, 218
Pulp and paper industry, 40
Putnam, Robert D., 82, 106, 247

Q
Quah, Danny, 47
Question marks, in market share matrix, 200

R
Raiborn, Cecily, 208
Rain forest, 40, 43–44, 55
Rands, Gordon, 83
Rangaswami, M., 105, 112, 143, 144
Rare resource, 118
Raven, Peter H., 12
Reciprocity, in coevolutionary relationships, 12

Recycling, 83, 144
Reed, R., 119, 220
Reinhardt, Forest L., 145, 148
Related diversification, 176, 177
Reorganizational bankruptcy, 189–190
Reporting, sustainability, 209–210
Reputational capital, 101, 105–106, 123, 146, 163
Resin rosins, life cycle assessment of, 130
Resource assessment
   audit of capital/resources, 99–108
   components of, 99, *100*
   of core competencies, 117–121
   data-gathering tools, 109–117
      footprint analysis, 112–114
      life cycle analysis, 112, 130
      stakeholder analysis, 114–117, *115*
      value chain analysis, 109–112, *110*
   of eco-and socio-effectiveness, 125–128
   of eco-and socio-efficiency, 121–125
   expansion of, 108–109
Resource-based view (RBV) of the firm, 99–100, 220
Resource heterogeneity, 102
Resource immobility, 102
Resources, defined, 100, 101
Responsibility audits, 211
Responsible Care® principles, 229
Responsible Care® program, 4, 5, 97–98, 124, 210
Restructuring strategies, corporate, 187–190, 201–202, 203
Retail Link inventory system, Walmart, 80, 85
Retrenchment strategies, corporate, 172, 187–190, 201–202, 203
Reverse innovation strategy, 138, 162–163, 172
Reverse LBO, 189
Reverse positioning, 165
Rexrode, Christina, 237
Rhodia, climate change strategy of, 155–156
Ricart, Joan Enric, 161
Rice, James, 53
Richard, O., 108
Rivalries, intensity of, 74
Robust ecosystem, 84
Rocketship Education, 69
Rodrigues, Susanna, 222
Rodríguez, Miguel Angel, 161
Rogers, Jim, 3, 58, 129, 167, 198, 202–203, 205, 227, 228, 248–249
Rokeach, M.J., 215
Rosinski, Niki, 124
Ross, Nancy, 42

Rothaermel, Frank T., 15, 20, 21, 24, 108,
    118, 119, 133, 135, 136, 170, 171, 172,
    174, 175, 176, 177, 178, 179, 180,
    181, 182, 183, 185, 195, 196, 232,
    233, 234, 236
Roth, Kendall, 217
Roudi-Fahimi, Farzaneh, 39
Royal Dutch Shell, 92, 144
Russo, Michael V., 108
Rwanda, genocide in, 54

S
Sachs, Jeffrey, 54
Sachs, Sybille, 78
Samsung, 86–87
Sánchez, Pablo, 161
Satellite technology, 194–195
Scenario analysis, 92–95, *94*
Schaubroeck, John M., 242
Schmidheiny, Stephen, 122, 194
Schmidt, Eric, 87
Schoemaker, P.J.H., 119, 220
Schön, D.A., 18
Schultz, Howard, 83
Schumacher, E.F., 15, 25, 29, 30, 55–56,
    60, 218
Schumpeter, Joseph A., 194, 222
Schwenk, Charles R., 215
Scope of firm's operations, 170–172
Scope of marketplace, 61
Second mover advantage, 138
Securities and Exchange Commission
    (SEC), 154, 185
Self-organization, optimizing, 222
Senge, Peter M., 6, 14, 15, 18, 20, 25, 68,
    127, 142, 196, 221, 240, 243
Servant leadership, 244
Shah, Anup, 47
Shaich, Ron, 159
Shake out/maturity stage of industry
    coevolution, 75, *76*
Shamsie, Jamal, 12, 222
Shared value, 111, 139
Shareholders, 231
Sharma, Sanjay, 116, 121, 127
Shemwell, Don, 52
Sherman, W., 209
Shireman, Bill, 10
Shrivastava, Paul, 116
Sierra Club, 148, 149
Silent Spring (Carson), 6, 96
Simultaneity, in coevolutionary
    relationships, 12
Singh, Harbir, 78, 106, 181, 183, 195, 197,
    246
Sisk, D., 219
Slums, urban, 53

Small share firm, 150
Smith, Aaron, 233
Smith, Adam, 36, 55
Smith, Geoffrey, 189
Smith, Mark K., 106
Snow, Charles C., 206
Social capital
    defined, 101
    and ecosystemic competencies, 106–107
    and entropic relationships, 246
    as intangible resource, 120
    socio-effiency of, 123–124
Social complexity, in business
    organizations, 119
Social entrepreneurship, 68–70
Socially responsible investment (SRI) rating
    agencies, 124
Social performance. *See* Socio-efficiency
Social responsibility, 4
    in triple-bottom-line performance, *11*, 11
Social sustainability, 55
    and food insecurity, 49–51
    gender inequity, 51–52
    and globalization, 53–54
    health inequity, 51
    and income/wealth distribution, 47–48
    and literacy rate, 52
    and population distribution, 46–47
    and urbanization, 53
Socio-effectiveness
    in economically depressed market, 159
    high-level strategies, 139
    poverty reduction strategy, 193
    resource assessment, *126*, 126–128
Socio-efficiency
    categories of, 122
    competitive advantage of, 139
    and human capital, 122–123
    in labeling, 146–147
    measuring value added from, 124–125
    and social capital, 123–124
Solus 2300 performance additives, 169
Solutia, 204–205, 230
Solution stacks, 79
Somalia, state failure in, 54
Sommer, Brian B., 208
Southwest Airlines, 110–111, 137
Space, in business ecosystem, 81
Specialization, of niche player, 152
Species extinction, 39–40
Specificity, in coevolutionary relationships,
    12
Speth, James Gustave, 6, 26, 35, 42, 68, 201
Spin-off, 188, 189
Spiraling coevolutionary process, 12–13, *13*
Spiraling integrative process, 16
Spiritual capabilities, 218, 220–221

Spiritual capital, 101, *102*, 107, 120, 218, 219, 220
Spiritual fulfillment, 218
Spiritual intelligence (SQ), 218, 219, 220
Spiritual leadership, 243–244
Stakeholder analysis, 114–117, *118*
Stakeholders
  citizen sector, 83
  community, 84
  engagement process, 85, 158, 186–187, 223
  expectations of, 65, 92
  fringe, 127
  green wave of concerns, 61–62
  internal, 231–232
  multiple, 62, 81, 108, 127
  in multisector ecosystems, 192
  self-organization by, 62
  strategy input of, 24–25, 162
  sustainability-conscious, 116
Stakeholder value
  and eco-efficiency, 121–122
  measuring, 124–125
  and socio-efficiency, 122–124
Stanwick, Peter A., 122
Stanwick, Sarah D.., 122
Staples, eco-efficient supplier relationships of, 144
Starbucks
  in business ecosystem, 83–84, 152
  concentrated growth strategy of, 173
  emergent strategies in, 24
  product stewardship of, 147
  recycling program of, 144
  sustainability reputation of, 105
Starik, Mark, 83, 116
Stars, in market share matrix, *199*, 199
Starwood Hotels and Resorts, 69
State failure rate, 54
Stead, Edward, 22, 52, 116, 139–140, 142, 145, 156, 216, 217
Stead, Jean Garner, 22, 52, 116, 139–140, 142, 145, 156, 216, 217
Steingard, D., 209
Stern, Nicholas, 104
Stock options, 236
Strategic alliances, 179, 181–182
Strategic business unit (SBU), 22, 170, *171*, 171
Strategic choice
  and accounting systems, 208–209
  benefits of, 226–227
  at competitive level, 211–212, *212*
  at corporate level, 212–214
  defined, 206
  enterprise resource planning system, 207–208

Strategic choice *(continued)*
  at functional level, 206–207
  sustainability-centered value system, 214–217
Strategic fit, 211
Strategic group analysis, 74–75
Strategic intrapreneurship, 186–187
Strategic management. *See also* Sustainable strategic management
  defined, 15
Strategic objectives (goals), 21–22
Strategic planning, 15
Strategic vision, 18–20
Strategies. *See also* Competitive strategies; Corporate strategies
  emerging, 24
  hierarchy of, 22–23, *23*
Strengths and weaknesses, 117, 211
Stuck in the middle, 135
Stumpf, S., 82, 85, 101, 104, 246, 247
Suárez, S.L., 2, 52
Subaru, eco-effective strategies of, 145
Success factors, critical, 61
Sudan, 46
Suppliers
  bargaining power of, 73
  eco-efficient solutions of, 143–145
Support activities, in value chain analysis, 109–110
Sustainability. *See also* Ecological sustainability; Social sustainability
  barriers to achieving, 54–56
  carrying capacity/human footprint in, 33–38
  consciousness of, 68, 218
  defined, 6, 59
  and economic growth, 37
  growth of, 6–7, 158
  and profitability, 10, 217
  science of, 28–33
  spiritual foundations of, 218–219
Sustainability Calculator, 146
Sustainability committee, 234
Sustainability performance
  auditing, 211
  balanced scorecard approach to, 208
  enterprise resource planning (ERP) systems in, 207–208
  performance gap analysis, *238*, 238
  reporting, 209–210
  spiritual capabilities in, 218–221
Sustainable enterprise economies (SEEs), 83
Sustainable Food Lab, 196
Sustainable Forestry Initiative (SFI), 124
Sustainable innovation, 4, 5
Sustainable Packaging Coalition (SPC), 144

Sustainable strategic management (SSM).
    See also Eastman Chemical Company
adaptive/generative learning in, 18
coevolutionary process in, 16–17, *19*
competitive level strategies. *See*
    Competitive strategies
concepts of, 18–23
corporate level strategies. *See* Corporate
    portfolio, SSM; Corporate strategies
defined, 16
environmental analysis. *See*
    Environmental analysis
implementation. *See also* Strategic choice
    and board of directors, 234–235
    at Eastman Chemical Company,
        227–228
    incremental, 224–225
    organizational structures for, 221–224,
        226
    spiritual capabilities in, 218–221
    and transformational change process,
        14–15, 215, 224–225, 226
leadership of. *See* Leadership, strategic
planning process of, 23–24
resource assessment. *See* Resource
    assessment
stages of, 18
stakeholders in, 24–25
triple-bottom-line framework for, 10–11, *11*
Sustainable value, 112
Svobodo, Susan, 112
Swanson, R.A., 95
Swatch watches, 165–166
SWOT analysis, 211
Symonds, William, 189
System level resources, 119

T
Takeover strategy, 185
Tangible resources, 101, 103–104, 220
Target stores, 123–124, 173
Tata Group, 177
Technical nutrients, as product material, 125
Technologies
    change in business environment, 62, 64,
        65
    disruptive, 194–195, 223
    and efficiency, *34*, 34, 37–38
    flexible manufacturing, 136
    information, 60
    and product stewardship, 167-168
Tender offer, 185
Thain, John, 234, 236
Thermodynamics, laws of, 31
Thompson, Jonathon, 41
Threats, in external environment, 60, 65–68,
    211

3M, 142, 214
Throwaway society, 42–43
Tickle, Phyllis, 68
Tolle, Eckhart, 31
Tong, Vinnee, 190
Top management teams, 25
Torrance, E., 219
Torres, Oliver, 78, 85, 86, 106, 181
Total quality environmental management
    (TQEM), 143
Toyota, 118
Trade, illicit, 67
Trade associations, 83
Transaction costs, 183
Transformational change, 14–15, 215,
    224–225, 226
Transnational (glocalization) corporate
    strategy, 70, 179
Trimble, Chris, 138, 139, 160, 163, 178
Triple-bottom-line-anchored business
    ecosystems, 246
Triple-bottom-line data, 114, 117
Triple-bottom-line performance, 10–11, *11*,
    16, 58–59, 90, 139, 148
Tritan copolyester, 5, 58, 168, 230
Trusting relationships, building, 246–247
Turnaround strategies, corporate, 187–188
Tymon, W., 82, 85, 101, 104, 246, 247

U
Undeveloped/developing markets
    competitive strategies for, 158–163
    consumer class in, 91
    diffusion of power to, 53–54
    socio-effective strategy in, 193
    state failure in, 54
    untapped, 90–91
UN Global Compact, 124
Unilever, 105, 158, 161–162, 196, 221
Union Carbide, 4, 96–97
Unlimited growth economy, 7, 16, 36–37,
    46, 56
Unrelated diversification, 176, 177
Urbanization, 53

V
Valuable resource, 118
Value chain
    cradle-to-cradle view of, 127–128
    ecosystemic-based, 125
    hybrid, 111–112
    life cycle assessment (LCA), 130
    new industries created by, 155
    open-system, 99, 112, *113*, 122, 123, 128,
        208
Value chain analysis (VCA), 109–111, *110*
Value creation, 100, 121–128

Value system
core, 215–216
in decision making, 215
in enterprise-strategy context, 216–217
and spiritual capabilities, 218, 220–221
sustainability-centered, 214–215, *217*, 217
and transformational change, 14–15, 225
van Bastelaer, Thierry, 106
Van Den Bosch, Frans A.J., 12, 221
Vaughan, F., 219
Venture capital, corporate (CVC), 182
Vertical integration strategies, 172, 175–176
Vertical scope, industry, 71
Violence
urban, 53
against women, 51
Vision, strategic, 18–20
Volberda, Henk W., 12, 77, 206, 221, 222
Vredenburg, Harrie, 121

W
Waddock, Sandra, 68, 83, 106, 211
Walmart
in business ecosystem, 84, 134, 152
concentrated growth strategy of, 173
cost-leadership strategy of, 134, 135
eco-efficient supplier relationships, 144
in global market, 179–180
Retail Link inventory system, 80, 85
Walter, F., 219
Waste disposal, 42–43
Waterman, Robert H., 173
Water pollution, 41–42, 49
Water scarcity, 38–39, 49
Waters, James A., 24
Watts, Phillip, 122, 194

Wealth distribution, 46, 47–48, 51, 91. *See also* Poverty
Wealth of Nations, The (Smith), 36
Weil, Richard, 49
Wernerfelt, B., 99, 220
Wetlands, 39
Weyerhauser, vertical integration of, 175
Wheelen, Thomas, 75
Whitney, Diana, 225
Whole-pyramid perspective, 163, *164*, 190–192, 195, 197, *198*, 202
Wicks, Andrew C., 216
Wilber, Kenneth, 13, 219
Williamson, Oliver E., 183
Winerip, Michael, 52
Winn, M., 157, 160, 161
Winston, A., 61, 62, 112, 121, 124
World Economic Forum, 65, 67
Wright, Jonathon, 208

X
Xerox, product stewardship at, 146
XTO Energy, 177

Y
Young, G., 105
Yunus, Muhammad, 162, 243

Z
Zaheer, Akbar, 181, 195
Zakaria, Fareed, 50, 53
Zambia, socio-effective strategy in, 193
Zhexembayeva, Nadya, 65, 81, 104, 108, 112, 148
Zohar, D., 107, 218, 219
Zuckerberg, Mark, 184

About the Authors

Jean Garner Stead is a professor of strategic management at East Tennessee State University (ETSU). Born and raised in Birmingham, Alabama, Jean earned her BS (1971) and MA (1973) in economics from Auburn University. After graduation she worked as an urban planner and consultant in Baton Rouge, Louisiana. She later moved to Illinois, where she earned her MBA (1979) from Western Illinois University while serving as an instructor of economics. She earned her PhD (1983) in business administration from Louisiana State University (LSU) in Baton Rouge, with a minor in ecological economics. Her appointment as an assistant professor at ETSU was her first job after graduate school at LSU.

Jean had always dreamed of living where her spirit and work could be nurtured, and she found that place in the Blue Ridge Mountains of Tennessee, where she and Ed raised their daughter, Garner Lee. Jean and Ed have written extensively for more than a quarter of a century on business ethics, organizations and the natural environment, sustainable strategic management, and social issues in management. The first edition of their book *Management for a Small Planet* received a 1992 *Choice* Outstanding Academic Book award, and their 1990 *Journal of Business Ethics* article "An Integrative Model for Understanding and Managing Ethical Behavior in Business Organizations," was named as a citation classic. In addition, Jean was a founding member of the Organizations and the Natural Environment (ONE) Division of the Academy of Management, and she has also been active in the Social Issues in Management (SIM) Division.

Jean's passion is teaching, and she received East Tennessee State University's Faculty Award for Outstanding Teaching in 1995. She has also been involved with the Melting Pot Ministry of Munsey Memorial United Methodist Church, a ministry serving the physical and spiritual needs of the homeless in Johnson City, Tennessee, for over a quarter of a century. She currently serves as the chair of the Melting Pot Ministry team.

W. Edward Stead was born and raised in Birmingham, Alabama. An interviewer once asked him what early events in his life shaped his strong commitment to environmental responsibility and social justice, and he responded, "My inspiration came from growing up in Birmingham at a time when it was one of the most environmentally polluted, socially unjust cities in America." Indeed, Birmingham during Ed's childhood had choking air pollution from the miles of open-hearth steel mills that spread across the north side of the city, and it was the scene of untold racial hatred and human tragedy that earned it the nickname "Bombingham," in the 1960s.

Ed is currently a professor of management at East Tennessee State University, his institutional home since 1982. He earned his BS (1968) and MBA (1972) from Auburn University, and his PhD in management from Louisiana State University (1976). He has also served as a lieutenant in the U.S. Army, worked in banking, and taught in the business colleges at Auburn, LSU, Western Illinois University, and the University of Alabama in Birmingham.

Ed and Jean have researched and written extensively together for more than thirty years on business ethics and organizations and the natural environment. Their articles and books have been widely cited: Their first book received a *Choice* Outstanding Academic Book award, and one of their articles was recently named a "citation classic" by the Social Science Citation Index.

Ed was a founding member of the Organizations and the Natural Environment (ONE) Division of the academy of Management. Ed served ONE as program chair, chair elect, and chair during its formative years from 1996 to 1998. He has also been an active member of the Social Issues in Management (SIM) Division of the Academy, and he has served as a strategic management, team building, and community sustainability consultant to numerous business organizations, communities, and nonprofit organizations.

Ed is currently at the end of his long and satisfying academic career. He chose this profession because he loved it, and that has never changed over forty-three years of teaching and writing. But now is a time for a new beginning for Ed, and he intends to make the best of it. He plans on spending his newfound time and energy doting on his grandchildren, nurturing his relationships with Jean, and with Garner and Mike, writing stories and poems, spending as much time as possible with family and friends, doing yoga, walking, enjoying the beautiful outdoors, cheering for his beloved Auburn Tigers, and getting closer to his God.